# AFRICANISTAN

# AFRICANISTAN

## Development or Jihad

SERGE MICHAILOF

# OXFORD
UNIVERSITY PRESS

Oxford University Press is a department of the University of Oxford.
It furthers the University's objective of excellence in research, scholarship,
and education by publishing worldwide. Oxford is a registered trademark of
Oxford University Press in the UK and in certain other countries.

Published in India by
Oxford University Press
2/11 Ground Floor, Ansari Road, Daryaganj, New Delhi 110 002, India

© Oxford University Press 2018

The moral rights of the authors have been asserted.

First Edition published in 2018

ISBN-13 (print edition): 978-0-19-948566-6
ISBN-10 (print edition): 0-19-948566-6

ISBN-13 (eBook): 978-0-19-909270-3
ISBN-10 (eBook): 0-19-909270-2

Typeset in Bembo Std 11/13
by The Graphics Solution, New Delhi 110 092
Printed in India by Gopsons Papers Ltd., Noida 201301

The Ferdi foundation (Fondation pour les études et recherches sur le développement
international), which promotes research activities to study development issues,
supported the translation of this book.

Any map reproduced from OECD/SWAC (2014), *An Atlas of the Sahara-Sahel:
Geography, Economics and Security, West African Studies* included herein, are without
prejudice to the status of or sovereignty over any territory, to the delimitation of
international frontiers and boundaries and to the name of any territory, city, or area.

# Contents

## Part III: Lessons the Sahel Can Draw from Afghanistan

## Part IV: What Is to Be Done?

# Foreword

This book carries an important message; fortunately, it is also well written and so highly readable. The message is that a region on Europe's doorstep, and which in a decade will have 150 million people, is on track to becoming a mega-Afghanistan. The Sahel is our neighbour, and it could easily become our nightmare. Yet, by learning the lessons from past failures, we could still avert it.

Serge Michailof is deeply knowledgeable about both Afghanistan and the Sahel. He is similarly knowledgeable about the deficiencies and potential of international development and security interventions. Despite recent international efforts, the countries of the Sahel have deteriorated. He explains why, without substantial international help, they are likely to deteriorate further. They are already too poor to secure their territory from the violence of radical Islam, and their demographic explosion is resulting in a rapid increase in unemployed and impoverished youth who are easy fodder for radicalization.

Yet, even if international interventions equivalent to those in Afghanistan were politically and financially possible in the Sahel, they would be no more likely to work. The key lesson from the failures in Afghanistan is that international assistance needs to strengthen the key institutions of government, and not substitute for them. The security forces of the Sahelian region must be supported to become operationally effective without gaining licence to victimize minorities; the police and judiciary must become dispensers of justice rather than vectors of corruption. These objectives are more difficult than the photogenic social agenda with which donors and non-governmental organizations (NGOs) are comfortable, but in conditions of deepening fragility, they are essential, and the generic skills that donors have learned in other sectors can be deployed to good effect.

I have come to regard state fragility as the core development challenge of our time. After the catastrophes of Afghanistan, Iraq, Syria, Mali, Somalia, and South Sudan, we should be under no illusions as to either the extent of the problem, or the inadequacies of past approaches. That is why I am currently co-directing an academic Commission on State Fragility, funded by the British Academy. In pursuing our work, we have realized that there is a dearth of studies that combine analysis with deep knowledge of context. Academics have produced theory detached from experience, and practitioners have produced descriptive accounts of individual situations insufficiently analytic to provide lessons for other situations. The comparative approach of this book is a truly valuable bridge between two worlds that seldom meet. It will be an invaluable resource for our work.

The world of development assistance, both official aid and NGO charities, is accustomed to uplifting messages. For decades, the narrative has been how our money is enabling poor people to lift themselves out of poverty, sickness, and illiteracy. How United Nations (UN) peacekeepers are doing just that: keeping the peace. Juxtaposed against this, has been a counter-narrative that such aid is the problem: without it, people would soon learn to stand on their own feet. Both these narratives are revealed as convenient falsehoods. What has been happening in Afghanistan and the Sahel is not an uplifting story to celebrate. Money has not brought jobs and hope to youth; foreign troops, whether under the American flag as in Afghanistan, or that of the UN in Mali, have not brought peace. This book will make uncomfortable reading for the many people who have been involved in these efforts. But it will illuminate the many more people who have been paying for them, and whose future tranquility is likely to depend upon whether they can be reshaped to achieve success.

Michailof's critique of the past, though devastating, is constructive. Some of his stories of past errors are excruciating: his account of the meeting in a French security bunker that determined France's contribution to the recovery of Afghanistan in 2002 hovers on the borderland between tragedy and farce. That of the UN peacekeeping operation in Mali, which despite costing a billion dollars a year and suffering over a hundred dead, has no possibility of operational effectiveness, is firmly in the domain of tragedy. Such truths are necessary given the willful denial habitual in the development agencies. But Michailof's constructive message is the key value of the book. The international efforts must not merely be scaled up, but radically redirected from the cheering task of delivering social services to the frustrating one of building the sinews of the state. Without effective states, the Sahel will implode and Europe will notice the consequences.

**Paul Collier**
Professor of Economics and Public Policy,
Blavatnik School of Government, and Professorial
Fellow of St. Antony's College, Oxford, UK

# Preface

For some time, the general view has been that Africa is doing well. And it is true: Africa is no longer the 'hopeless continent'. Progress can be seen across the board. Billions of dollars are pouring in. People are doing good business in Africa. But the question is: Is this upturn sustainable? And is it comprehensive enough?

Mali's collapse in 2013 when confronted by a few-hundred jihadists came as a surprise and marked the end of euphoria. Who could have also anticipated a few years ago, the emergence of a 'Boko Haram-land' in Nigeria or a 'Shebab-land' in fast-growing Kenya? Every week—perhaps every day—migrants are risking their lives and dying in the Mediterranean. Should we really believe all is well?

The continent is, in fact, a powder keg. The powder is demographics. And the detonator is unemployment. The equation is simple: by 2050, the population of Sub-Saharan Africa will be one-and-a-half times that of China. But the number of young people of working age will be three times that of China's. How will they feed themselves or put a roof over their heads? Above all, what jobs will be available, and where will those jobs be?

What is troubling for the continent as a whole is even more dramatic for the Sahel, a huge region covering 7 million square kilometres and facing severe ecological challenges. What can a country like Niger do with a population that has risen from 3 million when the country became independent in 1960 to 20 million today, and is set to reach between 63 and 89 million by 2050? Will this country, also threatened by global warming, be forced to rely upon food aid to feed its population?

In the Sahel, insecurity is spreading like a bushfire, bringing with it refugees, terrorism, arms-trafficking, hostage-taking, and mass migration. Foreigners can no longer travel freely. This is just as in Afghanistan. What is striking is that, despite major differences in history, geography, and culture, there are huge similarities between the Sahel and Afghanistan: a demographic impasse, stagnating agriculture, widespread rural misery, high unemployment, deep ethnic and religious fault lines, weak states, a lack of law and order, regional instability, drug trafficking, and the spread of radical Islam.

Drawing on an extensive knowledge of Afghanistan and of the failure of both foreign military intervention and foreign aid there, this book is a wake-up call on the extent of risks if the security situation in the Sahel continues to deteriorate. And it will definitely deteriorate if the same recipes that failed in Afghanistan are again put into practice in the Sahel, as is presently the case. Stabilizing the Sahel is possible, but not by relying on foreign troops or aid practices that have consistently failed in fragile countries.

The mass unemployment of young people with limited education, far more than jihadist propaganda, is the primary explanation for the dramatic collapse of countries such as Afghanistan, Syria, Yemen, and Iraq. Now, Africa is producing huge numbers of young people with limited education. With a very small manufacturing sector and a neglected agricultural one, where are the jobs today, and where will they be in the future?

Without a rapid turnaround and a radical change in the type of assistance provided by the international community in the Sahel, there are good reasons to fear that we will soon be confronted with, first, a 'Sahelistan' and then an 'Africanistan': an African Afghanistan, but five- or ten-times worse. In Europe, we are only now beginning to grasp the consequences of the implosion in Syria and Libya. What would be the consequences for Europe's stability if an immense region with a population of 100 million now, or 150 million in 10 years, were to implode, thus destabilizing all of West Africa and a fragile Maghreb?

If the international donor community does not bring some order to the shambles of international aid in the region, the future looks bleak. We need to ask ourselves what the impact of a collapsing Sahel would be on our societies and on the political balances in a world where populist leaders are on the rise. This is what *Africanistan* is all about.

# Introduction

'The Western world had no idea what Sahel was, because history has focused NATO and Western countries' attention on Iraq and Afghanistan; but Sahel is potentially even more dangerous ... than Afghanistan.'

—Romano Prodi, Special Envoy of the
Secretary-General for the Sahel

## Niamey, May 1985

It's almost noon. As usual, the heat at this time of the year in Niger is stifling. I push open the metal gate of the 'concession', a makeshift camp enclosed by a wall of beaten earth, and feel my wife gripping my arm. We come face to face with the horror of it. I had thought myself hardened, having worked and travelled in the poorest countries of the world for more than fifteen years. But we are appalled by the sight before us. Outside this 'concession' in a Niamey suburb, life, though tough, of course goes on. Last year's rains had been scanty. In fact, in 1984, the entire Sahel region reeled under the worst droughts since the 1973–4 disaster. Over six months, tent camps housing numerous refugees mushroomed up all around the city. They were run by the Nigerien administration with support from humanitarian organizations— an 'almost normal' situation that has little impact on life in a city congested by mopeds. Yet, right behind this wall, a child had died this morning. Some 150 people seek shelter from the sun, in vain, under cardboard and plastic sheets held up by improvised stakes. They do not stir at our arrival.

Our friends had told us about a camp of Malian Tuaregs who had taken refuge in this suburb; because they were foreigners, the Nigerien authorities felt they had no responsibility for them and had abandoned them to their fate. The group was literally dying of starvation right in the city. The impending rains would obviously destroy their fragile shelters and accelerate their end. For the first time, I had found myself confronted with the tragedy of the Malian Tuaregs, ostracized in their own country and ruined by the drought that had caused their herds to perish. Seeing this suffering, we rallied a few expatriate couples, needing only a modicum of effort and little money to bring food and water to tide them over, have a doctor friend provide them with medical care, negotiate their access to a few fields 15 kilometres away, pay for some tools and seeds, and help them buy a few goats, thus ensuring the survival of a group we had grown fond of as we had gotten to know them. We were able to speak to them through Amar, who was literate. I will never forget what Amar once said after we had overcome the initial period of suspicion and mutual observation: 'Once, we were lords …'

## Paris, 22 March 2012: Military coup in Mali

I am stunned by the news on the radio. The President of Mali, Amadou Toumani Touré—popularly called ATT—has been deposed by a military coup just a few weeks ahead of the presidential elections, even though he had announced his decision not to run for office! True, the situation was still dicey. About a year ago, a new insurrection had flared in the north, led by the National Movement for the Liberation of Azawad (MNLA), a group demanding independence for the Tuareg-dominated area. Bolstered by the defection of a few Tuareg units of the Malian armed forces and an influx of arms from Libya, the MNLA had entered into an alliance with Al-Qaeda in the Islamic Maghreb (AQMI, a regeneration of the Algeria-based GSPC[1]) and two

---

[1] Salafist Group for Preaching and Combat.

local Islamist outfits actively involved in trans-border trafficking and hostage-taking: Ansar Dine and the Movement for Unity and Jihad in West Africa (Mujao). The Malian army had suffered defeat after defeat in the north. Obviously, it wanted to make a scapegoat of poor ATT for its rout. ATT, it must be said, was a big disappointment. He was a big *personal* disappointment.

ATT was the general who had overthrown the president/dictator Moussa Traoré in March 1991, after the brutal crushing of a revolt in Bamako had claimed 200 lives. Contrary to the prevalent practice, ATT had organized elections in which he refused to run and transferred power to civilians, which resulted, thanks to a transparent and democratic process, in the installation of President Alpha Oumar Konaré in the presidential palace for ten years. ATT was obviously a deeply estimable man who had restored democracy in Mali. I had the World Bank invite him to Washington, DC, in 1995, where he delivered a brilliant speech on democracy that earned him a standing ovation. Thereafter, I met him at various international conferences and, making the most of my travels, called on him twice in Bamako. I found him to be open and accessible, and we got on well. He developed the habit of calling me by my first name and addressing me with the familiar '*tu*'. His house, always teeming with visitors, was run like a headquarters. He had not concealed his intention to run for office in 2002 from me.

Each time we had met, we'd had lengthy discussions about the Malian economy, an area in which reforms were long overdue, and about which he did not have a strong grasp, despite his interest in the subject. Hence, I was not surprised when, upon being elected, he sent his personal adviser to discuss economic issues with me in Paris where, at the time, I headed the operations of the French Development Agency (AFD). Based on these discussions, I had one of my teams prepare a detailed note about urgent reforms needed in the agricultural sector, and ATT discussed it over the phone with me once he had carefully read it. He assured me that he was in agreement with the proposals and that the reforms would soon be undertaken. But the reforms never materialized, despite a few gentle reminders from me. I was not really surprised; I knew politics follows its own logic, and I understood that the reforms were politically difficult to carry out.

The real disappointment for me came a few years later, when a friend in whom I had confided my hopes and concerns for Mali exclaimed, 'How come you don't know this? Paris has accused ATT of entering into a non-aggression pact with the Islamists. It has even been reported in *Libé*.[2] I think that the country is going astray'.

## 10 January 2013: 6,000 foreigners have just avoided being kidnapped by jihadists in Bamako!

For several years then, I had been badgering the French authorities, trying to draw their attention to the deteriorating security situation in the Sahel, particularly in Mali. The deterioration was due to both the collapse of rural economies of the northern fringe of this vast region, and the weakness of the state apparatus of all the countries in the zone—all exacerbated by bandits of all hues having free access to weapons at the Libyan arms bazaar after Kaddafi's fall. I had tried, in vain, to persuade our political leaders to reorient French aid to attack the root of these problems instead of merely addressing their effects through sporadic military and humanitarian interventions. In the 1980s, I had travelled through the whole region with my family, sleeping on the roadside with the car doors wide open, feeling absolutely secure. Things had now reached a point that the famous Paris Dakar Rally had to cancel its cross-Sahara itinerary and move to Latin America, a point where peaceful tourists were kidnapped from a café terrace in the heart of Niamey. A book I had published in 2010 entitled *Notre maison brûle au Sud* (*Our House in the South is Burning*) had obviously not disrupted the routines of the French ministries of Economy and Finance, and Foreign Affairs, which were supposed to pilot our development-aid policy.

On 10 January 2013, I watched the worst possible scenario unfold on my television screen: shortly after ATT's fall, the alliance between the jihadists and the MNLA ended. The three Islamist movements turned against the Tuareg-dominated, nationalist MNLA and crushed it. The jihadists then proceeded to occupy the major cities of northern Mali, particularly Timbuktu,

[2] Thomas Hofnung and Fabien Offner, *Libération*, 23 March 2012.

causing a de facto partition of the country. The Mujao, AQMI, and Ansar Dine outfits had just routed the Malian Army—not a real surprise since it was widely known that corruption had deeply eroded the Malian armed forces. Then, the jihadist groups swept across Mali, this time threatening not the few northern cities that they had not yet occupied, but the capital city of Bamako, which no longer possessed any credible military force with which to stop them. Around 6,000 expatriates, mostly French citizens, lived in Bamako. Thus, we were not just at risk of having four or five hostages taken, but several thousands! It was stupefying to watch on live television, a country of 18 million inhabitants—which the international community had long held up as a model democracy with a flourishing economy and a flattering annual growth rate of 7 per cent—falling before a few hundred bearded men on pickups!

## Mali's collapse revealed a far less dazzling situation than had been thought.

Was Mali's collapse an isolated case—an aberration? Or, on the contrary, did it prefigure a general collapse of the Sahel region? Preceding, by a few months, the disintegration of Iraq's over-equipped army at the hands of the Islamic State (ISIS), did Mali not show the surprising fragility of many states of the developing world? Mosul, an Iraqi city of 3 million inhabitants, was captured by fewer than 2,000 jihadists, and we tend to forget that Abidjan and the Ivorian regime had almost been toppled in September 2002 by a much smaller group of rebels.

Before returning to the case of Mali and other Sahel countries, it is useful to review Africa's overall situation. If there indeed is an Africa[3] that is winning, there is also an Africa that faces huge difficulties and is sometimes in the throes of crisis. And even in 'winning Africa,' not everyone is winning, and the economic success that has been widely highlighted since the turn of the century appears, upon scrutiny, quite fragile.

[3] Although I refer to 'Africa' for ease of use, I am speaking here exclusively of Sub-Saharan Africa, North Africa being, as is well known, a very different world by its culture, its geography, and the constraints it is subject to.

Having lived for more than fifteen years on the continent, having worked on it for half a century now, and having compared the advances made by Africa during this period with those of Latin America, Central, South, and Southeast Asia, and the Maghreb where I have also travelled and worked since the late 1960s, I have reservations about the current optimism about Africa. It seems to me almost as excessive as the pessimism with which it was regarded in the 1990s. Experienced Africa observers share this nuanced position: it was the subject of Sylvie Brunel's latest book,[4] which traces the fault lines of the continent. And reporting on the conclusions of the World Economic Forum on Africa that took place in June 2015 in Cape Town, South Africa, Sébastien Hervieu stated, 'Africa is still waiting for its real economic boom'.[5]

Sub-Saharan Africa has made remarkable advances during the last two decades.[6] But notwithstanding the extraordinary diversity of the continent, it is affected by common weak points not only at the economic level, but also at the political and societal ones. These weak points are particularly serious in the Sahel region and are so worrisome that the very future of Sahelian societies is under threat, particularly due to uncontrolled population growth, the consequences of which can be, literally, explosive. The picture that emerges of the entire region—with its lack of job prospects, its internal tensions, and transnational influences such as that of Wahhabism—is so disquieting that we must now be concerned about seeing the vast Sahel zone gradually transformed into ... a new Afghanistan.

## It is perhaps still possible to stabilize the Sahel, but there is little time left.

Clearly, burying our heads in the sand is no longer an option. Most European countries are in denial about the situation. This has to cease if we are to correctly identify the nature of the dangers

---

[4] Sylvie Brunel, *L'Afrique est elle si bien partie?*, *Éditions Sciences humaines*, 2014.

[5] *Le Monde*, 6 June 2015.

[6] These advances are brilliantly described in Jean-Michel Severino and Olivier Ray's *Le Temps de l'Afrique* (Odile Jacob, 2010).

and figure out how to face them. As far as France is concerned, the administration has to break with its present routine; the only department seriously concerned is the Defence ministry, whose armed forces are on the front line. Although they live up to their appellation 'la grande muette (the silent service)', they are deeply worried about the current impasse and the lack of a clear exit strategy.

The 2013 Mali conflict, which marked the outbreak of war in the Sahel, has only just begun. It is likely to be long and frustrating. It may even become an endless conflict. One of the characteristics of this kind of conflict is that the military can win all the battles, and yet lose the war. That's because the war must be won first on the development front, aiming at employment for all and drastic improvement in the living standards of massively deprived peoples.

If France and Europe—I include Europe because the problem is no longer restricted to France—do not quickly understand these challenges and organize themselves accordingly, there will be drastic consequences not only for the Sahelian peoples and all of West Africa, but also for our European suburbs and the political stability of our democracies. We have just seen how the populist Marine Le Pen, who made her political fortune criticizing immigration, came close to the French presidency in May 2017. A poorly managed Sahelian conflict would lead to a massive influx of desperate people that no sea, no wall, no 'limes' could halt.[7] If things go wrong in the Sahel region, the current tragedy of migrants in the Mediterranean will turn out to be but a prelude. The whole of West Africa will convulse. We will have a new Afghanistan at our doors, only closer, infinitely bigger, and more dangerous.

The purpose of this book is to help dispel illusions, expose the considerable risks that loom over Africa in general, and especially over the Sahel, and raise a constructive alarm. In light of the lessons to be drawn from the failed Western 'adventure' in Afghanistan, French military engagement in the Sahel is fraught with huge risks

---

[7] In this context, it is worth reading Jean-Christophe Ruffin's premonitory book, *L'Empire et les nouveaux barbares* (Lattès, 2001).

of stalemate and, in the end, of failure that would have daunting consequences not only for France, but for all European societies.

## Methodological outline

Given the variety of subjects dealt with in this book, I have grouped the chapters into four main parts.

The first part looks at the current situation, characterized by the end of euphoria in Africa. The continent is indeed still perceived by many as an Eldorado for investors and the great new land of opportunity for the twenty-first century. I will try to dispel, somewhat, this highly optimistic vision by focusing on four unresolved issues: the new threats to Africa's stability and growth, linked to the expansion of insecurity on the continent and the collapse of some regions into lawless areas run by mafias and jihadists; the demographic impasse in which many African countries are presently locked, creating considerable social and political tensions; the increasing marginalization of some rural regions and the exceptional level of unemployment in most of rural Africa, due essentially to inadequate investment and policies; and the questionable nature of both the current industrial development in Africa, which creates too few jobs, and the long-term political sustainability of the existing African development model.

The second part focuses on the 'weak states' problem, which affects most of Africa. In this section, I analyse the causes of fragility in certain states and the links between the weakness of public institutions and the weakness of states. I focus on the specific governance problems faced by multi-ethnic countries, an issue that goes well beyond African borders and can also be found in the Middle East, the Caucasus, and Central Asia. I then provide some historical perspective that explains how a rich and successful country such as Cote d'Ivoire can easily derail, descend into Hell, and even after recovery, remain highly fragile, unstable, and susceptible to falling back into chaos.

The third part concentrates on the weakest part of Africa. Because the most fragile countries of Africa are in the Sahel, just south of the Sahara desert, I focus my analysis on that region. It is striking to discover how similar the problems confronting Sahelian countries are, to those confronting Afghanistan. Both regions are beset by uncontrolled demography combined with extremely weak economic bases; unacceptable poverty and lack of jobs for youths; complex multi-ethnic societies with deepening fault lines; the recent spread of an intolerant brand of Salafist Islam; increasing insecurity due to the presence of jihadist groups and lack of law and order; parallel economies based on drugs and other trafficking controlled by powerful mafias; poor governance and high levels of corruption; and, finally, hollow states and Potemkin democracies. This analysis vividly illustrates how much the Sahel region resembles Afghanistan and why, since the fall of the Taliban in 2001, despite billions expended in military and other aid, Western countries have clearly failed to eradicate poverty in the country, to restore security, or to establish a reasonable democracy. My hope is that this comparison of the fateful Afghan drama to current circumstances in the Sahel will provide important lessons that can help prevent the Sahel from becoming a new Afghanistan.

Centring around the question of what is to be done, the final part of the book is devoted to exploring options for the Sahel, drawing on twelve key lessons learned the hard way in Afghanistan, from which new approaches, new concepts, and new policies might be drawn and put into execution to restore security and bring development to a region now in deep crisis.

# PART I

Sub-Saharan Africa: The End of Euphoria

# CHAPTER ONE

# The New Threats to Africa's Stability and Growth[*]

Our judgments are often influenced by the 'clichés' propagated by the media, and these clichés tend to impair both nuance and perspective. As a result, we tend to get a distorted view of the African continent, where skyscrapers and traffic jams on urban highways in Abidjan, Nairobi, and Abuja mix with massacres in South Sudan and Central Africa. Let us try to replace this blurred picture with an accurate and detailed view of the diverse continent called Africa.

## Africa is doing better than 15 years ago.

Any productive discussion of Sub-Saharan Africa must take into account its great diversity. Africa's ecosystems are as varied as its peoples and the legacies of its colonial past. The continent is just as diverse in terms of its countries' economic situations and

[*] A preliminary version of this chapter was presented at the Emerging Market Forum in Abidjan on 27 March 2017, and has been reproduced in Harinder Kohli and Ted Ahlers (eds), *Africa Reset, a New Way Forward* (Oxford University Press, 2017).

income levels. A simple example could be the stark difference in the average annual incomes of an inhabitant of Equatorial Guinea (at USD 20,000) and that of a resident of Niger (at USD 400).

Despite this diversity and the obvious differences across countries, trends in Sub-Saharan Africa were fairly uniform between 1970 and 1990. These years were marked by weak long-term economic growth, chronic productivity deficits, largely rentier-based economies, wide-ranging demographic changes, strong urbanization, stalled industrialization, and the persistence of poverty traps. It is often forgotten that these very countries, after gaining independence, enjoyed rapid growth from the 1960s until the oil crisis of 1973.

In the new millennium, however, many countries in Sub-Saharan Africa have experienced growth rates that stand in sharp contrast to the previous two decades of stagnation. Some of the countries with the highest levels of growth in the world, in the first decade of the new millennium, are from Africa. Five of them—Angola, Ethiopia, Chad, Mozambique, and Rwanda—have witnessed an average growth of over 7 per cent, a rate at which an economy doubles in size in ten years. The growth has not been limited to these five countries alone. In fact, almost everywhere on the continent, trade, construction, and services have seen spectacular growth. In 15 years, African market capitalization has almost quadrupled, private equity has boomed, and both migrant remittances and foreign direct investment have far exceeded official development aid. The so-called 'awakening' of Côte d'Ivoire since President Alassane Ouattara took office in 2011 is a stunning case in point.

The reasons for this widespread success are well established. They begin with the high prices of raw materials that were driven by the extraordinary growth of China until 2013, which increased Africa's revenues from exports. This economic success was reinforced by major infrastructure projects, including the construction of highways and freeways, expansion of ports, rehabilitation of major railroads, and commissioning of numerous power stations. The growth of new information and communication technologies and of the financial sector over the past two decades has been similarly spectacular. Today, even the smallest market trader has two, three, or even four mobile phones in their pocket. A scene from the remarkable film *Timbuktu* (2014) that shows a Tuareg child trying to get a signal on a phone at the top of a sand dune underscores the importance of the mobile phone in even the poorest communities.

Africa's economic success is also grounded in the macroeconomic stability that was rediscovered following the instability of the 1980s and the 1990s. Throughout the 1980s, severe structural adjustments sometimes provoked social disasters that led to collapses in the public services responsible for education and health. In some countries, they also caused breakdowns in state structures and major increases in corruption. Yet, the adjustments ultimately resulted in the restoration of balanced budgets and external accounts that, for more than a decade, had accumulated enormous deficits.

The adjustments made it possible to lower inflation and more broadly implement rigorous budgeting due to the rise of a new generation of technocrats accustomed to working with the Bretton Woods institutions. For the countries on this path, the cancellation of most of their external debt, which had risen to unmanageable levels, greatly facilitated these budgetary adjustments. Today, many observers predict for the growth of the past 15 years to continue into the future. However, the African horizon is, unfortunately, darkening.

## Several new clouds loom on Africa's horizon.

One of the issues looming over Africa's growth is linked to the decline in commodity prices exported by Africa, particularly to China, and the slowing down of the Chinese economy. The continent's growth has suffered considerably from the major shifts that took place in the Chinese economy. The decline in commodity prices has led to African GDP growth dropping to unexpected levels (1.4 per cent in 2016 and about 2.6 per cent in 2017). Unfortunately, commodity prices are likely to remain depressed for the near future. Given the demographic growth rate of the continent (about 2.7 per cent), this means that per capita income has, at best, been stagnating in most countries. This troubling situation is likely to lead to a rise in social and political tensions if it continues for several years.

Another factor that makes Africa's future look not too promising is that while there are successful countries that have seen remarkable growth, there are others that appear doomed to fail. Countries such as the Democratic Republic of Congo, Central African Republic, Somalia, and South Sudan are cases in point, being plagued by poverty, disastrous management of public affairs, and unresolved internal conflicts.

Moreover, even the successful countries have not been able to prevent the emergence of deep social and geographical inequalities, which are often accompanied by rising tensions and increased insecurity. In many cases, these phenomena combine with an erosion of authority as the state loses control over peripheral regions, which become lawless zones.

The continent's extraordinary economic successes reflected itself in the development of urban infrastructure, the proliferation of skyscrapers, traffic jams of Mercedes and SUVs, and the emergence of not only an opulent class of millionaires, but also an authentic middle class. But these impressive developments tend to be limited to particularly dynamic regions and to the capitals. The foreign businesspersons who invest in capitals often forget that the peripheries of these very cities mostly comprise miserable shantytowns and poorly integrated neighbourhoods that lack public services such as roads, drainage, drinking water, and electricity. More importantly, they also forget that rural areas that have not benefited from economic growth now face stagnation that is expected to last and the risk in such contexts of entering alarming cycles of violence. These are some of the new threats now confronting Africa.

### The destabilization of the northeast of Nigeria is emblematic of such new threats.

The Nigerian economic boom has not prevented the emergence of a caliphate in the north of the country. While the Nigerian economy largely stagnated from the late 1960s up to 2000, it experienced remarkable growth afterwards—until the 2014 collapse in oil prices. This growth coincided with the end of military regimes and, combined with a change in statistical procedures,[1] made it the largest economy in Africa. Nigeria is currently the seventh-most populous country in the world, with 190 million inhabitants. It is on track to becoming a global giant by 2050, the third-most populous country (after China and India), with 400 million inhabitants, and one of the world's twenty largest economies. It also recently held a non-permanent seat on the UN Security Council.

Nigeria is a working democracy. The most recent elections, in March 2015, saw the replacement of President Goodluck Jonathan, who hails from the south of the country, by General Muhammadu Buhari, who come from the north. The education system is fairly robust, the administrative elites are highly qualified for the most part, and some institutions (though not all) function remarkably well. Nigeria was one of only two African countries affected by Ebola that were able to rapidly and effectively contain the epidemic (the other being Senegal). Still, it suffers extraordinary inequality between the largely deprived north, where per capita income is among the lowest in the world, and the capital city and the south, which have experienced an economic boom.

The troubling issue today is that despite its considerable financial resources, administrative structures, and huge military budget, the Nigerian government is unable to guarantee security in the Niger River Delta, where mafia gangs rule, and has allowed maritime piracy to develop to the extent that the Gulf of Guinea is now more dangerous than the Somali coast. In recent years, it has also largely lost control of the northeast of the country, a territory ravaged by the armed group, Boko Haram.

The advances made by Boko Haram are of great concern to the neighbouring countries of Chad, Niger, and Cameroon. Chad feared economic suffocation because Boko Haram was threatening its main access route to the sea via north Cameroon and Douala. At the end of 2014, Chad, Niger, and Cameroon decided to commit their forces to loosening this stranglehold,

---

[1] There was a methodological change introduced in the way GDP was assessed in Nigeria, which resulted in a significant increase in the overall GDP. African statistics may sometimes be surprising.

but with mixed success. The offensive resulted in the destruction of Boko Haram's most visible military structure, especially its armored equipment (stolen from the Nigerian army's inventories), and its ability to mount coordinated offensives. In spite of its claim of having established a caliphate, Boko Haram, unlike ISIS, is incapable of administering the regions under its control. None of its stated objectives—to establish a caliphate covering all of northern Nigeria, southern Chad, southeastern Niger, and northern Cameroon; to impose an extreme version of Sharia law; and to eradicate all Western traces, in particular public education—were achieved.

**A tiny sect has been able to destabilize a whole region.**

The resilience of Boko Haram and its ability to challenge the combined armed forces of Nigeria, Chad, Niger, and Cameroon is surprising. The nihilistic savagery apparent in the Boko Haram insurgency is, in a way, reminiscent of the infamous Lord's Resistance Army (LRA), which has long terrorized northern Uganda. It is difficult to imagine its sustainability as an organized movement, as its activities are now largely confined to looting and massacring. But it is also too early to think that the threat has been conclusively removed. The very mixed results after a coordinated offensive by the armies of four countries—supported by the UK, the US, and France—justify probing the reasons for the emergence and expansion of a movement of such magnitude in the richest and most powerful country in Africa.

Northern Nigeria was a land of jihad throughout the nineteenth century, and its impact was felt as far away as Mali and Senegal. The Sokoto Caliphate led by Usman dan Fodio, which emerged at the beginning of the nineteenth century, covered the whole of what is now northern Nigeria, southern Chad, and northern Cameroon. It even exercised nominal sovereignty over a group of emirates covering part of present-day Mali and Burkina Faso. In addition, the establishment of Pax Britannica gave rise to a series of revolts (that were led by preachers) throughout northern Nigeria, particularly in the northeastern states, where Boko Haram is currently established. This rebellion, thus, has historical and religious roots.

It is surprising that the Boko Haram movement started in 2000 as a tiny Islamic sect comprising only a few dozen followers, all strongly influenced by the Wahhabi teachings disseminated by Saudi Arabia. This marginal sect, ridiculed by some for its isolationism and sectarianism, became progressively more radical after 2003 and adopted an ideology rejecting what it considered the remnants of colonial influence; in particular, Western-style education, and both national and local forms of government.

Although its aim is to establish an Islamic state 'purified' of all Western influence, Boko Haram's success is largely explained by the deprivation in northern Nigeria. Poverty in the north of the country, which stems from extreme population density, the consequent environmental crisis in the countryside, and the lack of prospects and employment for the youth, allowed Boko Haram to prosper. Even viewed from an airplane, the overexploitation of land in the region, with the disappearance of fallow land, due to demographic pressure, is striking. As in many other countries, the struggle for access to land is often the source of violent conflict. Boko Haram has skillfully played on such tensions, as well as on inter-ethnic and inter-religious rivalries. Since 2009, it has established links with jihadist networks in Niger, Mali, Libya, Algeria, and even Somalia.

While Boko Haram has now seriously weakened, it still poses a threat to the whole region. The linguistic and ethnic proximity of Niger and Nigeria along their 1,500 kilometre shared border means that insecurity in northeastern Nigeria is gradually corrupting southeastern Niger in the Diffa region. This is of considerable concern to Niger officials, who fear that it could jeopardize the unity of the country.[2] They are well aware that the threat cannot be addressed by military means alone, and that it demands a rapid acceleration of economic and social development programmes at the local level.

## While conflicts in Africa have been quite common, Boko Haram shows that a new type of menace is emerging.

Conflicts in Africa are not a new phenomenon—quite the contrary. There have been many conflicts, some of them devastating,

---

[2] In June 2016, the military base of Bosso, close to Diffa, was taken over by Boko Haram fighters, and 32 soldiers from Niger were killed.

in the decades following independence. These included both attempts at secession (Biafra) and long secessionist struggles (South Sudan, Eritrea). Some conflicts arose in the context of difficult decolonization (Angola, Mozambique, Guinea Bissau). Many took place in the context of the Cold War (Ethiopia, Somalia) and were supported by external players. Some of these conflicts were consequences of implosions of the economy and the state apparatus, and interference of neighbouring countries (Democratic Republic of Congo [DRC]), or the outcome of ethno-political crises (Rwanda). The rarest type consisted of classic conflicts between states, such as the one that once gripped Burkina Faso and Mali.

These wars and conflicts can be categorized according to various typologies, but they were essentially the result of internal political clashes and were only marginally driven by global ideologies. Even when regional coalitions were involved, for example in the DRC which, linked to the Rwandan genocide, has been considered by many observers to be the worst conflict in Africa,[3] each conflict was essentially unique in that it was linked to the specific characteristics, internal political tensions, and specific weaknesses of a particular state.

Francophone Africa was, for the most part, spared large-scale conflicts, if we omit the particular case of Chad and of the former Belgian colonies, the DRC, Rwanda, and Burundi. The reasons probably lie in a relatively well-managed decolonization process, concern on the part of the elites in power for the appeasement of ethno-political tensions through diverse redistributions, and the role played at the regional level by structured organizations such as West Africa Economic Monetary Union and the Franc Zone (Communauté Financière en Afrique or CFA). A final factor was the existence of defence agreements with France, which constituted de facto protection against external aggression but which, until recently, were perceived by local elites as insurance against internal uprisings.

With the end of the Cold War a quarter century ago, most African countries generally felt secure against external threats, and

[3] Gerard Prunier, *Africa's World War: Congo, the Rwandan Genocide and the Making of a Continental Catastrophe* (Oxford University Press, 2009).

their military budgets remained low.[4] But, for at least a decade now, new kinds of threats have developed from the depths of the forgotten countryside. These threats are arising in places where radical Islam has replaced the secular ideologies of the twentieth century (Marxism or fascism, for example), which had barely penetrated Africa. The broad ideology associated with these insurgencies gives the populations of these regions simplistic explanations for their misery and pushes them to believe that the West is responsible for it. The menaces are particularly dangerous because they are likely to spread to the many regions in Africa that, like northeastern Nigeria, have fallen behind in development.[5]

For a long time, the power elites in Africa assumed that the main danger came from rebellious armies or from the streets of deprived neighbourhoods. To deal with these dangers, they reinforced the presidential guards built on tribal loyalties and instituted populist policies ranging from low-cost cereal imports to subsidies for diesel fuel. However, rural people in peripheral regions were largely forgotten. It seemed their political weight did not count, for there was no effort to bank their votes. Their isolation was reinforced both by populist policies and by the lack of all-season road infrastructure. Surprisingly, the new menace is coming precisely from these peripheral rural areas long forgotten by the elites.

## The nature of the threats hanging over many African countries has changed.

New threats are emerging in countries subject to tensions that neither national institutions nor failing political processes are able to manage. Large-scale challenges weaken state structures that have been created too recently and are yet to develop deep roots.

---

[4] To some extent, the situation is comparable to Western Europe, where the US shielding and membership in NATO have led to a steady decline in military contributions until President Trump shook Europe's confidence in NATO.

[5] A full analysis of this issue has been recently developed in 'Linking Security and Development: A Plea for the Sahel,' FERDI Foundation, November 2016.

One striking characteristic is the similarity of the tensions and challenges that have appeared simultaneously in many countries, sometimes regardless of highly satisfactory rates of economic growth.

The causes are very often the coincidence of strong demographic growth, a narrow economic base principally focused on fairly unproductive agricultural activities, vast territories that are difficult for a weak state apparatus to control, populations fragmented into ethnic or religious groups, and the presence of a large Muslim population subjected, for several decades, to strong Salafist propaganda supported by social actions. The considerable underemployment among young men entering the labour market has also sometimes been heightened by marginalization or by economic or political discrimination.

These countries or regions, often described as 'fragile', are currently subjected to destabilization attempts, conducted by jihadist groups, on their poorly governed peripheries. These groups control specific economic circuits dealing with illicit trafficking of weapons, cigarettes, drugs, and migrants. While francophone countries, contrary to what occurred in the northeast of Nigeria, were generally spared large-scale conflicts, these threats have now developed in the countries of the francophone Sahel—Mali, Niger, Chad, Burkina Faso, and Mauritania—which have grouped together to confront them as the 'G5'. However, the regional nature of the menace also has an impact on nearby countries, particularly Senegal, Côte d'Ivoire, and Cameroon, as well as on the border regions of Kenya and Ethiopia[6] close to the 'failed' states of Somalia and South Sudan. Thus, the entire Sahel-Saharan belt and its neighbouring areas to the south, from Senegal to Kenya, are affected.

A series of events in 2012 and 2013 brought to light the severity of these threats. First, with the collapse of the Malian army, the whole north of Mali was taken over by jihadist groups. Emboldened by their victory, they soon attempted to take control of the south of the country but were stopped by the intervention

---

[6] The Ethiopian army, which is essential to the maintenance of order in Somalia, is currently withdrawing many of its troops from the country to deal with rural uprisings in Ethiopia itself.

of the French army. Meanwhile, the well-funded Nigerian army was unable to regain control of the area where Boko Haram was active. In short order, the ideological, financial, technical, and sometimes military links among these groups became apparent, particularly Al-Qaeda in the Islamic Maghreb (AQIM), Ansar Dine and Mujao in Mali, and Boko Haram in Nigeria. The symbolic attachment of jihadist groups in the Sahel and Nigeria to Al-Qaeda or ISIS signaled a connection to similar centres of jihad in the Middle East and sometimes even Afghanistan.

These new threats are evidenced by the presence of armed groups, often of foreign origin, linked to fundamentalist Islam, that take advantage of local tensions to slip into lawless, peripheral areas of fragile states. They result in a rising incidence of illicit roadblocks and taxation of road users, cattle rustling, assaults and kidnappings of traders, followed by targeted assassinations of hostile local authorities, and punitive attacks on recalcitrant villages. These actions clearly demonstrate the breakdown of the local state apparatus.

This first phase is frequently followed by terrorist acts carried out in local markets or capital cities by young suicide bombers. Less spectacular, but even more serious, is the everyday insecurity that is becoming widespread,[7] which paralyses travel and can lead to the collapse of the local economy. At the same time, in some cases such as Mali, attempts are made to set up parallel 'proto-state' structures that provide justice and security but impose religious and social norms on the population.

## The Sahel is specifically at risk.

The French intervention in Mali brought to light the enormous fragility of the entire region known as the Sahel, the definition of which varies. In its broadest sense, it connotes an area of some 7 million square kilometres south of the Sahara. Thus defined, the region encompasses about ten countries,[8] from the Atlantic

---

[7] We may recall here the transfer of the Paris–Dakar Rally to Latin America in 2009 for security reasons.

[8] Burkina Faso, Eritrea, Gambia, Guinea Bissau, Mali, Mauritania, Niger, Senegal, Sudan, and Chad.

Ocean to the Red Sea, and includes the northern parts of several states that border the Gulf of Guinea.[9] The four landlocked countries of the French-speaking Sahel, on which this analysis is focused, constitute an important subset of the region, covering a more limited (but still huge) area of just over 4 million square kilometres—almost eight times the size of France.

A climate map of this vast region would be marked by parallel bands of decreasing rainfall on the approach to the Sahara. The most northerly and arid Saharan-Sahel regions receive between 100 and 300 millimetres of precipitation per year, and no cultivation is possible outside of oases and a few low-lying areas surrounding small ponds. Only livestock herding, between lowlands and adjacent mountains, is practiced.

A little farther south, in the band where rainfall is between 300 and 500 millimetres per year—the true Sahel region—pastoralism continues to dominate, along with cultivation of short-cycle millet, sorghum, and some groundnut. Still farther south, where rainfall is between 500 and 700 millimetres per year, subsistence cereal crops based on millet, sorghum, and groundnut, as well as a little cotton, predominate. Finally, in the Sudan-Sahel band, where rainfall is between 700 and 900 millimetres, cultivation focuses on long-cycle sorghum, cotton, and maize. Only southern Chad and southwestern Burkina Faso are considered to be in the Sudanese region (rainfall between 900 and 1,200 millimetres), which has more agricultural potential.

I have focused my analysis on the landlocked French-speaking countries of the Sahel, in part because my recollections of Sudan, Gambia, Mauritania, and Guinea-Bissau date back to the 1970s and 1980s, and are now rather old. Among the French-speaking countries, these four landlocked nations seem, to me, to pose the greatest challenges. In the east, Sudan and Eritrea indeed face specific problems, as do the coastal nations of Mauritania, Guinea-Bissau, and Gambia in the west. Senegal has its own prospects due to the excellent port in Dakar. The four landlocked countries on which this analysis focuses—Burkina Faso, Mali, Niger,

---

[9] The Permanent Interstates Committee for Drought Control (CILSS) in the Sahel also includes the northern parts of Benin, Cameroon, Ethiopia, Guinea, and Nigeria.

and Chad (plus the northern hinterlands of two other important French-speaking countries, Côte d'Ivoire and Cameroon)—form the heart of the French-speaking Sahel and share a number of similarities. Thus, further in this text, the term 'Sahel' refers to these four landlocked countries which, as we will examine in detail later, are the most at-risk and have already been severely hurt by these new threats.

## These new threats are also worrying for many reasons.

These threats emerge in regions facing the serious problems previously described. They primarily affect low-income countries, with limited tax revenues, that have largely neglected their military capacities as well as their overall security and state structures. Most disturbing are the links between demography and natural resources, weaknesses and sometimes serious dysfunctions in the state apparatus, the lack of agricultural modernization and associated environmental degradation, and the lack of jobs and opportunities for young people who, without alternatives, easily become involved in illegal trafficking and may be tempted by looting, kidnappings, and attacks on villages.

The main victims of these threats are civilians, who are often unaccounted for because of the absence of local administration and records. In practice, clashes between armed groups and local armed forces are limited because they are asymmetric; control of entire territories and the populations residing in them is often achieved through a process that does not become visible for many years.[10] For jihadist groups, controlling territories and evicting state structures so as to conduct their trafficking, and undermining the morale of local armed forces through harassment, are more important than defeating them, which often is not within their capabilities.

Many armed groups that threaten these fragile countries have support networks and logistical bases in neighbouring countries

---

[10] To take the Afghan example, the calmest areas are those that are well-controlled by the Taliban. As the Afghan state no longer has the means to challenge the Taliban in these areas, the Taliban, in turn, has no interest in fomenting disorder.

that are subject to even greater insecurity and are virtually inaccessible, as is the case of Fezzan in Libya, and in parts of Somalia. Finally, these threats have a very strong ideological dimension based on a radical Islamism supported by foundations and networks in the Persian Gulf and promoted by skilled jihadist propaganda, backed by considerable financial resources and expertise. They are part of an arc of crisis that runs from Afghanistan to Mauritania through Iraq, Syria, the Sinai, and Libya, where failed democratic efforts, external interventions (such as in Iraq and Libya), religious conflicts, misgovernment, economic failure, and mass unemployment or underemployment have accumulated in multi-ethnic or multi-religious contexts.

These zones of insecurity behave like metastasizing cancers—exporting terrorism, arms trafficking, and jihadist propaganda, and taking advantage of local ethno-political tensions and problems to insert themselves and grow in fragile neighbouring countries. If they are not swiftly controlled, these threats risk spilling over from their areas of origin, spreading terrorism and giving rise to widespread insecurity in neighbouring countries, even those with relatively well-structured state systems.

The ongoing decline in security in the north and now in the centre of Mali clearly threatens the Malian state. But it also threatens western Niger, as evidenced by regular attacks. The October 2016 attack on the Tassalit camp in which the Niger army lost 22 soldiers and the October 2017 attack near Tillabery, 80 kilometres from Niamey, in which four US special forces green berets supporting the Niger army lost their lives, are examples of constant skirmishes with Malian armed groups. Finally, security deterioration in Mali also threatens Mauritania and, potentially, Senegal, as well as Burkina Faso and northern Côte d'Ivoire.

## The multidimensional nature of these conflicts makes them difficult to defeat.

In the Sahel, since 2000, 'the deterioration of the situation has accelerated exponentially when the various threats have combined their interests. Thus, when traffickers, highway bandits, autonomists, jihadists, etc., could reconcile their interests, the scale of the threat dramatically increased, whereas the previous compartmentalization that existed between the threats helped to keep them at low intensity'.[11] Just as a series of small waves, through the resonance phenomenon, can create a monster wave, this overlapping of formerly isolated threats now causes a greater threat of unexpected magnitude and reach.

A significant part of the African continent now faces a variety of threats whose determinants are not only linked to local politics or specific to the continent, but are also found in other multi-ethnic or multi-religious countries in the Middle East, the Caucasus, and Central Asia. These threats reflect the messianic ideology of jihadism, with its hatred of the West and its values, and are fostered by poverty, mass underemployment, a loss of bearings and hope among young people, the absence of the state, and missing or inept local governments. This takes place in a context of increased access to information which allows dispirited young men to watch Al Jazeera even from remote villages.

The collapse of the great secular ideologies of the twentieth century was thus succeeded—and in spectacular fashion since 11 September 2001—by a new religious ideology that clearly identified its enemies: apostates, the West and its education system and culture, and local elites corrupted by Western culture. This ideological phenomenon has an ethnic dimension and is heightened by tensions linked to conflicts over land and access to water. Conflicts among individuals (such as the one illustrated in the film *Timbuktu,* mentioned earlier, in which a farmer butts heads with a breeder whose cow had eaten the farmer's lettuce and is finally killed by the breeder) now easily take on an ethnic dimension— for example, setting Fulani and Bambaras against each other in central Mali.

Throughout the Sahel, this new situation now gives rise to multiple flashpoints in regions that are as dangerous as powder kegs. The question facing both the countries directly affected by this phenomenon, and their neighbours, is how to deal with these new threats.

---

[11] General Clément-Bollée, former commander of the French Unicorn force in Côte d'Ivoire, in an exchange with the author.

# CHAPTER
# TWO

# Programmed Demographic
# Explosion in the Sahel?*

The most spectacular demographic changes in the whole of human history are currently taking place on the African continent, and this development is set to continue over the course of the coming decades. Europeans accustomed to stagnant population figures find it difficult to grasp the consequences of a 3 per cent annual growth in population, which leads to an approximate doubling of the population every twenty years.

## In terms of demographics, Africa is a special case.

Sub-Saharan Africa is in the midst of demographic development different from that of other continents. Due to the upheavals and unrest caused by the slave trade, Africa is the only continent

---

* This chapter is based on an article published in German and English in KAS International Reports. Cf. Serge Michailof, 'Programmed Explosion? The Potential Consequences of the Rapid Population Growth in Sub-Saharan Africa', *International Reports*, 32(4) (31 December): 41–54, available at http://www.kas.de/wf/en/33.47597/ (last accessed on 27 June 2017).

whose population virtually stagnated between 1500 and 1900, increasing from around 80 to only 95 million. Despite relatively low population growth rates elsewhere in the world during the same period (0.2 per cent during the seventeenth century and 0.5 per cent during the nineteenth century), they still led to a five-fold increase in population in Europe and China.[1]

During the course of the twentieth century, Europe's population doubled, China's tripled, India's grew fivefold, and Sub-Saharan Africa's increased sevenfold.[2] This immense increase in global population over the course of the twentieth century can be attributed to the convergence of two factors: the large decrease in mortality, particularly child mortality, and persistently high fertility rates (the average number of children per woman), until a gradual decline in fertility rates set in. Hence, demographic growth remained high, about 2 per cent, in most developing regions until 1960. But, from the 1960s on, fertility rates dropped rapidly everywhere, except for Sub-Saharan Africa.

Decreasing demographic growth—often referred to as a demographic transition—is characterized by a gradual decline in the fertility rate, which usually follows a large decrease in child mortality due to improved sanitary conditions.[3] Such a decline in the fertility rate usually relates to several factors, particularly girls' education, access to modern contraceptive options,[4] and urbanization. But a key element has certainly been the implementation of family planning programmes, initiated mostly by governments in Asia and civil society organizations in Latin America.

---

[1] Jean Pierre Guengant, '*La démographie africaine entre convergence et divergences*', in Benoit Ferry, *L'Afrique face à ses défis démographiques, un avenir incertain* (Karthala, 2007).

[2] Jean Pierre Guengant and John F. May, '*L'Afrique subsaharienne dans la démographie mondiale*', *Études: Revue de culture contemporaine*, 415(4) (October 2011).

[3] The definition of a demographic transition is the shift from a traditional situation where fertility and mortality rates are near equilibrium, but at a high level, to a situation in which both fertility and mortality are near equilibrium, but at a low level.

[4] John F. May, *World Population Policies: Their Origins, Evolution and Impact* (Springer, 2012).

In Africa, however, fertility rates remained very high through-out the period and have almost stabilized at about 5.4 children per woman; during the last few years, the rate actually exceeded seven children per woman in most countries in the Sahel. This significant disparity between the rapid decline in the infant mortality rate and the stability in fertility is the main driver of Africa's demographic circumstances. This situation has resulted in continuously high population growth rates, averaging 2.7 per cent in Sub-Saharan Africa and over 3 per cent in most countries in the Sahel. So how will this African population develop in the course of the twenty-first century?

In view of the persistently high fertility rate, it seems likely that Africa is set to experience a second population explosion during the twenty-first century, following the initial one that took place during the twentieth century. But how big will it be? In view of the inertia that characterizes demographic phenomena, one can already forecast with some accuracy that the population in Sub-Saharan Africa will reach between 1.3 and 1.4 billion by 2030. In this region, the decline in fertility rates is considerably slower than one would expect based on the classic model. Disregarding the five countries of southern Africa, it appears that fertility rates are, in fact, currently stabilizing at more than four children in the most highly developed and urbanized African countries.[5] There has been no serious analysis of how cultural and religious factors, lack of access to contraception, and lack of interest on the part of the authorities may affect the situation. Research indicates that there has been no significant progress in the use of contraception—this only increased by 0.2 per cent per year in the first decade of the twenty-first century.

## The demographic transition has just begun.

While one can predict the size of the African population in 2030 with a fair degree of precision, predictions for 2050 are much more difficult because the trend in fertility rates until 2050 is highly uncertain. Several worrisome issues are involved.

[5] The five countries which are exceptions to the high fertility rates are South Africa, Botswana, Lesotho, Swaziland, and Namibia.

In Sub-Saharan Africa, the decrease in fertility is much slower than anticipated from the standard demographic model. It even seems to stabilize at approximately four children for the most developed and urbanized countries of southern Africa. Also, according to various surveys, most African women seem eager to have large families with five to nine children and even up to nine to twelve in the Sahel. In a context where access to modern contraceptives is very difficult, high fertility rates should not come as a surprise.

Authorities have shown a lack of commitment to the active promotion of family planning. External donors also show little concern for resolving this issue. The amount disbursed by the member states of the Organization for Economic Cooperation and Development (OECD) to run population programmes accounts for merely 0.2 per cent of its overall aid budget. In addition, numerous religious authorities, ranging from the American Right to jihadists from the Sahel, are vehemently opposed to birth control. The George W. Bush administration bears particular responsibility in this respect, as it decided to cut financial support to all aid organizations involved in this area, which led the World Bank, for instance, to basically dismantle its unit in charge of demographic issues. The new Trump administration has recently reconfirmed this decision.

Accordingly, there is a great deal of uncertainty about the population figures that can be expected by 2050. We do not know, for instance, how quickly the mortality rate among children under five can be reduced. In Africa, this rate declined from 256 per 1,000 children in the early 1970s to 120 per 1,000 today. That said, child mortality is almost ten times lower in Asia and 20 times lower in Europe. Significant progress is therefore to be expected in this area. However, while this progress is in itself highly desirable, it will undoubtedly affect population growth rates.

The population of Sub-Saharan African countries—about one billion in 2017—will most likely at least double by 2050. If the fertility rate throughout Sub-Saharan Africa were to decline from 5.4 children per woman (as in the 2005 to 2010 period) to 2.6 at the beginning of the 2050s, the population would rise to 1.8 billion by 2050. However, if the fertility rate were still as high as 3.5 children per woman, the population would rise to 2.3 billion.

## The case of Niger is characteristic of the Sahel demographic impasse.

When it gained its independence in 1960, Niger had a population of approximately 3 million. The figure has since risen to 20 million. And one can safely assume that whatever the expected development of the fertility rate and family-planning efforts, Niger will have more than 40 million inhabitants by 2035. The previous estimate for annual population growth of some 3.5 per cent was revised upwards to 4 per cent in 2015, and may even exceed the 4.3 per cent mark by 2035 based on the latest developments.

Forecasts for the period between 2035 and 2050 differ greatly depending on the assumed decline in the fertility rate. They range from a very optimistic 63 million at a fertility rate of 4.1 by 2050 to 76 million at a rate of 5.1, and finally to 89 million if the fertility rate were to remain at the current 7.6. One can conclude that by 2050, twenty times as many people will live in Niger as in 1960. Yet, is it not the children who are a family's wealth and a people's future?

Niger has a land mass of 1,267 million square kilometres, making the country roughly two-and-a-half times the size of France. But more than 85 per cent of the population lives in a narrow band along the Niger River and the border with Nigeria. Indeed, less than 8 per cent of the land area receives average rainfall exceeding 400 millimetres and is suitable for agricultural use. In these areas, population density varies from 60 to more than 100 inhabitants per square kilometre—even up to 150 inhabitants per square kilometre in some districts.

In view of the irregular rainfall, great disparity in soil quality, extensive cultivation methods, and scarcity of irrigation, population density becomes problematic as soon as the threshold of some 40 inhabitants per square kilometre is exceeded. This is because higher population density results in reduced fallow periods, land overuse, dramatic deforestation to cover the demand for firewood, and increased conflicts with cattle herders, who no longer have sufficient space for their nomadic herding. Documents in the public domain already indicate that the amount of arable land per working-age resident has been halved in 30 years, declining from 11.8 hectares in 1980 to 5 hectares in 2010.

This uncontrolled population growth has led to areas—by now even entire regions—that suffer from dramatic rural poverty, where tensions surrounding land use are severe and situations arise that can only be described as localized Malthusian crises. As we will examine in Chapter 3, 'Marginalization and underemployment in rural Africa', these problems are exacerbated by the lack of appropriate public and private investment in agriculture and inadequate agricultural policies.

## Will Malthus be right in the Sahel?

In the debate about population development, proponents of the doctrine put forward by Jean Bodin in 1576—which says that it is people who generate power and wealth—frequently find themselves opposed by the followers of Thomas Robert Malthus, who argued in favour of limiting population growth to prevent famine, wars, and epidemics, in his 1798 publication *An Essay on the Principle of Population*. Of course, each proposal reflects the problems confronting society in its particular periods. Jean Bodin's writings were published after a long period of demographic stagnation in Europe following the Black Plague. Malthus's work[6] came after a period of strong demographic growth at the end of the eighteenth century, when yields in agriculture were stagnant. But, of course, there have been many changes since the two authors published their works. The nineteenth and twentieth centuries were also marked by famines, wars, and epidemics of various kinds—not solely demographic ones.

By and large, events proved that Malthus was in error as scientific progress, particularly in agriculture, has confounded his predictions. However, experts are also aware that at a local level—for example, in a valley in Afghanistan or in a certain area of the Sahel—the combination of exceptional population growth and a lack of investment in agriculture and technical progress can result in Malthus's predictions coming true. Niger and other Sahel countries, for instance, are experiencing an increasing exodus

---

[6] Thomas Robert Malthus, *An Essay on the Principle of Population* (Oxford University Press, 2008).

from rural areas and greater dependence on humanitarian aid—situations that are only likely to get worse.

Cereal consumption in Niger is in the range of 4.7 million tonnes. Once every three years, Niger suffers from cereal shortages in excess of 500,000 tonnes. In periods of severe drought, this deficit can easily rise to a million tonnes or more. This deficit is generally covered by regional trade with neighbouring countries and by the efforts of the *Office des Produits Vivriers du Niger* (OVPN), the authority for strategic supply and national intervention. However, when the drought affects the entire sub-region, as was largely the case in 1973 and 1984, the situation quickly takes a dramatic turn. Even in 'almost ordinary' periods of moderate drought, such as 2009 and 2010, as many as 2.3 million Nigerians suffered from malnutrition.

In most of the Sahel, people are engaged in subsistence farming, which often does not even cover their own needs. They have to seek resources elsewhere, resulting in the rural exodus to major cities, Nigeria, or Ivory Coast, where they are not always welcome, and where many do not find work.[7] A minor climatic event can cause supply shortages and even famines.

Regularly recurring periods of drought result in catastrophic chains of damaging events. Besides spectacular crop failures due to water shortages, fairly regular swarms of locusts devastate crops and grazing land, epidemics spread through herds of cattle, food prices rise (going up fourfold or even fivefold), livestock numbers decline, the number of people making a living from farming and cattle breeding declines, debt proliferates, nutritional standards deteriorate, and, of course, poverty increases. The correlations between these mechanisms indicate that the effects of a strong drought can be felt for several years. Given these conditions, it is understandable that young people dream of leaving their homeland.

In view of Niger's increasing dependence on imports and food aid, significant efforts are being made to develop large-scale irrigation systems, communal or individual small-scale irrigation, and

---

[7] According to a recent survey, six out of ten migrants from Niger to coastal cities had not been able to find work: cf. *'Enquête nationale sur la migration au Niger'*, ENAMI, 2011.

measures are being taken to improve the use of surface water. Despite these efforts, cereals grown on irrigated land account for less than 2 per cent of overall cereal production, and forecasts show that even if all areas suitable for irrigation were developed— that is, some 330,000 hectares—Niger would continue to depend strongly (around 75 per cent by 2050) on extremely precarious rain-fed agriculture.

## Excessive population growth leads to increased poverty.

Africa still looks very much like an empty continent. Its average population density of about 40 people per square kilometre seems quite low compared to Asia's 137 per square kilometer. However, when deserts, arid steppes, and forests with highly fragile tropical soils are excluded, the ratio does not look so favourable. Also, taking into account the extensive cultivation currently practised and the limited irrigation potential compared to Asia, the population density becomes problematic in many regions, and Bodin's principle does not hold true.

While the idea that large number of children represent a source of wealth may hold within the rural family context because it increases manpower, if we look at the overall picture at the national level, the principle no longer remains valid. First, very high population growth depresses per capita income growth. If GDP grows by 5 per cent and population by 3.5 per cent, effective GDP growth per person is only 1.5 per cent. At this rate, it would take more than 45 years to double the living standard per inhabitant. This problem is illustrated dramatically by per capita GDP in Niger, which has declined by a third since the country gained independence, dropping from USD 476 in 1960 to USD 297 in 2014, having reached a low of around USD 260[8] in the period from 2002 to 2010.

Secondly, if the population of a poor country increases by 750,000 children every year, as is currently the case in Niger, and infants and school-age children already make up half the population, covering their needs in the areas of education, training, and

[8] All data here expressed in 2005 constant USD terms.

healthcare becomes financially prohibitive. Niger has redoubled its efforts with respect to schooling over the last fifteen years. The primary school enrolment ratio rose from 31 per cent in 2000 to almost 84 per cent in 2014. But the quality of education has lagged, and the average period children spend at school is under 1.4 years, while it takes at least five years for a child to become proficient in reading, writing, and arithmetic.

In principle, the growth of the working-age population (individuals aged 15 to 64 years) leads to a phenomenon described as the 'window of demographic opportunity' as working-age cohorts reach the labour market. To be transformed into a 'demographic dividend',[9] however, this 'window of demographic opportunity' requires a reduction in the number of dependents, be it children under the age of 15 years or elders over 65 years. If fertility remains high, the number of dependent children also remains high. As a result, contrary to expectations, very few African countries can hope to benefit from this 'demographic dividend'. John May from the Population Reference Bureau and Hans Groth from the World Demographic & Ageing Forum make this point in their recent work, *Africa's Population: In Search of a Demographic Dividend* (2017). Several econometric studies have also concluded that economic growth in emerging countries has significantly benefited from a decrease in the number of dependents.[10]

Young people flooding into the labour market need to find decent jobs if they are to benefit from a demographic dividend. In Africa, however, such prospects remain largely illusory. Again, regarding the situation in Niger, there are almost no jobs in manufacturing; the mining and oil sector employs some 5,000 to 6,000 people and presently create no new employment opportunities, while some 240,000 young men enter the job market

---

[9] The demographic dividend is the economic benefit accruing to a country undergoing a demographic transition. The number of working age adults reaches a high level while the number of dependents (young children and elders) is low. In such a situation, the population is extremely productive and the transfers to the young and elders limited. It facilitates high economic growth.

[10] B.J. Ndulu, *Challenges of African Growth: Opportunities, Constraints and Strategic Directions* (World Bank, 2007).

every year. Due to land scarcity, poor soil fertility, and meager returns from agriculture, many young people are driven out of rural areas. Unfortunately, they have a far greater likelihood of entering the masses of unemployed workers living in slums than of obtaining a skilled job; the same applies to young people in the cities, including graduates.

All in all, it appears virtually certain that the demographic transition in Sub-Saharan Africa, and particularly in the Sahel, has only just begun and will take decades to conclude. The next 30 years will see a spectacular rise in population figures and the number of young people, which will pose a challenge to food availability, improvement of living standards, social benefits, and, above all, the job situation. Both in rural areas and megacities, there will be vast numbers of unemployed people with little hope of social advancement, including many frustrated graduates ready to engage in risky endeavours.

Large numbers of young Africans in the cities belong to the group referred to as 'NEETs'—Not in Education, Employment, or Training. These young people either live off their parents, survive by taking small temporary jobs, or indulge in thefts. It is worth noting that the same phenomenon plays a significant role in the increasing tensions in the Middle East, which led to the famous Arab Spring and to the catastrophes taking place in Syria, Iraq, and Yemen. This means that the coming decades in Sub-Saharan Africa will be beset by all kinds of dangers.[11]

## The demography of the Sahel region can destabilize all of West Africa.

How can a landlocked country like Niger—with only limited agricultural potential, adverse climatic conditions, and a poorly educated population—hope to be capable of offering 60 to 80 million inhabitants a normal life in 35 years' time? And how can the group of the four countries forming the core of the Francophone Sahel Zone—whose population is set to increase from 67 million

---

[11] I have discussed this in detail in my book *Notre maison brûle au Sud* (Fayard, 2010).

in 2015 to between 120 and 132 million by 2035, and then to 170 to 210 million by 2050—hope to master first a doubling and then a tripling of its population in such a short time, knowing that the population will continue to increase after 2100 even if substantial efforts are made in the area of family planning? West Africa, south of the Sahara, with its 400 million population and 700 million in 25 years, is a bomb. The Sahel can act as a detonator.

With agricultural research largely in ruins in most countries of the Sahel, it is hard to believe that technical progress will allow the region to overcome the problems caused by such a large increase in population, or that such demographic growth in a region facing so many disadvantages and threats would not have dramatic consequences. Crop failures due to climatic catastrophe could result in large-scale regional famines in which food and humanitarian aid are overwhelmed. One can hardly expect to feed 30 to 50 million people with food aid for the simple reasons that the required volumes of cereals would not be available on time, mobilizing the necessary financial resources would take too long (and may not even be possible), and logistical systems could not cope with distributing the aid even if, by some miracle, the first two problems could be overcome.

In fact, humanitarian aid would be largely ineffective if a severe drought affected an entire region, because that would preclude intraregional trade from making up for local deficits. In September 1984, while I was the local representative of the French aid agency (AFD) in Niger, I was summoned to the presidential palace in Niamey by the then President Seyni Kountche when it became clear that, due to insufficient rains, the agricultural campaign had failed not only in Niger but in the whole sub-region. Clearly, the country would soon be confronted with a massive food crisis similar to the 1974 crisis, which had devastating consequences. The president, a former officer in the French Army, had a very direct way of addressing his visitors; many of his ministers were almost paralysed in front of him by the mix of fear and respect that he instilled. Even before I could sit, he asked me, 'Hey, Michailof, you know that the agricultural campaign has failed. In your view, during colonial times, what would the French have done?'

I had no idea what the response of the French governor would have been in such a situation, and in fact the president had already made up his mind and just wanted to test his ideas on me. He knew that about half the population—some 3 to 4 million people—would be at great risk. Maybe half-a-million tonnes of cereals or more would be needed, and he knew that, due to lack of rail facilities, his country would be unable to mobilize that volume of food from donors through 1,500 kilometres of dilapidated roads in time. His plan was to import seeds and tools by plane for off-season horticulture, using the thousands of small basins in the country where some water had accumulated. He wanted the army to identify on maps these basins and organize the supply of seeds and tools to farmers as a military operation.

In fact, his plan saved the country from catastrophe. I remember seeing bags of seeds being unloaded from cargo planes at night and army trucks waiting with maps and written orders to rush delivery of their cargo to distant parts of the huge country. But is it realistic to think that what was done in 1984 with a population of 7 or 8 million would be feasible once the population reaches 40 million in 2035 or 60 to 90 million in 2050?

Throughout human history, overpopulation has led to the collapse of whole civilizations. In his remarkable book entitled *Collapse: How Societies Choose to Fail or Succeed* (2005), Jared Diamond gives several examples of societies that did not survive environmental crises that they brought up themselves. Dramatic famines have cost the lives of millions of people. Leaving aside the major twentieth-century famines in Ukraine and China, which resulted from despotic and erroneous policies, Ireland is a case in point. There, around a million people starved to death between 1846 and 1851 when the potato blight devastated several harvests in succession, and the population had grown from 4 to 9 million within four decades. The famine caused mass emigration to the United States of America.

A drama of similarly historic dimensions is likely to take place in the Sahel long before its population has tripled by 2050. The final report of the multidisciplinary conference on the Sahel crisis that the University of California, Berkeley, organized in 2013 in collaboration with the OASIS Initiative stresses that 'there is no escaping the conclusion that climate change and population growth in the Sahel will rapidly outstrip the food supply'.[12] Malcom Potts from the University of California, Berkeley, adds: 'By mid-century, a business-as-usual scenario in the Sahel would turn more people than live in the USA into involuntary migrants with unprecedented challenges for humanitarian relief and profound threats of spreading extremism in an already unstable region.'[13]

The first serious famines will indeed trigger migration flows to regional capital cities, to coastal countries, to the Maghreb, and to Europe, as we have witnessed this year in the northeast of Nigeria and around Lake Chad. In this region, insufficient rainfall during the 2016 agricultural season has added to the insecurity caused by the Boko Haram insurgency that dismantled economic circuits and regional trade. About 2 million people are currently affected by famine, and most are already on the move at the regional level. Some have already reached Italy, having endured horrendous travel conditions in Libya. While representing the most natural 'safety valve', such a migration would inevitably spark a xenophobic response of unprecedented severity and, as seen several times in the past, result in massive deportations and widespread turmoil. The unrest in both Ivory Coast and Libya in 2010–11 resulted in the repatriation of 210,000 Nigers, triggering a great deal of tension.

A more likely consequence, even before such famines set in, will be that the impoverishment of rural areas and the hopelessness felt by the young will boost jihadism. This threat is already ubiquitous in Niger. Being caught between Boko Haram in the southeast, Libya in the north, and the persistently unstable northern and central parts of Mali, insecurity may become so

---

[12] 'Crisis in the Sahel: Possible Solutions and the Consequences of Inaction', OASIS Conference, Berkeley, April 2013. This is an issue that is currently flagged by the OASIS Initiative at the University of California, Berkeley, initiated by Alisha Graves and Malcolm Potts. The OASIS (Organizing to Advance Solutions in the Sahel) focuses on the imperative to educate adolescent girls, make family planning accessible to slow the most rapid population growth in history, and to help some of the poorest societies in the world adapt to global warming.

[13] Recent exchange with the author.

widespread that economic life is paralysed. One telling example is again the disastrous situation in northeastern Nigeria and around the Chad Lake area, where the insurgency by Boko Haram still paralyses economic activity and a humanitarian catastrophe is looming. The insecurity that is still increasing in the Sahel may well spill over into Ivory Coast, Cameroon, Senegal, and Nigeria, whose fragility people tend to underestimate.

A security note published as early as 2014 by the French embassy in Niamey prohibited French citizens from leaving Niamey without an armed escort. It reminded me of a similar note published by the French embassy in Kabul in 2006. One thing is certain: if the current demographic trend in the Sahel continues, the situation will become unmanageable.

## Such worrying developments are not yet irreversible.

While the current situation and events in the Sahel are very worrisome, appropriate policies could mitigate the negative consequences of the extraordinary population growth and at least help buy some time.

Suitable measures in agricultural policy and rural development could slow the rural exodus and initiate genuine and sustainable growth in the rural areas for a period of time. René Billaz, former Scientific Director of the French tropical agronomy research institute Centre de coopération international pour la recherche agronomique et le développement (CIRAD) and subsequently president of the NGO Agronomes et Vétérinaires Sans Frontières (AVSF), has just published a remarkable book summarizing his 60 years of experience in tropical agronomy and his extraordinary expertise in agriculture in the Sahel. The title of his book, which translates to 'Turning the Sahel into a Land of Plenty',[14] paints a clear picture of the challenge. Although the funding available for agricultural research is very modest, the systematic application of knowledge acquired over half a century of agriculture in the Sahel would make it technically possible to at least minimize the agricultural consequences of ongoing climate change in the immediate

---

[14] René Billaz, *Faire du Sahel un pays de cocagne, le défi agro-écologique* (L'Harmattan, 2016).

future. It would even allow the doubling of agricultural yields without the use of expensive chemical fertilizers and pesticides. We will examine these issues in Chapter 3, 'Marginalization and underemployment in rural Africa'.

These initiatives would require many policy and technical changes and adaptations. The measures range from protecting and restoring soil fertility to controlling the rainwater cycle, developing a special way of working the soil, the introduction of animal traction and low-level mechanization, and the use of biopesticides. All this should be accompanied by a literacy drive and the introduction of solar electricity, which is essential for the development of craft businesses. The problem lies in managing the leap from the micro to the macro level—from pilot projects demonstrating what is feasible by the example of a dozen villages to the extension of the lessons learned to millions of beneficiaries.

The application of these fundamental principles requires significant investment and the effective implementation of comprehensive development programmes for rural areas where local budgets include ridiculously small amounts for rural development and international aid organizations have scandalously withdrawn from the sector. One simple example illustrates the huge discrepancy between current realities and needs: Burkina Faso would need 250,000 so-called *Kassines*—lightweight ploughs that can be pulled by donkeys—yet only 400 such Kassines are produced each year.

But gaining some time does not necessarily mean the fight will be won. There is an urgent need to control human fertility, and population control programmes have a poor reputation. While China's one-child policy has been a success—maybe too big a success given the needs of China's ageing population—it took a dictatorial regime to implement it successfully. In India, bureaucratic activism led to forced sterilizations and other human-rights violations. This issue is highly sensitive on cultural, religious, and ideological grounds, yet people still indulge in the hope that the problem ultimately will resolve itself 'spontaneously' through education, urbanization, and the proliferation of modern contraceptive techniques as economic development progresses.

In Europe, North America, and Russia, this approach of relying on economic development and education was successful. In those countries, however, the demographic transition stretched over some one hundred years, and the natural population growth rate did not exceed 1 per cent a year. In Latin America and Asia, where Nobel Prize-winner Gunnar Myrdal forecasted dramatic famines in a famous book published almost half a century ago,[15] natural annual growth rates of over 2 per cent were short-lived. In how many decades can one seriously expect population growth rates of around 1 per cent a year, as is the case in Asia and Latin America these days, in Sub-Saharan Africa? In how many decades will this be a realistic objective in the Sahel region, where population growth has been above 3 per cent since 1960?

## Birth control is unavoidable, but is it politically feasible?

The situation in the Sahel is unique in recent history. Unemployment both in rural areas and in the cities, which is already very troubling, will turn into one of the most urgent problems that the governments of the Sahel countries have to address.

Is the introduction of family planning programmes possible? Technically speaking, it certainly is—there are plenty of examples of success (and of instructive failures) with such programmes in other parts of the world. Thanks to his World Bank experience in this field, John May has reviewed such projects and published specific proposals in *Agir sur les évolutions démographiques* (2013). This should enable authorities to promote the development and introduction of national programmes to facilitate fertility control. Such programmes will need to be conducted with caution, taking the culture of the respective countries into account. The costs would be reasonable—between USD 6 and USD 35 per family per year in a country such as Niger, depending on the type and objective of the programmes involved.

The question remains: is it politically feasible? Launching comprehensive family planning programmes to reduce fertility rates as quickly as possible will be very difficult for Sahel governments. They are likely to not only face opposition from religious

---

[15] Gunnar Myrdal, *Asian Drama: An Inquiry into the Poverty of Nations* (Pelican Books, 1968).

authorities, but also be challenged by the prevailing culture and mindset.

Will the governments have the courage to go against prevailing opinion, against religious conservatives, knowing that armed opposition groups might use the issue as a political argument, which could have destabilizing effects? In fact, the government of Niger has just taken the very important and courageous step of adopting such a birth control plan. But are the international donors, who have always avoided the issue, now prepared to come out of their comfort zone and offer support for these efforts? Are they ready to defy the prohibitive edicts of the religious right in the USA, which has considerable influence, particularly under a Trump presidency? This is likely to require a very ambitious lobbying programme to bring on board numerous influential partners, including the Catholic Church and the Republican religious right in the USA, and get them to at least remain neutral on this issue.

Will carefully thought-through strategies that have worked in well-organized countries such as Iran—where the fertility rate dropped from six children per woman in 1986 to 3.5 in 1994 (that is, in less than a decade) ultimately also work in countries such as Niger, Chad, or Mali, with their poor infrastructure and inefficient institutions? Will the approach that worked in Bangladesh be successful in the Sahel? We do not know the answer to that question yet. But the answer will be of crucial importance to the continent's future.

# CHAPTER
# THREE

## Marginalization and Underemployment in Rural Africa

The preceding chapters brought to light the vastly varied situations among African countries and regions, some experiencing an economic boom, others lagging behind or even in a downslide. But even the situations of countries experiencing economic booms raise many questions. The continent that many consider *the* emerging continent is following a development model that, unless overhauled swiftly, is likely to become socially and politically unsustainable as it does not generate sufficient employment to meet the demographic challenges that have been outlined.

### Employment is the major problem.

International institutions always maintain an optimistic outlook in their policy papers on Africa's economic prospects. And yet they too are now voicing their concerns. The deputy director of the African Department of the International Monetary Fund (IMF) wrote in September 2014: 'The potential for economic growth in Africa is still enormous, and investment, both domestic and foreign, is rising rapidly. Africa's major challenge for the next

20 years is now to ensure that this growth is job-rich and pro-poor. ... There will only be a demographic dividend if employment opportunities are there to match it.'[1]

It has earlier been noted that Africa's young working-age population (15–24 years old) will be three times larger than that of China by 2050: some 362 million versus 124 million. Thus, the ongoing demographic explosion in Africa, marked by the unexpected stabilization of a high birth rate, augurs serious problems if jobs do not materialize. Intensive family farming and upstream and downstream rural entrepreneurship are the only areas of activity that can generate large-scale employment sufficient to meet the job challenge, at least in the short term. The development of the kind of efficient, labour-intensive industry needed to complement a dynamic agricultural policy and generate the skilled jobs expected by the younger generation necessarily takes time and will be examined in the next chapter. This chapter examines how difficult launching an efficient and labour-intensive agricultural development process is, and why doing so will demand much more than merely continuing the current approaches. Because rural development is a critical issue for the Sahel, I go into it in some detail in this chapter and introduce technical elements that some readers may prefer to skip.

## All talk, no walk in agriculture.

Touting the development of agriculture and its myriad related activities as a priority in Africa is a ritual slogan. The number of conferences I have attended on this theme defies count; yet, agriculture in Africa is still lagging. In Sub-Saharan Africa, both agricultural output and cereal production per capita decreased between 1970 and 1990 and have only marginally recovered since. As CIRAD[2] economist Bruno Losch writes, 'Agriculture in the subcontinent could only partially support population growth and urban expansion. There has been a gradual deterioration in the

[1] Roger Nord, 'Regional Economic Outlook', *International Monetary Fund*, April 2014.

[2] Centre de coopération international pour la recherche agronomique et le développement, the French tropical agronomy research institute.

balance of trade in agricultural products which was accompanied by a general decrease in land and labour productivity as compared to other regions of the world.'[3]

Two points should be noted here. First, the rise in agricultural output and cereal production that helped at least partially support population growth was essentially the result of an expansion in cultivated area that cannot continue indefinitely. Regarding intensified farming, little progress was achieved, if one sets aside irrigated lands and contract farming (which is when small farmers enter into agreements to supply agro industries or export traders, as in the cases of cotton, cashew, tobacco, or rubber). Intensified agriculture has been generally limited to the periphery of urban centres, thanks to their denser networks of roads and proximity to urban markets.

The second point is that, due to geographic constraints, irrigation in most of the countries of Sub-Saharan Africa remains marginal. Irrigated lands make up no more than 6 million hectares in all and account for a mere 5 per cent of cultivated land. By comparison, South Asia alone has 90 million hectares of irrigated land. Handicapped by local conditions and the lack of rural electrification, the annual growth of irrigated land remains very low in Africa, standing at 0.7 per cent annually for the decade 1997–2007, with the outlook for the coming decades being even lower, at 0.5 per cent.

In this context, the heightened demographic pressure becomes a problem in many regions. Sub-Saharan Africa, as we have seen, is the only continent where the rural population continues to grow significantly. The average growth rate of this rural population is 1.85 per cent in Sub-Saharan Africa, whereas it is under 0.5 per cent in China and India. By 2050, the rural African population will likely have increased by 310 million, a surge of 57 per cent. This phenomenon is already triggering a reduction of cultivated land per inhabitant which, combined with stagnating or decreasing land productivity, resulted in a 13 per cent decline in cereal production per capita between 1961 and 2010.

[3] Bruno Losch, 'Urban Africa still needs agricultural Africa to meet the continent's challenges', CIRAD, Demeter, *Économie et Stratégies Agricoles* (Economy and Agricultural Policy), 2014.

In this regard, the situation in the Sahel—where population growth will be highest and land resources most limited—is deteriorating rapidly. In the conclusion of an in-depth study in Burkina Faso, which is certainly not the worst-off country in the Sahel, René Billaz writes: 'Food security, environment, education: the state of affairs in these three areas, which is already a matter of serious concern, will have reached alarming dimensions by 2025 and be disastrous by 2050; both the population and ecological clocks are ticking.'[4] He points out that some of the technical and scientific data that would bring about the much-needed agrarian revolution are yet to be defined. Given demographic trends and current agricultural policies, a major tragedy on the scale of a huge Malthusian crisis is brewing. This is an issue that is currently flagged by the OASIS Initiative at the University of California, Berkeley, initiated by Alisha Graves and Malcom Potts, which studies the interaction of demographic growth, health conditions, and food production on the future of the Sahel.[5]

## International aid bears a major responsibility.

This worrisome situation arises from the fact that very few countries—with the notable exception of Côte d'Ivoire—have based their economic development on dynamic small-scale farming. The fine speeches we hear at international conferences typically hide the fact that this sector is systematically neglected in economic policies. Many indicators confirm this situation. The share of the national budgets dedicated to agriculture, for example, is almost always very low; in 2015, despite the Maputo declaration which laid out that African countries should devote at least 10 per cent of their budget to agriculture, only eight countries were able to meet this target and only eighteen countries earmarked over 5 per cent. In fact according to the Arcadia report, on average, the share of

---

[4] René Billaz, 'Burkina 2050: comment nourrir et éduquer 47 millions d'habitants tout en luttant contre la désertification?' (Burkina 2050: Feeding and educating 47 million inhabitants while combating desertification), *AVSF*, 6 July 2013.

[5] Cf. the OASIS Conference organized in 2013 by the University of California, Berkeley.

public expenditures devoted to agriculture has been decreasing from about 6 per cent to less than 3 per cent between 1990 and 2012.[6]

In some countries—the Democratic Republic of the Congo until recently, for instance—agriculture accounted for about 2 per cent of the overall budget, which allowed it to cover only the salaries of the overstaffed Ministry of Agriculture, the offices of which were mostly abandoned! Even with very low budgets, in many countries, the quality of spending is mostly mediocre, the bureaucracy's salaries often absorbing a substantial part of the budget, most of which should have been devoted to investment in research, infrastructure, irrigation, and training. Resources are often subsidizing a small fraction of the peasantry instead of focusing on downstream activities which are critical for a healthy agriculture. Finally, it is telling that only 2 per cent of African students study agronomy.

International aid is also to be squarely blamed for this. It is paradoxical to observe that agriculture-development issues were not even mentioned in the much-discussed Millennium Development Goals (MDG) that international donors set for themselves in 2000 to eradicate extreme poverty by 2015. In the past few years, aid in the agriculture sector at world level has remained at about 5 per cent of the total aid granted;[7] In Africa, aid in this sector remained fragmented and erratic, the smallest difficulty or change in management often leading to projects being abandoned. We are nowhere close to the 30 per cent of development aid that was earmarked by the World Bank for small farmers at the end of the McNamara era in 1981!

Yet, most of the African population still lives in rural areas, the proportion reaching 80 per cent in some countries of the Sahel, such as Niger. Since this population depends first and foremost on low-yield family farming for its survival, boosting productivity remains the best way to increase incomes and reduce poverty.[8]

---

[6] Philippe Chalmin and Yves Jegourel, 'Arcadia: Annual Report on Commodities Analytics and Dynamics in Africa', *Cyclope Economica*, 2017.

[7] 'Agriculture Action Plan 2013–2015', World Bank Group.

[8] I would like to refer to the old, but remarkable, work of Michael Lipton that those who decided on the Millennium Development Goals should have read: Lipton, *Why Poor People Stay Poor? Urban Bias in World Development* (Harvard University Press, 1977).

This fundamental point seems to have been largely overlooked by the major donors.

## The right diagnosis and an appropriate policy had already been outlined in 1973.

In September 1973, in a famous speech he delivered in Nairobi, McNamara had very clearly identified the major problem of rural poverty and framed a suitable strategy to address it. By shelving the McNamara strategy after his departure, the World Bank committed a major mistake from which it has yet to recover. Unlike what it now pretends is the case, expertise in this area is no longer to be found at the Bank, but rather at the Gates Foundation (which recently launched the AGRA programme[9]), International Fund for Agriculture Development (IFAD) in Rome, bilateral aid organizations such as US Agency for international Development (USAID), Britain's Department for International Development (DFID), and Agence francaise de développement (AFD) in France, research institutes like CIRAD and Institut de Recherche pour le Développement (IRD) also in France, and, increasingly, in specific funds like Terra Africa and NGOs such as Groupement de Recherche et d'Echange Technologique (GRET) and Agronomes et vétérinaires sans frontières (AVSF).

In the early 1970s, I had the opportunity to work for the outstandingly competent and motivated team that McNamara had tasked with carrying out his policy, led by Leif Christoffersen, a dynamic young Norwegian. It was a fulfilling period of my life. Considerable expertise had been brought together under one umbrella. The division was made up of highly experienced agronomists—many of whom had worked for the former British colonial services, sported luxuriant grey moustaches, and harboured a marked fondness for whiskey—and young economists who made up for their inexperience with their enthusiasm.

We worked from north-eastern Brazil to India, from North to Central and Eastern Africa. We learned a great deal, although we sometimes made mistakes. We launched overly ambitious rural-development projects without having adequately taken into

[9] Alliance for a Green Revolution in Africa.

account the institutional complexity, socio-economic contexts, and specific technical issues involved. We sometimes underestimated the importance of the macroeconomic context, too. But the team acquired exceptional expertise in a few years. Thus, I was appalled to see the team scattered after McNamara's departure, and the advancement of its managers blocked by bureaucratic jealousy. I watched with even greater consternation as a kind of illusionist was hired to become a special advisor in this sector in the late 1970s and remained there for almost twenty years.

Strangely enough, this person managed to garner the trust of successive World Bank presidents by selling his proposals like an anti-hair-loss lotion, with before-and-after photos. The before picture showed a rocky desert, and after the application of his precepts, smiling farmers stood amidst fields rippling with crops bent under their own weight. This illusionist's agenda was only driven by the concept of extension services, forgetting the importance of agronomic and climatic conditions, pricing policy, the availability of inputs at acceptable prices, risks, market conditions, and a host of other factors that determine agricultural productivity. Seeking to impose measures in Africa and northeastern Brazil (which he was not familiar with) that did succeed in some prosperous regions of India and Turkey, he squandered both resources and the institution's reputation. Terrorizing his teams, he succeeded in making a large portion of the most experienced staff leave.

One still finds seasoned agronomists with extensive field experience at the World Bank. But their numbers have been declining for more than twenty years as they have been replaced by young economists unable to tell a sorghum plant from a cotton plant. The agronomists are now mostly scattered around an institution that has been unable to rebuild a full-sized department with the dynamism and experience of the one that McNamara had set up. Only in 2008 did the institution rediscover the importance of this sector through its annual World Development Report devoted to 'agriculture development'. However it did not lead to a significant shift in policies. In 2012, four years after the publication of this report, aid granted for the development of agriculture was still at 4.8 per cent of the total aid flow,[10] even though the whole

---

[10] 'Agriculture Action Plan 2013–2015', World Bank Group.

world recognizes that the best way to deal with the problem of poverty in the least-developed countries is by increasing agricultural productivity and rural incomes.

## The transition from extensive farming to sustainable intensive farming is difficult.

Availability of land is now a major constraint to the extensive-farming model, which requires long fallow periods. African agriculture will have to transition to intensive farming. Stagnant cereal yields—statistics are available over a long period—show how Sub-Saharan Africa is lagging behind Asia and Europe in this area and how much room there is for improvement. Maize yields, for example, which were practically the same in Africa and Asia in 1960, have soared in Asia over fifty years to more than 4 tonnes per hectare, compared to about 1.8 tonnes per hectare in Africa. Rice yields doubled during this period in Asia, rising from 2 to 4.2 tonnes per hectare, while they have generally stagnated in Africa, moving from 1.9 to 2.2 tonnes per hectare. The important question now is why the agriculture transition to intensive farming has not occurred in Africa. How can agriculture be intensified? And which agricultural-development model should the continent follow?

Behind the stagnation of Africa's production, lies of course, the lack of irrigation and the shortening of the fallowing period, which causes soil fertility to drop. However attempts to undertake intensive farming face many other obstacles: the lack of rural roads, the related difficulty of getting surplus product to the market, the unavailability of inputs at affordable prices, and, of course, the unavailability of credit. Historically, the growth in population density all over the world has triggered gradual agricultural intensification. But in Africa, especially in the Sahel, the high rate of population growth is thwarting progress in agricultural intensification. Quite simply, population growth is too rapid for extensive agriculture to shift gradually to sustainable intensive agriculture, as occurred in Europe throughout the nineteenth and twentieth centuries. This means that, in landlocked Sahel countries, traditional farming systems are no longer sustainable in the current demographic context.

Focusing on the growing gap between agricultural output and food consumption, and the increased dependence on global markets that this implies, many African leaders are considering a swift transition to a European- or even American-type agricultural model.[11] However, this model has several serious drawbacks for Africa: to begin with, it requires extensive use of chemical inputs and mechanization. Production costs are therefore largely indexed on fuel prices. In the long term, they are likely to rise significantly. The second drawback creates even more concern: large-scale mechanization will only accelerate an already problematic phenomenon of rural–urban migration and destroy existing as well as potential jobs. Finally, the conventional tillage utilized in such mechanised farming systems could have a disastrous impact on the very fragile tropical soils, as pointed out by Daniel Nahon, former CIRAD president and one of the foremost experts on tropical soils.[12]

Thus, the continent's demography and the political 'sustainability' of the development model requires not so much a rapid shift towards large-scale mechanization, but rather a focus on the development of small-scale farming. There is considerable room for progress in small-scale farming once the market is assured, inputs are available, and the output prices are attractive and relatively stable. This is why intensification based on peasant farming is occurring on the outskirts of urban hubs but does not spread spontaneously very far.

## Agroecology is an interesting approach.

While various models of small-scale farming intensification can be adopted, the conventional model is based on the heavy use of chemical inputs. But other models can also be considered—particularly, an ecologically intensive farming model as recommended

---

[11] I devoted an earlier book to analysing these mistakes: *Les Apprentis Sorciers du Développement* (Development's Apprentice Sorcerers) (Economica, 1987).

[12] Daniel Nahon, *Sauvons l'Agriculture* (Let's Save Agriculture) (Odile Jacob, 2012).

by, among others, Vincent Ribier and Pierre Baris.[13] Not only does this model not make agricultural income dependent on fuel prices, it also maximizes the biological processes for carbon and nitrogen fixation, thus preserving soil fertility. This is also the model that the famous French agronomist René Dumont recommended fifty years ago.

René Billaz also pleads for agroecology: 'The Green Revolution's limitations have been revealed in fragile environments. This has been seen for chemical inputs as well as improved varieties whose genetic potential struggles to be realized when the environmental constraints are too severe. Agroecology is therefore necessary. That is why we are urging that a regional research-and-development programme on agro-ecological management be initiated.'[14]

These techniques are quite effective, and one may wonder why they are not put in practice on a large scale. It is true that some technical obstacles are yet to be resolved, such as agro-forestry practices in places without enclosures, and the development of bio-pesticides that are effective against certain types of pests. But the main obstacle, I feel, is that this requires agronomic intelligence as well as considerable investments in research institutions and major infrastructure and, therefore, substantial resources. What is needed, in particular, is an extension network dispensing agronomic advice that is radically different from the existing ones, which most often depend on young extension workers of urban origin, trying to disseminate standardized technical messages to a mass of farmers they treat as ignorant.

In fact, ecologically intensive agriculture presupposes the establishment of a comprehensive dialogue between agricultural experts and farmers whose technical knowledge is far from negligible; and, along the way, soil fertility can be improved. It also requires well-maintained rural roads, storage facilities, small

---

[13] Vincent Ribier and Pierre Baris, 'Vers un renouveau des politiques agricoles en Afrique' ('Towards renewed agricultural policies in Africa'), *Demeter Economie et Stratégies Agricoles*, 2014.

[14] René Billaz, *'Faire du Sahel un pays de cocagne : Le défi agro-écologique'* (*'Making the Sahel a land of plenty: the agro-ecological challenge'*) (L'Harmattan, 2016).

processing plants (requiring electricity supply), agribusinesses, and so on. All of this is expensive and also demands greater ease of doing business.

Already grappling with serious budgetary issues, many African leaders find these steps to be too long and complicated. Often, they prefer procuring tractors—a symbol of modernity—and subsidizing fertilizers. Tractors, however, can end up displacing people for whom there is no alternative employment. And fertilizer subsidies can end up dismantling private commercial networks that some traders are trying to establish.

The historic success of southern Mali's rural development project, financed by the World Bank together with AFD during the years 1980–2000, shows that a rationally planned pairing of agriculture and animal husbandry is quite possible. In this kind of environment, animal traction and small-scale motorization along the Asian model can be successfully developed, provided that a mechanism for providing research/extension, appropriate institutions, and infrastructure is established. A significant part of all this, obviously, can be thwarted by mismanagement, financial crunch, and budgetary choices.

## Beyond technical constraints lie political obstacles.

A recent survey[15] estimated West and Central Africa's domestic food markets at around USD 35 billion. This is 'big business'. Whereas half a century ago, on-farm consumption was the rule, the market has now become largely monetized, which means that African households are increasingly dependent on prices.

This market is urban as well as rural, including not only the entire swathe of rural towns that are extending and multiplying, but also poor farmers. These urban and rural markets are very important outlets for local agricultural production, with market size varying according to the produce. Yet, as the aforementioned study points out, in the West African Economic and Monetary

---

[15] Nicolas Bricas, Claude Tchamda, and Marie Cécile Thirion, *'Consommation alimentaire en Afrique de l'Ouest et Centrale'* ('Food consumption in West and Central Africa'), *Demeter, Economie et Stratégies Agricoles*, 2014.

Union (UEMOA) zone, imported wheat and rice account for over two-thirds of all cereals consumed regionally.[16]

The continent's cereal-production deficit has been growing steadily since the 1970s. While cereal output until 1973 met local needs, the continent's deficit surpassed 25 million tonnes from 2010 onward.[17] This worrisome situation makes Sub-Saharan Africa the only part of the world where food security is not assured and malnutrition remains widespread. Sahel countries, particularly Chad, Niger, Mauritania, and Burkina Faso, run the most risk in this regard.

It is true that imported cereals constitute only a fraction of the calorie intake in these countries, which continue to depend mostly on roots and tubers, restricting dependence on food from abroad. However, the cities, particularly the capitals[18], depend increasingly on large imports of rice and wheat for their food security. They also depend on the import of basic food products such as milk, sugar, and cooking oil. Yet, apart from wheat, everything can be grown locally and profitably as long as supportive policies are adopted. Thus, there is great interest in programmes substituting imports with local production in order to reduce dependence (and its related risks) and create outlets, and therefore local jobs.

However, there are many obstacles to this substitution process. A key problem is the new food habits that have developed over the last half century among those living in cities: people now want a bowl of rice or a loaf of bread. Apart from this thorny issue and some pending technical problems, one wonders if the real obstacles aren't political in nature.

Indeed, it is far simpler for political leaders to take advantage of the availability of food products at low prices from global markets to feed the urban populace, than to embark on the tough and uncertain process of modernizing the agriculture practiced by small farmers living far away. We have seen that urban populations

---

[16] Bricas, et al., 'Consommation alimentaire en Afrique de l'Ouest et Centrale'.

[17] Each year, Sub-Saharan Africa imports about 10–12 million tonnes of rice and about 17–18 million tonnes of wheat.

[18] Bamako is an exception since, here, it is mostly local cereals that are consumed.

can easily topple a regime, as happened recently in Burkina. Successfully implementing intensified agriculture implies raising agricultural prices and/or depreciating the currency, which would be ill-received not only by city dwellers, but also by the inhabitants of small towns and by the rural poor who now have to buy a major share of their food.

Food imports enable urban residents, who will make up half the population of Sahel countries by 2030, to benefit from the huge rise in agricultural productivity in the United States, Europe, and Brazil. In general, those countries enjoy much greater soil productivity than Africa—a ratio of 1:2, according to ACET (African Center for Economic Transformation) analyses. In addition, labour productivity is reaching the ratio of 1:100 thanks to the huge progress in mechanization in the US, the EU, and Brazil.

## Monetary policy can also be an obstacle.

Food imports are always made easier with overvalued currencies, which place local production at a disadvantage. In this context, the West and Central Africa CFA franc is a serious hurdle. Despite its 50 per cent devaluation in 1994, due to lack of a periodic review mechanism, the African CFA franc, which is pegged to the Euro, is still overvalued. Here I am treading on what are very controversial grounds in France and broaching a subject that earns me brickbats from the French bureaucracy whenever I raise it publicly. But setting up an exchange rate for thirteen African countries in Frankfurt, according to German economic needs, does not seem to me an optimal option for raising African agricultural productivity. I strongly believe that the European Central Bank, which is a competent institution, cares little about African agriculture. This issue has recently been flagged by a very able African economist (and former minister of the economy in Togo), Kako Nubukpo.[19]

You could counter this by pointing out that Côte d'Ivoire is flourishing with the current parity of the CFA franc. This is true,

---

[19] 'Sortir l'Afrique de la Servitude Monétaire, A qui profite le franc CFA?' Kako Nubukpo, Martial Ze Belinga, Bruno Tinel & Demba Moussa Dembele, ed La Dispute, 2016.

but Côte d'Ivoire is reaping the benefits of the well-conceived agricultural policies of the 1960s–1970s, which enabled it to build remarkable comparative advantages (I elaborate on this in a later chapter on the Ivorian crisis). You could also object that the current exchange rate has not stopped the monetary zone from showing healthy operating accounts and surplus trade balances until recently. So what is the problem?

The problem is that this buoyant economic situation was largely due to the exceptionally high prices of oil and mineral exports until 2015. The trade-balance deficits or surpluses created by China's demand are not the only critical issue that needs to be addressed. The real challenge is employment.[20] Currency overvaluation favours food imports to the detriment of local agricultural production. I am not advocating a repeat of the 1994 operation that tackled an emergency situation. I am just arguing that Africa's economic decision-makers should analyse the linkage of employment problems and agricultural productivity with the CFA franc exchange rate without prejudice. I am also making a plea for setting up an adjustment mechanism to adapt the CFA exchange rate to economic needs in Africa and not in Germany. This was planned in 1993, when initial discussions on this subject were held. I was part of a World Bank team which discussed these issues with the West African Central Bank (BCEAO), which never implemented it. An alternative would be to peg the CFA franc to a basket of currencies including the US dollar and the Chinese yuan.

Apart from the CFA franc, many other African currencies are overvalued due to the significant export volume of mining and petroleum products, which generally trigger currency appreciation. However, the ruling groups in Africa have little incentive to hinder this kind of currency appreciation, which enables them to import Mercedes at more convenient prices. The import of

---

[20] The interests of Central Africa's oil-producing countries—whose concerns manifestly lie elsewhere—and those of West Africa, particularly the Sahel, are clearly divergent on this point. Thus, even the unity of the CFA Franc Zone is in question. A long-term vision of the Sahel's geopolitical stability is necessary in a world dominated by short-lived—even extremely short-term—considerations.

cereals is also an attractive business for a class of wealthy traders who, as in Senegal, do not hesitate to use their financial weight to influence not only trade policies, but also elections.

Finally, these policies subject the output of the poorest farmers in remote areas of Africa to competition from highly mechanized cultivation in the EU, the US, and Brazil, dooming them to a subsistence economy bordering on poverty. This helps explain the huge urban–rural wealth gap in Africa, which is evident when one compares urban gross domestic product per capita with that of the rural world: the ratio for Sub-Saharan Africa is 5.5, which means that, on average, a city dweller is five-and-a-half times richer than a rural inhabitant. This ratio stands at only 2.7 in India, even though poverty is a major problem there as well.

## Irrigation is part of the solution, but has limited prospects.

Given the limited prospects of extensive agriculture and the challenge of intensifying rain-fed agriculture, irrigation should be a major part of any solution. It offers many advantages. For example, it helps reduce the exposure to climatic shortfalls and fluctuations, allows the application of technical itineraries developed by researchers, and thus facilitates outputs comparable to those of India and China.

There are many methods of irrigation, but for the sake of simplicity, two main approaches can be considered. On the one hand, there are large irrigated schemes with complete water control, usually linked to a large dam and managed by a sometimes heavy bureaucratic structure. Good examples of such large irrigation systems, the development of which generally began during the colonial period, are the Ghesirah Board in Sudan and the Office du Niger[21] in Mali. On the other hand, many small, irrigated areas rely upon diverted streams, water accumulated in basins during the rainy season, or pumped water in areas where the water table is relatively close to the soil surface. Double cropping is usually difficult, if not impossible, on such small-scale plots, when irrigation and water use are managed by individual farmers or groups of farmers.

[21] On the Niger River.

In Sub-Saharan Africa, large irrigation systems are linked to exceptional sites; it is estimated that around 2 million hectares with full water control could be added to the existing 6.2 million with full water control, which represents only 3.4 per cent of total cultivated land. These large scale and sometimes spectacular projects can become extraordinary development hubs, producing considerable cereal surplus and attracting a wide diversity of upstream and downstream economic activities, as can now be observed at the Office du Niger. Much more than the 2 million hectares mentioned have been identified as possible sites, but many projects are likely to be constrained by a lack of water, which will soon be aggravated by global warming.

These large projects, however, have significant drawbacks. First, they are very costly; to make such investments profitable, most dams will need to generate power and will therefore require significant electricity demand at a reasonable distance. The other serious drawbacks are the complexity and cost of water management, the difficulty of recovering irrigation fees and maintenance costs, and the fact that the general design of networks must take into account how the rural population will be organized. All this requires careful consideration and extensive accumulated experience, if such projects are to be developed properly. While the feasibility studies of such projects usually suggest very high returns, in the real world it often takes decades to reach an acceptable result in terms of water management, acceptable levels regarding waste of water, and proper management by the bureaucracy, which sometimes plunders the system. All in all, rarely is the outcome completely satisfactory.[22]

Visiting the Ghesirah Board in Sudan many years ago, I was fascinated by the sophistication of a system, conceived by the British Colonial Office, whose Sudanese employees still wore khaki shorts and polished-leather shoes in the fields. On the other hand, it took the Office du Niger almost eighty years to achieve an output level that was satisfactory. These large projects are often in poor condition due to lack of maintenance and, after a few decades, require extensive additional investment for

[22] This situation is far from being specific to Africa; the same difficulties are faced in countries as diverse as Cambodia and Venezuela.

rehabilitation. Thus, these are extremely complex, cost-intensive, protracted projects to implement, as Vatche Papazian and Pierre Ponsy point out.[23]

Small irrigation programmes,[24] managed directly by farmers, while less productive, generally offer considerable advantages. The development and management costs per hectare are much lower and the modestly sized plots usually meet local needs. By carefully investing in areas located close to communication networks and at a reasonable distance from urban centres, it is also possible to have a better geographic distribution of the surplus production and more easily address the problem of local food scarcity. Last but not least, cost recovery and water-system management on a human scale is much easier. Private, individual irrigation, generally based on solar energy or diesel water pumps, can also be developed. Finally, these locally managed programmes are often very successful and well managed by farmers or group of farmers. They may, however, present implementation problems because they are scattered, and this would also require designs to be adapted to specific local conditions. This often makes external donors—wrongly—suspicious.

Many studies highlight the importance of such farmer-driven irrigation schemes often based on partial water control, particularly in Sahel countries. They also reveal farmers' interest in small-scale irrigation with wells or bore wells and, eventually, drip irrigation. Nevertheless, development of this type of irrigation is severely constrained by the lack of rural electrification and sometimes the maintenance costs of diesel moto pumps. It is striking to see the number of small initiatives supported at a village level by NGOs but that remain low-impact pilot projects and to recognize that major donors are usually uninterested in expanding these operations to a regional level for poor reasons (too much hassle ...).

---

[23] Vatché Papazian and Pierre Ponsy, 'Irriguer le Sahel, le pari difficile des grands projets en Afrique de l'Ouest' ('Irrigating the Sahel: The tough challenge of major projects in West Africa'), in Serge Michaïlof (ed.), A quoi sert d'aider le Sud? ('What is the point of helping the South?') (Economica, 2006).

[24] This is a simplification, of course, because obviously there are many intermediate forms.

In Niger, despite substantial efforts, irrigated cereal production accounts for less than 2 per cent of total cereal production while a mere one-third of the irrigable potential has actually been developed. In 2012, authorities launched an important programme called '13N'[25] to overcome this problem. However, farmers can bear only a small fraction of the overall development costs, so this very poor country must largely rely on the interest that international donors might express in these issues.

## Global warming and population explosion are driving the Sahel to a dead end.

There is every possibility that global warming will soon aggravate this already tough situation. Various studies estimate that the temperature rise will be around 2 degrees Celsius by 2035[26] and 3 to 5 degrees by 2050.[27] This phenomenon will weaken Africa's agriculture[28], and is likely have a particularly tragic impact in the already hot and arid Sahel countries. A literature review in a recent study[29] estimates that the consequences will be particularly drastic in Sahel countries, including northern Nigeria, Sudan, and Ethiopia, triggering a scarcity of cereal production—particularly that of maize, whose output could fall by 40 per cent—accompanied by surging prices and a significant increase in child malnutrition.

As is often the case, the expected impact of global warming on rainfall in the Sahel is disputed,[30] but experts agree that,

[25] 'Initiative: Nigerians feed Nigerians.'

[26] 'Population and Climate Change:Who will the Grand Convergence Leave Behind?', University of California, *The Lancet*, vol. 2 (May 2014).

[27] A difference of five degrees is what separates us from Ice Age.

[28] The International Food Policy Research Institute estimates that, on the basis of current policies, food production in Africa will fall by one-fifth by 2050.

[29] Théodore Ahlers, Hiroshi Kato, Harinder Kohli, Callisto Madavo, and Anil Sood (eds), *Africa 2050: Realizing the Continent's Full Potential* (Oxford University Press, 2014).

[30] Some studies stress that in East Sahel rainfall has increased since the early 1990s, and certain modelling studies conclude that, contrary to expectations, this rise in rainfall will continue. But most agree that there will be greater annual variability, with the rainy season becoming shorter and the occurrence of lesser rainfall.

regardless of changes in the overall rainfall volumes, the increasingly irregular rainfall that is expected implies repeated alternating periods of flooding—washing away seedbeds—and drought. This will seriously affect the ability of the region to feed its people. A significant fall in output can be expected unless there is an exceptional breakthrough in agronomic research and GMOs. In Niger, the National Environment Council for Sustainable Development (CNEDD), which has examined various climate-change scenarios, estimates that with the 3-degree rise expected, millet and sorghum outputs will fall by 15 to 25 per cent in 2040/2050.

Decision-makers in the Sahel must also retain a lesson learned from recent dysfunctions in the world cereals market: global markets can indeed no longer be fully trusted to guarantee lasting regional food security. This wariness is already guiding the response of some Asian countries, such as Vietnam, Thailand, Cambodia, and Myanmar, who are already implementing policies to foster self-sufficiency.

It has also prompted the decisions of China, South Korea, and some Gulf countries to negotiate the purchase or leasing of land in Africa to secure their food supply. These projects risk leaving vast tracts of land infertile in the long term because of large-scale mechanised farming, which would deplete and ruin fragile soils. One shudders at what would have occurred had the Daewoo Logistics project to lease 1.3 million hectares of land from Madagascar in 2008 materialized, given the island's extremely fragile soils and the peasants' deep attachment to their lands. Conducted under a shroud of complete secrecy, the South Korean company's plan hid the fact that around fifty other projects were also under preparation, which would have ultimately led to a 'land grab' of more than 3 million hectares.

At the time, I was working with the economic team of the Malagasy President's office. I was advised to refrain from raising the matter during my meetings with the President, even though there were persistent rumours about the issue. I disregarded their advice, of course, and that day, the conversation took a sour turn. I was stunned at the transformation of the President. I had first known him when he was the mayor of Tananarive, concerned about the welfare of his constituents, then as a young president mindful of running his country like a company, and now all of a sudden he was cut off from reality. This mad project which, if implemented, would have added to the country's persistent poverty, contributed soon thereafter to the protests and then the massacre that brought down the Ravalomanana regime. Let's hope that this project has been put off for good.

## The successful, region-wide cotton-development programme shows how a first step can drive a whole development process.

The picture I have painted should not be taken as a reason for discouragement. Contrary to prevailing opinions, reviving agriculture in the Sahel is perfectly possible, as I explained in detail in a paper with Pierre Jacquemot, following the launch of the French military 'Operation Serval' in Mali in 2013.[31] Remarkable success was achieved in developing cotton production in southern parts of the Sahel from the late 1960s until now. Although it was not expected to have a direct bearing on food production, this massive programme had a significant impact on both cereal production and regional development. It offers valuable lessons.

Within a few years in the late 1960s, cotton yields tripled. The programme received French support for more than thirty years and covered vast regions, from southeast Senegal to southern Chad via south Mali, Burkina Faso, northern Côte d'Ivoire, and from Benin to Togo. Fibber exports—which were marginal when these countries became independent—exceeded 2.5 million tonnes in the 2000s and come close to the USD 4 billion mark, making this francophone region of Sub-Saharan Africa the second biggest global cotton exporter, behind the United States.

Developing cotton helped trigger a systematic process of agricultural modernization. Sometimes, one step is all it takes to get a remarkable process rolling: The revenues from cotton, and the contractual agricultural system implemented on a large scale, helped farmers increase the use of modern inputs (seeds, fertilizers, pesticides). They helped finance the development of animal

[31] Pierre Jacquemot and Serge Michailof, '*Le Développement du Sahel et en particulier du Mali*' ('The Development of the Sahel and particularly Mali'), May 2013, IRIS. (IRIS is the leading think tank on geopolitics in France.)

traction and light mechanization. The combination of cultivation and animal husbandry spread the use of manure and helped stabilize shifting cultivation, leading to the creation of true agricultural landscapes. The by-products of cottonseed made cattle-fattening possible.[32] Unexpectedly, significant increases in cereal production were experienced in most of these regions, due to the need for crop rotation, and not the substitution of cereals for cotton that one might have feared.

Rural roads were maintained to help transport the raw cotton, thus improving the transport problem that hinders the development of food trade. Small-scale private service providers for assembling and maintaining agricultural equipment were established. Literacy campaigns helped farmer organizations manage the primary commercialization of cotton, and the organizations increased in scale and political importance. There was a measurable drop in poverty in the cotton-growing areas, which also increased the demand for food crops. Thus a whole process of agricultural modernization took place for several decades, particularly in southern Mali and southwest Burkina Faso.

All in all, it is clear that an ambitious process of agriculture modernization on a large scale is possible in the Sahel region and that a real green revolution, based on the organizational and technical assets of cotton development, is finally within reach.

## This region-wide scheme has been confronted by many ups and downs.

Nonetheless, the benefits of this remarkable programme—which, directly or indirectly, still provides livelihoods for more than 15 million persons, and should be one of the foundations of the Sahel's green revolution—differ widely among countries. A key issue has been the increasing mismanagement of public sector cotton companies subjected to organized predation by corrupt managers and local political networks just as they were undergoing an expansion of their unfunded public service missions. In Burkina, which implemented sound reforms, the programme is very successful. In

---

[32] This practice involves using cottonseed meal, a high-protein supplement, to fatten livestock.

other countries such as Mali, where key institutional reforms were not implemented and where the public company is still a 'milk cow' of the regime, the programme has run out of steam and its future is uncertain. This political context likely explains President ATT's refusal to follow my recommendations on the privatization of the company.

A critical issue has been the distortion of the global cotton market brought about by the export of subsidized cotton from the United States and Europe and by China's fairly unpredictable behaviour.[33] The subsidies, which have exceeded USD 3.5 billion in some years, benefit only a few thousand producers and have caused global prices to slump by putting cotton on the market that otherwise would not have been produced. The well-known French writer Erik Orsenna, who is also an expert on Africa, has condemned this situation with his usual talent.[34]

The private sector is also hesitant about engaging in a highly politicized sector, given that its profitability is influenced by the foreign exchange rate, American and European subsidies, and China's unpredictable behaviour. This global context and specific mismanagement in Mali explain why labour-exporting regions, not cotton-exporting ones, prevail in this country in terms of relative wealth, as can be seen on a poverty map recently published by the 'Club du Sahel'.[35]

Finally, the major donors also bear a significant responsibility. France no longer has resources to support this kind of programme, and neither the European Union nor the World Bank took a serious interest in the matter.

## How Brussels turns a deaf ear and Washington sometimes derails

I cannot help expressing my disappointment that in 2003, Brussels gently but firmly turned me down twice—twice, because I am

---

[33] China is sometimes an importer and at other times an exporter of cotton, depending on variations in its production and consumption.

[34] Fayard Erik Orsenna, *Voyage aux pays du coton. Petit précis de mondialisation* ('Travels to cotton countries: A small essay on globalization') (Fayard, 2006).

[35] '*An Atlas of the Sahara-Sahel: West African studies*', OECD/Club du Sahel, 2015.

stubborn. On the second occasion, I had my 'boss' and friend
Jean-Michel Severino, CEO of the French Development Agency,
accompany me. We went to Brussels to plead that the European
Union make a financial contribution for the recovery of the
Sahel's cotton sector.

We asked for 300 million euros spread over five years,
crumbs really, given the deep pockets of the European Union,
while France contributes 800 million euros annually to finance
EU-managed aid programmes. The requested amount was all
the more justified as the European Union's subsidies to Greek
and Spanish producers at the time amounted to nearly 700 million euros per year, which contributed to undermine the African
industry. The only answer Brussels offered was: 'Sorry, but your
proposals had not been accounted for in our planned programs.'[36]

The World Bank had long opposed these programmes as relying too much on what it viewed as a gangrenous state system,
which was quite true; but its resolve to privatize without planning
any safeguards to protect the successful contract-farming system
led to an incredible bureaucratic guerrilla war between the French
aid system and the World Bank, which lasted throughout the
1980s and 1990s.[37]

[36] Said budget having been fixed for five years just one year ago.

[37] By way of anecdote, in Washington (in 1999), after having blocked
the privatization of the admittedly very poorly managed Chad Cotton
company, dreamed up by my staff, my dear comrades, probably seeing
me as a congenital traitor to the house dogma on account of my nationality, they attempted to impose their ideas on me by sneaking in their
reform proposals as an IMF condition, without my knowledge. As I was
their boss, they could not entirely bypass me or seek direct arbitrage
from higher Bank authorities. Their idea, of course, was to either make
me bend to their will or to have this esteemed organization's Executive
Board give me a rap on the knuckles. I refused to bend and was summoned by the IMF board. As luck would have it, that day, the Board
was presided over by Alassane Ouattara, the current President of Côte
d'Ivoire and then IMF Deputy Director. He and I had known each
other for many years. After a thorough dressing down from the American
administrator, Ouattara—whose curiosity I had pricked—let me lay
down my arguments in front of the entire board, the key argument being
that only crooks would buy this company. This enraged the American

## Is it time for a paradigm shift?

Flourishing small-scale farming requires not only considerable private and public investment, but also far-reaching reforms to the institutions concerned, as well as to agricultural and commercial policies. Reforming institutions—be they national development agencies, marketing boards, or, eventually, stabilization funds—is tough. Many of these institutions have been dissolved due to appalling mismanagement. Those that survived have often fallen prey to networks of nepotism that, as we will see later, keep cash flowing to the ruling parties. Agricultural and commercial policies that influence food prices are, in fact, determined by the political balance of power between rural and urban populations.

Far-reaching reforms require a paradigm shift that only the African elite can impose. Favouring urban dwellers to the detriment of rural ones now entails considerable political risk. While discontented urban consumers' protests may bring down a government within a few hours—as we've recently seen in Burkina Faso—demoralized youths in rural areas can join Boko Haram-type movements, which end up undermining both state and society. The Kalashnikovs in circulation have brought about a readjustment in the rural–urban balance of power. But the urban populace is a constantly looming immediate threat, whereas the slow deterioration of security in the back of beyond is a problem that can be ignored—at least for a while.

Readjusting and injecting dynamism in small-scale farming is even more necessary because the model, based on feeding urban hubs through imports has been working to the satisfaction of African leaders since the independence of their respective countries. It will, however, gradually become dysfunctional. The years 2008 and 2010 saw numerous riots provoked by sharp rises in world food prices. These riots were a symptom of tensions that have been surfacing periodically in cereal markets since 2008 as a result of the impressive growth of emerging countries—particularly

---

administrator and earned me a summons from the World Bank president to explain myself. He had, of course, been thoroughly briefed about the whole story. Ah, the ambience....

China. Over the next thirty-five years, the world population will rise by approximately 2.5 billion inhabitants—the equivalent of the world population in 1950. And this growth will be coupled with the expected affluence of some 3 billion new Asian consumers by 2050,[38] to trigger a colossal boom in direct and indirect demand of cereals.[39]

The continuation of the world population's strong and sustained growth and Asia's increasing affluence will run up against the constraints of available farmland on the global scale, the ambitions of biofuel production, and the wariness about GMOs. Under these conditions, many experts believe, the historic global trend of falling agricultural prices observed since World War II, due to impressive productivity gains, will be reversed. They have, for instance, not yet returned to pre-crisis levels. The tensions expected to flare up then will be heightened by the predictable behaviour of major exporting countries that—as in 2008, and particularly in Russia in 2010—are very likely to ban exports to prevent domestic scarcities, thus sowing chaos in the global market.

## A coherent region-wide plan is essential for stabilizing the Sahel's rural areas.

Obviously, in the context of high population growth, the marginalization of the poor rural population, locked in poverty, will lead to considerable social and political risks. The revival of agricultural development must therefore become a real priority, not only for long-term food security but also for the sub-region's social and political stability. Without it, there will be no viable agriculture in the Sahel capable of feeding the people, raking in revenues, generating employment and halting an exodus. Drawing up a coherent plan is, therefore, necessary. Such a plan requires global policy changes by Sahel governments and major donors alike. While each donor and each institution has a host of long-prepared

[38] Estimated in the Centennial Group's ASIA 2035 long-term perspective report commissioned by the Asian Development Bank.

[39] Let's not forget that producing one kilogram of beef requires six kilograms of cereals and that growing affluence of households translates into a strong growth in meat demand.

'Sahel strategies' that are generally restricted to listing and justifying the projects they are financing—there must be at least fifty of them—to the best of my knowledge, this kind of global plan does not exists today. Preparing such a plan should be a priority. Since the 'Club du Sahel' unfortunately does not have the necessary political authority to prepare such a policy document, here is an area in which the Gates Foundation could usefully assume leadership if, as anticipated, France refuses to move.

Such a plan requires abandoning the isolated project approach that each sponsor prefers, to move towards national or region-wide programmes requiring strong coordination among donors. These programmes must include substantial investment in all-weather road infrastructure to link the zones with agricultural potential to urban centres, in order to reconnect the cities to their rural hinterlands. They imply reviving the cotton-growing programmes in the south of the Sahel zone and, therefore, implementing much-needed reforms. They require initiating soil-regeneration programmes through reforestation and assisted natural regeneration, along with soil protection and restoration boosted by erosion-control measures, stone barriers, mulching, and weirs, along the lines of the programme now being conducted on a significant scale by Niger. This also requires that we seek to get out of the small number of traditional forms of speculation (in cotton, rice, cattle) to aim at breakthroughs in export horticulture, as Senegal or Kenya have done. This requires intellectual investment in market knowledge as well as the development of concerted strategies with local and foreign private sectors.

Such programmes should aim at increasing productivity by combining credit, support for animal-traction agriculture, and small-scale mechanization. They should also be required to multiply small-irrigation infrastructure. In arid, densely populated areas where irrigation and construction of riverbeds and basins is possible, investments in land upgrading and rehabilitation, which only public development aid can finance, are also required. Finally, ambitious rural electrification programmes are imperative.

## Rural electrification is crucial.

It is critical for rural populations in the Sahel to have access to power. In Niger, the rate of access to electricity is around 10 per cent for the population as a whole, and around 0.2 per cent for rural areas—a situation characteristic of the entire region. This is no longer acceptable: there is absolutely no hope of retaining the younger generation in rural areas without electricity. While access to electricity in cities is mostly a matter of proper governance and the ability of production and distribution companies, public or private, to recover user fees and borrow to invest in production capacities, access to electricity in the countryside was, until recently, a very serious challenge.

That's because the cost of available technologies, low rural incomes, and low population density made these programmes financially unsustainable without significant recurrent subsidies that no one was willing to pay. This is no longer the case. Today's solar technologies offer decentralized solutions that are technically and financially suitable at low cost. The production costs per solar kilowatt have been reduced by a factor of three to four since 2000.[40] For large villages and small towns, conventional technologies based on diesel generators and more recent hybrid diesel-solar technologies associated with decentralized mini-networks offer attractive options[41] that can be managed by local investors.

Contrary to common belief, however, this type of development cannot be brought about simply by turning to private initiatives without serious state supervision and support to standardize the equipment, impose quality norms, and test options through pilot projects to check adaptation to local needs and conditions. All this requires significant public support and subsidies to cover initial development and investment costs. We already know that such resources are difficult to mobilize in the various countries' budgets. Donors now need to move in with important resources and the will to shift from pilot schemes to large-scale programmes with ambitious objectives.

My view—and I recently discussed the matter with Niger officials—is that now that some pilot schemes have demonstrated

[40] The kw/h produced by solar energy fell from 70 US cents in 2000, to 25 to 40 cents in 2008, and 10 to 20 cents, depending on the place, in 2014. The development of mini-networks and individual pre-electrification now helps envisage ambitious solar electrification programmes.

[41] New technologies using prepaid cards enable operators to minimize the risk of defaulters.

the technical and financial viability of decentralized solar electricity in the Sahel, it is time for these countries to forget about past unmet interconnection objectives between the usual national production companies and rural areas. These public companies basically have no expertise in decentralized solar energy. Niger, Mali, Chad, and Burkina Faso, with the support of some key donors, should move aggressively by contracting out the development of financially viable rural electricity programmes to international private companies,[42] once initial development costs have been paid by foreign aid.

## How can agriculture in the Sahel be supported?

Rural development requires profitable prices for farmers, which is where things start getting complicated in regions where the main and, sometimes, unique agricultural activity is in food production. It certainly will be difficult to implement long-term policies that ensure that rural producers receive sufficient prices for upgrading their production systems in environments that have become vulnerable due to global warming. The good news, paradoxically, is the expected rise in global agricultural prices. The World Food price index recently published by FAO shows that food prices which basically multiplied by 2 between 2006 and 2011 have not yet recovered to their pre- crisis level and are still about 50 per cent above the 1990–2006 trend.

If such a trend continues, it will be tragic for the poor in African cities and villages, but it may also be a chance for Sahel's agriculture. Of course, nothing can be taken for granted. If the likely trend is a rise in global cereal prices, their extreme volatility will pose a problem, because building efficient and modern small-scale farming is a long-term project. This is evidenced by the West African cotton-production programme which took 30 years to reach full maturity (and in some cases went south when donors and governments lost interest). Gains for producers engendered by a few years of high agricultural prices on the global market can be swept away by two years of depressed prices.

---

[42] Such as the French utility and oil giants Veolia, Engie, or Total.

During the 1980s and the 1990s, an ideological controversy developed between advocates of agricultural price stabilization and those in favour of simply correcting the impact of price volatility in food commodities through emergency food aid and private insurance mechanisms. This latter doctrine has largely collapsed in the aftermath of the 2008 food crisis. It is worth noting that Niger's 2010 food crisis was well-handled thanks to measures taken by the office in charge of managing food stocks (OPVN), cereal purchases made by donors throughout the sub-region, and facilitation of regional cereal exchanges made by traders. These measures were quite different from the idiocies perpetrated by Mali's agricultural commodities office, OPAM, in the 1970s, and we thus see that some Sahel institutions are now able to elaborate and implement complex strategies.

The gradual upward trend in food prices, if it materializes, may require that the social costs for the poorest be borne in the future by social redistribution mechanisms such as social safety nets and cash transfers similar to 'bolsa familia'[43] programmes commonly implemented initially in Latin America and now, throughout the world. Having said that, I am quite aware of the difficulty involved in setting up any mechanism for agricultural price regulation. But, it should be remembered that Côte d'Ivoire became the world's top cocoa producer thanks to the remarkable action of a stabilization board, the well-known 'Caisse de stabilisation,' and the guarantee of minimum producer prices for coffee and cocoa—that is, until the institution went completely astray with corruption, as we shall see in a later chapter.

In an ideological context that despises protectionist measures, and in the face of pressure from urban consumers, the feasibility of a policy supporting agricultural prices supposes that African elites would clearly accept the importance of having a dynamic

---

[43] Brazil's social programme 'bolsa familia,' inspired by Mexico's 'oportunidades' programme, ensures financial aid to particularly disadvantaged families with the provisos of compulsory education and health checkups for children. This is a common approach not only in Latin America but in many developing countries. The logic behind these programmes benefitting tens of millions of Latin Americans is to bring families out of conventional assistance programmes and ensure better schooling and better health for children.

agriculture based on small farmers. Deep uncertainty over the smooth functioning of global cereal markets in the future should prompt them to ensure food security in these countries. Such a step would also generate employment for youth while the demographic transition is completed. Once again, the implementation of such protections would be illusory if it had to depend on customs duties, given the porosity of African borders. An intelligent handling of the exchange rate, on the other hand, could offer a solution.

## In Northern Sahel, environmental disasters and growing instability go hand in hand.

If agricultural development in the southern part of the Sahel, which has the best potential in terms of rainfall and fertile lands, is now vulnerable, what is the state of affairs in the less-fortunate zones in northern Sahel and the Sub-Saharan fringes? The situation there is very worrisome. Alternating bouts of drought and heavy rainfall, in the context of a rapidly growing population, are leading to efforts to convert land previously used as pasture to agricultural production, triggering increased tensions between nomads and farmers. Each drought then sets off a downturn in agriculture and a fall in pastoralism, bringing misery in its wake.

The combination of overpopulation and a deteriorating environment leads to drastic local impasses. Youth no longer have significant job prospects in agriculture, but there is no local alternative apart from involvement in trans-Saharan trafficking (stolen cars, fuel, cigarettes, migrant labour, and now cocaine), which has overtaken the old trans-Saharan trade in gold, salt, and slaves. The collapse of the Tuareg economy, the Tuareg's ostracism in some countries, arms circulation, bandits, increased trafficking in these regions—ill-controlled since time immemorial by the central authorities—have combined to create zones where law and order have broken down, leading to the disaster that burst out in Mali.

In this environment, the increasing presence of the jihadi extremists of al-Qaeda in the Islamic Maghreb, Ansar Dine, Mujao, and other groups offers disaffected youth an appealing ideology, significant revenues, and the only prospects for social mobility. The events in Mali, which came about after protracted deterioration in security in the northern Sahel area, prove—if any proof is necessary—the deterioration of the global situation. Should one therefore despair of these regions?

In the winters of 1984, 1985, and 1986, my friend Mano Dayak, who was to later become spokesperson for the Tuareg rebellion in Niger, drove me across Niger's vast Sub-Saharan zone in search of Tuaregs and members of other remote groups to examine prospects for local development. There is no need to emphasize the tough ecological conditions in these regions. But these visits—the hours spent under trees or in tents with the inhabitants and the analysis of the many technical surveys on these zones, some dating back to colonial times—convinced me that it is still possible to bring significant improvement to the standard of living there.

## Even in the Sub-Saharan fringes it is possible to improve people's livelihoods.

In semi-arid zones, the collapse of the Tuareg economy poses the major challenge of implementing programmes for saving oases, which are environmentally very fragile. These oases have been the subject of research projects for almost a century, and there is no dearth of proposals—such as building small underground dams to raise the water table—that would improve the situation, at least marginally. And much can be done to improve healthcare, basic education, and vocational training so that migrants who move towards the coast are not restricted to seeking employment as street sweepers!

In zones with better agricultural potential, the proposals of Michel Griffon,[44] former scientific director of CIRAD, need to be implemented more ambitiously than merely through pilot projects. Griffon reminds us that the restoration of what he calls 'basic ecological functionalities' is feasible even in arid regions. For this, water needs to penetrate the soil instead of flowing on its surface, which can be aided by terracing, stone lines, afforestation, and protection of natural forest regeneration.

[44] Michel Griffon, *Pour des agricultures écologiquement intensives (For Ecologically Intensive Agriculture)*, Éditions de l'Aube, 2010.

Of course, these projects cannot be implemented throughout the vast semi-arid regions, but, by focusing on temporary riverbeds and water basins, as well as in zones where soil is degraded but has promising agricultural potential, they can offer concrete local solutions. The costs of soil restoration, ranging from USD 100 to USD 300 per hectare, are essentially charges for labour—which is abundantly available during the dry season. Implementation can be spread over time, generating employment. These techniques had already been developed when I was working in Niger in the mid-1980s, and technical manuals are still available.[45]

Pilot projects set up during this period led to major programmes in Niger, where the surface area benefiting from soil restoration is about 350,000 hectares. But this type of programme should cover a major portion of the 10 million hectares currently under cultivation in this country. Cereal output from these regenerated soils could increase by 30 to 50 per cent, or more than double if conditions are favourable.

The situation regarding animal husbandry is very complex, but numerous studies and pasture-development projects have helped build effective programmes. These programmes take into account the initial failures that occurred due to the ignorance of traditional transhumant husbandry rules, which were often frustrated by the public wells that sprang up. These wells, which 'belonged to nobody,' led to chaotic management and the destruction of adjacent pastures. Recent, well-conceived programmes that organize and facilitate transhumance help reduce tensions and conflicts between pastoralists and sedentary farmers[46].

Clearly, even in the poorest zones of northern Sahel bordering the Sahara, solutions exist for reviving agriculture and animal husbandry. Of course these zones cannot be turned into agriculture development poles, but it is still possible to begin countering prevailing trends before they lead to the looming tragedies that can be anticipated. It is important to draw on the intellectual capital

---

[45] Such as: Michel Bonfils, *Halte à la désertification au Sahel* ('Stop Desertification in the Sahel') (Karthala, 1987).

[46] An excellent book had already been published on these issues: Brigitte Thébaud, *Elevage et development au Niger* (BIT Genève, 1988)

accumulated through many experiments and proceed to scaling up—moving from pilot projects to programmes on a larger scale. However, the unfortunate turnover of staff in major development agencies means that accumulated experience disappears very fast as local experts grow old and retire without being replaced due to a lack of projects and financial resources.

## Between population growth and insecurity, time is of essence!

Time is of the essence because the current response to a deteriorating security situation is essentially a military one, yet one knows that a military response is insufficient. The disastrous situation in Afghanistan show us how dangerous it is to neglect rural development when security starts declining. We still await courageous measures from the Malian government, putting the affairs of its cotton company in order, which probably requires privatizing it, as well as the reform of the Niger Office, which continues its shambolic management of tens of thousands of irrigated hectares in the river valley.

Time is of the essence for efficiently supporting the Sahel's agricultural and broad rural development by kick-starting massive programmes for small-scale irrigation and organizing community-driven development (CDD) to provide rural areas with small-scale investment in rural roads, small dams, and irrigated plots that are so badly needed. Such CDDs are a necessary step and have been quite successful in Indonesia, Brazil, Ethiopia, and even in Afghanistan, as we will see in a later chapter. Such programmes face colossal constraints arising from the vastness of the territories and the limited resources that national budgets and international donors are inclined to earmark for them because of sheer myopia. Then comes in the difficulty of coordinating the actions of donors, an important subject that I will come back to later. There is so much to do!

Time is of the essence because, as René Billaz writes, 'As of now, the density of population has attained or surpassed 100 inhabitants per $km^2$ in certain areas, and agricultural productivity per head must be more than doubled to ensure national food security.' He adds, 'The Sahara is not stretching out towards the

Sahel, but the desert is growing right under the feet of farmers and their animals.'[47]

Time is also of the essence because jihadists crushed in the Mali desert by the French armed forces are reinforcing their stronghold in the bend of the Niger River between Gao and Mopti. In this densely populated region, France cannot conduct air strikes without causing collateral damage. French soldiers, now up against a guerrilla force that is getting tougher, run the risk of being exposed to the kind of asymmetrical warfare that a Western army respectful of human rights can no longer win. As representatives of a former colonizer, they will soon find themselves in an impossible situation.

Finally, time is of the essence because all along the vast, 1,500 kilometer border between Niger and Nigeria, while the people on either side are very close ethnically, linguistically, and through family ties, Boko Haram is ever present. It is true that the group has been crushed as an organized military structure following the offensive by the coalition armies of Chad, Niger, and Cameroon and a rebuilt Nigerian army. But the scattered survivors are always present in the bush and able to launch guerrilla attacks on the Nigerian, Nigerien, Chadian, and Cameroonian territories.

## The West has mostly offered pipe dreams to Sahel's poorest.

Living conditions in rural Sahel remain appalling, a situation that, while shocking from an ethical point of view, is full of even greater threats from the political point of view. In this regard, I have statistics only on Niger, but it is pointless to think that the situation is better in Chad (despite its oil production), in Mali (despite much higher agricultural potential), or in Burkina Faso.

The poverty in all these countries is devastating. Only half of Niger's rural population has access to safe drinking water. We've already noted that a mere 0.2 per cent of the rural population has access to electricity, which means it is impossible in villages to store medicines, recharge mobile phones, transform local production with small mills, irrigate fields with pumps, or establish small

[47] Billaz, 'Faire du Sahel un pays de cocagne: Un Défi Agro écologique'.

services with an electrical point for welding—and the situation is similar in Chad and Mali. Again in Niger, healthcare coverage, which has improved over the past few years, still benefits to only 50 per cent of the population.

One understands better the attraction of Boko Haram's messages to a poor population that has gained nothing from school, having attended it too briefly, while this organization criticises Western education and offers disaffected youths immediate profits from looting. More than 240,000 young men now reach Niger's job market every year. In twenty years, they will number 570,000, a fairly accurate figure because many of the future job searchers have already been born. The country's employment agency, ANPE, currently has 1,500 youths on its rolls. Where will the future jobs come from?

As early as 2010—eight years ago—the Algerian daily *El Watan* wrote: 'It is clear that the situation in the Sahel is dangerous to the point of being explosive. It calls for the states of the region to react urgently before others turn it into a second Afghanistan.'[48] Five years after the military Operation Serval, and in the background of the ongoing military Operation Barkhane, aid to Mali and to the Sahel is no longer a matter of charity and compassion, but a question of geopolitical equilibrium and the prevention of conflicts in an extremely unstable region. The situation in northern Sahel today reminds us of Afghanistan in the 2000s, where the collapse of agriculture, state's absence or corruption, and the lack of jobs in vulnerable rural areas opened a broad avenue for the Taliban.

[48] Salima Tlemçani, '*Sahel, towards the 'afghanisation' of the région?*' (El Watan, 20 September 2010).

# CHAPTER
# FOUR

# Will Africa Skip the Industrial Development Stage?

Newspapers and conferences that heaped criticism on Africa twenty years ago now abound with encomiums on its many success stories. I must say, these highly optimistic articles weary me when I contrast them with the squalor of the slums that I still visit regularly. I have had a special interest in slums since my first encounter with their reality in 1959 when, as a high school student, I spent a month in Casablanca on a study trip. I am also annoyed when people cite flattering figures on foreign investments in the continent. It is true that foreign investments, which were almost negligible throughout the 1980s and 1990s, shot up from about USD 6 billion in 2000 to USD 35 billion in 2012 and stabilized at about USD 40 billion until the 2015 commodity prices crisis. This is good news. But the fact is that these investments were made chiefly in the mining and petroleum sectors. In many countries, by contrast, the manufacturing industry has seen deep stagnation since the mid-1990s.

## Industrial development in Africa is marking time.

Some industrial wastelands in Africa are so grim that they could be converted into sets for angst-ridden films. It is difficult to imagine a better future for some of them. They are ill-conceived, ill-scaled, ill-positioned factories sold by corrupt brokers or equipment manufacturers to buyers who were either gullible or shamelessly bribed. I sometimes think that the best service I have rendered to Africa is torpedoing the construction of some of these white elephants, which earned me serious threats from equipment manufacturers—who openly told me that they would 'take care' of my career—as well as the wrath of a few ambassadors, who complained to my boss. Fortunately, these colossal projects petered out over the last two decades due to French tied aid being cut off[1] and state intervention in the industrial sector becoming outdated. A new generation of private African investors appeared, who are usually well informed and maintain a healthy distance from these kinds of projects.

Still, progress in Africa's industrial sector is very slow. The share of the manufacturing sector's contribution to gross domestic product in the long term stagnated at around 9 per cent for the entire Sub-Saharan region between 1970 and 2010, and even slipped in certain countries. The industrial component of the GDP is above 10 per cent in only 18 African countries. In the 15 African countries retained by the African Center for Economic Transformation (ACET) in one of its key studies,[2] the ratio fell from approximately 12 per cent in 1970 to 10 per cent in 2010. The corresponding ratio for comparable non-African emerging countries during the same period rose from around 15 per cent to almost 25 per cent. Africa's urbanization is thus disconnected from the industrialization process, unlike the cases of Europe in the nineteenth century and Asia since World War II.

Under these conditions, despite the mining boom and given the low labour demand in the mining and petroleum sectors, secondary sector jobs in Sub-Saharan Africa improved only marginally in 15 years. Thus, despite incorporating the significant industrial

[1] Tied aid finances only local goods and services or those provided by the donor country. This type of aid most often helps bypass the procedure of calls to tender and quite systematically leads to excessive prices being charged.

[2] *Growth with Depth*, African Transformation Report, ACET, Accra & Washington, DC, 2014.

development in Mauritius and South Africa, which are clearly two exceptions, secondary sector jobs rose from a mere 8 per cent of the total jobs in 1995 to 8.5 per cent in 2010. African countries are thus massively transiting from agricultural economies with low productivity to service economies with equally low productivity, or with negligible impact on employment in the high productivity information and communications technology (ICT) sector, which is experiencing a boom. If current trends continue, Africa runs a strong risk of never passing through the intervening phase of industrialization and the expansion of a labour-intensive manufacturing sector, as emerging countries elsewhere have done.

## Industrialization in Africa still faces a number of hurdles.

The reasons behind this stagnation are many. To begin with, the business environment leaves much to be desired. Every year, the World Bank publishes its famous 'doing business' report in which countries are ranked on the basis of a composite index measuring the ease of doing business.[3] This index reveals the many differences among countries. While Mauritius is among the 50 countries leading the global ranking, of the 39 countries beyond the 150 rank, 26 are African, essentially occupying the lowest positions.

One area in which Africa is particularly open to criticism is compliance with the rule of law, which is measured through the Worldwide Governance Indicators (WGI) rule-of-law index. This index shows that while Mauritius and Botswana rank close to OECD countries, many others—particularly the Congo, Kenya, Angola, Nigeria, Sudan, and Côte d'Ivoire—plummet disastrously due to their highly corrupt judiciaries. Let us not forget that the reason the headquarters of the African Development Bank Group was transferred from Abidjan to Tunis in 2003 was an unlawful judgment in a civil case condemning the institution in complete disregard of the rule of law. The judgment having been upheld on appeal and all other recourses exhausted, the president of the bank decided it was no longer possible for his

---

[3] Though controversial, the index does provide useful information.

flouted the rule of law.[4]

The labour codes in francophone countries—as currently in France—are also a very serious issue that impedes competitiveness. Indeed, they are largely based on the French labour code and are inappropriate for the region. The presence of unions that once benefited from the advice of the *Confédération générale du travail* (CGT), the French national trade union confederation closely linked to the Communist Party, also frightens willing entrepreneurs.

Labour costs are, relatively speaking, high, at least in the formal sector. They are indeed driven by the historically high level of civil service salaries which are easily six to ten times the GDP per inhabitant. Other reasons include the use of a guaranteed minimum wage disconnected from the informal sector and from any concern for maximizing employment. Finally, also worth noting is an often forgotten aspect: the salaries and benefits-in-kind offered to expatriate managers, which local managers seek to match. Clearly, the combination of these constraints, which are understandably seen by those concerned as social progress, is a barrier to the development of the type of labour-intensive industries that have arisen in Bangladesh or Cambodia.

Several other factors also adversely affected industrial investment. Foremost among them was political instability in numerous countries, a typical example being Madagascar since 2008. Political instability also paralysed Côte d'Ivoire's economy for fifteen years, as we will see in detail in Chapter 7, 'The ignored fragility of Côte d'Ivoire and its descent into hell'. Also critical was the lack of proper dialogue between political authorities and the private sector, which in many countries incentivizes unwarranted rents from parasitic institutions and local predators.

## Africa continues to be a continent of parasitic institutions and predators.

This situation, which is not readily apparent, seriously harms many activities. In the 1990s, at the request of Senegalese businessmen

---

[4] The ADB HQ was restored to Abidjan after Alassane Ouattara assumed power as the president of the Ivorian Republic in 2011.

involved in the tuna-processing industry, which was then facing a deep crisis, I had one of my teams conduct an in-depth survey of the tinned-tuna industry in Senegal, a major domestic activity. These businesspersons were vociferously complaining of unfair competition from Thailand and overvaluation of the CFA Franc. The survey led to quite different conclusions and the discovery of no less than 18 different unwarranted 'rents' that were jeopardizing the profitability of the sector. The rents ranged broadly and included rents for having to use the port's pilot services, which small tuna boats have absolutely no need of, paying unionised dockworkers for zero services rendered while other crews actually unloaded cargo, and paying higher charges for transporting food-can metal sheets through Dakar port than the cost of transporting them from Rotterdam to Dakar. These little 'rents', taken individually, were quite modest. But the sum of all 18 rents rendered the activity unprofitable, even though one would be hard put to find more favourable conditions for tuna fishery than Dakar. Behind each rent, of course, was a group of 'rent-seekers' who fought tooth-and-nail to maintain their advantages.

There are of course many other significant hurdles to industrial investments in Africa. The first is insufficient infrastructure and its poor management, especially in three main areas: A notorious obstacle is the poor quality and high cost of energy, which can be four to nine times that of emerging countries.[5] Also problematic is the poor functioning of port platforms, where it can take weeks for containers to be unloaded, whereas in Asia it takes hours. This is particularly important since the fluidity of international trade is a key element of all modern industrial processes. Delays translate into significant overruns: The average import cost for a container is more than USD 2,500 in Africa versus less than USD 1,000 in Asia.

A third infrastructure-related issue is poor road transport due to the disregard for axle-load limits and poor road maintenance—this, in addition to the myriad roadblocks and checks by multiple parties, including customs officials, 'gendarmes', police, military personnel, and even game wardens, all of whom want their cut. To counter these illegal collections, some countries are

[5] USD 0.45 per kw/h as compared to the prevalent rates of USD 0.05–0.10 per kw/h.

administrative departments present at borders.

The cost of these 'abnormal practices', to borrow official terminology, is sometimes exorbitant. The World Bank has expressed the cost in 'equivalent additional transport distance'. Thus, the costs involved in a truck's crossing the border between the Democratic Republic of the Congo and Burundi is the equivalent of transport charges for 1,824 kilometres, crossing the DRC–Rwanda border is the equivalent of transport charges for 1,549 kilometres, and so on.

Added to the list of obstacles are education systems that are disconnected from the needs of the economy. Sixty years after independence, one still finds French plumbers in Libreville and Portuguese tillers in Luanda. African universities hold mediocre rankings in technological areas, and a mere 4 per cent of African students enroll in engineering, versus 20 per cent in Asia.

## Industry is still constrained by narrow domestic markets.

A longstanding, fundamental hurdle to Africa's industrial development is the small size of national markets, the combined result of the continent's political fragmentation, and its low per capita purchasing power. The small size of domestic markets makes it hard for modern industrial plants to achieve economies of scale and be profitable. Progress has, however, been made. The gradual growth of a small middle-class and higher household income have helped expand domestic markets. And significant steps have been taken towards regional integration—two zones, Economic Community of West African States (ECOWAS) in West Africa and the East African Community (EAC), have been especially successful in diminishing the impact of borders.

Progress notwithstanding, the growth of Africa's domestic markets does not compare to developments in Asia; interstate trade remains hampered by the lack of complementarity between economies, insufficient road networks, and bureaucratic hassles. In terms of industrial development, regional integration mostly benefits the major coastal countries, which, like Côte d'Ivoire, already have significant domestic markets and more favourable production costs, and, in comparison to landlocked countries, can more easily ship exports to neighbouring countries. The industrial development of Sahel countries thus remains an unresolved issue, and regional integration, though useful, cannot be a panacea.

For a decade now, Africa's industrial problems have also been exacerbated by China's export of manufactured goods. China produces practically every imaginable manufactured product for people with low to medium purchasing power. These goods are specially adapted to demand in Africa, and a network of small-scale Chinese traders is developing there thanks to immigration spurred by major public-works contracts awarded to Chinese companies. Thus, trade in Chinese consumer goods is choking a good part of Africa's manufacturing activity. This is particularly so in Nigeria, where the fast-moving-consumer-goods (FMCG) manufacturing sector struggles against competition from Asia. The textile industry in Nigeria, which provided work to some 300,000 labourers 30 years ago, has shrunk considerably, employing less than one-tenth as many today.

Apart from industries that process local raw materials, only those producing heavy goods, such as construction materials, or products whose value-to-volume ratio is low—such as mattresses, PVC pipes, bulky plastic goods, beer, and other beverages—are able, today, to challenge the Chinese competition.

## Industrialization in Africa remains a frustrating process.

To sum up, owing to insufficient market size, efforts at import substitution industrialization made throughout the 1960s and 1970s still face the challenge of achieving economies of scale sufficient to ensure profitability while also facing competition from China's exports. It is also hampered by the overvaluation of currencies such as the CFA franc and by labour laws, inspired by European and, particularly, French ones that do not help counter competition from Asia.

It is thus no surprise that the textile industry died more than 20 years ago in most of West Africa, as illustrated by the case of the Ivorian Company Cotivo in Côte d'Ivoire, which was trapped in the 1980s between high labour and energy costs and extremely cheap Asian imports. Today, manufacturing productivity in Africa, defined as the value added per worker, is currently about a

third (USD 11,700) of that achieved by emerging countries (more
than USD 36,000) listed by ACET. In fact, Africa's manufacturing productivity has been on the decline since 1990.

Apart from the structural problems encountered by old import-substituting industries, it is not so easy for African manufacturers to become profitable in raw-material processing and export industries, such as in food processing and agro-industrial sectors. Success demands natural comparative advantages on the agronomic front and efficient management, which most often require know-how from foreign investors. Côte d'Ivoire excels in this area and thus provides an interesting development model. Its complete control over the palm-oil-processing industry—as also over the rubber, banana, and pineapple industries—is truly remarkable. Still, the difficulties involved should not be underestimated.[6] In many countries, rent-seeking and rackets stalk small investors who cannot gain access to political authorities when they are being blackmailed by local authorities or the bureaucracy.

Some time ago, when I was in charge of monitoring the investments of Proparco, the French Development Agency's (AFD) private-sector arm, I ran into just such a racket set up by a local bureaucracy. A French investor, observing the abundance of octopus on the coast of an African country, decided to open a processing plant to export processed octopus to the Japanese and European markets. The project looked as though it could be very profitable, was supposed to produce value out of a formerly neglected product, offered jobs to around 80 employees, and provided new outlets for traditional fishermen. I thus gave my approval to the investment, along with a major French group and Japanese interests. Japanese and European health norms being very stringent, delegations from Japan and Europe visited the factory while it was under construction and after it became operational, to monitor work conditions and check compliance with norms, and thereafter issued appropriate certificates.

---

[6] For example, Côte d'Ivoire had to close three out of its six sugar mills built at great cost in the northern region during the 1980s. The cocoa industry has invested heavily in Côte d'Ivoire, which is an excellent idea. But manufacturing high-quality chocolate precludes the sole use of local cocoa beans and demands the expert blending of cocoa beans from various countries, as done by European chocolate-makers.

The factory began production and exports, and everything was working well until the formal inauguration, which I had the opportunity to attend, about a few months after production began. A few days after inauguration, the owner of the firm called in a panic to tell me the factory was to be closed by order of the local health–inspection department. Smelling a rat, I called the minister in charge and explained that the project had a certain political visibility and that I found the closure order incomprehensible when all due health and sanitary precautions had been taken and proper certification received. I also said I would have to apprise both the French ambassador and the president of the Republic of this matter, as the latter had pressed firmly for attracting foreign investment to the country. The minister had not been informed about the matter and asked for a little time to be briefed on it. He then called me back: '*Cher ami*, it was a complete misunder-standing—there is absolutely no problem', he assured me. What had happened, of course, was that the local health and sanitation department had simply tried to cash in on their nuisance value.

Industrialization in Africa thus remains a frustrating process characterized by many difficulties and failures. A worrisome con-sequence is that industrial jobs, apart from the very special cases of Mauritius and South Africa, remain marginal and, given current conditions, cannot meet demographic challenges.[7] Côte d'Ivoire is certainly an interesting model for many African countries, but even there, the growth of the industrial sector is insufficient to meet the employment needs of the masses of youths entering the labour market every year.

## The desired reforms, though long known, come up against powerful lobbies.

Despite these challenges, the African continent is in no way con-demned to be trapped by the shallow development model currently

---

[7] South Africa is a special case because the country's isolation during the last years of the apartheid period had obliged it, on the one hand, to produce many consumer goods and, on the other, inserted it into certain international value chains for obtaining foreign currency. Thus, it manufactures most of the left-hand-drive BMWs and exports helicopter turbines.

followed by all the Sub-Saharan countries except South Africa and Mauritius. The African Center for Economic Transformation draws up detailed strategies for changing the model, incorporating recommendations made by most of the industrial economists who have worked on these issues. These recommendations, which are quite conventional, stress two aspects that are definite prerequisites.

First, establishing a strengthened partnership between the state and the private sector is essential. Very often, a wall exists between governments and the private sector. I strongly urged—albeit sometimes in vain—the many heads of state and government I advised, to organize regular meetings with the local business communities at which grievances, mostly over bureaucratic hassles and red tape, could be expressed. Second, in line with other recommendations I have long been making, is the need for more stringent management of the economy, which often requires the overhaul of ministries of finance, budget, planning, commerce, industry, and the like. A key objective should be to transform these departments into centres of excellence along the lines of the Asian and Latin American models. I will have more to say on this important topic particularly in Chapter 13, 'Other key lessons for the Sahel and the donor's drawn from the West's failure in Afghanistan'.

The other recommendations, most of them also fairly conventional, include the need to systematically improve the business environment; clean up the judiciary; develop technical and vocational training, thereby bringing the business community and the state into closer association; encourage the establishment of subcontracting links between formal and informal sectors; better manage mining and petroleum revenues so as to gain greater budgetary leeway; and vigorously foster export activities, including non-traditional ones, perhaps by establishing special industrial zones, along the lines of the successful Ethiopian model, in which the business climate can be more easily improved than at the national level.

To this long list of (rarely followed) recommendations, must be added the quest for greater efficiency to ensure the fluid circulation of goods at ports and airports—which, as seen earlier, requires attacking the system of local extortions—and cleaning up national banking systems so as to improve savings and investment rates, the latter being still too dependent on international aid in Africa.

That these recommendations have been reiterated regularly in seminars and conferences for more than a quarter century without much effect is depressing. Yet, implementing them requires having political will to throw out illegal levies and associated rent mechanisms, which means accepting the short-term political consequences. Many African governments hesitate to shake some fortresses. It is hard to criticize them, however, when one considers that successive French governments have, for 50 years, been unwilling to contest outrageous advantages benefiting strongly unionized public sector employees and that it took four months and considerable outrage, controversy, and mass demonstrations in France to adopt a very modest relaxation of obsolete and Kafkaesque labour-law constraints.

Apart from political will, the operational conception and implementation of these measures should be entrusted to a robust technical team. In my view—and following the sound advice of Robert Wade[8]—such a team should include engineers with solid international-business experience and must be positioned at the core of the local power system so it has constant political support. The way Taiwan industrialized in the 1960s and 1970s offers an inspiring model, albeit a difficult one to emulate given that the world has changed quite a bit since.

## Can Africa enter the value chains of globalization and follow the Asian industrial model?

To overcome the massive unemployment problem, African countries must go beyond their traditional roles as exporters of unprocessed raw materials. They must work to weave their mining and petroleum complexes into the local economic fabric, which several countries are doing with some success. The Gabonese Republic's development should not be cited as a model, but at least it has let its private sector develop an efficient service activity around the regional petroleum industry. African countries must also develop their food-processing capacity, as Côte d'Ivoire is doing. Wherever feasible—and despite the difficulty

[8] Robert Wade, *Governing the Market, Economic Theory and the Role of Government in East Asian Industrialization* (Princeton, 1990).

due to Chinese competition—they must try to develop conventional import-substitution manufacturing industries, as Nigeria and Ghana have done in the past. But one has to recognize that all these various approaches that have been implemented over the past fifty years have not really helped the African industrial sector generate substantial wealth and employment.

In fact, Southeast Asia and, more recently, East European countries and Turkey have clearly shown that to develop swiftly, industry in African countries must throw off the constraints imposed by the low growth of domestic demand and regional markets. They should attempt instead to enter the 'value chains of industrial globalization'. What does this phrase mean? Quite simply, that industrial processes are now extraordinarily fragmented among multiple chains of sub-contractors who are constantly competing against each other. Consider the case of Apple's rollout of the first iPhones in 2007 from a Chinese factory, Foxconn International, located in Shenzhen. The factory actually assembled parts produced by two companies in Singapore, six in Taiwan, and two in the US—all of which had been designed in and coordinated from the Silicon Valley. China's value-added accounted then for only 5 per cent of the iPhone's price. Since then, China has 'climbed up the value chain', and some of its companies are manufacturing all the components of new smartphones, even in the face of competition from other Southeast Asian countries.

Developing countries eager to enter such value chains must take the initial step of manufacturing very basic components. Thereafter, they must try to move up the value chain by producing more complex components, gaining a greater share of added value as a country's technological skill grows.

## A process that is neither simple nor 'spontaneous'.

This is the approach that brought about China's industrial success. China now controls the value chains that enable it to produce the most sophisticated products, from communications satellites to fighter jets. But two important points should be highlighted.

First, the significant reforms enumerated above indicate that industrialization will not occur spontaneously or through laissez-faire. It will require political will expressed in appropriate sectoral and macroeconomic policies—each country, for instance, should be capable of controlling its exchange rate. Here, the states have an important role to play, both in protecting nascent industries (for a period of time), while pushing local companies to pursue competitiveness, which requires the intelligent management of protection systems that need to be progressively relaxed. Companies would likely be satisfied with simply collecting protection money and so would lobby to keep the protections. But management of protection mechanisms requires firm political will and solid technical and economic capacities—which accounts for my earlier paragraph about transforming economic bureaucracies into centres of excellence.

A little historical reminder is needed here. The standard neoclassical economic theories that still govern the World Bank and the IMF thought process roughly posit that if the price system is adapted and the market is free, industrialization takes place almost spontaneously, depending on the comparative advantages of the country, without state intervention. State intervention, they feel, could in fact lead to serious distortions through tactlessness or the influence of lobbies. Unfortunately, these theories have clearly been disproven by the manner in which some Asian dragons, especially Taiwan and South Korea, have handled their respective industrializations. An old but remarkable work on this I have already quoted[9] draws parallels between neoclassical economics and the economic policy measures implemented during the first 20 years of industrialization in these two countries—and underlines the extreme state intervention that was astutely masked so as not to alarm the American donor.[10]

---

[9] Wade, *Governing the Market, Economic Theory and the Role of Government in East Asian Industrialization*.

[10] In 1993, the World Bank published a thick book entitled *The East Asian Miracle*. The author, who candidly explained in his first work that Asia's success had largely come about through state intervention, faced severe censure from the organization's ayatollahs, pressuring him to adapt his analysis to the classic model. The unsatisfying result sparked controversy and the publication of a collective 'counter-work' in 2001 co-edited by two independent minds, Joseph Stiglitz and Shahid Yusuf, entitled *Rethinking the East Asian Miracle*.

Also, the world has changed considerably since these Asian dragons, followed by China, launched their prodigious industrialization movements. The potential for insertion into world markets isn't what it was 30 years ago. This holds true not only for the textile industry, in which Asia offers stiff competition, but also for various other sectors that have enabled Taiwan and South Korea to attain—and perhaps soon, improve upon—our own standards of living. Competition will make this effort even more difficult than before.

Nancy Birdsall, who was the director of economic policy and research at the World Bank and founding president (currently President Emeritus) of an important think tank, the Center for Global Development, has explained how new entrants will find themselves in an open field swept by a storm.[11] The asymmetrical competition requires that new entrants possess clear comparative advantages, particularly in terms of labour and energy costs, if they hope to attract foreign investors. But comparative advantages are not linked solely to natural conditions, a fact that enabled Portugal to produce better wine than England, as Ricardo explained more than two centuries ago. They are, above all, specific conditions that are built in the long term through appropriate policies.

A favourable point is that China and other countries, such as India and Turkey, that have become part of global markets are following the North American and European companies that delocalized massively in the 1990s. These countries, themselves facing major increases in production costs, are delocalizing large parts of their operations to countries with very low labour costs. Thus, China has made massive investments in Cambodia and Bangladesh, which are now major hubs handling a good share of global textile production. Industrial development through insertion in world value chains enables beneficiary countries to take advantage of foreign investments and the expertise that often accompanies them, while shedding the constraints and limits of domestic or regional markets. For many countries, this is clearly the key to rapid industrialization.

[11] Nancy Birdsall, 'Stormy Days on an Open Field: Asymmetries in the Global Economy', Working Paper 81, Center for Global Development, Washington, DC, 2006.

Two recent examples show that this is possible in Africa.

As Africa has begun benefiting from these processes (which implies, at a minimum, a drastic improvement in the business environment and smooth transits at ports and airports), a few experiences, mainly involving countries with very low labour costs, seem to hold promise today. They mainly concern the textile sector, in which two countries, Madagascar and Ethiopia, stand out.

### The textile industry in Madagascar had a promising start before being thwarted by political instability.

In Madagascar, an outmoded textile industry, dating back to the 1950s and the 1960s, that processed cotton and produced garments for the domestic market, was largely dismantled in the 1980s following the country being hastily thrown open to international trade and the uncontrolled import of second-hand clothes from Europe—all courtesy of ill-conceived adjustment programmes and, ultimately, destructive charitable actions. But, in the late 1990s this sector, which was on the road to ruin, was stitched back together thanks to Indian investments that had multiplied in Mauritius, in the textile-export sector. Due to its high labour costs, Mauritius sought an alternative to its low-end products. Within ten years, thanks to a free trade zone set up by the government and to a free trade agreement with the US, established in the context of the African Growth and Opportunity Act (AGOA), these investments helped generate around 120,000 jobs, thus providing sustenance to more than half million people. This was no mean feat.

This activity, however, was strongly thwarted from 2008 on due to political turmoil and instability that brought investments to a halt and due to the collapse of global economic growth. This political instability also led to the suspension of the AGOA agreement by the US, which penalized the textile workers while having little impact on the government. About half the jobs in the sector were lost. Including related jobs upstream and downstream—close to 100,000 jobs were lost in the blink of an eye, contributing to the domestic slump and crisis. The heart of the capital—which had looked to me, as a student hitchhiking across the country in 1960, like a shiny new penny—looked like a disaster area in 2010, with thousands of homeless people sleeping in the cold night using cardboard sheets as mattresses.

Political instability persisted until the confirmation of a new president in 2014; meanwhile, the sector continued to falter despite trade facilitation agreements with Europe, and with African, Caribbean, and Pacific (ACP) group countries and the opening of the South African market. Despite uncertain political stability, some Mauritian investors have opened new factories since 2013, and Chinese investors have come on prospecting trips. While the programme is not yet conclusive due to the political upheaval the country underwent and its permanent instability, it highlights the dynamics of job creation through foreign investments that bring a strong component of know-how and the advantages of a free trade zone that shakes up pre-existing, non-competitive local industries.

## The textile and footwear industries in Ethiopia offer a successful model for insertion in global value chains.

A second, very interesting example are the textile and leather industries currently developing in Ethiopia. I first visited Ethiopia in the early 1970s for work on a remarkable agricultural project on the banks of the magnificent Lake Awasa in the south. I took the opportunity to travel through the entire country, which had been ravaged by terrible food, social, and political crises. The Negus was then under house arrest in his palace while rebellions erupted throughout the country, and there was appalling poverty in the capital. On several recent trips to the country, I found Addis Ababa to be completely unrecognizable. What I saw during an inland trip, however, led me to feel that the countryside hadn't changed much.

Like Madagascar, Ethiopia possessed an old national textile industry dating back to the Italian occupation. But starting in 2011, it began drawing significant foreign investments and, today, is home to some 120 textile factories, 80 of which are foreign-owned, covering the entire gamut of production (cotton-ginning, weaving, knitting, and garments). Over the past few years, Ethiopia has drawn the interest of corporations with global distribution networks, such as Walmart, Primark, and Tesco.

These companies were not only looking for cheaper production costs, but were also interested in diversifying their supplies in the aftermath of the Rana Plaza factory scandal in Bangladesh, where 1,100 workers lost their lives when the building collapsed. In 2014, the Swedish group H&M, the world's second-largest garment manufacturer, decided to buy a wide array of textile products in Ethiopia, which attracted the attention of the sector's major investors. The Turkish group Ayka Textil established what would become the biggest textile factory in Africa with an investment of a quarter billion dollars; that was followed by a huge Saudi investment. Soon the major global distributors[12] realized that Ethiopia was on the textile world map, and the dynamics of investment and employment generation have been at work ever since.

Turkish, Indian, and Pakistani groups are also laying the groundwork for substantial investments. Prospects are that 2017/18 will generate an additional 40,000 jobs and exports reaching billions of dollars. A new industrial zone of 340 hectares has been opened on the outskirts of the capital. Close to it stands a vast industrial area—the Eastern Industry Zone—where several Chinese groups have invested in the automobile industry and in manufacturing shoes for Guess, Clark's, and Tommy Hilfiger. The Huajian group from China is planning an investment of USD 2 billion and the construction of a city of a 100,000 inhabitants. The dynamism of the textile sector will at last revive local cotton production, which had gone into hibernation.

Clearly, the major global buyers and investors did not choose Ethiopia at random. First, the country is a demographic power with close to 100 million inhabitants, expected to reach 150 million by 2040. Economic growth, despite the lack of significant oil or mining resources, exceeded 8 per cent since 2004 and even happened to reach 12 per cent some years, which suggests excellent economic management. Per capita income remains low (USD 400 per annum), as do salaries, which hover at USD 50 per month—almost one-tenth the average in China. Ethiopia is

---

[12] Calvin Klein, Hilfiger, Wrangler, Lee Jeans, Diesel, Carrefour, Oxbow, Zara, Marks & Spencer, Kappa, and Delta.

also politically stable, ruled with an iron fist very much in the Asian style.

A number of elements attractive to investors are notable. Institutional corruption is quite low, there is effective dialogue between the private sector and political authorities, and major efforts regarding education have been made in the past decade, with some 100 vocational training centres having been set up. A huge Grand Ethiopian Renaissance Dam under construction on the Blue Nile will add 6,000 megawatts—output equivalent to that of six nuclear power plants—to current power capacity, which already generates some of the cheapest electricity in the world. Addis Ababa has also become an important regional air hub thanks to Ethiopian Airways, which many regular travellers to Africa now choose to fly.

Thus, we have before us an example of African industrial development through insertion in the global value chains. Clearly, this is possible in Africa. Yet the system is still fragile, as we have seen in Madagascar, and political instability may cost dearly. Apart from political stability, macroeconomic stability must also be ensured. Inflation in Ethiopia has been oscillating between 18 and 20 per cent over the past few years following the strong stress on food-product prices arising from agricultural stagnation. Meanwhile, inflation in China is below 7 per cent. This means that Ethiopia's exceptionally low salaries can swiftly increase and the country could lose its key comparative advantage. In the meantime, however, considerable industrial and managerial expertise will have been built and the country might soon be ready to move along to a new value chain.

Ethiopia is clearly showing the way to Africa in term of export-based manufacturing, which seems to now develop quickly. Manufacturing exports have doubled over a decade in Africa from about USD 50 billion in 2005 to more than USD 100 billion in 2014. Rising wages in China and policy improvements in many countries have provided the region with a unique opportunity to attract foreign investment in manufacturing. Given the recent decline in commodity exports, manufacturing exports are also making countries more resilient to the current slowdown. Textile and leather are promising sectors, as demonstrated by Ethiopia; as are fertilizer, agro-processed products, and inorganic chemicals as explained in a recent DFID/ODI study.[13]

## Unfortunately, Ethiopia's example shows that few African countries can follow this path.

Ethiopia's example, though instructive on many points—particularly regarding a South–South relationship[14] with an emerging country—also sadly illustrates that not all African countries can hope to follow its path.

Candidates to be put aside include those where political stability and security are not assured; those where the dialogue between government and the private sector is unsatisfactory; those with a corrupt judiciary; those whose ports and airports are riddled with corruption and inefficiency; those with poor macroeconomic management; and those with high energy costs due to poor choices of investments and/or poorly managed local production and distribution systems. Add to this list countries where the exchange rate is overvalued and where labour laws inherited from former colonial countries do not yield the low wages that can compete with Asian countries; add also countries whose financial situations do not allow them to invest in modernizing infrastructure which is needed to create an environment welcoming to foreign investors.

Ultimately, that leaves few candidates. The ODI/DFID report previously quoted[15] highlights Ethiopia, Kenya, Mozambique, and Zambia as the most promising countries in this regard, since they are particularly able to attract foreign direct investment in manufacturing. Unfortunately, all of the previously listed criteria specifically eliminate the Sahel countries that so urgently need huge employment-generating opportunities.

---

[13] Neil Balchin, Stephen Gelb, Jane Kennan, Hope Martin, Dirk Willem te Velde, and Carolin Williams, 'Developing export-based manufacturing in Sub Saharan Africa', ODI/ DFID, April 2016.

[14] See Philippe Hugon, *Géopolitique de l'Afrique* ('Africa's Geopolitics') (SEDES, 2012).

[15] Balchin et al., 'Developing export-based manufacturing in Sub Saharan Africa', ODI/DFID, April 2016.

Current obstacles to industrial development in most of Africa, all linked to a poor business environment, are extremely worrisome when considered along with demographic factors. Youths entering the labour markets of Sub-Saharan Africa each year number close to 20 million and this figure is increasing at a fast pace. By 2025, the total will stand at 330 million—the current population of the US. The disturbing question for the continent's stability is this: How can the economy be reoriented to absorb this influx of young workers in a region dominated by low agricultural productivity and output?

Should efforts be focused on the development of light industry based on 'outsourcing', as Ethiopia seems to be doing with some success? Or should efforts be concentrated on improving agricultural output because it employs the huge masses of the countryside? What is certain is that dynamic small- and medium-sized enterprises involved in downstream or upstream activities linked to the primary sector must be strongly supported. This is precisely what a number of private investment funds now do—one such being 'Investor and Partners' led by Jean Michel Severino, former CEO of the French Development Agency—even though the managers of such funds know that this approach alone cannot fully resolve the problem due to its sheer magnitude.

The challenge of employment in Sub-Saharan Africa has been clearly identified by the World Bank, which devoted its 2013 World Development Report to the issue. It must be noted, without malice, that the solutions recommended by the World Bank in this report, emphasizing ambitious industrialization and urbanization policies, somewhat contradict the recommendations of its 2008 report, which emphasized agricultural development. Clearly, in terms of global strategy, the greatest minds are still floundering.

# PART II

Fragile States in the Eye of the Storm

# CHAPTER
# FIVE

# What Causes Fragility in Certain States?

In the preceding chapters, we dealt with a number of 'factors of fragility' that are essentially linked to a clash between economic constraints and population growth in many African countries. Economic growth, although significant, does not generate enough jobs to meet the huge flow of young men reaching working age into the job market. As we have seen, the main problem is largely due to a delay in the demographic transition as countries move from high birth and death rates to lower rates of birth and death.

The so-called Arab Spring that took place in the Middle East a few years ago—and which led to the present disasters in Syria—was largely caused by a similar contradiction. There is reason to fear that the discrepancy between job expectations and economic opportunities might cause similar violence in Sub-Saharan Africa. As we have seen in most African countries, unless major changes occur in the corresponding sector policies, neither agriculture nor industry will be able to offer young men jobs that allow them to earn a decent living. In describing these countries, I have used the term 'fragile' and outlined 'factors of fragility'. Is this a serious concept?

## Is it appropriate to apply the concept of fragility to specific countries?

Applying the concept of fragility to states is now common. But where does this characterization come from? Is it a purely subjective idea or is there an objective basis for ranking states on a 'fragility scale'? The evolution of an international consensus on the idea of a fragile state has been remarkably described by Jean-Marc Chataigner and Hervé Magro in their book *Etats et sociétés fragiles*.[1] They explain how the concept was developed through studies conducted in the early 2000s by aid agencies, particularly USAID, the UK's DFID, and the OECD's Development Assistance Committee.

These organizations aimed to identify troubled countries struggling to make efficient use of international aid resources. To the extent that aid resources are allocated, at least in theory, on the basis of economic performance, the troubled, unstable countries that fall prey to conflicts run the risk of being 'aid orphans'. Identifying such countries allowed the earmarking of specific resources for them. To assess and compare the performances of all the countries receiving aid, the major multilateral aid agencies usually refer to composite indices based on multiple criteria.

A standard approach is the one devised by the World Bank that ranks all countries according to a specific index, the 'CPIA'.[2] In a nutshell, donors used to consider that all countries with a low index were 'fragile' and those that ranked well were not. Such a rough approach owever, has sometimes led to significant errors. For instance, due to its progress on development policies, Niger had a favourable CPIA ranking and was not classified in the category of fragile states by the World Bank, although few countries in the world display so many obvious factors of fragility.

This rough approach has gradually been refined and other competing indices have been developed, the most common being the 'State Fragility Index' devised by the George Mason University, the 'Mo Ibrahim Index of African Governance', and the *Foreign*

---

[1] Jean-Marc Chataigner and Hervé Magro, *États et sociétés fragiles, entre conflits et reconstruction* ('Fragile States and Societies: Between Conflict and Reconstruction') (Karthala 2007).

[2] Country Policy and Institutional Assessment. I will delve later on what I call the pseudo-scientific nature of these approaches.

*Policy Review*'s 'Failed State Index'. The major international banks also have various scoring systems to detect—and therefore stay away from—what they consider to be 'countries at risk'.

The main problem with these indices is the relatively subjective ways of assessing parameters. Value judgments and subjectivity reign beneath mathematical constructions. These analytical weaknesses are the reason that, for all the attention aid agencies pay to scoring methods in research papers, they are rarely used operationally. Fortunately, economists (being what they are) have defined a more analytically rigorous concept—that of 'vulnerability'. On this matter, I highly recommend an article published by Patrick and Sylvianne Guillaumont, 'State Fragility and Economic Vulnerability: What is Measured and Why?[3]

Without getting lost in a labyrinth of details, the concept of vulnerability can be developed on the basis of objective, measurable data, such as the number and frequency of droughts and similar events, price variations for exported raw material, terms of trade, and the like. Statistical studies help define composite indices based on such objective factors. The best known is the Economic Vulnerability Index (EVI), defined by the UN. So why not base my analysis on the vulnerability concept, which has the advantage of being built on objective data? In a word, because this index is overly simplistic and does not take into account the extraordinary variety of situations.

Having clarified to some extent what the concept of fragility conceals, and having underscored the subjective nature of this approach, let us now explore another aspect of the fragility of African states, which is linked not to economics and demography but to other social sciences: history, geography, anthropology, and political science.

## Some states are at a nascent stage, while others are just being formed.

Historians and sociologists have taught us that modern states are supposed to exercise a monopoly on violence throughout their

---

[3] Patrick Guillaumont and Sylvianne Jeanneney-Guillaumont, 'State Fragility and Economic Vulnerability: What is Measured and Why?' policy paper prepared for the European Report on Development, 2009.

territories and ensure that law, order, and security are maintained. To this end, they have specific institutions, such as armed forces, police, territorial administrations, and the like, at their disposal. States are also supposed to fulfil functions ensuring the welfare of their citizens, particularly in social matters; further, they must maintain, to the extent that is possible, peaceful relations with their neighbours. Finally, they have control over taxation.

When some of these functions cannot be carried out or are jeopardized due to conflicts caused by external or internal sources, affected states are deemed 'fragile', 'at risk', 'poorly perform-ing', or in some extreme cases—as in today's Somalia or South Sudan—'failed' or 'collapsed'. Many such states are affected by current conflicts or sequels to past conflicts, be they inter-state— although this is rare in Africa today—or internal, which is by far the most prevalent type. In this respect, some African wars can be compared to European wars during the slow and painful processes of state formation in the thirteenth and fourteenth centuries, some of which are described by Barbara Tuchman in her well-known book about the hundred-year war in France.[4]

The term 'failed state' here is unrelated to the terminology used by former French Prime Minister François Fillon, who described France a few years ago as "*un pays en faillite*". He used the term in reference to France's troubled public finances—that is, a nation at risk of bankruptcy. At no time in the 2000s, of course, was France in a predicament like that of Somalia or Afghanistan, unable to offer minimum public services to their people and prey to many armed conflicts in their territories.

France is, of course, a very sophisticated nation and state, the culmination of a gradual process of state construction since Kings Clovis, Charles VII, Louis XIV, and Emperor Napoleon. State formation is not a linear process—far from it; it is often marked by failures and regressions generally related to episodes of internal or external conflicts. Hence, some states disappear, absorbed by their neighbours—as Poland was over the course of centuries—or they disintegrate, like the Austro-Hungarian Empire or Yugoslavia.

---

[4] Barbara Tuchman, *A Distant Mirror: The Calamitous 14th Century* (Ballantine Books, 1978).

That is why the processes that render some states fragile should be studied through the dual perspective of history and politics.

## Some states were never really built and largely remain 'pseudo-states'.

Some states—a typical case certainly being Afghanistan—were never really built as modern states and ultimately did not emerge from 'pseudo-state' chrysalises. The former Afghan president, Hamid Karzai, understood this deeply and therefore conceived of his role as that of a mediator among tribal powers that controlled various valleys and warlords reigning over various provinces. Thus, he spent his time negotiating unstable alliances with the diverse local powers, rather like a Merovingian king. When I was travelling in Afghanistan in 2002/03, my mission order, duly signed by the ministers of Agriculture or Finance, held no value once we had passed the suburbs of Kabul. Every 30 kilometres I had to negotiate with the local 'commander' for a pass, which was, in fact, a plain piece of paper he had signed, a process with its own set of hassles when the commander was nowhere to be found.

The manner in which President Deby rules Chad today is quite similar. The tribal fragmentation of the country is such that, in the absence of solid administrative and political structures, he is obliged to constantly negotiate unstable alliances with tribal chieftains and heads of major families and tribes, who are constantly falling out with each other—just as in Afghanistan. This problem explains why ministers are shuffled so quickly; with each change of alliance, some ministers are dismissed, though they often can make a comeback a few months later. This rotation of ministers, which is worse than that of France under the Fourth Republic, made me despair when I was working there, as my interlocutors would change by the time I next visited.

Even now in Afghanistan, some of the fabulously wealthy warlords do not really answer to the central government in Kabul. They collect their own taxes, and despite the 2004 UN-led disarmament, they still have significant militia on their payrolls. Several of them received me at a time when one could still travel the country in relative security. I especially remember my reception in 2007 by one of the most powerful warlords, Mohammed

Atta, who still reigns over the province of Balkh in northwest Afghanistan. Word has it that he is worth billions of dollars. On the coffee table, between our teacups, lay a laptop, the latest models of two satellite phones, three or four mobile phones, and VHFs. He led the conversation and was perfectly informed about the economic subjects on which I questioned him.

After twenty minutes, I sensed that I was about to be dismissed by a man who was as organized and as much a stickler for his calendar as the CEO of a top Wall Street company. But, perhaps interested in what I had to say about local agricultural prospects, he took me to lunch at his residence in a convoy of armoured Mercedes SUVs with tinted windows, followed by a convoy of Toyota pickups overflowing with armed men. It felt like being in a Francis Ford Coppola film. The welcome I received as part of a World Bank delegation from Moise Katoumbi, the then extremely powerful governor of Katanga in the Democratic Republic of Congo, wasn't too shabby either. I must acknowledge that in both cases I knew I was in the company of exceptional men.

## Building a state is rarely a long, quietly flowing river.

If some countries never came together as modern states and therefore never emerged from deeply entrenched fragility, others have progressed swiftly in building a state endowed with functional institutions to help ensure that law and order are obeyed. Some states have also embarked on building a nation, implying shared common values and a sense of belonging to the same community. Such was the case in Côte d'Ivoire during the rule of President Houphouët-Boigny, who was—let's not forget—a state minister under France's Fourth Republic. This was also the case in Tanzania, where President Nyéréré—though he had undoubtedly ruined his country's economy throughout the 1960s and 1970s with his absurd decisions—succeeded in forging a nation and making ethnic divisions gradually fade away.

On the other hand, reminding us that the process of building a state and nation is not a long, quietly flowing river, certain countries have fallen into fragility after years of progress. I will dwell in detail in Chapter 7, 'The ignored fragility of Côte d'Ivoire and its descent into hell', on the interesting and very instructive case, mentioned earlier, of Côte d'Ivoire. In fact, the history of each state's formation helps chart its particular situation according to a very theoretical scale. This scale varies from a chaotic ethnic or tribal situation (which rather resembles the situation in Libya today) to a semifeudal system, and then to the classic Weberian state model which gradually gained ground in Europe after the Thirty Years' War in the seventeenth century. This does not mean that each state must necessarily go through the same steps, but it illustrates the gamut of possibilities and the major historic trends of evolution.

If one accepts this presentation, some fragile states—whose institutions have yet to grow deep roots—are simply at an intermediate point in the historical process of building a state. A typical case is that of Libya, mentioned earlier. While I am not in the least a Gaddafi fan, I strongly disagreed with the Franco-British military action in that country.[5] Gaddafi had not bothered to build any state institution and maintained an autocratic reign over a group of tribes, alternating between repression and alliance. Once the 'Guide' died—none of the foreign powers that had initiated military action being willing or capable of building a state apparatus in such a challenging country—the situation ended in the chaos we are now witnessing and has grown even more dangerous due to the presence of ISIS.

Other states have simply regressed on this scale due to recurrent crises or conflicts. A state's fragility can thus be caused by an incomplete process of formation, and be hampered by circumstances as in Afghanistan. It can also result from a deviation from the expected trajectory—as in Côte d'Ivoire from the 1990s—or even a downslide that, in the worst-case scenario, can lead a relatively structured state to become a failed or collapsed one, as in the case of Somalia.

These situations are not necessarily overdetermined and sometimes leaders' actions can change the course of events. However, often, the weight of constraints paralyse such leaders. Hence I feel that if the current Afghan president, Ashraf Ghani, could implement the policies he has in mind—a tall order given the

[5] A point that shocked many during my address to a group of former World Bank officials in Paris a few days after the Franco-British military strikes began.

expanding insecurity, the political imbroglio, and the critical financial situation he faces—the process of building an Afghan state would accelerate quickly. Unfortunately, this is likely to now be just a dream.

## In Africa, the slave trade has long been an obstacle to the process of building a state.

When states have been forged over the course of several centuries and have thus been able to gradually shed most of the regional, ethnic, religious, and linguistic divisions, they have every chance of exiting the zone of fragility. In addition, when they have been able to establish legitimate political systems and their people feel that they belong to a single nation sharing common values and a vision with wide consensus, their resilience to upheaval is considerable. But, such resilience is seldom achieved in recently constituted countries where the institutions are weak, the legitimacy of political authorities is challenged, ethnic divides remain a serious problem, and belonging to a religious community provides a stronger bond than the sense of belonging to a nation.

Most of Africa's young states that are just over fifty years old thus retain latent elements of fragility that time alone can erase. Such latent fragility can be found not just in Africa but almost everywhere in the world, especially in places where states have been established by colonial or imperial powers under power-sharing treaties in zones of influence and not on coherent ethnic or religious bases. This holds true for most African countries as well as some in the Middle East, such as Syria, Lebanon, Jordan, and Iraq.

In Africa, the process of state or kingdom formation on a large scale began in Ethiopia in the year 800. It continued later in West Africa in the eleventh century with the kingdom of Ghana (now in Mali), then the constitution of the empire of Mali in the thirteenth century, and the Songhai empire in the fifteenth century.[6] Other states began being formed in various regions throughout the fourteenth and fifteenth centuries, such as the kingdom of

---

[6] For details, see Kevin Shillington, *History of Africa* (St Martin's Press, 1995) or Bernard Lugan, *Histoire de l'Afrique—Des origines à nosjours* ('A History of Africa: From Its Origins to Our Times') (Ellipse, 1995).

Kongo in Central Africa. But the process remained at the embryonic stage in most regions.

From the sixteenth century on, the few organized empires and vast kingdoms were dismantled and their structures transformed by the slave trade. This chaotic period of constant wars and razzias, which lasted till the mid-nineteenth century, severely disrupted the traditional agrarian economies, destroying state structures located well away from the coastal zones. Instead, a succession of small kingdoms sprang up along and near the coast, their economies fuelled by the slave trade.

A typical example is the kingdom of Abomey, now in Benin which, founded around 1600, became a regional power in the eighteenth century during the height of the slave trade. It is estimated that around 20 per cent of the African slaves shipped to the American continent during this period were captured and sold by this kingdom, whose unceasing wars and razzias contributed to the disintegration of the entire region. Anyone who has attended—as I had occasion to do in the 1960s—a major traditional celebration featuring thousands of dancers at the Royal Palace of Abomey can gauge the power that these kingdoms, established on slave trade, wielded historically.

Through the second half of the nineteenth century, these small kingdoms were conquered by European powers and consolidated into colonies of a size that made administrative and military staffing cost-effective. These colonial 'states' were organized according to different rationales by British, French, Belgian, Portuguese, Spanish, and German colonizers. But none of these 'states' aimed to gain enough of their people's adhesion to build modern states, let alone forge nations.

These 'states' were organized around the exploitation and export of raw materials from mining and tropical agriculture and were essentially focused on the control of production zones and communication networks (ports, roads, and railways). Various authors have written about 'gatekeeper states' whose essential function was to keep control of transport routes for the export of the region's wealth.[7]

---

[7] Frederik Cooper, *Africa since 1940: The Past of the Present* (Cambridge University Press, 2002).

This rudimentary state set-up was swiftly replaced, after the independence of African countries, by a supposedly 'modern' state system. But as is abundantly clear, the colonial powers had drawn the borders without taking the ethnic and religious aspects into account. This reveals the general fragility that ultimately affects almost all the African states, given how recently they were formed, the considerable ethnic and religious diversity within them, and the process of state-building that initially had neither the aim of establishing Weberian-type states nor commanding the adhesion of the peoples concerned.

## Other obstacles have thwarted state formation in Africa.

### Geography

The topography of certain countries is challenging: Some areas are covered with very dense forests, others have extensive deserts; both conditions make it hard for a government to exercise control over the entire territory.[8] This is true of Afghanistan's mountainous areas, the jungles of East Colombia, and Chad's deserts.

In these specific cases, the government's first failure generally is its inability to build or maintain an all-weather road network criss-crossing the entire country. The reasons for this may be technical, economic (due to low population density), or linked to the presence of insular irredentist groups in these regions. In the colonial era, the use of forced labour meant that people were sometimes pushed into these tough terrains, a case in point being that of the DRC.[9]

This situation explains a major part of Mali's tragedy: No central authority in Bamako has ever been able to control the vast stretches of desert in the north of the country. Even today, French and African troops under international mandate struggle

[8] On this subject, I recommend the remarkable book by Jeffrey Herbst, *State and Power in Africa: Comparative Lessons in Authority and Control* (Princeton, 2000).

[9] On this, read the horrifying description of the quasi-genocide under Belgium's colonization of the Congo under King Leopold's reign: Adam Hoschild, *King Leopold's Ghost: A Story of Greed, Terror and Heroism in Colonial Africa* (Mariner Books, 1998).

to control these vast spaces despite sophisticated surveillance equipment (drones, reconnaissance aircraft, and satellites). It is easy to understand how in these regions where, historically gold, salt, and slaves were actively traded, networks for illegal activities have developed with impunity in recent decades. Absence of the rule of law forced traffickers to turn to armed groups for protection; armed groups that ultimately largely took control of trafficking activities.

It came as no surprise to me when, upon my arrival in Niger in the early 1980s, I was given the option of acquiring an 'almost new' Mercedes or Peugeot. I could specify the model I desired and even the colour, at unbeatable prices. All I had to do was wait a few months—not much longer than a car showroom waiting period—and expect to find a layer of sand under the seats. Stolen in Europe and then crossing the Sahara in convoys, or stolen on the Lagos port, accompanied by well-forged documents, these cars were sometimes offered—as in my case—by none other than the franchisee's own salesman.

In the 1990s, these traffics expanded into cigarettes and gasoline, taking advantage of price differences with Algeria. Soon thereafter, the trafficking was controlled by local goons and included migrants attracted to the European mirage, cocaine for the European market sourced from South America, routed via Nigeria or Guinea-Bissau, and hashish coming from Morocco, routed via Mali, Niger and Libya towards the European market. This kind of trafficking being extremely profitable, it corrupted—as in Afghanistan—police, customs officials, territorial administration staff, and even highly placed politicians.

Such high profitability also enabled traffickers to diversify modes of transport. Thus, in November 2009, 200 kilometres north of Gao in Mali, a Boeing 727 flying from Venezuela was found on a makeshift airstrip. Originally loaded with cocaine, it had been quickly emptied and abandoned when it was unable to take off. Illegal trafficking diversified further to include the lucrative business of kidnapping expatriates and local traders. All in all, extreme geographical features and the challenge of controlling vast desert tracts almost devoid of human population contributed to rendering all the Sahel countries fundamentally fragile, regardless of their respective economic performance.

War and conflicts, including those in neighbouring countries, also contribute to making a country fragile, though their consequences can be contradictory depending on the conditions. Civil war usually has such a drastic impact on economic development that some economists view internal conflicts as reverse development. Thus, after ten years of horrific conflicts that followed Mobutu's plunder of the DRC and the invasion of this country by Rwanda after the 1994 genocide, the wealth per capita of the DRC in the early 2000s fell below independence-era levels.

In certain remote areas of the DRC, the poverty level was, until recently, unimaginable. In Kindu, a former rail, road, and river hub in eastern Congo that used to connect the DRC with East Africa, to the port of Mombasa, I saw the first train from Lubumbashi arrive in 2006. Not a single window remained in the coaches, which probably dated from the 1940s, and the train had taken fifteen days to cover 900 kilometres. The road I tried to follow east to Mombasa petered out after a few kilometres and disappeared completely in a forest. River traffic was paralysed by sunken barges. About 10 kilometres from Kindu, farmers toiled with wooden implements, unable to afford metal blades for their hoes. Their threadbare clothes were held together with patches. In the end, the governor was particularly eager to see our delegation leave—because he couldn't guarantee our safety at night.

In contrast, and paradoxically, the perpetual rivalry among states—and the accompanying wars—were part of the process of building European states from the thirteenth to the nineteenth centuries. The conflicts made it necessary for them to maintain standing armies and develop increasingly sophisticated administrative, fiscal, and financial systems to pay for them. Fiscal and financial institutions thus grew along with administrative systems to maintain gendarmeries,[10] build strategic routes and fortresses, initiate major construction projects, and so on. Some authors thus think Britain's military success throughout the eighteenth century

---

[10] Security in rural areas in France and many African francophone countries is provided by a special police force from the army, the 'gendarmerie'.

was due largely to the superiority of its fiscal administration and its ability to borrow, and astutely manage its debt.[11]

But there is a fundamental difference between inter-state wars that oblige the warring parties to reinforce their apparatuses of national sovereignty, and internal conflicts that, on the other hand, tend to weaken them. When states are still being built, civil wars wreck their consolidation and even lead to the disintegration of some, as happened not long ago in South Sudan. When one pores over the very complex map summing up the ten years of war in the DRC—which dragged seven neighbouring countries into the conflict—one is struck by its resemblance to the map of the Thirty Years' War, which saw most of Germany's neighbours clash with one another, sowing chaos and destruction throughout Central Europe.

In twenty-first century Africa, as in seventeenth-century Europe, the line between war and organized plunder or massacres for religious or ethnic reasons is quite blurred.[12] Often, the primary goal is plunder. In short, such conflicts can lead some countries to 'choose' between consolidating their state apparatuses and disintegrating. This, as I read it, is now the dilemma facing the leaders of the DRC. The huge conflict that ravaged the country through the 1990s is probably a step in the highly complicated and bloody construction process of a state, or perhaps even a nation.

## Hierarchy in state functions

Various authors have attempted to identify indicators of a state's fragility. For Rotberg,[13] former director of the Program on Intrastate Conflict, Conflict Prevention, and Conflict Resolution at Harvard, these indicators of fragility include growing criminal violence, the state's inability to offer its people fundamental

---

[11] Carmen Reinhart and Kenneth Rogoff, *This Time is Different: Eight Centuries of Financial Follies* (Princeton University Press, 2009).

[12] The remarkable book edited by Jean-Christophe Ruffin, '*Économie des guerres civiles*' ('The Economy of Civil Wars') (Hachette, 1996).

[13] Robert Rothberg, 'Failed States, Collapsed States', in *State Failure and State Weakness* (Brookings, 2003) and 'West Africa International Drug Trade', in *African Affairs*, vol. 108, 2009.

security, the emergence of warlords, and the failure to control its borders or significant parts of its territory. Rotberg identifies a hierarchy in the duties assumed by a state, beginning with security and proceeding to the ability to make the rule of law prevail and meet justice, to settle internal conflicts, and to ensure that property rights are respected. Added to these primary indicators, he posits, are guarantees of participation in political processes and the legitimacy of the political power, as well as providing access to basic infrastructure, such as roads and elementary social services in healthcare and education.

Other authors, especially Collier and Sambanis,[14] have flagged ineffective governance and poor economic performance as indicators of how the weakening of a state can lead to its implosion. They have also highlighted the role that poor management of oil and mining resources can play, and the correlation between the fragility of a state and the availability of natural mining or oil resources. Through various statistical analyses, they show that countries possessing rich natural resources are more likely to fall prey to violent internal conflicts. It is true that the knife tends to decide how booty will be shared.

On the basis of these various indicators of fragility—to which must be added whether the state's monopoly on taxation is respected or not—it is easy to see that a particular country may be weak in discharging certain duties and yet solid in others. Uganda, for example, has shown a considerable level of sophistication in the management of its economy, registered exceptional long-term growth rates, offered its people a significant range of healthcare and education services, and maintained a reasonably fair and legitimate government. Yet during twenty years, Uganda has been unable to control or ensure security in some of its border areas ravaged by the guerrilla war waged by the infamous LRA.[15]

Identifying a fault line that signals when a country will tip over to a general state of fragility as weaknesses affect various state functions, requires in-depth analysis. Colombia, where I spent a good part of 1967, experienced periods of civil war and

[14] Paul Collier and Nichola Sambanis editors, 'Understanding Civil Wars, Evidence and Analysis', The World Bank, 2005.

[15] Lord's Resistance Army.

insecurity—the famous *La Violencia*—from 1948 to 1960 that left more than 300,000 people dead. After this tragic period, armed groups inspired by Castro—particularly the FARC—played on the glaring inequalities in rural areas. Countered by paramilitary militias, they were confined to parts of the jungles in the east, adjacent to Venezuela, which they controlled until the 2017 peace agreement. These groups were quick to turn to drug trafficking. The lack of safety, at its worst in the 1980s, receded without quite disappearing. Yet this modern state, with established institutions, is hardly in the category of fragile states. A long culture of violence does not in and of itself make a country a fragile state.[16]

On the other hand, the case of Sri Lanka is unclear. In 1973, I spent almost a year there working on a particularly complex project. I had noticed the tensions between the country's two major ethnic groups and the fairly systematic persecution of the Tamils. But I never imagined that just a few years later, a horrific civil war would erupt between a government leaning on the Sinhalese majority population and a Tamil minority mobilized by a totalitarian party. From 1983 to 2000, much of the country was ravaged by war.

The government's forces crushed the Tamil uprising in 2009. Thereafter, political parties alternated power from election to election, offering hope that the situation had eased and the country would gradually emerge from the critical zone. But the deep-rooted causes of the conflict, which involved land grab as well as contempt and racism aimed at the Tamil people, lead one to feel that tensions still prevail and the risks of renewed insecurity are far from negligible.

### The hierarchy of national sovereignty functions helps assess how fragile a country is.

The last few examples show how difficult it is to define composite indicators of fragility; some aid agencies attempt to do so, but are

[16] My first encounter with the climate of violence in Colombia left a lasting impression on me: In 1967, having just landed, I went to exchange money at a bank in Bogota. I had to step over the dead body of a gangster who had been shot down by the guard at the entry and left there all morning, as a message to other gangsters.

ultimately reluctant to apply them in practice. What I can do is provide some insight into how I personally proceed when I work in a new country.

My approach is completely subjective and based on an analysis of multiple qualitative criteria without attempting to define a composite index. I use more of an analytical framework. I select three main criteria: the political context, the quality of institutions and governance, and the expected ability of the country to overcome the challenges it faces.

The questions I set myself regarding the political situation are whether the country's national history has been calm or turbulent; whether previous and current leaders have the ability to build a nation based on common values and a shared vision; the degree of homogeneity within the society; whether there are persistent ethnic, religious, and cultural tensions; the level of control national-sovereignty institutions exert over the territory; how inclusive the political system is; and the extent of consensus on the regime's legitimacy.

Regarding institutions and governance, my questions usually have to do with the magnitude of corruption; the possible involvement of the regime with organized crime and illegal trafficking; the impact of clientelism and nepotism on the functioning of the main institutions; the scale of mechanisms for extorting internal levies; the impact of all these phenomena on public service; the nature of the country's relations with 'friendly' states and the latter's ability to extend support in the event of crisis; and the scale of aid given by the international community.

Regarding the ability to surmount persistent challenges, apart from the classic macroeconomic analysis, I consider the past and anticipated resilience of institutions of national sovereignty in the face of unexpected crises, such as conflicts in neighbouring states spilling over into the country in question, extremely severe drought, et cetera. Thereafter, I examine a series of questions, the main ones being the scale of the slum problem, if any, and local authorities' urban-planning capacity; the government's ability to supply the usual public services, such as water, electricity, healthcare, and education; unemployment and underemployment levels, as well as job prospects in keeping with demography and the dynamism of the agricultural and industrial sectors; the fragility or resilience of the agricultural sector, as well as the quality of institutions and policy in this area; and the ability of the sector's institutions to support farmers' efforts with regard to agricultural intensification, modernization, and climate-change mitigation.

This is my usual checklist. As mentioned, it does not culminate in a composite criteria index. But after conducting this kind of investigation, it's possible, in principle, to gain a reasonable idea of a given country's 'degree of fragility.'

Applying this analytical framework to Uganda, I feel that, despite the continued lack of security in the northern areas still under LRA threat, this is not a particularly fragile state. Niger, which presents a fairly healthy macroeconomic management, a fairly legitimate and reliable government, and some success in social matters despite quite terrifying indicators, is, on the other hand, the prototype of a fragile country. The reasons are easy to identify: The north is a vast, semi-arid and desert zone that is largely uncontrolled; demographic growth is the highest in the world; arable land is in limited supply, and the entire country experiences periodic drought; environmental degradation has become a major concern; the Tuareg problem has not been fully resolved; and the geopolitical surroundings are extremely worrisome. The Fezzan region to the north in Libya has been a hotbed of jihadists since the fall of the Gaddafi regime. Boko Haram looms over the southeast border, not to mention the northwest frontier with northern Mali, which is yet to be pacified. As early as the 1980s, President Seyni Kountché—who did not lack in humour—was acutely conscious of this fragility and once commented to me: 'Poor Niger, with its terrible neighbours! If we were at the cinema, we'd have had to exchange seats.'

## Ethnicity remains an important factor in Africa.

The artificial borders drawn by colonizers have contributed to making most African countries home to numerous ethnic groups, sometimes hundreds, with great linguistic and cultural diversity. People adhere to various religions, both traditional and modern. A well-known religious fault line runs through the continent from east to west and separates the Muslims from the Christians and/or animists in the south.

Latent tensions exist all along this fault line. These sometimes degenerate into conflicts that have particularly affected Mauritania, Côte d'Ivoire, Nigeria, and Sudan. These conflicts attained their peak in the Central African Republic, where France somewhat naively thought it could ease a serious conflict between Muslim and Christian communities, with a backdrop of natural resources being plundered and disastrous governance. A word now on the role of ethnicity in this violence.

African leaders often deny the weight of ethnicity, especially to Europeans, in order to convey the idea that these issues are from a bygone era. But the genocide in Rwanda and many other conflicts, such as the one in South Sudan—recently independent and torn by the conflict between native Dinkas and Nuers—show how important ethnicity is.

Ethnicity still weighs heavily on the African continent and has a major influence on local politics: In many countries, political parties have very strong ethno-religious bases. A typical example is Guinea, where the Malinke ethnic group overwhelmingly supports President Alpha Condé while the Fulani group supports the alliance led by his opponent, Cellou Dalein Diallo. Similarly deep cleavages can be found in countries as different as Kenya and Côte d'Ivoire.

It should be noted that ethnicity often has no clear historic, biological, or racial roots. Intermarriage and the intermingling of peoples have helped gradually erase the boundaries between the original social groups that were composed into ethnic groups. Moreover, colonial powers sometimes contributed to artificially assigning ethnicity, particularly in the cases of Rwanda and Burundi, with the good old colonial policy of divide and rule. Some politicians also manipulate ethnic situations to build their power based on fear and hatred of the other.

Thus, ethnicity is often a social construct. Increasingly, one belongs to one ethnic group or another depending on people's perception.[17] To cite a non-African example, the head of the

---

[17] In this regard, see the article by Mélégué Traore: 'Le Fait Ethnique' (Ethnicity) in Jean-Pierre Vettovaglia (ed.), Déterminants des Conflits et Nouvelles Formes de Prévention ('Determining Factors of Conflicts and New Forms of Prevention'), Ed Bruylant (Bruxelles, 2013).

Afghan executive branch (and unfortunate runner-up in the last presidential election), Abdullah Abdullah, was born of a Pashtun father and a Tajik mother, but he is perceived as a Tajik and is the candidate of Tajiks.

## Ethnic divides and religious heterogeneity are specific elements of fragility.

History tells us that states that are home to ethnically heterogeneous people are far more fragile than those that have an ethnically homogeneous population. There is no dearth of examples. Yugoslavia's disintegration reminds us that the phenomenon is not confined to Africa. Is the fragility of ethnically heterogeneous states not similar to the fragility of empires that bring together very different nations and peoples under a single entity? Remember the end of the Ottoman Empire. Remember also how the Austro-Hungarian Empire's leaders perceived it to be highly fragile due to its heterogeneity, which artificially grouped various nations together; it was this very perception of fragility that made them 'overreact' to the assassination in Sarajevo in 1914. The assassination was perceived as a fresh and intolerable Serbian aggression that, left unpunished, would imperil the empire's unity, thereby justifying Austria's attack against Serbia, which led to consequences with which we are very familiar.[18]

The existence of many religions or variations of the same religion in one country can also be a source of fragility if the demographic weight of various religious groups is significant, and an additional source of fragility if it changes over time as has been the case in Lebanon. This obviously holds true for Nigeria, torn between a Christian South and a Muslim North. In the Middle East, Fromkin's famous work[19] reminds us that the whole stretch encompassing the three nations already constituted as Turkey,

---

[18] The recent bestsellers on the 1914 war: Margaret MacMillan, *The War That Ended Peace: The Road to 1914* (Random House, 2014) and Christopher Clark, *The Sleepwalkers: How Europe Went to War in 1914* (Penguin Books, 2012).

[19] David Fromkin, *A Peace to End All Peace* (Henry Holt and Company, 2001).

Persia, and Arabia was divided into areas, under direct French and British administration, into five spheres of influence under the 1916 Sykes Picot Agreement. This dismemberment, in complete disregard for the distribution of tribes and religious groups, and ignoring the demand for nationhood made by certain peoples, particularly the Kurds and Armenians, led to the creation of artificial states that were never able to forge themselves into real nations.

These artificial states imploded—Iraq in 2003, Syria in 2011—and the maelstrom that followed is shattering their local societies. Observers wonder whether Lebanon and Jordan can continue resisting for long. A remarkable case is that of Iraq, where the senseless dissolution of the armed forces and the Baath party apparatus by the US pro-consul Paul Bremer[20] in 2003 triggered the events that the entire world is witnessing: terrorism, a civil war that has been going on for 14 years, and the emergence of ISIS. This historic reminder from a non-African country shows how difficult it is, even now, to form a state or nation in countries that are ethnically and religiously heterogeneous. I shall dwell on Iraq in greater detail later.

In all societies fractured along ethnic or religious lines—especially when the state has been recently formed, as in Africa—each individual's first loyalty beyond immediate family lies with extended family, and beyond that with the tribal, ethnic, or religious group with which the person feels an affinity. This point is borne out throughout Africa, as well as in countries as different as Afghanistan, Syria, Lebanon, and many Caucasian and Balkan countries where the state is regarded with some suspicion or even with much distrust. Unfortunately, this phenomenon undermines the authority and legitimacy of the state, encourages uncooperative behaviour, and, in certain cases, spurs revolt against the existing political power if it is wielded by a different ethnic or religious group that is unwilling to share political and economic power.

[20] A remarkable book tracing Iraq's disintegration due to this mad decision is Thomas E. Ricks, *Fiasco. The American Military Adventure in Iraq* (Penguin, 2006).

# The process of nation-building is complex and protracted.

One can gauge both the effort and the time necessary for building a homogeneous state and a nation that shares the same values by considering the case of France. The process of forging a state in France involved centuries of systematic destruction of all elements of cultural, ethnic, or religious diversity, from the Revocation of the Edict of Nantes in the seventeenth century to the repression of the Breton language in the early twentieth century. To the best of my knowledge, only three African countries have embarked on a truly deliberate policy of obliterating ethnic identities to reinforce national cohesion: Tanzania, as already noted; Rwanda, after the genocide for reasons one can easily imagine; and Botswana, which has imposed a common language and, like France, crushed the use of regional languages.

Despite the efforts of generations of African leaders to build nations and develop a sense of national adhesion among very heterogeneous populations, progress on this front has been uneven. In most ethnically heterogeneous countries, such as Guinea, political affiliations closely follow along ethnic or religious lines, complicating every policy aimed at erasing the divides. This point is examined in detail in chapter 7 dealing with Côte d'Ivoire's descent into hell in the 1980s and 1990s.

The tendency of political affiliations to fall along ethnic or religious lines is less rigorous in areas of relative ethnic homogeneity when one group exercises, de facto, a strong domination, such as the Wolof people in Senegal, though the cases of Rwanda and Burundi show that there are numerous exceptions to the rule, particularly if a political or ethnic group oppresses minorities. In cases of major ethnic fragmentation when hundreds of ethnic groups coexist in one country, as is the case in the DRC and Nigeria—parties usually align according to regions.

It is true that, ethnically, more homogeneous countries, such as Senegal, or those whose leaders have instituted deliberate integration policies, as in Tanzania and Botswana, have made significant progress in nation-building. But in most African countries, ethnic and religious fragmentation remains the rule rather than the exception, which introduces specific factors of fragility.

As we shall see, these factors are particularly visible when the distribution of power and wealth is inequitable; it is therefore always important to see if political and economic factors underlie ethnic tensions or conflicts. These factors of fragility are enhanced when political leaders play the ethnicity or religion card and manipulate fear and hate to divide society and secure their power. In this regard, unfortunately, democracy—at least as it is generally practiced in Africa—is not a miracle remedy at all and, paradoxically, can instead exacerbate tensions, as has been so clearly explained by Paul Collier.[21]

## Communal polarization is a frequent phenomenon in times of crisis.

We have seen that in countries where the weakness of the state prevents them from providing the commonly expected services (security, justice, and basic economic and social services), tribal, ethnic, or religious loyalties become more deeply entrenched. In parallel, loyalty to the state tends to wane, if it existed at all, especially as tribal, ethnic, religious, or mafia groups substitute for the malfunctioning state to provide basic services, from elementary schooling to security.

Various events can hasten the withdrawal of individuals and families into ethnic, tribal, or religious groups, resulting in extreme polarization. A typical example is the resumption of civil war in Iraq following America's withdrawal in 2011. This non-African case is worth pondering.

In December 2011, despite the many serious political mistakes made by the occupying authorities, the withdrawal of US forces from Iraq opened a window of opportunity to normalize the situation. Al Qaeda-affiliated outfits had been defeated militarily in the successive battles of Fallujah and the departure of foreign troops had removed its main justification for continuing the insurrection. Further, Sunni Arab organizations had started participating in the political institutions, having even led the polls during the 2010 legislative elections. The optimistic scenario that

[21] Paul Collier, *Wars, Guns and Votes, Democracy in Dangerous Places* (HarperCollins, 2009).

then seemed possible—the establishment of a democracy based on shared power and wealth and gradually freed from religious divisions—soon shattered.

The responsibility for this lies squarely at the door of Prime Minister Nouri al-Maliki and the Shiite political organizations that supported him—and that continued marginalizing the Sunnis. Negotiations concerning the sharing of oil revenues led nowhere. The Sunni regions gained little from the economic recovery. The Sunni Sahwa militia, which had defeated the jihadi insurrection, was dismantled. The armed forces and the police were purged and recomposed based on religion, excluding the Sunnis. Members of the Sunni political elite were targets of harassment. Even so, no one in 2012 imagined that civil war would return.

The fire was ignited by the brutal repression of peaceful demonstrations about local economic claims and respect for rights, as in the Hawija clashes in April 2013 that caused dozens of deaths. The Sunni people fell back on their own organizations and, harassed by police clearly guided by a sectarian agenda, were driven to despair and insurrection. When Baghdad decided on military action instead of negotiation to repress the insurrection, civil war spread like wildfire in early 2014, leading to Fallujah falling into the hands of Sunni insurgents.

As the regime mobilized Shiite militia (supported by Iranian advisers), the desperate Sunni organizations, bombarded with TNT barrels, found themselves constrained to enter into a pact with the best organized—and most extreme—group: ISIS. 'We are very clearly opposed to the practices of the Islamic State in Iraq and the Levant,' explained a leader of JRTN, an armed Sunni movement, 'but the current situation is no longer tenable, and all armed Sunni groups must unite.'[22] But as the nationalist project of the Sunni groups clashed with the transnational project of ISIS/ ISIL, in July 2014 the latter began purging Sunni groups to grab full control.

As in Syria, protest movements stemming from local concerns and initially containing a small religious dimension became

---

[22] Quoted by Arthur Quesnay in 'The Sunni Revolution and the Outburst of Community Divisions in Iraq', Noria research paper, 19 December 2014.

radicalized on a purely communal basis, thus supporting the most extremist group. The movement led to systematic ethnic and religious purges of, among others, the Yazidis, the Shabaki people, and Christians. Massacres took place aimed at 'homogenizing'—a horrible term in this context, but the very aim of ISIS/ISIL—the mixed Arab-Kurd and Sunni-Shiite territories to oust non-Sunnis. The sectarian segregation and accompanying polarization make it now much more difficult for the new Prime Minister Haider Al Abadi to work out a negotiated solution and the reconstruction of a pacified, modern Iraqi state.

This example shows how a modern, secular, and structured state, run by a brutal dictatorial regime, stays intrinsically fragile when nation-building remains incomplete and strongly assertive ethnic and religious communities subsist. It also shows how the destruction of the cementing institutions of national sovereignty can lead to civil war and to a communal polarization likely to jeopardize the survival of the state. It is now time to turn to the role that state institutions can play in consolidating or weakening a state.

# CHAPTER
# SIX

# Weak Institutions Create
# Fragile States

## 'Extractive' versus 'inclusive' institutions: A recent North American view

Fragile states are characterized by highly ineffective public institutions often incapable of providing the goods and services expected by the population in areas as basic and diverse as drinking water, security, justice, and road maintenance. Why do such institutional weaknesses occur? Why, in particular, do technical and managerial support only rarely result in long-term solutions? Is there a curse that condemns institutions in certain countries to ineffectiveness?

In their bestselling book *Why Nations Fail*, American academics Daron Acemoglu and James A. Robinson[1] set out a comprehensive theory on fragile states. The authors seek to identify the reasons why some nations are prosperous while others remain poor and, in some cases, collapse. In doing so, they draw a distinction between two major situations: one in which 'extractive' economic institutions focus on extracting revenues to benefit a

---

[1] Acemoglu, Daron and James A. Robinson, *Why Nations Fail* (Crown, 2012).

small elite, and another in which 'inclusive' economic institutions support a broad distribution of resources. This premise explores the link between economic institutions and political institutions: the first case increases the power of a small elite, while in the latter, political power is distributed more evenly.

The authors take the view that creating inclusive political institutions requires a degree of state organization and centralization, which would explain why Sub-Saharan Africa lags behind in this area. The alleged synergies between economic and political institutions lead to vicious or virtuous cycles, depending on the situation. In vicious cycles, the extractive institutions become entrenched, impede development, and create internal tensions, which lead to political instability when groups that are excluded from economic and political power try to overthrow the established order. In virtuous cycles, inclusive economic and political institutions foster political stability and an environment that supports development and the kind of creative destruction described by Schumpeter in his famous book titled *The Theory of Economic Development*, which enables rapid growth and a diversified economy.

In their analysis, the authors emphasize that these virtuous or vicious cycles are the product of history, even if they are not historically determined. Chance, the decisions made by leaders, and unexpected events that may upset the political balance can all have an impact on a country's fate. But there is no magic formula to ensure that the scales tip the right way. Acemoglu and Robinson describe, in detail, some dramatic downward spirals that have resulted in African countries becoming failed states. They point out that such states have collapsed because the process of state building began late and because the weight of 'extractive' political institutions ultimately 'boiled over', leading to civil war.

One of the book's most interesting points is its observation that 'extractive' economic and political institutions are perfectly capable of allowing periods of strong growth, but that the political instability that accompanies this type of social organization will not support such growth over the long term. By highlighting the fundamentally unstable nature of regimes that exclude the majority of the population from power and wealth, the authors emphasize the underlying fragility of many African countries despite their impressive economic performance. Applying the argument put forward by Acemoglu and Robinson to countries such as Cameroon or Congo Brazzaville raises concerns about the sustainability of their spectacular growth despite their wealth and the increasing sophistication of their economies. Ultimately, the capacity of both countries (and many others) to ensure better distribution of wealth and power will undoubtedly determine their future stability.

## 'Politics of the belly' and 'Potemkin' states: The older French vision is not so far removed from the previous one

The reference to Cameroon leads me, of course, to a well-known French researcher, Jean-François Bayart, whose field work in that country has made a significant contribution to thinking about the African state ever since the publication of his first book on the subject some time ago.[2] First, Bayart comments that since various African countries became independent, control of the state apparatus has been the fastest and most effective method for accumulating wealth and that this wealth has been the key to retaining political power. This is a vicious cycle: Knowing that it is not their salaries as heads of state that allows political leaders to buy the many loyalties they need to exercise and retain power helps explain the role of corruption in the operation of African political systems. It is therefore essential that leaders mobilize a significant level of resources, and they have two main tools for doing so: corruption and trafficking.

Corruption—and we are talking here, about large-scale corruption, not the kind perpetrated by the police officer who stops you at the corner so he can pay his rent—takes multiple, infinitely imaginative forms. The more traditional methods involve misappropriating a proportion of state revenues: customs, tax, oil and mining revenues, port revenues, revenues from stabilization funds, and so on. Other mechanisms are so sophisticated that even seasoned analysts can have difficulty identifying them. I have had the opportunity, for example, to work with a team from the International Monetary Fund (IMF) to examine in detail the oil revenues of one African state, a significant exporter of crude oil. It took a highly experienced specialist to spot the multiple

---

[2] Jean-François Bayart, *L'État en Afrique: la politique du ventre* (Fayard, 1985).

minor and unjustified variations and discounts in the price of the crude oil exported to get even a rough estimate of the significant amount of money being diverted.

Analysing the funds misappropriated from the coffee-and-cocoa stabilization fund in Côte d'Ivoire in the early 1990s, before it was liquidated under pressure from the World Bank, was a simpler matter. That said, I believe the liquidation was a mistake because it did not, in any way, tackle the political power relationships that underpinned the pillaging taking place in the sector. It would have been easier to introduce transparency into the institution, which had a useful role to play, than to get clear insight into the convoluted mess that replaced it under President Gbagbo's scheme. That scheme was, of course, intended to serve the same plundering purpose, and under President Gbagbo a comparable amount of money was most likely misappropriated. The experts from Côte d'Ivoire and the economists from the World Bank and the European Union who met in Washington and Abidjan in 1994 and 1995 had some epic discussions, in which those, like myself, who supported retaining the institution and cleaning it up found themselves in the minority.

Trafficking is another method that presents significant advantages: In general, unlike large-scale corruption, it does not affect the operation of the national economy, provided it takes place outside the country. One of the great trafficking specialists was the well-known president of a Sahel country who has since been overthrown by a popular uprising. This was a man of great intelligence who is alleged to have been involved in trafficking diamonds, arms, and counterfeit bank notes, and to an extent, drugs, until he was called to order by the US State Department. I had the chance to meet him on one occasion, and while he talked to me about his commitment to transparency and good governance, I could not keep from thinking about everything that was being peddled through his alleged trafficking. The way he operated meant that he was able to ensure that his country's economy, which had an efficient and honest administration,[3] worked properly. But one

[3] One of my friends, who worked as an economist in Zaire in the mid-1980s, told me how surprised he was at the progress made in terms of governance at the time, saying ironically, 'Where the hell is Mobutu off to now?'

has to shudder at the idea that President Hollande of France once thought that this man might run the International Organization of La Francophonie.

Back to Jean-François Bayart. He was almost certainly the first person to theorize that in spite of their modern Western appearance, impressive head offices, boards, and audit committees, many African institutions are, in reality, often entirely different. Although I had spent more than 15 years on behalf of AFD on the boards of major African companies, from mining companies, public banks to major utilities, he helped me understand that many of them simply put up a facade similar to those erected by Potemkin when Catherine II travelled through Russia. And behind these façades lay an entirely different world. This other world is characterized by loyalty networks based on ethnic and political affiliations, which sit alongside the official organizational structures. The main purpose of these networks is to discreetly extract income from the institution to support the party, ethnic or religious group, or politician that effectively controls the institution from the shadows. This is the 'politics of the belly', as eloquently described by Jean-François Bayart.

Such rent-extraction mechanisms are not always discreet. While representing AFD in Gabon in the 1980s, I was summoned, one day, to an exceptional meeting of the board of the Development Bank of Gabon, into which the AFD had put some money. Only upon entering the room did I receive the documentation for the loan that was to be discussed, a fairly bulky file with many appendices. The loan amount was significant for an individual borrower—the equivalent of about of 10 million euros—and the purpose was to finalize the construction of a villa. The documentation showed that the borrower was able to reimburse the loan thanks to his current real estate income. Most surprising was what was written against 'Activity' on the information sheet about the borrower: *'President de la République'*.

There was deep silence for several minutes as the Gabonese board members digested the information in front of them. I decided to launch the discussion and said that, in my opinion and that of my institution, the purpose of a development bank should not be to finance a head of state. My statement was followed by a deeper and longer silence. And then one of the Gabonese administrators raised the only other point made during the meeting: 'Gentlemen, I believe the interest rate is too high for the President.'

The tension between loyalty to one ethnic, political, or religious group and loyalty to the state lies at the heart of large-scale corruption. This tension goes a long way towards explaining the weakness and ineffectiveness of numerous state institutions in Africa, which in turn contribute to the weakness of the state itself. Why are they so ineffective? Quite simply, because the actual purpose of the institution tends to drift under the influence of these predatory networks. In the more benign cases, the network simply takes a cut on a few contracts. In serious cases, the institution loses sight of its aims so that generating rents becomes its primary concern. Then, the managers who witness the pillaging tell themselves they might as well take advantage of it too and start pillaging in turn. Serious pillaging of this kind is not a long-term option and quickly leads to disasters.

### Controlling a fragile state means controlling rents and corruption.

Ultimately, in Mobutu's Zaire, it hardly mattered if the national airline could fly its planes once the networks of internal predators and the airline's executives were able to sell kerosene and spare parts for their own profit. In the end, of course, it all collapsed. When I took over as director for Central Africa at the World Bank in 1996, the port of Douala, whose tariffs for docking vessels were some of the highest in Africa, was no longer accessible to cargo ships of a certain draft. Because the port no longer had the resources to dredge the access channel; I had to have the World Bank finance it. So, where had the money gone?

Situations of this kind are not a purely African phenomenon, of course. The famous 'Elf affair' showed that even in modern France, predatory networks can pillage a national company, very probably to the benefit of a political network at the outset and, then, taking advantage of the situation, to their own benefit. Yet, in these circumstances, the corrupt individual who is dragged through the courts is not the faithful manager who extracts funds for the benefit of his group, but one lost sheep who takes advantage of the situation to fill his own pockets.

Fortunately, situations of this kind are the exception in France, where control mechanisms are, in fact, effective; nor are they specific to Africa, but rather are characteristic of societies that are profoundly heterogeneous in ethno-political or political-religious terms. In this situation, each group is in direct competition with others for the control of resources that enable them to gain or retain power.

I have found similar—often worse—situations in countries such as Afghanistan, Syria, and Lebanon. How else can we explain the scandal of Kabul Bank, whose directors bankrupted it after embezzling almost a billion dollars? Or the extraordinary losses at the Lebanese energy company which, in spite of operating a monopoly over a country the size of two French departments, lost a billion dollars a year, which the national budget was forced to cover to avoid the country being plunged into darkness?

Generations of experts have pored over this last mystery and produced enough technical reports to fill several cupboards. But the problem is not in any way technical or managerial. It is simply that one of the 18 religious/political organizations recognized by the Lebanese state was bought off with this unfortunate energy company as part of the Taief Agreements that put an end to the civil war in 1989. Staffs were therefore appointed on the basis of religious affiliation rather than competence. But, above all, the organization in question avoided demanding payment for electricity bills from its poorest members, thus securing the loyalty of several hundred thousand people quite peacefully, since the state had to cover the deficit to avoid the risk of a general blackout. Some years ago, I took part in a series of discreet audits of the Lebanese public accounts. I concluded that the only solution was an unlikely political agreement, since the organization in question had the capacity to cause harm far in excess of the billion dollars being lost each year.

This small example illustrates the fact that in fragmented societies where clans, tribes, ethnic or religious groups, and political parties are at odds over the control of revenues and power, state institutions—whether the army, the ministry of finance, the port authority, or the energy company—cannot readily become the impersonal social constructions that we find in our own institutions in homogeneous, developed countries. Most frequently, they are structures based on very strong personal, tribal, ethno-political, or political-religious ties.

Such highly personalized operational rules have a decisively negative impact on the performance of the institution in question, as emphasized by Douglass North, the leading specialist in institutional economics.[4] The famous 'poor governance' we hear so much about, and what is commonly known as neo-patrimonialism, characterizes the confusion between public goods and private goods. It must therefore not be judged according to ethical criteria, but on the basis of the history of a society, its political organization, the level of effectiveness sought, and, finally, the degree of mistrust and suspicion among groups.

I recall the reaction of an Afghan minister to whom I was advocating the benefit of a recruitment mechanism for officials in his ministry based on merit rather than membership in a particular ethnic group: 'But I'm not going to recruit someone who might cut my throat!' he replied with an eloquent gesture to make sure I understood his English. This is a perfect illustration of the lack of understanding, in some societies, of conflict of interest. The argument is: 'I appoint someone because I know him, he belongs to my tribe, and therefore I trust him.'

## Good governance: The mythical vision of donors

In general terms, what we call corruption—a phenomenon we judge from an ethical standpoint—is most frequently a mechanism in these countries for extracting rents from an institution controlled by a specific social group. It is therefore, in fact, a social mechanism that can sometimes even be useful as a means of buying social peace. President Houphouët Boigny embezzled billions from Côte d'Ivoire's stabilization fund. But he redistributed a large proportion of these resources, ensuring that each ethnic group, regardless of size, received a share and that the redistribution was seen as fair.

This mechanism allowed him to maintain civil peace in Côte d'Ivoire for 30 years. Let's not judge him too severely for practices

[4] Douglass North, *Institutions, Institutional Change and Economic Performance* (Cambridge University Press, 1990).

that, we hope, date from another era. In fact, behind this notion of good governance, we have a tendency to project an idealized vision of the operation of our own 'impersonalized' institutions, which exist in what are now ethnically homogeneous societies that have set up control mechanisms to avoid the diversion of assets and where pension funds provide for a peaceful old age. But let's not forget the level of poor governance that existed in our own societies just a century ago—or how corrupt some of our own institutions still are. One day, the finance minister of Nigeria, Ngozi Okondjo Iweala,[5] responded at a hearing before members of the U.S. Congress questioning her about corruption in Nigeria: 'Gentlemen, what you call lobbying is called corruption in my country.'

Finally, we should note that most state institutions in fragile states characterized by ethnic or religious heterogeneity have a 'Potemkin' dimension to a greater or lesser extent. The customs authorities, ministries of finance, ministries of trade, energy and railway companies, and port authorities look like their Western counterparts. They have broadly similar organizational structures and are supposed to collect customs revenues and taxes, facilitate trade, distribute electricity, transport passengers and freight, and handle container ships as efficiently as possible, for the collective good. If their performance is mediocre, we tend to think that they lack certain technical or managerial skills or computers or other equipment, and that technical assistance, training programmes, and a bit of investment will soon sort things out.

Unfortunately, although these traditional solutions do have their uses, they generally miss their target. We can only transform failing institutions of this kind by 'turning them on their head' and challenging the entire system for recruiting and selecting executives, the methods used to manage human resources, and their organizational structure, in order to introduce management by objectives. Yet, it is a political problem more than a technical or organizational one. It means accepting a dismantling of internal predatory mechanisms, breaking up networks that are based on ethnic or political affiliations, and rebuilding the institutions to

---

[5] Before being appointed Minister of Finance, Ngozi Okondjo Iweala was the managing director of the World Bank.

make them as effective as possible. It is not an easy task but nor, as we will see, is it a lost cause.

In fragile states that are largely heterogeneous in ethnic or religious terms, loyalty towards your ethnic or religious group does not demand any particular effectiveness with regard to the production of goods or services for the population. You will therefore not be judged on your performance, but on your capacity to serve the social group that placed you in your position. Your role is therefore to facilitate access to employment for the members of your group, offer some of them free services, as the Lebanese energy company does, transfer funds extracted from contracts, and make sure that some of these contracts are granted to 'friends.'

This situation is not specific to Africa but, as we have seen, is typical of numerous heterogeneous societies. Unfortunately, this way of working is profoundly ineffective in terms of achieving the objectives of the institution concerned. The result: the hospital falls apart; the electricity company survives only because of subsidies that undermine the budget; the trains only run occasionally; the roads are no longer maintained; water is no longer fit for drinking, and the supply is available only a few hours a day; customs revenues disappear; police officers get involved in racketeering; and so on.

### The ineffectiveness of public institutions contributes to the fragility of the state.

The ineffectiveness of the main public institutions clearly impedes the ability of the state to provide the basic services expected by any population. In these conditions, it is illusory to believe that states can hope to command respect and loyalty from citizens who have a canny sense of the origins of the mismanagement. People then tend to make increasing use of parallel services offered by the social groups to which they belong on the basis of ethnic or religious affiliation. The various churches or mullahs take charge of education, health, and social services while the tribal chief hires out bulldozers to maintain the roads in the region he controls, arranges for a bridge that has collapsed to be rebuilt, dispenses justice or keeps the neighborhood safe, and receives various taxes for doing so.

Ultimately, this all triggers a vicious cycle that increases the need for loyalty towards one's ethnic group to compensate for the ineffectiveness of the state. This process has been seen on a large scale in Afghanistan since 2002 and goes a long way towards explaining the failure of the Western coalition. This was described in sober but accurate terms in late 2009 by General Stanley A. McChrystal shortly after taking up his position as commander of the Allied forces in a report that, unfortunately for him, did not remain confidential.[6]

To return to the case of Iraq, there can be no other explanation for the collapse, in just a few weeks of 2014, of an Iraqi army of more than 260,000 men, over-equipped by the United States, in response to a few thousand ISIS jihadists. Religious cleansing had led to the removal of experienced military officers, mostly Sunnis from the time of Saddam Hussein. New recruits were brought in on the basis of their religious or political affiliations in a process designed to offer jobs to specific groups rather than to build an effective army; the exclusively Shiite officers were part of these groups and engaged in all kinds of trafficking, including selling their own equipment to the jihadist groups they were meant to be fighting.

Is it any surprise, under these conditions, that discipline disappeared and diesel evaporated, paralyzing the tanks? Some 50,000 soldiers were actually phantom troops, which allowed a few senior officers to pocket the corresponding wages, as happened in the DRC a few years ago. Does this not also explain the inability of the Nigerian army, with its 100,000 men and USD 6 billion budget, to deal with the Boko Haram gangs? The spectacular collapse of the Iraqi army opened the door for the Shiite militias to replace its troops. Prime Minister Nouri Al-Maliki's regime was a perfect example of power based on a sectarian logic, which resulted in ineffectiveness that made it impossible to restore order to the army on which he depended for his survival. Finally: Maliki, Mobutu, same logic, same failure.

Unless political leaders adopt an entirely new approach and create a real nation, distancing themselves from tribal and

[6] 'Commander's initial assessment,' Commander, US Forces in Afghanistan, 2009.

religious affiliations and an approach commonly described as 'state neo-patrimonialism,' to use Pierre Jacquemot's term,[7] national institutions are condemned to a high level of ineffectiveness, which significantly weakens the state. The decision to distance themselves from the tribal, ethnic, or sectarian/religious field is not simple, since this type of state has been built over many years and an upheaval of this kind would therefore mean challenging the political equilibrium in a way that is sometimes impossible to imagine. Yet that is the condition for creating 'modern' institutions, which need to be driven by effectiveness, and not rents.

This is the problem that paralyzed the Afghan government for eight(!) months after the last presidential elections in 2014. Although President Ashraf Ghani is convinced of the absolute necessity of 'turning things on their head' to build a modern and effective administration, he is faced with the tribal logic of many of his supporters and associates, such as the Uzbek warlord Dostom—number two on his electoral list—whose approach is to view public institutions as spoils to be shared.

We will see later that building modern, effective, public institutions is possible—sometimes on a small scale to avoid overly dramatic political challenges. However, in order to consolidate a fragile state, it is essential to establish a critical mass of such 'modern' institutions based on impersonal rules and driven by the need for effectiveness.

## Inclusive political systems are highly praised but are not a panacea.

It is quite clear that political systems that exclude major social groups from power on the basis of ethnic or religious affiliations are particularly fragile. We might therefore think that inclusive political systems, which are committed to including all social groups in political and economic life, must be a source of stability. But it is not as simple as that.

Inclusive political systems can certainly be democratic, as in modern-day Ghana. But they can also be autocratic, as in

[7] Pierre Jacquemot, *L'Économie politique de l'Afrique contemporaine* (Armand Colin, 2013).

President Houphouët Boigny's Côte d'Ivoire, which, as we have seen, made sure the rents extracted from coffee and cocoa was redistributed to all ethnic groups. President Houphouët even had a 'kitty' and would sometimes personally distribute bundles of 10,000 CFA franc bank notes; he was personally involved in almost all appointments to public posts, even the lowliest ones, and was careful to ensure that each ethnic group received a fair share.

In general terms, inclusive systems undoubtedly bring stability, while systems that exclude certain social groups can only create stability through repression (generally on a temporary basis); even then, this only continues while the repressive system retains its effectiveness and the level of repression does not exceed certain limits, as shown in the case of Syria. But, it is also important to distinguish between inclusive systems that give everyone a social role as a citizen, with equal rights and an equal ability to influence policy, and inclusive systems based solely on a redistribution of rents to remain in power. The former obviously creates more stability than the latter.

Inclusive systems also have other areas of fragility. Autocratic inclusive systems rarely survive the autocrats who have implemented them because their successors do not necessarily have the political skill and talent to pursue a redistribution policy of this kind. The successor may, on the contrary, take advantage of the control he has over rents to increase his personal power and enable extravagant spending. The exceptional length of President Omar Bongo's regime in Gabon relied on the same redistributive approach as that of President Houphouët Boigny, using a proportion of the income generated—in this case from oil—to maintain social peace.

It is well known that some African heads of state had also become accustomed to ensuring that representatives from all parties of the French political class benefited from their largesse.[8] Allow me to indulge in a little gossip. A very close

[8] I recommend that readers with an interest in the numerous historic links between France and Africa refer to the well-known book by Antoine Glaser and Stephen Smith, 'Ces Messieurs Afrique. Le Paris village du continent noir' (Calmann-Lévy, 1992).

friend of mine who occupied a senior position in a Gabonese bank, where I was head of AFD's office just before the French presidential elections in 1988, told me that some people really were dishonest—they didn't even send back the empty brief-cases! I have also often noticed the unusual number of senior French political figures standing patiently in the waiting area of the Hôtel Meurisse when President Omar Bongo was passing through Paris. Let's hope all that is now in the past, whether we quite believe it or not.

President Bongo, whom I met many times while I was work-ing in Gabon, was an infinitely wily, superbly informed man, whose political intelligence was often underestimated because of his sometimes unorthodox command of French and his extrava-gant tastes. I still remember his amused expression on the day his head of protocol literally kidnapped me as I stepped off the plane and took me directly, in jeans and a safari shirt, to his immense office with its multiple clocks and constantly flickering televi-sion screens. I felt practically naked in front of the president of a country whose elites are constantly dressed to the nines. But he could not have cared less about my jeans and had a very clear message he wanted to give to avoid my making a mistake on a very modest operation. Rumor has it that his son and successor, for having spent too much time in France as a student, is less skilled at this kind of careful and well-informed management, which requires detailed knowledge of Gabonese society and its infinite complexity.

## Democracy also has its limits.

It might be tempting to think that 'democracy' magically offers a satisfactory solution to the problem of political instability in a multi-ethnic or multi-religious context. That was the mad gamble taken by the American neo-conservatives who triggered the war in Iraq. But, it is important to remember the definition of democ-racy, which is the exercise of power by the majority in accordance with the rights of the minority. After all, Nouri Al-Maliki was elected in Iraq on an essentially uncontroversial vote. But he then established a dictatorship that violently repressed the Sunni population.

Democracy, at least in the rudimentary form implemented in Africa since the 1990s, is not in itself a solution to the problem. Once elected, the victorious faction tends to exercise dictatorial power and has no qualms about excluding the various minorities. Above all, it takes advantage of its control of the state apparatus to rig elections, buy off undecided voters, and perpetuate its own power. There is nothing inclusive about this kind of democracy, as Paul Collier highlights in his well-known best seller.[9] In fact, how many times were presidents such as Biya, Compaoré, Dos Santos, Deby, and others 'democratically' elected?

A second problem is the difficulty of pursuing an equitable distribution of rents in a democratic system. Indeed, while an intelligent autocrat with an interest in remaining in power has everything to gain by engaging in widespread redistribution of rents, such practices are extremely difficult for an elected president confronted by an opposition based on ethnic or religious affiliations. If he redistributes a share of 'his' rents to his opposition, he strengthens it rather than weakening it, giving it the resources to fight him.

This helps explain the criticism leveled at President Houphouët Boigny's successor in 1995–99: 'Bédié doesn't share!'. Faced with strong opposition, President Bédié had no intention of strengthening it by generously redistributing rents as his predecessor had done routinely. But in doing so, he contributed to the polarization and ethnic stratification of political life. One preliminary conclusion we can draw from this situation is the incompatibility between democracy and the still-widespread *rentier* system.

A third difficulty relates to the electoral issues at stake in multi-ethnic societies where there is a degree of balance among political forces and an approximate demographic balance among ethnic or religious groups who confront each other in elections. Paradoxically, even when elections are free and fair, democracy and the issues associated with it can still provoke an increase in tension at the extremes, which can seriously threaten civil peace. This is because the operation of democracy in Africa too often implies a method of governance based on the notion of 'winner

---

[9] Paul Collier, *War, Guns and Votes: Democracy in Dangerous Places* (HarperCollins, 2009).

takes all,' a lack of status for the opposition, an absence of anti-establishment force, and the use of political power either to accumulate wealth and use it to ensure re-election or to rely on the state apparatus to remain in power.

## Election time: The danger period

In Kenya, Guinea, the DRC, and elsewhere, elections are often a period of extreme tension feared by everyone, when electoral confrontations can degenerate at any time into bloody riots and even conflict between ethnic or religious groups. A typical case was the 2007 elections in Kenya, in which clashes between supporters of the opposition leader Raila Odinga and outgoing President Mwai Kibaki resulted in more than 1,500 deaths and the displacement of 650,000 people.

The Nigerian elections in 2007 were a scandal: more than 30,000 fake polling stations meant that the ballot boxes were stuffed with false voting papers. It is therefore easy to see why, in early 2015, pre-election tensions developed in a climate of profound mistrust; a Gallup poll found, at that time, that just 13 per cent of Nigerians had confidence in the electoral system. The climate worsened as a result of the hoarding of oil rents by the parties in power, the build-up of weapons stocks by armed groups in the Niger delta which supported the outgoing president, and preparations for demonstrations and violence that many observers feared would likely lead to organized chaos to prevent votes from being counted.[10]

Fortunately, the concerns came to nothing. But this kind of situation leads some seasoned observers to advocate forms of 'consensual democracy' in Africa, inspired by the operation of traditional African chiefdoms, involving opposition status and power-sharing, among other things. These observers take the view that the Western model of conflictual democracy, where two parties confront each other and one is cast into obscurity or simply trampled underfoot, is inappropriate. This line is advocated

---

[10] Cf. the article by Jean-Philippe Rémy: '*Au Nigéria, report des élections sous tension*', *Le Monde*, 10 February 2015.

vigorously by Aldo Ajello[11] who, having led the post-conflict process in Mozambique on behalf of the United Nations and in the Great Lakes region on behalf of the European Union, has undeniable experience in this area.

Other observers advocate building democracy from the ground up, resulting in indirect electoral systems where negotiations among major electors replace mass confrontations to appoint both the head of state and opposition leaders. If we consider the political impasse resulting from the electoral mechanism in Afghanistan in 2014, with the two main opposition parties divided along ethnic lines, it is clear that there is a major problem. Without the danger represented by the Taliban threat, it is likely that the two camps would have found themselves involved in armed confrontations in the streets of Kabul in the summer of 2014. Skillful negotiations among the elected representatives on the development committees, if transformed into small municipalities, undoubtedly would have resulted in a representative *Loya Jirga*,[12] avoiding a general election that, like the one held in 2009, turned into a farce that could have ended in tragedy and that dangerously undermined democratic power.

## Political interference thwarts institutional effectiveness.

Even in coalition governments, which one would hope would be 'inclusive,' political game-playing inevitably affects how institutions operate. This is particularly true of governments formed after a conflict in which there has not been a decisive victory for any single camp. In these situations, the temptation is always to buy loyalty by sharing not only the income and rents derived from various sources, but also by granting public institutions to particular groups as a kind of booty. On this basis, one faction gets the port, another the customs authority, et cetera. This type of fragmentation dramatically increases the ineffectiveness of public institutions, which, as we have already seen, goes far beyond

---

[11] Aldo Ajello, *Brasiers d'Afrique: Mémoires d'un émissaire pour la paix* (L'Harmattan, 2010).

[12] Grand assembly of elders.

managerial shortcomings. Each social group will try its best to 'milk' the institution it has been 'given.'

This mechanism results in an ethnic or religious stratification of public institutions, intended to extract rents in order to 'buy' political allegiances. There is, therefore, a powerful driver behind the phenomenon, which can be indispensable in certain post-conflict situations as a means of 'buying' peace. This, clearly, has a negative impact on institutions and ultimately contributes to extending or even aggravating the fragility of the states concerned.

The most powerful political groups are obviously given the most 'profitable' institutions in terms of extracting rents, such as the customs authority, ministry of finance, stabilization funds, port authority (which offers the advantage of access to foreign exchange from offshore accounts), and the like. The weakest groups will make do with poorer institutions capable of paying a few per diem allowances. In these circumstances, as we have seen, Potemkin institutions flourish to the detriment of any drive for effectiveness.

The entire system then runs completely contrary to rules that, since the time of Napoleon and Bismarck, have ensured that institutions operate effectively. These are, namely, selecting leaders on the basis of merit, results–based management of human resources, establishing written procedures as the objective basis for sanctions, systematic implementation of controls based on transparency, and management principles free from the constraints of ethnic, religious, or party affiliation.

## Is it possible to combine merit and ethnic or religious origin?

Breaking the deadlock in these circumstances generally means implementing a dual system in which merit and results are taken into consideration alongside membership in ethnic or religious networks. Introducing mechanisms to establish transparency through independent audits is fundamental as a means of curbing the misappropriation of resources, or making it more complicated to misappropriate resources.[13]

---

[13] The simple existence of independent audits has a significant impact on curbing embezzlement. A good example can be found in the

Dual mechanisms of this kind cannot aim to cover all public institutions from the outset, many of which will remain vulnerable to predatory behaviors. They need to concentrate on a few key institutions, such as the ministries of finance, budget, and planning, the national audit office, the general state inspectorate, the ministry responsible for the civil service, the ministry of the interior, and others, in order to form a critical mass of effective institutions that are also well equipped to implement reforms. All of this obviously implies a clear understanding of the issues by political leaders, many of whom are now well aware of the fact that continuing with traditional malpractice results in deadlock.

These situations are not entirely divorced from those of multilateral institutions and multinational companies, which also need to combine the drive for effectiveness and constraints that impose ethnic diversity. Some multilateral institutions have been remarkably successful at managing this type of contradiction, in particular, the World Bank, which successfully combined an incredibly diverse range of talents, at least until Paul Wolfowitz's presidency from 2005 to 2007.[14]

Other institutions, particularly the main United Nations agencies and even the European Union, are not always successful at combining the need to balance their executives' national origins with considerations of merit and a culture of effectiveness. Certain malicious pieces of gossip claim that coming from an underrepresented country such as Latvia or Bulgaria is more useful than competence for those who wish to rise in the Brussels hierarchy. These are difficult questions to answer, even for international institutions, but there are nonetheless some remarkable examples of success, even in multi-ethnic countries that are plagued by corruption.

---

role played by Senegal's audit committee, which scrutinizes the accounts of public corporations. Many very 'sensitive' audits have remained confidential. But the simple fact that such audits have been carried out has significantly reduced malpractice.

[14] Wolfowitz, one of the main architects of the Iraq War, was appointed by George W. Bush and was dismissed for nepotism by the bank's Board of Directors following an intense press campaign denouncing his managerial practices.

We should not allow ourselves to be misled on this point. Not all multi-ethnic or multi-religious societies fit the 'chemically pure' description I have set out, whose dysfunctionality seriously undermines the sturdiness of institutions and state building. In reality, states exist on a continuum that ranges from an exceptional model based on an unfettered commitment to transparency and institutional effectiveness, free from any clan-related concerns, of the kind undoubtedly found in Sweden or Denmark, to the equally extreme case of Guinea-Bissau. Here, any desire for effectiveness that the country's public institutions might have once had has long ago given way to an opaque system of clan-based affiliations previously masked by Marxist discourse and now bogged down by wheeling and dealing.

## The scourge of 'crony capitalism'

Finally, we cannot address the problem of the fragility of states without also referring to 'crony capitalism.' Essentially, this refers to those within the circles of power monopolizing a significant share of economic activity. The usual procedure involves stakes in private companies being granted to individuals free of charge in exchange for 'protection' or 'facilitation' or even taking control of certain businesses on the basis of unlawful judgments, or pure and simple looting, as practiced shamelessly in Putin's Russia. Another classic practice involves establishing private monopolies to the benefit of the family or friends of the head of state based on unscrupulous legal decisions. 'Friends' can thus benefit from monopolies in importing essential goods such as rice, oil, or cement, thereby generating scandalous margins.

Western public opinion 'discovered' the scale of the problem during the revolutions that took place in the Arab Spring, particularly the collapse of Ben Ali in Tunisia, although in practice, people had long been aware of what was going on. This type of situation is particularly common in the Middle East and contributes to the stifling economic activity by introducing major legal uncertainties and thus paralysing serious investors. Unduly taking income out of the main economic activities also contributes to driving up local costs, resulting in a loss of competitiveness; all of this limits economic development and inevitably contributes to unemployment.

I witnessed this phenomenon first-hand in Syria in the early 2000s. The context was a rapprochement between President Bashar al-Assad and French President Jacques Chirac. President Assad was aware of the increase in unemployment, the mediocre performance of the Syrian economy, and the country's uncertain oil prospects, but he was also very keen on avoiding a potentially intrusive mission by the IMF/World Bank. He therefore preferred to ask French authorities to send a team to review the options for accelerating the growth of the Syrian economy.

Largely out of curiosity, I headed up the first two of a series of missions. Our main contact was the new Minister of Planning, a young, relatively inexperienced economist who had just spent several years with the United Nations Development Program (UNDP) and very courteously opened numerous doors for us. He had a clear idea of the reforms needed and was probably looking for external support in order to try to get them accepted. But it did not take us long to discover the extent to which the system was locked down by those within the circles of power. My impression was that even if the President had been truly committed to liberalizing the system, it is far from certain that it would have been politically possible given the entanglement of the 'clan's' economic interests and political power.

The attack that cost Rafic Hariri, the Lebanese Prime Minister, his life in 2005 and provoked President Chirac's anger against President Assad (who probably instigated the attack) put a stop to any further advisory missions. Our contact was later appointed Prime Minister. Yet, in spite of his promotion, he has been unable to make much progress with his ideas or our proposals. It is not the first time a prime minister has found himself confronting the realities of power.

This type of situation is frequent in Latin America, but it is perhaps less common in Africa than in the Maghreb or the Middle East, no doubt because the industrial and economic fabric is much weaker. We saw malpractice of this kind in Mobutu's Zaire, but everything was swept aside by the economic collapse of the 1980s. Mugabe's Zimbabwe, whose economic development was fairly remarkable during the British colonial period, is now an outstanding example of 'crony capitalism.' These mechanisms, combined with aberrant economic policies, have contributed to the country's catastrophic economic collapse.

## Fragile states: Concluding remarks

I would like to highlight a few points on fragile states that strike me as important in the specific case of Africa.

The fragility of African states is not always very visible, and states with elements of fragility do not always correspond to the image we usually have of them—namely, very poor countries with militias roaming around. Numerous African states, including some of the wealthiest and most developed, such as Kenya[15] and, as we will see in the next chapter, Côte d'Ivoire, are ultimately fragile states as well. In practice, they have had too little time to put down roots deep enough to ensure a high level of resilience for state-building; as a result, the nations are weak, and antagonism among ethnic groups has led to political conflict. This kind of 'underlying' fragility is not in any way incompatible with strong growth, which could, over time, improve the situation by increasing the influence of the private sector and civil society, which in turn require institutional reform.

A fundamental problem in Africa is that democracy, as it is commonly practiced, often under pressure from Western countries, shows scant concern for the 'inclusive' approach to minorities that is needed in multi-ethnic societies. The uncertainty in the rules governing changes of leadership and the common practice of election-rigging is another aspect of fragility.

Factors of this kind stem from the heart of the social structures and histories of the societies concerned, which explains why it is so difficult to emerge from these situations. Exhortations and pressure exercised by the outside world are likely to have little effect. The heterogeneous nature of a society is a product of its history; it is resistant to external orders and can require skillful

---

[15] Where the number of people employed in the private-security sector now exceeds both those employed in tourism and the number of police officers.

Periods of crisis may trigger the process of emerging from a situation of fragility and building resilient states. These crises might be a change of regime, the arrival of a new generation of leaders, external or internal threats, or a combination of factors. A few typical examples come to mind: outside Africa, the way Mustapha Kemal reformed the Turkish state, which had collapsed after emerging from the ruins of the Ottoman Empire following the First World War; in Africa, the way Yoweri Museveni reformed and brought Uganda out of the situation it had been plunged into by Idi Amin's disastrous management, and the way Meles Zenawi rebuilt Ethiopia after Mengistu's bloody regime.

The main challenge faced by numerous African countries over the coming decades will be their capacity to react to the stress and shocks caused by the combination, in the major cities, of the unsatisfied demand for skilled jobs and uncontrolled urban development, and in rural areas by environmental crises associated with the decline in soil fertility and demographic growth. The main question is whether the states whose underlying fragility we are identifying will be able to adapt quickly enough to address these challenges. Will they become bogged down and plunged into conflicts and chaos, as we are currently seeing in Syria? Or conversely, will they contribute to 'imposing' change on rebellious societies in the way the American irruption into Japan prompted the Meiji era?

Some future stresses, such as the impact of demographics, are easy to identify. But the policies that could help limit their effects require cultural change over a period that extends beyond normal political timeframes. There is, therefore, an awkward contradiction between the urgency of launching reform and modernization processes and the fact that the results may well benefit only the political successors. We have seen an example of this type of contradiction in Europe, where the labour market reforms introduced by Gerhard Schroeder in Germany very probably cost him his re-election to the advantage of Angela Merkel, who was their main political beneficiary. We should therefore remember that in the near future, many African states will be confronted with these kinds of challenges which, according to Toynbee[16] can, depending on the response to them, either strengthen or destroy civilizations.

Next, we move to a particularly interesting case study in which we see a well-structured and organized country succumb to both internal and external shocks, leading it into civil war and bringing it within a hair's breadth of tipping it into chaos.

---

[16] Arnold Toynbee, *A Study of History* (Oxford University Press, 1972).

# CHAPTER
# SEVEN

## The Ignored Fragility of Côte d'Ivoire and Its Descent into Hell: 1980 to 2012

If the previous two chapters seem a bit abstract, we move, now, to a concrete account of some of the stress factors listed earlier for a country long-considered—and justly so—to be a model: Côte d'Ivoire. We shall see how accumulated tensions—population growth being perhaps the most important—weakened the social fabric of a country that plays an important regional role. The health of the Sahel states depends, in good part, on that of Côte d'Ivoire. Indeed, it is difficult to envisage a prosperous Sahel with a crisis-ridden Côte d'Ivoire.

### A success story goes awry: The end of an era

I was in Abidjan in December 1993 when the rumour of President Houphouët-Boigny's death began to circulate. The president had been resting in Switzerland, as he was wont to do, due to his advanced years. His demise was kept secret to enable political games to play out between the president of the National Assembly, Bédié—who, as provided for by the Constitution, was supposed to step in as acting president and organize the elections—and Prime Minister Ouattara, who actually wielded power and went all out to secure his place as the president's successor.

The official announcement of President Houphouët's death came quite some time after the initial rumours. I recall being on the lawns of Hotel Ivoire attending a garden party to bid farewell to a diplomat on the evening the president's death was announced. The atmosphere became grim, the dance floor emptied, and, deep inside, Ivorians and outsiders alike felt that they were witnessing the end of an era. A World Bank colleague and I were there to discuss in secrecy with Ivorian authorities, a devaluation of the CFA franc that was being contemplated, and we, too, felt as though we were dancing on a volcano, to borrow Gustav Stresemann's phrase.

The economic situation was a disaster, the state's coffers were empty, the banks were on the brink of bankruptcy, and great uncertainty loomed over whether the devaluation would be carried out or not. The operation seemed critical to reviving the entire CFA Franc Zone and pulling it out of crisis, but it was a technically complex operation with considerable political risk given its likely impact on the social situation.

A rumour made the rounds a few days later that the French ambassador was playing a crucial role in the fight for the president's succession. According to the rumour, he had just driven presidential candidate Bédié, almost paralysed by the critical importance of the event, to a television studio to read a prepared statement announcing that he would take over, thus relegating Ouattara to the side. Was this astonishing step taken by the ambassador because of his personal ties with Bédié? Was the ambassador acting under instructions from the famous 'cellule Afrique' located near the Elysée Palace? Or was it, as the ambassador pretended later, linked to the fear that a military coup would take place if the 'half-Burkinabe Northerner'—as Ouattara was described—attempted to seize power? A widely shared opinion in both the ruling Ivorian milieu and the French community was that the country was the de facto property of the Akan ethnic group, which occupies most of its centre, and whose chief representative was Bédié. Therefore, the thinking went, someone hailing from the North had no place in the president's office.

In December 1999, President Bédié, whom I had met on several occasions with the World Bank teams since 1994, and had been unable to engage in any serious discussion on the economy—which was, fortunately, not the case with his remarkable Prime Minister, Kablan Duncan—was toppled by demonstrations organized by dissatisfied military personnel. I was visiting Cameroon at the time and was shocked by the news. According to the bits of information making the rounds, soldiers had been marching through the streets protesting about their living conditions, for the past few weeks. Apparently, they had no munitions. President Houphouët surely would have settled this kind of problem in 48 hours by cajoling some of them and opening his famous kitty to others.

Bédié's collapse, however, also meant the collapse of Ivorian democracy in what appeared to be a military putsch. The rebels called on an unknown general, Robert Gueï, to assume power until October 2000. Elections were subsequently organized, but General Gueï and his rival Gbagbo connived to have both Bédié and Ouattara thrown out of the electoral fray on questionable grounds even though, together, they represented at least two-thirds of the electorate. The elections ended with the victory of Gbagbo, Houphouët Boigny's historic rival, a wily schemer and the leader of a small party forged on a narrow ethnic base, the Bété. General Gueï's political base was even narrower. Democracy was thus restored, but the president's legitimacy was highly questionable.

In September 2002, a group of ex-servicemen of 'northern' origin, probably financed and armed by Burkina Faso's President Compaoré, and led by a brilliant young Ivorian politician, Guillaume Soro,[1] captured northern Ivory Coast all the way to the central city of Bouaké in a series of daring raids conducted over a few days. The group then attempted to carry out another raid on Abidjan to bring down the Gbagbo regime. After routing the Ivorian army, the rebels came up against the gendarmerie, which held out for an entire night in its barracks. They also faced

---

[1] Now president of the National Assembly.

the threat of intervention by French forces that had occupied a base camp near the airport since 1960 under a Franco-Ivorian cooperation agreement. Difficult as it is to imagine that preparation for the invasion had escaped the notice of French secret services in Burkina, the French ambassador and military personnel in Cote d'Ivoire were clearly taken by surprise. Communications are not always shared in the French system.

Taking advantage of the general chaos in Abidjan during this night, Gbagbo had General Gueï and his spouse assassinated; he also tried to have Ouattara assassinated, but Ouattara narrowly escaped. Gbagbo accused them of being responsible for the raids, which was untrue. At dawn, fearing French intervention, the rebels withdrew to Bouaké and sealed the division of the country into a North occupied by irregular forces, which would live off racketeering and plunder, and a South controlled by the Gbagbo government. France refused to accede to the president's request to help him reconquer the North, an action that could have led to full-scale civil war. The regular Ivorian troops suffered defeat after defeat each time they tried to penetrate the North.

In October 2004, as head of operations for the French Development agency (AFD), I took a brief trip to Abidjan for meetings with the Minister of Finance. The city had an alarming, pre-rebellion kind of feel. We had to zigzag around roadblocks and demonstrations by young Gbagbo militants to reach the minister's office, and were pelted by insults (and even a few stones) along the way. Inside an office on the twentieth floor of a tower, I found a light-hearted finance minister apparently unaware of—or indifferent to—the once-again disastrous economic situation, in very good humour. According to rumour, he had just hit the jackpot, amassing the fastest fortune in the country's history.

A few days later, casting, with a heavy heart, a final sweeping glance from my plane window at the skyscrapers of the 'Plateau', the central business district of Abidjan, I felt a deep rage at seeing the sinking of a country that could have been a role model both for African development and for exemplary partnership with France.

Thus, it came as no surprise two weeks later when I watched the city catch fire on my television, a gory new episode of a serial on dramatic political developments; leading, this time, to a rupture between Ivorian authorities and France. Two Ivorian Air Force fighter jets piloted by Ukrainian mercenaries had just killed nine French soldiers in Bouaké. On President Chirac's orders, the jets were destroyed when they touched down. President Gbagbo and his entourage unleashed anti–French riots across the city. Protestors launched a hunt of French nationals and tried to occupy the airport, which had just been secured by French soldiers to help evacuate French citizens.

I was aware of the gravity of the situation, having lunched during my recent visit with General Poncet, commander of French forces in Côte d'Ivoire, who had confided in me that the idea of having to organize the evacuation of thousands of French people scattered over a city of 3 million inhabitants kept him awake at night. French combat helicopters were now shooting real bullets to keep protestors from occupying the two bridges that split the city to allow French citizens to gather at the airport.

Years later, in April 2011, at President Sarkozy's behest, French helicopters destroyed the tanks guarding former President Gbagbo's residence, allowing forces supporting the newly elected President Ouattara to arrest his opponent. For months, Gbagbo had refused to acknowledge the results of an election that, according to all the international observers present, gave a clear victory to Ouattara.

Military interventions of that type go against all my principles and fundamental beliefs, but I felt that this one had helped the country avert a fresh episode of civil war that it surely did not need. A new era was being ushered in after three decades of serious economic, social, and political crises. How did Côte d'Ivoire go from being a model of development to sinking into such chaos?

## The failure of the Ivorian model: France's share of the responsibility

Côte d'Ivoire had long dismissed the grave forecasts French agronomist René Dumont had made in the 1960s about Sub-Saharan Africa in his bestselling book.[2] Cote d'Ivoire was indeed

---

[2]  René Dumont, *L'Afrique noire est mal partie* (Black Africa got a failed start) (Seuil, 1962).

a model on three counts. First was its impressive economic success. Côte d'Ivoire had opted to go down the free-market path and, throughout the 1960s and 1970s, had registered a growth rate akin to Asia's, while neighbouring Guinea and Ghana, with their Marxist leanings, were sinking in crises. When one reached Abidjan from the airport, a glimpse of the impressive 'Plateau' skyscrapers while crossing the bridges was enough to make one feel that Côte d'Ivoire was no commonplace Sub-Saharan African country, but the first 'emerging' one.

It was also a model of social peace among very different ethnic groups—Krou and Gouro from the southwest, Akans from the centre, Yakouba from the west, and Malinkés and Mandés from the north—despite considerable gaps in the wealth of the diverse territories in which they were settled. (The weakness of the mechanisms that maintained this stability have already been mentioned.) Finally, Côte d'Ivoire was a model of successful partnership between a newly independent country and its former mother country; French technical staff and investors had worked toward this remarkable partnership for years.

The destruction of the partnership was the first and most visible failure after the 2004 crisis and its anti-French pogrom. In France, the disappointment ran deep: 'We believed so much in it!' recalled Éric Leboucher in Le Monde.[3] Combined with France's indignation was Côte d'Ivoire's deeper rancour: on the one hand, President Gbagbo's bitterness over his feeling that he had been abandoned by France during the 2002 attack by rebels coming from a foreign country, despite explicit military protocols between France and Cote d'Ivoire; and on the other, the disappointment of President Bédié and Ouattara's supporters. According to them, France, the mother of democracy, had shut its eyes and allowed Cote d'Ivoire to be run by what they considered to be a 'minority, unrepresentative, sectarian, and criminal power'.

But was this Franco-Ivorian partnership not doomed in any event? Among the matters that elicited a visitor's surprised reaction during this period was the excessive—even unreasonable—place occupied by French technical assistants, small French entrepreneurs, and specialized French workers, all of which ultimately

[3] Le Monde, 22 November 2004.

caused deep unease. In the early 1980s, as the AFD representative in a co-financing negotiation with the World Bank in Washington, I found myself facing an Ivorian delegation composed exclusively of French technical assistants—whom I knew quite well—except for the head of the delegation, who stayed only for the opening, as he was quite taken with his shopping expeditions. It so happened that the chief negotiator for the World Bank was Ghanaian, and I could not help but notice his astonished expression when the 'Ivorian' delegation entered. No wonder the Ministry of Planning (*Ministère du Plan*) was commonly known as the Ministry of the Whites (*Ministère du blanc*).

There were many—in both Paris and Africa—who pondered what a desirable end of the France–Africa arrangement might look like. Was this form of neo-colonialism—the de facto recolonization of the Ivorian administration by French technical assistants, at Houphouët Boigny's request—not senseless? Had France, which used to wield so much influence in the French-speaking part of the continent, not lost its touch; seeing its efforts at mediation among Ouattara, Bedie, and Gbagbo fail and being forced to call on the United Nations, or the Ghanaian and South African presidents? Hadn't France committed mostly blunders and mistakes[4] in Côte d'Ivoire?

Clearly, France had neither prepared for, nor been able to oversee the succession of President Houphouët-Boigny, a process it had perfected earlier when Jacques Foccart, the all-powerful adviser to Charles de Gaulle and then to presidents Pompidou and Chirac, made and unmade African heads of state. This time, France had allowed its ambassador to take sides in a conflict-ridden political succession, allowed the coup d'état that swept General Gueï to power in 1999 occur, and ignored the preparations made by rebels from Burkina Faso throughout 2002.

After the rebels' invasion, France had not been very skilful in attempting to broker peace. It tried to transform the crafty, manipulative, and stubborn President Gbagbo, who was supported by part of the French left, into a kind of powerless 'Queen of England', an attempt obviously doomed to failure. Was it not a mistake to have first humiliated him and then attempted to renew

---

[4] *Le Nouvel Observateur*, 16 December 2004.

ties with him, only to ultimately destroy his air force while he was engaged in a perilous re-conquest of the North? Should France have supported his attempt to end the country's division at the risk of being accused of complicity in an operation that could have turned into a settling of scores among ethnic groups?

## Seeking historical trends amidst the apparent chaos

Does France really have any business maintaining a standing army near Abidjan and meddling in any aspect of Côte d'Ivoire's domestic politics in the twenty-first century? Does the mere presence of a battalion of French marines near Abidjan not involve France in any conflict that occurs in the country, whether it intervenes or not? Should the cooperation agreements conceived during the Cold War, when the Soviet Union made several attempts to destabilize Cote d'Ivoire, be terminated? Was this military presence not more a risk factor than a guarantee of security for the French community? After all, the powerful Lebanese community, which was not involved in the country's political games, was never harassed during this period. Still, it must be acknowledged that without a strong logistical base in Abidjan and two others in Dakar and Ndjamena, it would have been impossible for the French army, in January 2013, to avoid a takeover of Bamako by extremist forces and push back the jihadist threat in the Sahel.

Finally, were the November 2004 events the convulsions of a second and real independence movement—as claimed by Gbagbo hardliners—after four decades of what they considered simply a phase of neo-colonialism? Was the Ivorian conflict a modern form of the tribal conflicts specific to 'Eternal Africa' complicated by a clash at the local level between Islam and Christianity? Apart from the events touched on above, it is important to explore the principal explanatory factors of this crisis, identify the major tectonic shifts, and identify long-term trends in the apparent chaos. Côte d'Ivoire had, in fact, to deal with three phenomena that seriously destabilized it.

Ever since its independence, Côte d'Ivoire has been experiencing a population explosion. It also endured a deep and persistent economic crisis from 1978 to 2012 with very brief remissions, the most significant one having occurred from 1994 to 1998 thanks to the CFA franc devaluation. And finally, the democratic system introduced in a rush after President Mitterrand's 'La Baule' speech in 1990[5] was not forged from an analysis of the Ivorian state, the peculiarities of Ivorian society, its history, or the constraints linked to its population explosion, its multi-ethnic composition, and its economic system.

Other political players might have better dealt with these shocks and constraints. Different behaviours and different decisions from the various players might have led to a quite different situation. As in all historical phenomena, chance and human decisions have played an important role. But history teaches us that when people are destabilized, they rarely choose a good guide. It also teaches us that, similar to military decisions in battle, political decisions in times of crisis are made on the basis of information that is not always accurate, and are made in a fog of passion, urgency, and stress.

## An incredible population explosion

As the last region to begin its demographic transition, we already explained that Africa has seen a particularly high natural growth rate in its population. But in Côte d'Ivoire's case, economic success—the famous 'Ivorian miracle'—attracted migrants en masse from neighbouring countries with lesser natural resources (particularly Mali and Burkina Faso) or suffering from economic and political crises (Ghana, Guinea). In just over half a century, from 1960 to 2017, the population of Côte d'Ivoire multiplied sevenfold, soaring from 3.3 to 24 million inhabitants—probably

---

[5] In a famous speech soon after the fall of the Berlin wall, President Mitterrand urged African countries to resolutely move towards democracy and made such a shift a condition of future French aid. The rumour is that he had not previously read the speech written by his then-advisor, the writer Erik Orsenna, and that he was quite unhappy when he realized the importance of what he was just reading and the problems that this new orientation would raise regarding the cozy relations France maintained with African dictators. The 'La Baule' speech had a major impact in francophone Africa and is still considered a momentous event. Advisors may sometimes make history...

a world record. If France had undergone a similar process during the same period, its population today would be around 350 million inhabitants—more than that of the US.

True, Côte d'Ivoire in 1960 was largely an empty country. But the average annual population growth rate from the 1960 to 1990 period was more than 4 per cent—higher than the rates of Burkina Faso and Mali. Their fertility rates being close means that these two countries exported workers in large numbers to Côte d'Ivoire, contributing to its rapid development.

These migratory phenomena were influenced by an initially weak sense of national belonging, historical traditions of mobility for people in regions not densely populated, and the demand for labour. In the early 1960s, President Houphouët had even considered introducing dual citizenship between Upper Volta (now Burkina) and Côte d'Ivoire. All this led to a considerable intermingling of people from very different geographic origins, ethnic groups, and even religions.

Added to the inter-state migrations were the intense inter-regional ones from the poverty-stricken north towards the central, west central, southern, and southwestern parts of the country, where there was potential for employment and high economic growth. This has also led to the extraordinary growth of cities, the most spectacular case being Abidjan. To those who, like me, remember the Abidjan of the late 1960s, the city is completely unrecognizable today.

The magnificent line of coconut trees bordering the beaches that ran along the road leading to Grand Bassam, where I used swim in the 1970s, have been razed and replaced by low-income housing. From 1960 to 1990, the urban population growth rate exceeded 8 per cent per year (it was just 3 per cent in Accra in Ghana), creating—despite considerable investments—huge urban-management problems, which were aggravated by the complex network of lagoons. Thus, residential areas for the elite have mushroomed, as have slums and poor districts, creating pockets of abject poverty, albeit well away from the eyes of visitors because there are no access roads.

Away from the cities, Côte d'Ivoire's success in agriculture during this period was exceptional due, largely, to the early construction of a remarkable road network and a particularly intelligent agricultural policy. Prepared in the 1960s and pursued through the 1970s, this policy established a daring mechanism for the stabilization of prices paid to cocoa and coffee growers, which turned out to be a great success until it was corrupted. The agricultural success also attracted migrants, Ivorians and foreigners alike, to rural zones, particularly in Bété and Krou regions in the west-central and southwestern regions. The rural population thus spiked 60 per cent during this period. The gradual densification of rural areas triggered rising tensions over property disputes between native and non-native dwellers, sometimes ending in fatally violent clashes.

These clashes even led to ethnic cleansing at the local level in the west-central and southwestern areas. From the late 1990s onwards, mostly due to increased rural density and related land issues, Côte d'Ivoire underwent not only an economic but also a social and political crisis, with racist discourse based on an Ivorian identity refused to northerners—and to Ouattara. Episodes of ethnic discrimination were a daily affair. To get a sense of the magnitude of these tensions over identity, imagine for a moment how France would react if confronted to similar events. While France had recently refused to accept 30,000 Syrians, it would be peopled by 350 million inhabitants, of whom around 150 million might be from North African origin. Jean-Marie Le Pen would have been elected president long ago.

## Agricultural success, failure to insert in global industrial value chains

Côte d'Ivoire became the top global producer of cocoa and a major coffee producer during the 1970s. It also diversified its agricultural exports, which now include cotton, rubber, palm oil, pineapple, banana, and cashew nuts. Côte d'Ivoire's agricultural miracle is not a mirage. The role of immigrant workers from the country's north, and French aid are often highlighted to explain this result. We tend to forget that this success was first and foremost the product of a remarkably intelligent agricultural policy crafted by Ivorians like Minister Abdoulaye Sawadogo (who was from Upper Volta) and Mohamed Diawara (who was of Malian origin) in the 1970s, when immigration was encouraged and talent from the entire sub-region was recognized and mobilized.

This agricultural policy was implemented with the backing of public institutions, which later became ridden with corruption, but helped accelerate agricultural development for more than twenty years. These were aided by sectoral development companies (Sodepalm, Soderiz, and others) and the famous CAISTAB (Coffee and Cocoa Stabilisation Fund). Significantly, this agricultural policy was backed by an ambitious infrastructure policy pushed by President Houphouët-Boigny.

The agricultural miracle was doubled by significant success in the agro-processing sector. Although most of the sugar agro-industrial plantations and processing factories built in the north of the country, at high cost in the 1980s, are now closed or struggling, the south and southwest of the country are covered by plantations of rubber, palm oil trees, bananas, and pineapples that have their own packaging and processing facilities. These privately managed sectors create added value locally, generate employment, and are remarkable drivers of growth.

On the other hand, for reasons already mentioned in the chapter on African industrialization, this agricultural and agro-industrial success has not led to insertion into the value chains of industrial globalization, which would have enabled the country to multiply its sources of growth and provided jobs for both skilled and unskilled labour. Thus, despite considerable efforts, Côte d'Ivoire saw its textile industry collapse. It has not been able to imitate the Southeast Asian countries in being included in the world subcontracting mechanisms, as Morocco and Ethiopia have recently been able to do. And yet, Côte d'Ivoire had tremendous assets that could have helped it carry out such diversification.

Indeed, until President Houphouet's death, it offered political stability, a pragmatic economic policy favourable to international investors, outstanding infrastructure in terms of ports, energy, road transport, and the like. But it remained a country exporting agricultural raw materials, agricultural products, and now oil, and is thus vulnerable to the fragilities linked to such international specialization. Being deeply subject to unpredictable international prices for raw materials, Côte d'Ivoire did not really get back on its feet—from the crisis that started in the late 1970s—until 2012.

# Structural adjustment: Surprisingly, a repeated failure

Let us rewind briefly to the crisis—truly a textbook case—triggered by the successive coffee- and cocoa-price surges from 1973 to 1977 and their drastic fall in 1978. As often happens in such situations, in Côte d'Ivoire, the soaring prices led to a reckless budgetary policy characterized by frenzied public spending and mounting indebtedness. Following the drastic drop in prices, the government maintained its spending by going deeper into debt—a rather conventional development in a raw-material-producing country. While adjustment policies implemented during the next fifteen years did help control the damage and stabilize the major economic indicators somewhat, they did not bring about a real adjustment in the economy and, as a result, everything—and I do mean everything—ended in failure.

The competitiveness of private and public companies continued to decline, the balance of payments deteriorated, and the public finance crisis reached dramatic proportions. Finally, attempts to manipulate cocoa prices in 1988, by the extremely unwise decision to stockpile the perishable raw material, helped weaken a banking system already in jeopardy due to outstanding payments arising from the economic crisis.

The prolonged impact of this failure is astounding.[6] Côte d'Ivoire's adjustment policies did not fail because it suffered from a deeper crisis than other major producers of raw materials. Thailand, for example, and other Asian countries whose production structures are not very different from that of Côte d'Ivoire, faced the same crisis during the same period and were able to get out without major problems.

It is now known that the adjustment in Côte d'Ivoire failed because the magnitude of the external shocks faced by the country meant that real recovery required a currency devaluation. To be precise, the dollar price of coffee and cocoa nosedived 40 per cent and 54 per cent respectively from 1977 to 1982. The plummeting prices, combined with constraints linked to the abnormally high

---

[6] A massive energy crisis, due to the lack of proper anticipation of consumption and a drought that had dried up the reservoirs of the major hydroelectric dams certainly did not help.

average salaries of civil servants,[7] rendered the recovery impossible without devaluation.

## The dogged refusal to adjust the CFA franc exchange rate

Despite the desperate need, adjustment of the currency parity was constantly rejected during this period for easily understandable reasons: such an operation—simultaneously involving the thirteen countries of the Franc Zone—was extremely complex, both technically and politically. Every little cyclical rise in cocoa prices rekindled hope of economic recovery. President Houphouët thought he would be able to swing the cocoa prices his way by halting purchases and exports in 1988, a measure that failed because cocoa was smuggled to Ghana. African leaders of the CFA Franc Zone did not grasp the advantages of the operation and were deeply worried about its social risks—and the spike in Mercedes prices that such a step implied. In the end, President Houphouët Boigny perceived it as bringing nothing but a loss of prestige, and therefore vetoed it.

It should be noted that the preoccupations of French decision-makers lay elsewhere, too. From 1983 on, their primary concern was to keep France's currency tied to the German Deutschmark in order to prepare for the euro. But the CFA franc's de facto anchoring to the Deutschmark, which was itself appreciating against the US dollar, only aggravated the non-competitiveness of the Franc Zone.

President Mitterrand's lack of understanding of economics (and that of some of his close advisers) did not help, either; despite being alerted to the problem, he did not address it, choosing only to criticize the action of the World Bank after the successful devaluation! Differences of opinion among French economists also muddied the debate. Many of them argued for continuing what is referred to as an 'internal' adjustment without devaluation, which Eurozone countries in the south of Europe are now trying to implement by reducing their production costs and salaries and undertaking austerity measures.

[7] Which is equivalent to more than nine times the GDP per capita, a ratio that is around two in OECD countries and a maximum of three in Asia.

It should be noted that the analytical work necessary for a full understanding of the problem was considerable, yet the French monetary authorities had imposed a total blackout on the subject, and had taken a dim view of independent work on the topic. 'I forbid you even to think about it,' said a high-ranking French Treasury official to my economist colleagues at AFD, who despaired of the situation. Added to this were the initial blunders of the World Bank which, exasperated by France's refusal to take action on the issue, tried to play the African authorities off against France, which of course did not help matters at all.

Though I was fully aware of the problem, its magnitude, and the ongoing impasse, I only discovered the full analytical work when I joined the World Bank. On my arrival in Washington, D.C., in 1993, my boss and friend, Olivier Lafourcade, then director of West and Central African countries at the World Bank, swore me to secrecy while handing over the enormous technical file on preparation for the devaluation. I was to be part of a small core team that would prepare for and steer the operation in close liaison with the IMF and the French Treasury.

To make a long story short, during almost 15 years, depending on how cocoa prices evolved, Côte d'Ivoire authorities were living either in despair, or in hope of seeing light at the end of the tunnel and avoiding a devaluation. The so-called internal adjustment (without devaluation) that was then attempted, was based on a policy of deflation, whose chances of success were impeded in Côte d'Ivoire—as it would have been anywhere—by the political impossibility of making substantial cuts in state spending: how can you cut nominal wages without triggering a revolution? How can you expect to fire bureaucrats without sparking huge strikes?

Thus, the financial crisis and the economic crisis fed off each other. With a quarter century of hindsight, it is now clear that the right decisions were not taken in time—that is, by the late 1970s or the beginning of the 1980s—and that if France had any real responsibility in the Ivorian crisis, it lies here.

## Social crisis and impoverishment

The economic crisis was kept under wraps for a long time. Bureaucrats received their salaries thanks to credit provided by

France, which had little hope of seeing the loans reimbursed. The urban elite and interest groups that controlled political life protected most of their consumption. Currency convertibility enabled the cities' shops to maintain well-stocked shelves. But the accumulation of arrears triggered liquidity crises that culminated in a deep banking crisis.

Even more worrisome was the declining competitiveness that stifled the economy and hindered the industrial diversification that could generate urban jobs. The loss of competitiveness, which reached 65 per cent, asphyxiated the economy. International experience has taught us now that a competitiveness gap of that magnitude cannot be resolved without currency parity adjustment.

The fifteen years of lost development for Côte d'Ivoire gradually decimated the middle class that had emerged during the two preceding decades and left entire swaths of the population impoverished. Per capita income halved during this period. Poverty tripled between 1985 and 1993, the rate soaring from 10 per cent—which was, then, exceptional for Africa—to 31 per cent. The impoverishment was intensified by budgetary difficulties that led to a massive reduction of public spending on healthcare and education and to the collapse of entire sections of fundamental public services. The deep and protracted crisis turned out to be greater for Cote d'Ivoire than the 1930s crisis in Europe was for Germany, a country that seemed well structured.

When it was finally undertaken—almost fifteen years after the opportune time—the devaluation of the CFA franc in 1994 was remarkably conducted by the World Bank–IMF–French Treasury trio along with certain African countries, including Côte d'Ivoire. I want to hail the role played by Olivier Lafourcade, whose work methods, and subtle coordination among Abidjan, Paris, Washington, and twelve other countries, I had the opportunity to observe and admire. The operation, which led the World Bank to disburse more than a billion dollars in a few months to the CFA franc countries, also benefited from a favourable world economic situation.

The economic impact was spectacular. While from 1990 to 1993, Côte d'Ivoire's economic growth had been negative or close to zero (corresponding to a negative growth of per capita income of about 3.5 per cent per annum), it bounced back to

Asian levels in 1995.[8] For the first time since the 1978 crisis, per capita income rose significantly. The impact turned out to be most impressive in rural areas. In November 1993, despair ruled the countryside. Farmers did not even bother to harvest their coffee and cocoa. A year later, there was euphoria in the same countryside. Still, despite the success of the devaluation, poverty declined only marginally—by perhaps 2 or 3 points—owing to rising regional and social inequalities and the fleeting nature of the recovery, which was hindered by appallingly poor governance.

## Governance gone astray, recovery hindered

From 1996, Côte d'Ivoire's relations with the Bretton Woods institutions were strained. International institutions were appalled by the country's prevailing corruption and poor governance, characterized by a plunder of the cocoa/coffee stabilization fund. This led to the suspension of the IMF programme in 1998, which dented foreign investor confidence and impeded the execution of the public-investment programme, which shrank drastically and brought growth virtually to a halt (1.6 per cent in 1999).

Under these conditions, the political background seriously deteriorated. As already mentioned a putsch led by disgruntled soldiers took place in late 1999, and General Guei assumed power. Per capita income continued to shrink. AFD's macroeconomic team estimated the loss in per capita income to be close to 20 per cent between 1998 and 2003. The gains made in per capita income during the post-devaluation period were swept away in less than four years. The economic recovery lasted for too short a period—four years after almost a quarter-century of stagnation or depression—to have any significant impact on per capita income.

Economic management by the Gbagbo regime, tarred again by abysmal corruption, did not improve an already troubling situation. Poverty worsened severely, surpassing 52 per cent in 2011. Life expectancy declined to 52 years in 2011, one of the lowest levels in the world.[9] In 2013, per capita GDP was about USD 1,000, a

---

[8]  7.1 per cent in 1995, 7.7 per cent in 1996, 5.7 per cent in 1997.

[9]  The world average is 71 years.

30 per cent drop from 1980. In terms of development, almost 35 years had been lost.

Opinion polls on governance and democracy in West Africa, conducted in Abidjan in 2002, revealed that Abidjanis, who widely complained about the economic difficulties, were well aware of their elite's hand in poor governance and their responsibility for the crisis; 95 per cent of those surveyed considered corruption to be the main factor behind the paralysis of the administration, and 93 per cent believed that the authorities' poor governance was the main cause of the crisis.

François Roubaud, who headed a survey at the time, noted: 'By at least partially exonerating foreign powers and international donors of Côte d'Ivoire's decline, the Abidjanis reject the accusation of some local elites and many intellectuals that structural adjustment played the prime and disastrous role. ... In a way, the Abidjanis follow in the footsteps of the donors, the Bretton Woods institutions foremost, in imputing responsibility for the failure to misgovernance by an irresponsible and corrupt local ruling class. Therefore, it is the 'higher-ups' who are to be blamed.'[10] A quarter-century of crisis, plunging per capita income, widespread corruption, a poverty rate multiplied by six: if France had been 'treated' in the same way, would the Fifth Republic have resisted?

## The complexity of democracy in a multi-ethnic country

The abysmally poor governance cannot be unlinked from the overall political situation of President Houphouët Boigny's succession. Again, far be it for me to indulge in facile criticism, but there is no avoiding reality. The introduction of democracy and the end of the reign of a man who had managed his country's development in an autocratic set-up for more than thirty years already presented serious challenges in a period of economic and social crisis, and impoverishment. As demonstrated in the many well-known works of Paul Collier,[11] history teaches us that

[10] François Roubaud, 'La crise vue d'en bas à Abidjan: ethnicité, gouvernance et démocratie' ('The Crisis seen from below: ethnicity, governance and democracy'), *Politique africaine*, Summer 2003.

[11] Cf. in particular Paul Collier and Ian Bannon, 'Natural Resources and Violent Conflict' (World Bank, 2003) and Paul Collier, *War Guns and Votes: Democracy in Dangerous Places* (HarperCollins, 2009).

democratic institutions are particularly unstable in low-income countries that essentially produce commodities.

These countries are subject to external shocks that trigger periodic financial, budgetary, and economic crises, which if managed badly—as in the case of Côte d'Ivoire in the 1980s—destabilize society. Further, the structure of their economies, which places political power at the core of trade negotiations on a macroeconomic scale, often leads to questionable modes of governance. In a context of widespread corruption, respect for politicians is swiftly eroded. History also shows that when democracy is being established in an ethnically heterogeneous country, special precautions are desirable to preserve minority rights and avoid exclusion that can create strong resentments and tensions.

A key problem is that French political culture does not recognize ethnic minorities. In France, one vote equals one voice, whether one is Basque or Breton. But what works for France is not necessarily suitable in a country like Côte d'Ivoire. Also, when democracy is established during a major influx of immigrants and amidst pre-existing inter-ethnic tensions, matters become very complicated. When democracy is established in a state where all the rulers, for reasons related to local social structures, have practiced the 'politics of the belly,' the situation becomes even more complex.

In such a context, the stakes are particularly high since controlling political power means controlling the rents that ensure its continuity. In short, unless a clear political deal has been made between the main factions, a democratic architecture must be carefully worked out if it is to function smoothly. The example of Switzerland in the early nineteenth century, with the formation of a confederation of cantons, teaches us that formulas for the democratic handling of these situations exist. But, that system was the fruit of an evolution that had begun as early as the thirteenth century. The bedrock principle is building a democratic architecture that reduces the domination of ethnic, religious, or other groups as much as possible, by defining, in detail, the rules for sharing power and wealth, and distributing it if there are serious disparities.

Without acknowledged rules for sharing power and economic gains, without appropriate constitutional framework or, at the very least, a clear agreement among parties and ethnic or religious groups, the winner garnering 51 per cent in a presidential election, even if fairly conducted, can legally appropriate all power and rents for his entourage and/or ethnic group. In such a situation, all the plum administrative or public sector positions will be systematically allotted to this group.

## Abuse of ethnic links

Examples of abuse of power along ethnic lines in Côte d'Ivoire, in the 1990s and 2000s, unfortunately abound. One that especially struck me occurred in early 2002. I was in President Gbagbo's office with the head of AFD, Jean-Michel Severino; Jean-Michel was born in Abidjan and was very fond of the country. He had personally prepared a PowerPoint presentation in the form of questions about the major challenges facing the country.

The president sent immediately for his 'brain trust'—to borrow his own words—and, holding all other matters in abeyance, organized a two-day seminar for us in Yamoussoukro with his team. We emerged from these meetings filled with consternation. We had found ourselves dealing with a team incapable of being engaged in serious discussion. We were accustomed to dialogues in Cote d'Ivoire with high-level officials, such as Tidjane Thiam, an alumnus of the prestigious *Ecole Polytechnique* and *Ecoles des Mines* in Paris who, as Director of the National Bureau of Technical Studies and Development (Prime Minister Duncan's de facto brain trust), was one of my main interlocutors during the tough economic discussions in 1994 and 1995.

God alone knows how many times Tidjane had pointed out my contradictions, highlighted weaknesses in my arguments, making all discussions on the Ivoirian economy like a tennis match that is at once fascinating and hopeless, in which a seeded player returns all your serves before routing you with an unstoppable backhand.[12] Hence, in this seminar, we felt lost by the lack of dialogue on even the simplest issues. Returning to Abidjan thoroughly frustrated, I consulted an Ivorian friend and showed him the list of our interlocutors. 'Come on, Serge, have you looked at these

[12] Tidjiane Thiam, after a career at McKinsey and having served as the CEO of the multinational insurance company Prudential, in London, is currently the chief executive of Credit Suisse.

names?' he said. The president had formed his economic team along purely ethnic lines, which were very narrow, supplanting the experienced men and women who had served before. The era of President Houphouët, who surrounded himself with the best experts regardless of their ethnic origin or nationality, seemed quite distant.

## Democracy paradoxically accelerated the race for controlling rents.

In the absence of a deal for sharing power and rents, the Ivorian political game for President Houphouët-Boigny's succession involved a race for their control. This race, which started as soon as President Houphouët died in late 1993, and was led by President Bédié's party, the PDCI, coincided with the post-devaluation period.

This race to control rents was intensified by two phenomena. The presence of a credible challenger in Prime Minister Ouattara, who already had an electoral base due to ethnic and religious ties, and a solid reputation as a good administrator from his terms at the head of the BCEAO and at the IMF. The other phenomenon was the liquidation, in 1998, of the Coffee and Cocoa Stabilization Fund—the famous CAISTAB—under the constraints of the Bretton Woods institutions. The CAISTAB had been a major source of rents that historically funded the party in power. The abrupt depletion of coffee and cocoa rents weakened the PDCI, which desperately sought to regain its former affluence.

The race for rents significantly contributed to the worsening management of the Ivorian economy in 1998 and the chronic misgovernance of the country, which brought discredit to the political authorities at both the national and international levels. It exasperated the donors to Côte d'Ivoire—including the European Union, which is usually reluctant to impose 'tough' conditions. The donors practically cut off funds for Côte d'Ivoire.

This rupture destabilized the country financially, given the debt accrued during the period preceding the currency devaluation and the impact of the devaluation on the debt; the cancellation of the IMF programme indeed paralyzed the debt's refinancing programme under the Heavily Indebted Poor Countries (HIPC) initiative. It also demoralised the highly qualified Ivorian economic teams that had handled the post-devaluation situation and almost revived, though only for three years, the economic miracle of the 1970s.

The race for rents was aggravated under President Gbagbo by the establishment of four parasitic institutions in the coffee-cocoa sectors to replace the CAISTAB, all of which functioned in complete opacity and siphoned off similar amounts of money[13] that the former CAISTAB had. Clearly, the national rulers' ability to bypass externally imposed reforms and constraints seemed boundless, demonstrating in retrospect that lasting reform ultimately, can only be the product of a political agreement reflecting an internal balance of power.

In that regard, President Bédié's launching of the slogan 'Ivorité' in 1996 to oust his challenger, Ouattara—allegedly of Burkinabé origin—was undoubtedly effective, as the latter had to struggle for many years to justify his eligibility. But the slogan was particularly irresponsible, as it symbolized the exclusion of a large section of the country's people—the poorest in the north of the country, who were already being bullied and were often treated as immigrants, deprived of all rights. To get rid of an opponent, President Bédié had deliberately tossed a torch in a powder keg.

Bedie, however, was not the inventor of this stratagem, which was also employed the same year in Zambia to evict its former president K. Kaunda from the political fray. President Gbagbo's reprisal of the slogan for the same reprehensible reasons led to the country's implosion and destabilization right until the 2010 election (which Ouattara won). What a contrast to the earlier policy of assimilating immigrants conducted by Houphouët-Boigny!

## 2012: Côte d'Ivoire's economy takes off again

President Ouattara's assumption of office in 2011, after almost a year of tension and fighting between the two presidents, marked the close of the period of civil unrest that had racked the country for twelve years, dividing it into a North occupied by warlords living off racketeering and a South run by an incompetent team

---

[13] In the range of USD 1 billion a year.

with dubious legitimacy. It also brought an end to a veritable civil war, whose toll remains unknown, but is assessed to be at several thousand between 1999 and 2011. Ouattara pacified the political situation thanks to a deal made with his long-time opponent, former President Bédié, and by recruiting Kablan Duncan, the former prime minister who had skilfully handled the post-devaluation period in 1994–1995, to become his own Prime Minister[14]. This new phase allowed the return of competent professionals to the Ivorian bureaucracy. Ouattara's political reconciliation with ex-President Bédié created, at last, an alliance of the two largest political parties and Ivorian ethnic groups, paving the way for a pacification indispensable to economic recovery.

This revival was spectacular, but the fact is that Côte d'Ivoire never became a 'failed state' despite episodes of bloody civil war and several horrifying massacres. In 2004, when the divided country was undergoing a serious economic and social crisis, and protests in Abidjan were escalating, I noticed with surprise that gardeners were still mowing lawns in the open spaces of the city. I also learned that, although the bills had not been paid since 2002 in the entire north under the control of rebels, those regions continued to be supplied with electricity. The country was in no way comparable to Darfur and still possessed remarkable infrastructure and institutions that continued to function despite the awful governance during the troubled period.

Economic growth remained negative during the entire 2000–04 period. It then fell below the demographic growth rate from 2005 to 2008 and briefly experienced a positive episode in 2009 before plunging to -2 per cent again in 2010, then to -4.7 per cent in 2011 during the difficult election and post-election period. However, it bounced up to 10.7 per cent in 2012, 8.7 per cent in 2013, 8 per cent in 2014 and 2015, and has hovered around the 9 per cent mark since 2016. This growth has been powered by major infrastructure programmes, such as the construction of the third Abidjan bridge in record time through a well-conceived public-private partnership—a project that had been discussed for

[14] Kablan Duncan is now Vice President of Cote d'Ivoire, a position recently established.

forty years—as well as the dynamism of the telecommunications sector.

Growth is particularly impressive in Abidjan. Construction cranes can be seen everywhere in a city that has expanded in a spectacular way. Having lived five years in Abidjan in the past, I was astonished, this year, to lose my way among the city's many bypasses and urban highways. I was unable even to find the villa I once occupied along the lagoon twenty kilometres away from Abidjan in a peaceful fisherman's village now transformed into a busy city. This growth is based on an economic structure that is the most balanced in West Africa, where diversified agricultural exports draw on a modern agro-industry. While the food processing sector does require considerable investment for modernization, it far outstrips those in all the other countries of the West African Economic and Monetary Union. The mining and energy sectors also boomed until the new drop in commodity prices in 2014. Around 80 per cent of Côte d'Ivoire's debt was cancelled in 2012, bringing it to around 30 per cent of GDP, thus freeing up substantial budgetary margins.

## Cote d'Ivoire is back!

As one of my Ivoirian friends recently told me: 'Côte d'Ivoire is back!' Confidence has surged, marked by the return of the African Development Bank to Abidjan and the raising of considerable capital from the financial markets. Champagne is flowing again in the luxury villas of Cocody and Deux Plateaux. Does this mean that the country is finally out of trouble? Things are far from being fully satisfactory. My driver from the 1970s, who was driving me again in Abidjan this year, made a telling remark: 'We do not eat concrete.'

According to the Ivorian National Institute of Statistics (INS), in 2013 almost 70 per cent of Ivorian families had serious difficulties feeding themselves. Urban highways are fine, but the slums around Abobo, where my driver still lived, have not changed much since the seventies, except that they are much bigger, the population density is worse, and sanitation conditions are now really awful. Most of the debt was cancelled in 2012, but new public debt is surging quickly. The education system, deeply corrupted by a politically motivated trade union (the FESCI) supported by Gbagbo since the 1980s, remains deeply dysfunctional. The overall human development index, at 0.45, ranks Côte d'Ivoire number 172 out of 188 countries. Per capita income is improving very slowly; growth remains insufficiently inclusive and the demographic flow has not abated. Hence, while the poverty rate has diminished, the overall number of poor has increased by about a million since 2008.

A critical issue for political stability is clearly the level of underemployment and unemployment. Attending the Emerging Market conference in Paris in 2016, I was struck that President's Ouattara's opening speech was focused on demography. I discussed this matter with the president when I met him briefly this year in Abidjan, and rising unemployment was at the top of his list of concerns. Even a 9 per cent GDP growth rate does not guarantee that sufficient jobs are created in the country. It is indeed urgent for Côte d'Ivoire to follow ACET's proposed agenda and 'deepen its development model,' which is still too dependent on a few agricultural and mineral commodities.

The fragility of the Ivorian economic model has again been highlighted by the significant drop in commodity prices since 2014. Oil prices (Côte d'Ivoire is now a significant oil exporter) have halved, and cocoa prices, which had held up until 2015 under the false assumption that there was world penury, plummeted between January 2014 and November 2016 to almost a third of its initial 2014 value, plunging Côte d'Ivoire again into a deep budget crisis. This crisis has worsened in 2017 due to an unexpected revolt in the army led by former rebels who had been integrated into the armed forces.

These former rebels had indeed been promised considerable benefits to placate them and help restore peace. Their mutiny has led to a renewal of unreasonable financial promises that the country has great difficulty funding, which led, by mid-2017, to instability harmful to Côte d'Ivoire's recently rebuilt reputation. Despite its many successes, one needs to recognize that the country is still fragile, too dependent on international prices of a few commodities and basically unable to create sufficient jobs for the huge number of young men entering its labour market each year, even as new challenges and threats appear on the country's horizon.

## The new challenges

Côte d'Ivoire has been stabilized, and despite the drop in commodity prices, its economy is still expanding. But the country also faces huge challenges:

First is the need for *reconciliation* with groups that have supported ex-President Gbagbo and are currently marginalized and refuse to accept the new political status quo. Gbagbo is facing trial at the International Criminal Court in The Hague, but his supporters continue to hold obstructionist attitudes that could become problematic.

A second challenge is returning to a *more balanced distribution of government and influential positions* on the ethno-political level; there is indeed much criticism of the overwhelming presence of ethnic groups from the north who think it is now 'their turn to eat.'

A third is *bringing in line the former warlords* of the northern insurgency who display uncontrolled behaviour, much to the exasperation of the people. Obviously, this process will require time. Their troublemaking-ability cannot be dismissed, and the government that benefited from their support during the last episode of the civil war, when Gbagbo refused to relinquish power, is obliged to share power with them. Some have been appointed to head some of the few well-trained and well-equipped army battalions, which worries some observers, especially since their role in the recent mutinies is unclear.

A fourth challenge is the necessity of *reining in the corruption unleashed* as much for the personal gain of some personalities as for stocking up reserves for forthcoming political battles. Many Ivorian and international observers are openly criticizing the government for its laissez faire attitude regarding the high level of corruption. It is also unclear how much of this corruption is linked to the need to stock up for future political battles and how much is due to the political weakness of the regime.

A fifth challenge, already mentioned, is the necessity of '*deepening*' *the growth model* and inserting the country into the industrial value chains of globalization. Despite the considerable progress made in the agricultural and industrial sectors, and despite remarkable growth rates, Côte d'Ivoire is struggling—and will continue to do so—to ensure decent jobs for the droves of young adults who will graduate from its high schools and universities. There is considerable political risk here, and the constant temptation of some politicians to exploit the disenchantment will persist.

Among the main impediments is the difficulty of doing business, which is still a problem in Côte d'Ivoire due, in particular, to a fairly corrupt judiciary and day-to-day corruption. Another issue is, again, the ill-adjusted parity of the CFA franc. The current parity level has ensured a comfortable balance of payments thanks to high cocoa and petroleum prices, which enabled authorities to deal with the situation; but the major shift that has taken place in this field since 2014 creates a new challenge.[15] The currently overvalued currency does not allow Côte d'Ivoire to engage in industrial globalization and to offer skilled jobs to impatiently waiting youth. Of course, managing a devaluation in a politically unstable period is fraught with dangers, so choosing an appropriate policy is difficult.

A sixth challenge will be *reorganizing and beefing up the security sector*. The recent mutinies indicate that the integration of former rebels into the Ivorian army has not worked, and that the whole security sector is extremely weak, since it has been unable to put down the mutinies via the standard recipe of combined threats and carrots-on-sticks, in large part because the threats were not credible.

With insecurity also increasing in Burkina, and Mali likely to fall apart if the French army moves away, reorganizing the security sector in Côte d'Ivoire is clearly a priority. However, the government seems almost paralyzed because of difficulties with the current balance of power; and the fiscal crisis also complicates the problem considerably. Insecurity is developing in the north of the country to the extent that, by mid-2017, traveling by car from Bouaké, the key city in the country's centre, to Korhogo or other northern cities had become dangerous due to roaming bandits and the risk of encountering Malian rebels. Businessmen now travel

---

[15] The challenge is even more important for the other CFA monetary zone, the CEMAC region including Cameroon and Gabon, which mostly relies upon oil exports. I personally do not see how a devaluation will be avoided if oil prices remain at their current levels.

by air—behaviour reminiscent of the situation in Afghanistan from 2005 on.

A seventh challenge, *and perhaps the most difficult to address,* will be *the political management of the post-Ouattara period* if rival candidates, relying on political parties supported by powerful ethnic groups, clash in elections. The fact is, if appropriate political 'deals' are not reached soon, for sharing power and providing satisfactory status to opposition groups, including Gbagbo's supporters, along with the establishment of checks and balances and an equitable distribution of wealth and rents, the old demons may well return to plague the country. Experienced observers are now clearly worried by the increasing political tensions (and corruption) that accompany the preparation of the post Ouattara era.

## What conclusions can be drawn from the analysis of the protracted Ivorian crisis?

Dealing with the problems of Sahel countries requires placing them in a regional context in which the two obvious economic drivers are Nigeria and Côte d'Ivoire. Because envisaging any kind of future for the Francophone Sahel with a ruined Côte d'Ivoire is unthinkable, it was important to decrypt the long period of economic crisis and social unrest this country has experienced. Four main conclusions may be drawn from this analysis.

First, all multi-ethnic and multi-religious societies suffer from a latent fragility that renders the smooth running of a democracy extremely complex. The transition from the Houphouët autocratic system, whose stability depended on intelligent rent-redistribution mechanisms, to a democratic system based on 'winner-takes-all' principles triggered extreme political tensions, the paroxysms of which manifested during elections. The establishment of a system of checks and balances is indispensable to avert inequities in this regard.

Next, countries like Côte d'Ivoire that have just begun their demographic transition are subject to massive population explosion, and the resulting tensions are often underestimated. Among them are the problem of access to land and property rights, tensions erupting from urban unemployment and slum-based urbanization, ethnic conflicts arising from migrations, the inability of social sectors to handle inflows of people, and political tensions having to do with nationality, identity, and voting rights.

Third, skidding off a political hairpin bend could send the country hurtling over the precipice. Huge population growth has triggered upheavals in Ivorian society, and these upheavals, along with economic stagnation, best explain the deep unrest the country has suffered. Even if Cote d'Ivoire's population growth slows, which is likely, the economic revival will attract migrants from the North, and the coming decades will require both economic management capable of generating numerous jobs and a political management capable of dealing with the tensions associated with a skyrocketing population.

Finally, the key cause of fragility in a country is the combination of ethnic and religious fragmentation with non-inclusive political systems. In such context, an inclusive political equilibrium is badly needed to provide stability. However, maintaining such equilibrium usually requires efficient public institutions, while a key difficulty is that efficient public institutions also require inclusive political systems... Breaking the circle to reach both political stability and efficiency in public institutions is difficult and elections are unlikely by themselves to solve this dilemma, particularly if they bring instability.

Côte d'Ivoire will, in fact, be like a cyclist riding along a ridge. Each political turn must be skilfully negotiated during elections to avoid exacerbating ethnic factors. The country will also have to maintain a high 'economic speed,' if possible double-digit growth rates in order to maintain social and political stability.

## Côte d'Ivoire 1980, Greece 2011: Same mistake, same failure

The last conclusion goes beyond the case of Africa and relates to the difficulty of implementing a structural adjustment policy aimed at regaining lost competitiveness in a fixed-exchange-rate regime. Readers who are put off by economics might prefer to skip these paragraphs, but they are unfortunately essential for all Eurozone citizens.

As Côte d'Ivoire was sinking after suffering the shock of nose-diving prices for its export products, Asian countries affected by the same shock managed to emerge swiftly from the crisis by combining adjustment policies and devaluation. In fact, economic history reveals that when the loss of competitiveness falls below a certain threshold (between 30 per cent and 40 per cent), what are known as policies of 'adjustment in real terms' (that is, without currency devaluation) are politically unsustainable and typically lead—as in Côte d'Ivoire's case—to failure, due to the people's rejection of the required austerity measures and the reduction of nominal salaries.[16] Such rejection often helps extremist parties ascend to power.

This is precisely the problem that concerns Greece today. In a 2011 article,[17] I predicted the failure of its adjustment programme, which had been imposed by the European Commission, the European Central Bank, and an IMF clearly under orders, and unenthusiastic because its staff certainly agreed with my analysis but was trapped by its European political bosses. If Greece were not allowed to exit the Eurozone at least temporarily for a devaluation, economic recovery would remain a pipe dream and the country would be a festering wound in our side.

Such a withdrawal from the Eurozone should have been based on a 'friendly exit' and accompanied by restructuring or cancellation of a substantial part of Greece's debt by dividing up the costs among the reckless big banks and, unfortunately, probably European taxpayers as well, to avoid any risk of systemic impact on the international financial system.[18] Of course, exit from the Eurozone alone would not have solved anything and would have

---

[16] For readers interested in economic theory regarding these issues, I recommend the remarkable (though dry) work of Larry Hinkle and Peter Montiel: *Exchange Rate Misalignment, Concepts and Measurement for Developing Countries*, World Bank Research Publication (OUP, 1999). (Larry Hinkle was the World Bank economist who prepared the technical documentation and guidelines on the CFA franc devaluation.)

[17] 'Leçon africaine pour la Grèce' ('An African Lesson for Greece'), *Libération*, 8 November 2011.

[18] The banks will protest vociferously, but the resolution of the 1992 Mexican crisis shows that they caterwaul long before they are actually strangled. On this subject, see the impressive memoirs of Robert Rubin, former Secretary of the Treasury during President Clinton's term: *In an Uncertain World: Tough Choices from Wall Street to Washington* (Random House, 2004).

to be accompanied by fundamental structural reforms aimed particularly at rebuilding institutions gangrened by clientelism.

I must say, I got so much criticism for this article from French circles eager to 'save the euro' and accusing me of being a 'pseudo-economist,' that I began to worry. Fortunately for my pride, in 2015, a talented economist—no less than former French President Valéry Giscard d'Estaing—recommended precisely such a 'friendly exit' for Greece from the Eurozone. [19]

For want of courageous decisions at the right time, nervous about the prospect of a breach in the 'Euro wall' and their banks being weighed down, and undoubtedly also due to the lack of competence in economic and monetary matters (as Giscard d'Estaing took the liberty of writing), German and French leaders condemned Greece to years of political austerity (that has not yet ended) and inadequate restoration of competitiveness sufficient to revive its economy.

Greece's GDP shrank 26 per cent, and despite successive debt cancellations, the debt-to-GDP ratio escalated from 120 to 176 per cent. The social sector is now in a disastrous predicament. Nominal salaries have shrunk some 30 per cent, a well-known recipe for pushing people out onto the streets and triggering the rise of extremist parties such as SYRIZA which, being stuck with the rejection of devaluation, is now implementing policies close to those of its predecessors—and just as ineffectively.

The responsibility of French and German leaders is considerable, as the lost time and the deterioration of Greece-EU relations could someday lead to Greece's disorderly withdrawal from the Eurozone and the collapse of its economy. We could and should have spared the Greek people the suffering that Ivoirians experienced during fifteen long years of crisis that preceded a devaluation that, in 1994, came too late.

---

[19] 'La Grèce doit sortir de l'Euro' ('Greece must leave the Eurozone'), *Les Échos*, 19 February 2015.

# PART III

Lessons the Sahel Can Draw
from Afghanistan

# CHAPTER
# EIGHT

# Is the Sahel in the Process of Turning into a New Afghanistan?

**The fragility of the Sahel must be a source of concern not only for all of West Africa but also for Europe.**

At the end of the day, how important is the Sahel, really, to our daily lives? There is already so much poverty in the world—why devote more concern to this region than to another?

I remember going to talk to a publisher, for whom I have a great deal of respect, about the reasons behind the disappointing sales of one of my books—which, I admit, was a little on the technical side—relating a series of development experiences that I found instructive. Opening my book to the contents page and pointing to one of the first chapters, entitled 'Improving impoverished neighbourhoods, approaches used in Burkina', he said to me, 'But no one cares what's happening in Burkina Faso. Who did you think was going to be interested in this stuff?'

Yet, a trawler carrying 700 migrants sank in the Mediterranean recently, prompting outpourings of emotion and contrition. And there is even more concern about those who do not sink, the thousands of migrants fleeing war and poverty, who are flocking to our coasts. However, we have seen nothing yet compared to what would happen if the Sahel were to collapse as Libya did and if, in the chaos, it were to drag the majority of West Africa along with it. Then we would not just be facing a chaotic Libya, with its 7 million inhabitants, but an enormous region that, counting only the four countries we are studying here, will have more than 200 million inhabitants in 2050.

There is no escaping the figures. If the demographic job-creation dilemma in the Sahel is not resolved or does not enter the process of being resolved over the next 15 years, it will become a problem not only for the people of the region itself, but for the whole of Europe, which, having so far failed to focus its radar in the right direction, is largely uninterested in these issues.

Through the previous chapters, we have reached an understanding that concrete does not feed a population, that rosy figures of economic growth do not solve every problem, and, in particular, are not likely—on their own—to result in jobs for the huge numbers of young people who will soon be entering the employment market in the Sahel. We have also been able to gauge the inherent fragility of the majority of African countries, which struggle to control their desert or forested border regions. Finally, we examined the reasons why so many of the institutions, even in the richest, most developed countries, are often dysfunctional. In the French-speaking nations of the Sahel, practically all of the factors contributing to fragility that I have previously discussed come together, compounding their ill effects.

This accumulation of these factors and their associated risks are inevitably of concern to the elite in the French-speaking Sahel. But they should also concern those throughout West Africa, since the entire region is vulnerable to destabilization if the Sahel falls apart. The economic links between landlocked and coastal countries, ethnic proximity, and the fluidity with which people move around within the region are such that it is hard to imagine West Africa prospering while the Sahel is in chaos.

These issues should also worry our own elite. France has significant interests in the Sahel. A third of the uranium supply for our nuclear power stations comes from the mines of northern Niger, representing huge investments. A resident French community in the sub-region numbers some 20,000 people. The pressure of events resulted in France's being at the forefront of the military action in Mali whether it wanted to be or not. Through Operation Barkhane, France has assumed responsibility for monitoring an area covering several million square kilometres and regularly carries out military operations there.

The destabilization of the Sahel would place our troops in a very difficult situation if they were called on to take action not against jihadi groups, who can be isolated in the desert, but against fighters hidden within the local population. The army of the former colonizer would inevitably get bogged down. Such instability would also have repercussions for Côte d'Ivoire, whose fragility we have recently witnessed, as well as Senegal, Cameroon, Ghana, and Nigeria—all countries in which France has substantial economic interests and significant numbers of people.

Finally, and most important, this kind of destabilization—likely to be rapid and brutal, as we have seen in recent years in Mali and Libya—would considerably increase the pressure on Western Europe from migration, which already has grown significantly since the beginning of the war in Syria and the resumption of fighting in Iraq. In this chapter, I review the factors contributing to fragility, which are similar to those seen in Afghanistan, and highlight the quagmire into which these countries are in danger of sinking.

## Is fire still smouldering under the embers in Mali?

For two years following the troubled period that extended through most of 2013, and despite serious incidents in Kidal in 2014, the situation in Mali has largely been perceived by outsiders to be returning to normal. In France, incidents in Mali were relegated to the inside pages of the daily newspapers. This perception was also linked to the Malian presidential election that was held extremely quickly in 2013, the undeniable legitimacy of the new president, Ibrahim Boubacar Keita, and the signing, in June 2015, of the Algiers Accord by the Coordination of Azawad Movements. French troops had apparently restored security throughout the country with the exception, of course, of the Kidal region, where Tuareg irredentism was still present. As then perceived in Paris and even Bamako, the situation seemed to be returning to normal.

A succession of events, however, proved that the situation—and particularly the restoration of security—was far from satisfactory. First, on the governance front, the purchase of a presidential plane for 30 million euros, using the Ministry of Defence investment budget and under disputed procurement conditions in the midst of accusations of overcharging, enraged the IMF and Mali's financial partners who temporarily suspended their funding in June 2014.

Then, on 20 November 2015, one of the main hotels in Bamako, the Radisson Blue, mostly used by expatriates, was attacked by a group of terrorists, and 20 people were killed. Even more troubling, security in the huge Gao region and in the Mopti tourist area in the centre of the country began to deteriorate. By the end of 2015, even before the Radisson Blue attack, while vigilance and governance had considerably relaxed in Bamako, it became clear that security was non-existent in a considerable part of the country where the MUJAO, Ansar Dine, and other jihadist groups were settling in.

As for the peace process, the Algiers accords remained empty promises. Both sides seemed reluctant to seriously implement its conditions, and several armed groups that had not been part to the accord were creating new troubles. In terms of vigilance, there was also considerable disappointment regarding the government's behaviour. We had seen neither the anticipated cleaning out of the Augean stables that are the main Malian government departments, nor the appointment of experienced technocrats to head the key ministries and public institutions.

The army and other security services had received training and equipment from French forces and benefited from two large-scale training programmes funded by the European Union, the EUTM and EUCAP programmes.[1] But according to discussions I had with both senior and junior French officers, its fighting capacity had not improved much. Misbehaviour by the police forces was a source of resentment throughout the country. The arrival of the UN peacekeeping force, the MINUSMA, did little

[1] European Union Training Mission and the European Capacity Building mission.

179

Is the Sahel in the Process of Turning into a New Afghanistan?

to improve security, as the UN troops quickly came under night mortar attacks that caused significant casualties[2] and pushed them to remain largely barricaded in their compounds.

In February 2016, I happened be in Bamako when the French Prime Minister paid a short visit to Mali, and I was invited to a cocktail party held for him at the French embassy. I had a chat with him, and a more serious discussion with members of his delegation I happened to know. They had been so positively impressed by the martial look of the Malian army with its brand-new uniforms and by the optimistic presentations made by Malian authorities that I wondered for a while whether we had been visiting the same country. I guess that when the 'boss' comes to visit the troops, local officials tend to present a rosy picture. Remember how McNamara was briefed when visiting Vietnam.[3]

The atmosphere in Bamako in 2016 was, in fact, a mixture of euphoria and anxiety. It reminded me of the feeling that reigned in Kabul in 2002–03 after the collapse of the Taliban regime: The Americans have gotten rid of the Taliban. Let's move on to serious business. Nothing is more deceptive, or full of risk, than this casual return to 'business as usual'—especially business that is not necessarily above-board.

This parallel with Afghanistan is not a trivial one, although the Sahel is situated 12,000 kilometres from Afghanistan, and the geographical and cultural differences make it appear that we are dealing with two worlds that have nothing in common. Clearly, the snowy peaks of the Hindu Kush bear little resemblance to the rugged, parched hills of the Adrar des Ifoghas. Yet, the previously cited challenges faced by Mali's leaders, and more generally by leaders in the Sahel, are remarkably similar those Afghanistan is confronting. Now more than ever, we should not forget some of the lessons learned the hard way in Afghanistan, and we should be clear that while stabilizing the Sahel certainly involves dealing quickly with some urgent security problems, it is also necessary to address fundamental needs: rebuilding states, and inclusive

---

[2] About 140 killed between 2013 and 2017 which makes it the most dangerous of the present peace keeping forces.

[3] See Robert McNamara, *In Retrospect, the Tragedy and Lessons of Vietnam* (Random House, 1995).

economic development. These are problems that cannot be resolved without a determined, long-term approach.

## The Sahel, of course, is not Afghanistan, but the similarities are unfortunately numerous.

### Demographic Impasse

As previously noticed, the Sahel is, broadly speaking, at the same demographic stage as Afghanistan, with a growth rate somewhere around 3.5 per cent a year, meaning the population doubles every 20 years or so. The 'demographic transition' in the region—and the situation is quite similar in rural Afghanistan—has barely begun. The total population of the main landlocked countries of the French-speaking Sahel—Niger, Burkina Faso, Mali, and Chad—was estimated at 67 million in 2015. It is likely to reach 170 to 210 million by 2050, depending on how quickly fertility rates decline. It could even be close to 260 million if fertility rates in these countries remain at current levels, a scenario that cannot be ruled out, considering that they have remained almost unchanged for the last 50 years.

Whatever the population trends, the next 20 years will witness a huge influx of young men into the lacklustre job markets of these countries because most of the future job applicants already have been born. This phenomenon provides a better explanation for the success of the Taliban in Afghanistan than the attraction of jihadi arguments. To break it down, young, rural Afghans have to choose between going to the city to swell the masses of the unemployed working small informal jobs, slipping into the opium-production chain, or being employed occasionally or permanently by the rebel groups—who pay either a fixed fee for this or that attack—or a higher salary for full-time service than is offered by the regular army, whose rate of loss is significant (7,000 troops killed out of 350,000 in 2016 and most likely more in 2017 [4]). The alternatives are just the same in today's Mali, where

---

[4] Taking into account that most of the fighting (and the heavier losses) is done by afghan special forces numbering about 20,000.

jihadists offer more than three times the minimum monthly salary for the laying of a mine![5]

*Stagnation of agriculture and the rural economy*

Beyond the constraints of technology and climate, we already noticed that agriculture in the region has been largely neglected and so faces colossal challenges. Re-energizing this sector will require considerable effort and investment. Investment in activities such as small-scale irrigation and protection and rehabilitation of damaged soils is as inadequate in the Sahel as it is in Afghanistan. With slight differences linked to specific local conditions, in both Afghanistan and the Sahel, agriculture, like herding, has suffered from environmental damage resulting from a combination of demographic growth, deforestation, loss of soil fertility, and over-exploitation of pastures. These phenomena are likely to worsen in the Sahel under the impact of climate change. All this is pushing certain regions towards localized Malthusian crises; in the Sahel as in Afghanistan.

Like some valleys in Afghanistan, parts of Niger, northern Mali, and Chad are dealing with recurring food shortages that are structural in nature. The spectacular growth of poppy cultivation in Afghanistan (production reached a peak of about 9000 tonnes in 2017) is a logical response to this agrarian crisis. The Afghan farmers I spoke to in front of their small poppy fields explained to me perfectly what I subsequently found in scholarly reports: in the absence of profitable alternatives (which do exist but are not available), only this type of cultivation enabled them to buy wheat and survive shortages during the hunger season. Even in Burkina Faso, which is not the worst-off country in the Sahel, the works of René Billaz—one of the most, if not *the* most, experienced French agronomist in Sahel agriculture—have highlighted the clear land deadlocks that, in the absence of a true agrarian revolution, will make themselves felt very soon.

---

[5] About 100,000 CFA francs (150 euros) for laying a mine, and 400,000 CFA francs (600 euros) if the mine kills a UN or French soldier. The minimum monthly salary in Mali is 32,000 CFA.

*Mass unemployment in a context of no industrial development and young people who have lost hope*

As in Afghanistan, agricultural stagnation in the Sahel is combined with weak growth in employment in the service industries, a lack of local craftsmanship because of the unavailability of electricity, an absence of small and medium-sized agro-industrial enterprises owing to barriers preventing the transition from the informal to the formal sector, and the lack of an industrial base and urban industrial development. In Afghanistan, creating enough jobs for the 400,000 young people who enter the employment market every year, in a country where industry is negligible and agriculture highly dependent on climatic conditions, is an immense challenge. And yet, the Afghan population is just over 36 million, while the four main countries of the Sahel, whose demographic structure is fairly similar, have a combined population of double that figure. In Niger alone, more than 570,000 young people will be entering the employment market annually in 20 years.

In Sahel, then, the main problem is, and will increasingly be, youth unemployment. The current drivers of the strong economic growth that began around 15 years ago in these countries are primarily mining, construction, services, and information technology. Evidence indicates that these sectors will be able to provide employment to only a fraction of the masses of young people who will enter the job market. Prospects for industrial development in these countries, whether through deeper integration with the West African Economic and Monetary Union (WAEMU) or by becoming part of global value chains along the Ethiopian model, are, as we have seen, extremely limited because of the landlocked nature of the countries, an unfavourable business environment, and abnormally high input costs, particularly for labour and energy.

Under these conditions, employment is, and will increasingly be, a ticking social and political time bomb in all of these countries. Just like young Afghans, young people in the Sahel can no longer find jobs that meet their aspirations—aspirations that have increased tenfold through access to education and information. They are unable to integrate into society and cannot marry due to a lack of money. Against this background, they are naturally tempted by illegal activities, the trafficking of arms, cigarettes,

183

Is the Sahel in the Process of Turning into a New Afghanistan?

migrants, hashish and cocaine. They are also tempted by job offers from rebel groups with substantial resources. As in Afghanistan, they are then subjected to the indoctrination of the jihadi networks that offer them both an explanation of the reasons for their misfortunes and attractive prospects in this world... or in the next.

## Anarchic urbanization

Very rapid urbanization—at annual rates of 4–6 per cent—is unavoidable when agriculture is unable to offer proper jobs, and also when insecurity expands. The kind of urban growth seen in the Sahel capital cities, in Kabul, and in some key provincial capitals in Afghanistan is impossible to manage in cities with meagre fiscal revenues and very little technical and managerial capacity. The too-quick growth of capital cities is leading to the chaotic expansion of shanty towns and areas unintegrated into the urban fabric and therefore deprived of the essential utility networks required to provide decent living conditions.

International aid bears part of the responsibility here, having largely moved away from funding urban infrastructure.[6] Such urbanization will lead to the loss of the traditional social structures that characterize rural communities, and to people's feeling uprooted due to the anonymity of the city, as highlighted by Sylvie Brunel in an article for *Le Monde* published shortly after the attack against *Charlie Hebdo*.[7] The pressure on social budgets, which currently receive substantial funding from external aid, is now considerable, but no one can guarantee the sustainability of this aid over the long term.

## Mass migration

When deep insecurity develops, mass migration is inevitable within each country and across the entire sub-region, intensifying demographic pressures in receiving regions. During both the

[6] The selection of the Millennium Development Goals (MDGs), which make only a brief mention of these issues and set a nonsensical indicator, was not neutral in this respect.

[7] 'Des bombes humaines globalisées', *Le Monde*, 15 January 2015.

so-called 'Russian war' and the Mujahidin war in Afghanistan, between 1979 and 1995, about 5 million Afghans moved to Pakistan and Iran. We should not expect in the Sahel the type of scorched-earth policy conducted by the Soviets in Afghanistan. But if a combination of insufficient rainfall and disorganization of the rural economy due to insecurity develops in the francophone Sahel, as is already currently happening in the northeast of Nigeria and South Sudan, and the horn of Africa, how many people will leave the countryside and move to capital cities, the coastal regions, and Europe?

We have seen the dramatic political impact such population movements have had in the past in Côte d'Ivoire. These new migrations will take place against the backdrop of an extremely complex ethnic patchwork, increasing the risks of friction and tension. Will Côte d'Ivoire, Cameroon, and Nigeria, all grappling with countless problems, be able to absorb huge numbers of migrants without incident? In 1986, I saw some of the 200,000 foreign workers expelled that year by Nigeria arrive in Niger crammed into open lorries in appalling conditions. Will we witness even larger expulsions?

### Ethnic, political, and religious splits

In Afghanistan, as in the Sahel, ethnic, political, and religious divisions, previously handled by complex systems of mediation and dispute resolution, have intensified as these traditional mechanisms have disappeared. In the Sahel, these problems occur along two main fault lines, between North Africa and Sub-Saharan Africa and between Muslim and Christian populations, in a setting where ethnic groups straddle artificially established borders, nations have been built only recently, and efforts to create shared values have been extremely limited.

These divisions are reinforced by environmental damage, increased pressure on natural resources, and the slow collapse of the formal economy. As a result, communities that used to exist in relative harmony are being torn apart. Access to modern light weapons makes the slightest conflict infinitely more lethal. As everyone knows, Kalashnikovs are part of the landscape in Afghanistan. Almost all groups of herders in the Sahel are now

185

Is the Sahel in the Process of Turning into a New Afghanistan?

armed, and in Mali, most villages in the centre of the country where insecurity develops quickly are now forming militias and buying weapons.[8]

### Extremely weak or non-existent state presence in peripheral areas

The spectacular return of the Taliban in Afghanistan was, in large part, due to the weakness of government structures, with the state abandoning huge areas in which lawless zones open to all types of trafficking were created. In these regions, physical and legal insecurity is a heavy burden for a population driven to despair either by the absence of the state or by the predatory nature of a state whose representatives are often corrupt. The similarity with regions in the northern Sahel, from which governments have, de facto, mostly withdrawn, is striking.

In the Sahel, the institutions essential to stability, security, and the proper functioning of states and their economies remain, for the most part, extremely fragile. The police, regional govern-ments, and legal systems are underequipped, underfunded, and remain disturbingly weak,[9] making it easier for organized-crime and drug-trafficking networks to penetrate them. Generally speaking, across the whole region, state or economic institutions that have achieved sufficient competence to effectively carry out their functions can be counted on one hand.

### Particular weakness of national armies

I will take up the particular situation of the Afghan army later on. But first, a few words about the armies in the Sahel. The Chadian army, which intervened alongside French troops in Operation Serval in Mali in 2013, is well equipped and highly trained. The small Nigerien army is largely underequipped and has nowhere near enough troops (around 15,000) to confront the threats that are pressing in on Niger from all four corners, but it is well led. That is why, after several rough confrontations with this army, the

---

[8] As illustrated in the excellent film *Timbuktu*.

[9] See Jeffrey Herbst, *State and Power in Africa: Comparative Lessons in Authority and Control* (Princeton, 2000).

jihadi groups chose Mali for their ruthless activities. We saw the Malian army collapse in a matter of weeks against several hundred jihadists, and more recently witnessed both its repeated failures in the Gao and Kidal regions and its inability to restore security even in the densely populated central and southern regions of Mali.

Niger should, however, be a particular cause for concern because it faces multiple threats. In the north of Niger, jihadists established in the south of Libya continue to transit through Niger to reach their normal business grounds in the north of Mali and are a direct threat to the Arlit uranium mines. The threat posed by the jihadists roaming in the Gao and Kidal regions of Mali weighs on its north-western border where clashes occur regularly in the vicinity of Tillabery, 80 km from Niamey. In the northeast, a gold rush is underway, which is transforming the desert region of Djado into a lawless area. Finally, Boko Haram still poses a considerable risk to the entire southeast of the country. Under these conditions, the small Nigerien army, which has already sent a battalion to Côte d'Ivoire and another to Mali under United Nations mandates, is spread thinly. The few well-trained and properly equipped battalions are constantly being transferred by French or US planes from one end of this immense country to the other to deal with emergency situations, and have no time to rest. And their very few attack helicopters are never present in the right place.

As the collapse of the Malian army demonstrated, there is also a 'Potemkin' element to many of these armies that is difficult to assess. There are several causes behind the weakness of these armies. The first is political and is linked to the persistent fear among heads of states, of a military coup by an army over which they have poor control. Consequently, presidential guard forces, usually recruited along ethnic or tribal lines, if not greater in number than regular armies, are at least much better equipped. But these forces remain in the capitals and intervene only rarely in the skirmishes that usually occur more than 1,000 kilometres away.

A second and related cause is that some armies as most state institutions in these countries are not immune to nepotism and cronyism. Most officers, whatever their ability, are only promoted to upper positions if related by family or ethnic/ political links to the head of state or its close associates. First because such close links appear to be the best guarantee against possible coups. Second because these are attractive positions where considerable money can be made by pocketing the salaries of 'ghost soldiers' or involvement into various traffics with gasoline and spare parts of military vehicles.

The third cause is budgetary. Any army is expensive to run, but the budgets of these states do not allow them to maintain armies larger than the ones they have, and the IMF hates military spending. When confronted with an emergency situation, officials in these countries are obliged to rob Peter to pay Paul—to reduce their budgets for economic and social development in order to respond to military crises. In Niger where I did a special analysis of the subject for the Niger Government, security expenditure was reaching 6.3 per cent of GDP in 2016, an amount much higher than that allocated to the agricultural sector at the beginning of the 2000s (3.2 per cent of GDP). Between 2009 and 2015, military expenditures have grown by a factor of 3.3 but are still far from sufficient to tackle external threats. All of these countries therefore find themselves in a budgetary and security impasse, unable to respond to security threats even when sacrificing essential expenditures on economic and social development.

A fourth cause is that the French army, once a regular provider of training and technical assistance to many African armies, has abandoned this function over time due to the increasing scarcity of its resources. For a long time, military agreements with France—and the implicit guarantee of French intervention when necessary—meant that these countries were not obliged to raise taxes and make budgetary decisions necessary to create sizeable armies supplied with modern equipment.

A final cause relates to the inadequate capacities of the police and other forces that are likely to occupy territory retaken from armed groups. Even a well-trained army like Chad's, which is capable of defeating armed groups, as it showed against Boko Haram and in the north of Mali, is not organized to maintain peace in a region it has temporarily secured. This army is, moreover, very much aware of, and has vigorously protested against, the failure of Nigeria's law-enforcement agencies to take responsibility in the regions recovered from Boko Haram. French forces face the same problem. They have no option but to limit their interventions to crackdown operations that are effective in the short term but cannot restore security to a region for the long term. They basically now realize that in such context, they are in a strategic impasse if the Malian government cannot put some order into its security services.[10]

## A very worrying regional environment

The geopolitical environment of the region could not be more disturbing. While eastern Niger and southern Chad are directly threatened by the Boko Haram insurgency, and northern Niger is threatened by the jihadi groups that abound in the Fezzan region of Libya, south-eastern Chad is threatened by Seleka groups from central Africa. Eastern Chad is threatened by regular incursions from Sudan. Northern Chad has been a region of insecurity since the end of the 1960s and experiences regular revolts by Toubou tribes. In northern Mali Tuareg factions compete to control illegal trafficking. Finally, a new Fulani insurgency is now developing in the formally touristic region of Segou and Mopti in central Mali.

Beyond the spectacular terrorist attacks that took place in Bamako in March 2015 and 2016, the most disturbing issue in Mali now is the rapid deterioration of day-to-day security in the countryside, where traders are kidnapped for ransom, cattle is regularly stolen, and whole villages are attacked and sometimes burned to the ground. Such security breakdown is very similar to the security collapse that occurred in much of Afghanistan after 2002 and has the same consequences, with militia organizing and, having recognized the superiority of the Kalashnikov over the traditional bow-and-arrow, buying modern weapons. In this chaotic context, groups of jihadi propagandists are now very active, providing minor social services, recruiting unemployed young men, and already killing the local leaders that dare resist their authority. Confronted to such rising insecurity and the inability of the local gendarmerie and police force to control it, Malian authorities are now considering asking French forces to take over. However of

---

[10] As I explained in a recent article published by the main French military review: *Une guerre sans fin* ('A war without end'), Revue de la Défense Nationale, février 2018.

course, sending in the French Foreign Legion in the Malian villages would send us back to a foregone colonial era.

The fall of the Gaddafi regime launched a tidal wave that swept through the entire sub-region, as numerous Sahel workers employed in Libya came home and mercenaries from Niger and Mali, who had been fighting for the regime, returned, sometimes bringing their 'equipment' with them, including, in Mali, heavy weaponry. After six years of crisis, Libya has become a failed state; the south of the country is an almost impregnable fall-back and resupply area for the sub-region's rebel groups. Local rebel groups have now established contact with the local Islamic State militias. They have access to the stockpiles of weapons accumulated by the former regime. In this context, most of Niger, Chad, and Mali as well as the northern part of Burkina Faso have become unsafe to travel in, even with a military escort.

Several regional aspects can no longer be ignored. As a leading nation, Algeria plays an often-ambiguous role throughout the sub-region. For example, the country's secret services have been manipulating Ansar Dine in Mali and attempting to infiltrate the various rebel factions to such an extent that, as was the case during the Algerian civil war, it is not possible to determine who is doing what.

Of greatest concern to much of the local elite, however, is the penetration of Wahhabi influence and the spread of radical Islam, which is alien to local traditions. For more than 25 years, thanks to funding provided by Saudi Arabia, Qatar, and Kuwait, foundations, religious schools, and mosques have proliferated. They support Wahhabi causes and often promote extremist propaganda.[11] This is reminiscent of the role played by the madrasas in the indoctrination of young Afghans exiled to Pakistan, who then joined the ranks of the Taliban insurgency, a topic discussed in detail in an excellent book by Ahmed Rashid,[12] who probably knows more than anyone about the world of the Taliban.

[11] Saudi organizations allegedly pay a monthly sum to some Sahel pilgrims returning from the Hajj, who are prepared to disseminate Wahhabi ideas and build koranic schools or mosques.

[12] Ahmed Rashid, *Descent into Chaos: The United States and the Failure of Nation Building in Pakistan, Afghanistan, and Central Asia* (Viking, 2008).

*Transition to an economy based on illegal trafficking and drugs*

Overall, as in Afghanistan, the economy of northern Sahel is increasingly based on illegal trafficking, including the transport of Latin American cocaine and Moroccan hashish destined for European markets. I have not been able to get any figures from the United Nations Office on Crime and Drugs (UNODC) related to cocaine traffic in the Sahel, but reliable sources indicate that the value of the traffic in illicit tobacco through the Sahel is in the range of USD 700 million.[13] Also, as in Afghanistan, the 'business' of taking hostages is increasingly common. Here, there is now less focus on the spectacular but risky kidnapping of Westerners[14] than on kidnapping local business owners and other notable figures for ransom, which is Boko Haram's speciality. Bit by bit, the Sahel is becoming part of Philippe Hugon's 'criminal globalization.'[15]

### Risk that jihadi groups will become embedded

This economic system was initially marginal but has now reached unhealthy levels with the aid of a variety of factors: the emergence of a militant, Salafi Islam, resulting in clever propaganda; the withdrawal of Algeria's Salafist Group for Preaching and Combat (GSPC), hounded by the Algerian military, towards the Sahara and northern Sahel; and the latter's integration within local mafia networks linked to drug-trafficking and hostage-taking. In Mali, as in Afghanistan, the most striking factor has been the progressive corruption by drug-money—of political power in the former regime, and in the administrative and political system.

Finally, throughout the region—again as in Afghanistan— jihadi groups combine mafia activities, social activities, and proselytizing to try and integrate themselves into local social structures through marriage, distributing money, and countless small actions

---

[13] This is quite easy to assess because the cigarettes are sold by well-established manufacturers, most of them being established in the Middle East.

[14] Income accruing to AQMI groups in the Sahel from kidnapping internationals has been estimated by French services at close to USD 160 million.

[15] Philippe Hugon, *Géopolitique de l'Afrique* (SEDES, 2012).

of a social nature. As in Afghanistan, they are already moving to eliminate traditional chiefs and local leaders hostile to them.

### Access of these groups to almost impregnable fall-back areas

At the regional level, these groups have access to almost impregnable fall-back areas, as is the case in the Libyan region of Fezzan, which no one now has control over, and in the territories of northwest Pakistan, to which most of the leadership and resupply structures of the Taliban groups and Haqqani network have withdrawn.[16] Fortunately, unlike in Afghanistan, where since 2003 the Pakistani special services (the ISI) have been routinely involved in destabilization, no regional power is actively supporting the jihadi and rebel groups in the Sahel. On the other hand, the difficulty of coordinating military action across five countries—the so-called G5—without active support from the two regional powers, Algeria and Nigeria, must be noted.

### Funding military action and development concurrently leads to budget impasse

Afghanistan's current budget impasse, which we will analyse in a later chapter, clearly illustrates the need for external funding when a fragile state with a poorly developed economy and no significant oil or mineral resources finds itself confronting a serious insurgency. To fight this kind of insurgency requires not only targeted military activity, which is always expensive, but also the construction and maintenance of infrastructure (roads, energy, public buildings, et cetera) in vast peripheral areas that are underequipped and underpopulated. It also requires the recruitment, training, and deployment of government personnel and infrastructure to guarantee security, respect for the rule of law, and proper administration on the ground.

In the Sahel, the situation is certainly less serious than it is in Afghanistan, but recent work carried out by the World Bank for

[16] The Haqqani network is an armed Islamist group that is independent, but has close links to the Taliban. It is one of the most formidable terrorist organizations operating in Afghanistan.

the first time in this very sensitive area, focusing on Niger, shows that the country does not have the budgetary capacity to continue to increase expenditures on security at the rate it has been forced to over recent years.[17] It would be surprising if the situation were any better in Mali or even in Chad, given the collapse in oil prices.

Across the world, the refrain is like a broken record: development without security is impossible. Security without development is also impossible. However, as long as the definition of development aid according to the criteria of the renowned OECD Development Assistance Committee (DAC) does not include security expenses, international donors will maintain a cautious distance from these issues. When can we hope to see the legitimate costs of strengthening government institutions in fragile states reflected in expenditures eligible for official development assistance (ODA)? It, clearly, will not be anytime soon. In this context, are oil and mineral resources the only factors capable of making a difference?

## Can mining and oil pull these countries out of their budgetary ruts?

The mobilization and allocation of oil or mineral resources to spending on priorities, in terms of the development and consolidation of states, poses a variety of problems. First, it is very difficult to exploit oilfields or mineral deposits in areas of insecurity. Doing so places staff at substantial physical risk, as evidenced by the kidnapping of French hostages at the Arlit mines in northern Niger and China's postponement of the commissioning of the Aynak copper mine in Afghanistan—despite protection provided by police and armed forces in the countries concerned.

The associated investments are huge, amounting to more than USD 8 billion for the Aynak mine. The tax income anticipated by states is as great as the investments made: the tax receipts expected from this mine alone would represent nearly 30 per cent of the Afghan government's total tax receipts. Different assessments of

[17] 'Public Expenditure Review of the Security Sector in Niger', World Bank, November 2013.

the notional value of Afghan mineral reserves quantify it some-where between USD 1 trillion and USD 3 trillion.

Statistically, mineral wealth is proportionate to the area of land controlled. The countries of the Sahel cover a considerable area. This suggests that as yet unidentified or unexploited mineral resources in the Sahel are enormous. Their notional value is prob-ably several times that of the reserves in Afghanistan—in the tril-lions of dollars. These resources, if developed and well managed, would certainly enable some Sahel nations to cover, as Chad was attempting to do, both their security expenses (currently unsus-tainable on their budgets) and their development expenses (now subject to the good will—or the lack thereof—of international donors).

That said, the case of Aynak shows that major international investors, whether Chinese or Western, are hesitant about invest-ing colossal sums in regions of insecurity. Whatever the potential mineral wealth of the countries of the Sahel, which is undoubt-edly considerable, the geopolitical uncertainty is such that we are unlikely to see new investments such as those made in the four uranium mines in northern Niger [18] in the near future, except perhaps in the oil sector, once international prices return to an attractive level for investors.

## How can immense potential mineral wealth be transformed into development?

Let's assume that the security problem is resolved and that signifi-cant investment can be made in mining. The second problem is to prevent the associated income from 'evaporating'—from disap-pearing via opaque routes and being spent on prestige items or deposited into bank accounts in the Bahamas or other tax havens. This is a fundamental question because the associated income can be two, five, even ten times the amount that these countries can raise through international aid. Effective use of income from oil and mineral resources can enable fragile states to consider devel-oping their infrastructure, particularly roads, and better control peripheral areas that have been neglected. It would also help them

---

[18] Somaïr, Cominak, Imouraren, and Azelik.

to strengthen their government institutions by equipping them properly and paying attractive salaries to civil servants.

This very important point has been the subject of economic research, surveillance mechanisms, and best-practice exchanges for some 15 years. At one time, I was involved with this difficult work, which is naturally impeded by a lack of goodwill from both the states concerned and the oil and mining companies, as well as the opacity that surrounds these issues. But the stakes are very high. Trillions of dollars lie beneath the ground in countries that are among the poorest in the world, some good part underneath countries in the Sahel. Putting these future resources to good use would, in principle, allow these countries to pull themselves out of poverty and to leave the fragility shores.

Some interesting initiatives have been undertaken. The 'Publish What You Pay' initiative, launched some time ago, attempts to put pressure on oil and mining companies to publish what they pay the countries in which they operate in an attempt to limit the 'evaporation' of funds that frequently occurs after the payments are made and before they become public revenue.

In 2005, I chaired a meeting in Paris, organized by the World Bank, that brought together academics, researchers, officials from NGOs and development institutions, and representatives of oil and mining companies. This gave me the opportunity to gauge, behind all the public displays of a desire for transparency, how extremely reticent oil and mining companies are about shedding light on these issues. Their arguments were not without merit: countries would refuse to make this kind of information public, and companies from non-OECD countries—and particularly from China—that had no intention of submitting themselves to such investigation would walk away with the best projects.

Currently, the best-known mechanism is the Extractive Industries Transparency Initiative (EITI),[19] an international organization created in 2003. It has set standards for transparency in oil and mining activities, which have been voluntarily accepted by 48 countries.[20] The World Bank, IMF, and numerous major

[19] The initiative came from Tony Blair during the 2002 World Summit on Sustainable Development in Johannesburg.

[20] Considered 'EITI compliant'—in other words, they adhere to the transparency standards laid down by the organization.

companies and civil society organizations have signed up with the initiative, which makes this institution particularly unusual.

These transparency standards oblige participating countries to provide a range of information on their mining, oil, and gas activities, thus eliminating—or at least significantly limiting—the risk of corruption. Personally, I continue to be somewhat puzzled by the list of countries considered to have accepted the EITI rules because it includes such 'usual suspects' as Nigeria and Congo, which are not exactly known for their transparency in these areas. At the international level, however, belonging to the 'EITI Club' has become almost obligatory. All that is needed now is for the organization to find the will to publicly exclude the black sheep from the club.

Other organizations are also looking into these issues. The two most important, the Revenue Watch Institute and the Natural Resource Charter, are in the process of merging both their technical teams and their governance and advisory structures. I was once part of a group of advisors[21] for the Natural Resource Charter because I had previously been at the centre of an operation seeking to promote the development of a significant oilfield in a very fragile country and introduce transparency in the use of the associated funds.

The experience turned my hair grey. A short personal story will help explain the difficulty of the undertaking and let readers better understand how decisions are made and how an institution like the World Bank operates with regard to an issue that was the subject of intense controversy from the end of the 1990s until very recently.

## Should a major donor have facilitated oil production in Chad?

When, in 1997, my vice president at the World Bank informed me that he wanted to move me from Cote d'Ivoire and Ghana issues to work on Central Africa, he said with a small smile: 'Serge, you will find two really thorny issues in these cases. Get out there quickly to gauge what's happening on the ground, and come back

---

[21] Technical Advisory Group.

so we can discuss it.' The first issue was the financial collapse in Cameroon, which had not been able to manage the devaluation of the CFA franc in 1994 and, incapable of paying its civil servants after failing to meet the conditions of three IMF programmes in three years, was going completely off track and threatening the integrity of the Franc Zone. Clearly this was not just a minor detail. But the second issue, related to a very small stake in the financing of a pipeline and development of the first oilfield in southern Chad led by Exxon, did not seem, at first sight, to be terribly complicated. How wrong I was!

On my return to Washington after meeting the relevant Cameroonian and Chadian officials in country, I had not even unpacked before I was summoned to both the State Department and the US Treasury. At the State Department, the message was very clear: 'I'm not kidding around here, the World Bank must participate in financing the pipeline or Exxon, the lead partner, won't want to go in there and then the Chinese will get involved and route it via Sudan. This is a serious issue—sort it out.' At the Treasury, the message from the official I met was a little different but could not have been clearer: 'This project has to go ahead, but I want complete transparency on how the revenue is used. I don't want to see a single quarter escaping your control.'

My predecessor had, of course, been involved in a dialogue with Chad for a number of years about a mechanism to facilitate the allocation of future oil revenue to development spending, but to go from there to demanding full transparency was a big step. As I tried to discuss the feasibility of what my interlocutor in the Treasury was asking of me, the remainder of the message was delivered with the candour and bluntness of which our American friends are capable: 'You heard me, son—sort it out.' All the while, his behaviour made it clear to me where he believed the power in the World Bank lay: right there in his office.

## A tough interlocutor

I spent the following week between IMF crisis meetings on Cameroon, on the telephone with Cameroon's Finance Minister, and in meetings with my team on the so-called 'Chad–Cameroon project,' which was to become the most complex and controversial

to tell him about my meetings with the American officials and
bemoaned the fact that he had given me an impossible task. I had
spent an hour with the President of Chad, Idriss Deby, and I had
quickly understood that this fellow was not likely to be daunted
by conditions imposed by the World Bank. Rumour had it that
Deby, leading a charge in pickup trucks—armed with French
anti-tank weapons—had destroyed a column of Libyan tanks...

I had found an interlocutor who was clear, precise, and capable
of delving into the technical details of the operations we were
then financing in Chad. His message was equally clear: 'If you
want to continue to work in Chad, you must finance our pipeline. Otherwise, it's not worth coming back.' Rather than console
me, Jean-Louis Sarbib, my vice president and friend, plunged me
further into despair by telling me: 'And on this matter, you also
need to pay attention to a very tough campaign against this project being fought by environmental NGOs; they will turn it into
a symbol and do everything they can to block it. Watch out for
trouble from this quarter and approach your task accordingly. But
my first question is this: What is your view? Should this project
go ahead or not?'

I was dismayed. The World Bank's financial stake in the
operation was very modest when compared to the overall cost,
a hundred million dollars in a project worth more than three billion, including the downstream pipeline and the development
of upstream oilfields. But the project was conditional on our
involvement. Exxon, the lead partner (together with Shell and,
initially, Elf), absolutely did not want to make a commitment in
Chad without a financial contribution from us, which seemed to
offer the companies reassurance in a region they did not know.
In return, the World Bank had laid down clear requirements with
regard to managing environmental aspects and on the use of oil
revenue by the Chadian authorities.

Fortunately, I had backing from the exceptionally high-quality
team responsible for preparing the project. I have always marvelled
at the capacity of the World Bank—which receives so much criticism (some of it justified)—to mobilize a team of colleagues with
extraordinary experience to work on major projects. In this case,
I could not have asked for better. The involvement of Philippe

Benoit, an American lawyer and graduate of Harvard Law School (Obama's *alma mater*) and Michel Layec, a French engineer with vast experience, boosted my morale.

I spent the next two weeks learning about the project. With Exxon as operator, it posed few problems from a technical point of view, apart from the likely difficulty of getting Exxon to adhere to the draconian environmental standards imposed by the World Bank. For three hours, I listened politely to a group of American NGOs specializing in 'advocacy'—otherwise known as lobbying. Their message was that the project was a disgrace, Deby was an awful dictator, and they would do everything they could to prevent the World Bank's participation in it. My attempts to engage them in dialogue about the project itself ran up against a brick wall. The environmental concerns associated with the project, which were clearly a justified topic for discussion, were of no interest to my visitors. But they had picked ingredients for the making of a great issue: a dictator, the much-decried big Bank, those dreadful oil companies. Good stuff for a campaign, right?

## Environmental battle ... in Washington

A few words on these environmental issues: my vice president and I met a member of the senior management team at Exxon and his project manager. The message that Jean-Louis gave them could not have been clearer: 'We want to see you working to the same environmental standards in Chad as you would in New Jersey. We will withdraw if we see the slightest slip.' The environmental studies filled an entire room and cost almost USD 25 million! One of my teams walked the entire length of the 1,100-kilometer route the pipeline was to follow, from the Port of Kribi in Cameroon to the first exploration wells in Doba in southern Chad, to check that the pipeline would avoid not only villages but also sacred forests, cemeteries, sensitive areas, et cetera. Detours imposed significant additional costs on Exxon. None of this prevented the launch of a multi-stage media campaign against us which, to my surprise, took a nasty turn.

My computer was attacked by a hacker who got hold of my professional and private emails and circulated them; fortunately, they contained nothing dramatic. After inviting TV channels along, climbers scaled the outside of our offices on 1818 H Street in Washington DC and attached banners to the top of the building denouncing the destruction of Chad's primary forest (which, in all likelihood, disappeared some 2,000 years ago). And a campaign was launched regarding the expected population displacements in the oil zone. All of these issues, of course, were subject to extremely rigorous and well-monitored procedures within the World Bank.

I met with the institution's managing director, Shengman Zhang, an exceptional Chinese economist, to brief him on the population-displacement aspect. I explained to him that 75 families would be displaced. He looked at me, a little surprised. 'Did you mean to say 75,000?' When I confirmed that the number was 75 and expressed my concern about the smear campaign, he was flabbergasted. The most serious attack, however, was the publication of full-page advertisements in the American press featuring a photo of the president of the World Bank accompanied by a note: 'Wanted dead or alive for environmental destruction in Chad.' As a result of these advertisements, Jim Wolfensohn had to be accompanied by a team of bodyguards for a while. This is indeed the US!

A fan of sailing and nature, I gave up my early desire to become an anthropologist after catching malaria on the Ouémé River, an amoebiasis on the Upper Orinoco, and losing a kidney while living with the Inuits of the Canadian Arctic (I do have my excuses). But, I have always been sensitive to environmental and social issues, and I have a lot of respect for the development NGOs with whom I had many, many meetings out in the field during my career. I even now sit at the board of one of the leading French NGOs …

So I despaired that I could not engage anyone on the actual project in a real dialogue, my interlocutors focusing chiefly on the scandal my work represented. It was particularly exasperating that my two main arguments were not heard: that it was impossible to develop a country, including its social services, without roads, and only oil money could maintain a road network in Chad; and that if the Bank did not get involved, the Chinese and money from Sudan would come in and implement the project in accordance with 'Sudanese standards'—the risk being that, as in South Sudan, these Sudanese standards would involve 'clearing' villages in the way of the pipeline with the help of combat helicopters.

## Dilemma

The main issue tormenting me was whether this project should go ahead or not. My team and I held a very open brainstorming session on the subject. After all, we could manage pressure from the State Department and US Treasury by playing for time, by putting off Exxon with additional requirements, and by relying on the Bank's executive directors most likely to be swayed by the arguments of the NGOs. The conclusions of our brainstorming session can be summed up in five points.

First, Chad was an extremely fragile state that did not have a year-round road network, with technical issues (sand, lack of laterite) complicating things significantly. Even if donors arranged to fund such a network, which was highly doubtful, the country's budget was so limited, its resources so meagre, that it would have been impossible to guarantee that the network would be maintained. Oil resources could be a unique source of funding for building and maintaining such a network and also launching a coherent development programme. We were being asked to help to develop Chad, but it is impossible to do anything without roads: a realistic health programme, a serious educational programme, an agricultural programme—all impossible.

Second, if we did not get involved, the Chinese would go ahead with the project, probably resulting in Chad's coming under Sudan's influence. If that happened, we could say goodbye to the IMF programme and any hope of improving governance and having a serious finance minister who managed his budget.

Third, President Deby was clearly no altar boy, but what altar boy would be capable of leading a country torn apart by tribal wars and regularly invaded by its Libyan and Sudanese neighbours or their henchmen? He seemed to manage the country, albeit with a firm hand. He had submitted himself for election and made an attempt, undoubtedly limited, at democracy. He was certainly someone we could talk to.

Fourth, the main justifications for our involvement were the proper management of oil revenue and ensuring that it was

201

Is the Sahel in the Process of Turning into a New Afghanistan?

allocated to development spending. The feasibility of implementing a transparency mechanism would be one of the main criteria in making our decision.

Finally, the environmental questions were not really major issues, as they would be, for example, with a large dam. They could be managed, and it was not up to lobbying NGOs in Washington who were indifferent to the fate of Chadians to dictate to us how we should act. In the end, it would be better to ask Chadian NGOs representing civil society—to consult them properly and leave it to them to decide, with full knowledge of the issues. If they told us no, we would arrange for the project to get bogged down. If they gave us the green light, we would go ahead and stand by it. This left us with the most difficult task: selling the position of the US Treasury to a hard-line, nationalist, and prickly Chadian President.[22] I got on a plane to N'Djamena—something that would become a habit.

## Interference and sovereignty

My idea was to propose to President Deby, a mechanism inspired by the way the French Development Agency (AFD) managed structural adjustment funding, whereby funds were paid to an account at the central bank and then disbursed via a system requiring signatures by both the donor and the recipient country. I was also considering setting up an independent monitoring body composed of representatives from Chadian civil society. Finally, a sanctions procedure was needed in the event of non-compliance, and to that end, a virtual atomic weapon was suggested to me by my vice president: the suspension of all World Bank support, and mechanisms entailing a parallel blocking of IMF support, and a probable halt to all external funding, on which Chad's budget was heavily dependent. I was worried, of course, about how the President might react to my proposals. I had requested a one-on-one meeting to try to sell him these ideas and, frankly, I felt quite uneasy.

[22] It is no coincidence that the cover of the February 20, 2015, issue of *Jeune Afrique* carried a photo of President Deby with the headline: *Le boss du Sahel* ('The boss of the Sahel').

As it turned out, my attempt to get a one-on-one was a complete failure. Ushered into his office after a long wait (to get me prepared, I suspect), I found myself face-to-face with the entire government and the President in his grand boubou robes. I did my best to explain the constraints, saying that the US Treasury was not leaving me any room to manoeuvre and so on, and outlined my proposals. After I finished my explanation, the silence that followed seemed as though it would never end, until finally the President asked me: 'Is that all?' And right there, I got the biggest 'tongue-lashing' of my life. There is no other way to describe it.

'Chad is an independent country. You are not going to submit us to your control. Colonization is over. Who are you? What is this imperialist institution? We don't need you. We would rather walk barefoot than have anything dictated to us.' And on it went. Throughout this diatribe, the other members of the government remained silent.

I had expected a difficult discussion, but this astounded me. Back in my small room at the Novotel, I went over the meeting in my mind: a complete failure. Perhaps I had not gone about it the right way, but it was surely an impossible task. The telephone line to Washington was down, as was the internet connection. The next flight was in three days, the swimming pool was empty, and the air conditioning, at best, reduced the temperature to thirty degrees Celsius from the forty degree heat outside. I had a serious case of the blues. I was furious with myself, and with the institution that was putting me in impossible situations. The worst thing was that I could not completely disagree with the President's arguments that our demands were untenable. I accepted his tongue-lashing. I was torn between relief at being rid of this project and the regret of knowing that my hopes of seeing the oil resources used wisely had just disappeared, perhaps due to my own blunder. What a job!

I had a very bad night, but at eight in the morning, a presidential driver was in front of the hotel: 'The President is expecting you.' I was very surprised. I told myself that I was in for another session. But the President was waiting for me, alone in his office and wearing a suit. Very business-like, he said to me, 'I have thought over your proposal. It's not a good one—I am going to propose an alternative to you'. I understood straightaway that the tongue-lashing I'd received the day before had been staged before the full government so that everyone would be convinced that the President was not going to have his policy dictated by bureaucrats from Washington. Now it was time to negotiate.

I have heard many bad things said about President Deby, but I have a lot of respect for him, for his sense of statehood, for his ability to grasp situations quickly, and for his physical courage, too. In February 2008, a rebel column from Sudan crossed the entire country from east to west, crushing his army and literally reaching the gates of the presidential palace. Everyone believed that Deby was finished. President Sarkozy offered to have French Army helicopters stationed at the airport extract him. At the head of what remained of his guards, with a portable VHF radio and four old tanks, he drove back the rebels, who fled to Darfur.

In any case, he made an impression on me during this negotiation. He had immediately grasped that my position was as difficult as his if he wanted, as he did, to work with Exxon rather than the Chinese (in which case he would have to depend on Sudan). He had understood my constraints perfectly, and overnight—by himself, I suspect—he had prepared a counterproposal that was largely a cosmetic dressing-up of the arrangements I had proposed. The account at the central bank was turned into an offshore account with an international bank that would be audited regularly. He also agreed to a monitoring body drawn from civil society. We reached agreement on the technical details within an hour.

## Too much interference kills interference.

For the next (exhausting) four years, I spoke to President Deby or his advisors by phone regularly. I went to Chad every three months. But the affair was made vastly more complicated by the campaign run against it, which had become symbolic. The Chadian president's political opponents mounted a campaign against the project, one that was taken up by the NGOs in Washington. The schedule slipped on several occasions. President Deby came to Washington, and I watched him cleverly trap the president of the World Bank. As he made his farewells, he naturally offered his hand, and a well-placed Chadian photographer got a shot of the handshake, which was published by the press in N'Djamena the following day with the headline 'Agreement in Washington on the pipeline.' In fact, we were far from an agreement. I had to take World Bank managing director Shengman Zhang to Chad, and we were given a ceremonial reception in Abéché by an unbelievable gathering of dignitaries in full regalia.

On this occasion, I witnessed, with great interest, the clash of cultures between the Chinese economist of short stature and President Deby in full traditional costume. But in the end, pragmatists that they both were, they got along very well. Still, we went from crisis to crisis because the project crystallized global opposition to the World Bank's involvement in major infrastructure projects, an issue that seems outdated today.

While criticized by some officials who were sensitive to the NGO lobbying campaign, the project was vigorously defended by Chinese and Brazilian officials who feared that its rejection by the World Bank would jeopardize funding of future large-scale infrastructure projects in their own countries. The costs of the internal review by my team alone exceeded USD 2 million, which was utterly outrageous and blew a hole in my budget. The message from the NGOs and civil society organizations from Chad that we brought to Washington could not have been clearer: 'We do not trust President Deby at all, but we need the oil resources; we are too poor. This is a unique opportunity. We need you to ensure transparency with regard to the revenue.' Finally, I was able to get the project approved by the World Bank board.

What followed was equally complicated. A few years after my departure from the World Bank, dialogue between the institution and President Deby broke down. The responsibility for this is shared, in my view. Deby challenged the agreement we had come to. I was not really surprised. The agreement was exorbitant. We had demanded too much. After all, it was naive on our part to seek to control all of the oil revenue of a sovereign state and allocate it exclusively to spending that we considered relevant in the fight against poverty. But the split between Chad and Washington did not last, and new foundations were discreetly established.

In retrospect, I am annoyed with myself for not having had the guts to engage in a serious discussion with the US Treasury which, to satisfy public opinion, imposed on me and on Chad exorbitant conditions that had no hope of lasting over the long term. I should have fought to limit our ambitions to allocating maybe half of the

205

Is the Sahel in the Process of Turning into a New Afghanistan?

revenue to objectives linked to fighting poverty while insisting on transparency with regard to so-called 'sovereignty' expenditures. Had I done so, of course, I might have found myself down on the pavement, banished from the offices of 1818 H Street. In any case, sovereignty expenditures cannot be ignored in a country like Chad, which is constantly confronted by armed incursions from its neighbours and internal rebellions. I remain convinced that a more balanced agreement would have survived.

Meanwhile, it is worth noting that, 18 years after these discussions, thanks to this project, Chad reached 7.3 per cent economic growth in 2014, according to the African Development Bank. Oil revenue then accounted for 70 per cent of tax receipts and was fully recorded in the budget. The country was complying with an IMF framework agreement that required it to adhere to strict governance criteria. In April 2015, it reached the completion point of the Heavily Indebted Poor Countries (HIPC) initiative, which allowed it to benefit from a substantial cancellation of its external debt. Finally, Niger now intends to connect to this pipeline, which will enable it to exploit its own oilfields in the far east of the country in the future.

Following the split with the World Bank, some of Chad's oil revenue was, unsurprisingly, used to purchase military equipment. At the end of the day, however, is there not a certain degree of legitimacy in wanting to guarantee security, without which there can be no development? On the other hand, as I had hoped, a large portion of the revenue was used to build roads, to develop government structures across the majority of the country, to transform N'Djamena, and to pay teachers and nurses. France also benefited from the support of an effective Chadian army in Mali in 2013. The Chadian army is currently the only one in the sub-region capable of taking on Boko Haram. Finally, In January 2015, *The Economist* published an article about the collapse of the Russian economy in the face of falling oil prices that also noted the success of the Chadian economy under the same circumstances. The article was entitled 'What Vladimir can learn from Chad.'[23] Of course the situation is now less rosy. Security costs,

[23] *The Economist*, 10 January 2015.

which reach up to 9 per cent of GDP, constitute a huge drain on budget resources, and persistently low oil prices render the 2017 fiscal situation very difficult.

### What additional conclusions can one draw from this example?

I sincerely believe that the first conclusion—which was my deep conviction throughout this case—is that it is unrealistic to seek to impose, on a sovereign country, conditions with which its leaders profoundly disagree. Conditionality works when it is local officials who demand and define them. This is how I helped design the reform programme that sort out the Cameroonian economy in 1997–98, and I was lucky to have interlocutors in Cameroon who understood the usefulness of an approach that let them define the conditionalities of their reform programme themselves.

The second conclusion, obviously, is that it is criminal to oppose a very poor country's gaining access to its own natural resources. There is no doubt that these resources bring potential dangers, Dutch disease being the best-known, but by no means the only problem: constant political intervention in commercial negotiations involving enormous sums heightens the risk of wide-scale corruption and abuses of authority.[24] But, a refusal to facilitate access to this potential wealth and to attempt to control it, even clumsily, risks condemning the country to remaining trapped in poverty. Before oil, Chad did not have a year-round road network. I defy anyone to develop a country without roads.

But, let us return to the Sahel as a whole.

### The entire region is entering a highly turbulent phase.

Considering the medium-term outlook, the overall situation in the Sahel is extremely worrying. As already mentioned, *Crisis in the Sahel* is the title of the report issued following the OASIS Conference organised in 2013 by the University of California,

---

[24] On this subject, see the following work, now a classic and which remains relevant today, about the abuses in Venezuela in particular: Terry Lynn Karl, *The Paradox of Plenty: Oil Booms and Petro States* (University of California, 1997).

Berkeley and the African Institute for Development Policy. The report rightly emphasizes that when the Sahel's problems are considered independently, it is possible to conclude that a set of classic policies founded on the principle of 'business as usual' will bring about improvement, whether the issue at hand is food security or economic development. Unfortunately, when demographic issues and climate change are added to the equation, it is 'highly probable that today's crisis risks turning into a colossal humanitarian calamity involving tens of millions of people.'[25]

Clearly, in geopolitical terms, the region is entering a highly turbulent phase, the conflict in Mali being only the beginning. We are, in fact, witnessing the progressive entanglement of localized crises and conflicts that have the potential to slip into a broader crisis, in the face of which we will all be helpless. At this point, it is useful to refer to a remarkable collection of texts compiled and published in 2013 by Jean-Pierre Vettovaglia, on the determining factors in conflicts, particularly to the pieces written by Vettovaglia himself, a Swiss diplomat who has given a great deal of thought to these issues.[26] For now, France has essentially mobilized its military resources. Its monitoring mechanism covers the entire Sahel band, from Mauritania to Chad, also including Djibouti. But France cannot police an immense area that faces masses of demographic, economic, political, social, and religious problems.

The French military intervention in Mali is just one episode that should help raise awareness among politicians and buy time to help Mali and neighbouring countries set up the structure and organization needed to tackle the challenges confronting them. At the regional level, the continuation of military efforts on the part of Algerian authorities and pacification/normalization of the situation in Libya are two important elements helping to stabilize the

[25] 'Crisis in the Sahel, possible solutions and the consequences of inaction', OASIS conference, Berkeley, April 2013.

[26] Jean-Pierre Vettovaglia, Bruylant (eds), Déterminants des Conflits et Nouvelles Formes de Prévention (Brussels, 2013). See, in particular, the article co-written by Vettovaglia and Philippe Hugon on the entanglement of determining factors in Africa ('Enchevêtrement des Déterminants en Afrique').

region. Particularly in Libya, however, nothing can be taken for granted, even if the international community were to intervene, as is sometimes rumoured—a possibility that could, moreover, end in disaster if poorly handled.

In any case, France's ability to contribute to the stabilization of the region cannot depend on military resources alone, especially since it can scarcely manage more than crackdown operations. How can France hope to pacify a territory of more than 5 million square kilometres (if we include Mauritania) with 4,000 men? Western forces in Afghanistan, numbering 150,000, have not managed to occupy a territory of 600,000 square kilometres, running into the same difficulties as the 120,000 Soviet soldiers who controlled only the urban centres of the country between 1979 and 1989.

The Soviets found themselves challenged by the Mujahedin not only throughout the rest of the country but even on the strategic routes, judging from the dozens of destroyed Russian tanks and armoured personnel carriers that I saw in 2002 along the length of the winding Salang Pass, the only road linking Kabul to the north of the country. So, what other tools of influence do we have in the Sahel? We have already mobilized our diplomatic resources, and we are almost certainly exercising political pressure, but the limits of such interventions are well known.

### Aid is another of the rare tools in the international toolbox that might help reduce instability.

In the end, there is not much left in our toolbox that might have a significant impact apart from international aid. There is a tendency to disparage aid and minimize its importance. It is true that at a global level, aid, amounting to around USD 140 billion per year, has become almost marginal compared to the private investment flowing into developing countries, which now exceeds USD 500 billion. Aid even accounts for significantly less than migrant remittances to less developed countries, which reached USD 441 billion in 2016. These figures, however, mask the significant role that aid still plays in the countries of the Sahel where, outside the oil and mining sectors, private investment is a very long time coming.

For the very poor countries of the Sahel, international aid still plays a major role. It usually represents between 8 to 12 per cent of their GDPs, approximately 60 to 90 per cent of their investment budgets, 60 to 70 per cent of their net external flows, and almost 40 per cent of their tax receipts. If properly targeted and managed, this funding can make a significant contribution to the economic development of the recipient countries by creating jobs for young people, improving the quality of social services, developing large-scale and small-scale infrastructure, and helping reinvigorate the rural economy—all important aspects in building social stability.

Such aid—and I stress again that it must be properly targeted and managed—can, in particular, help respond to two absolute emergencies in regions in difficulty: the need to provide jobs for idle or underemployed young people to reduce the temptation for them to join the ranks of traffickers associated with jihadi groups, and the need to reinvigorate the economy in the rural areas most affected by instability and underemployment. This is why rural development should be a priority.

The 'properly targeted and managed' aspect is critical because where they are poorly targeted and managed, these inflows of aid can actually have harmful effects. They can encourage dependent behaviour and exacerbate the resentment felt by the population towards both external donors and local political leaders, who are quickly accused of having 'stolen' international aid that does not meet the expectations and needs of the population. Moreover, where aid is excessive, as was the case in Afghanistan in 2008–09, when Western allies began to panic in the face of the progress made by the insurrection, it can have the same pernicious effect on fragile economies as oil revenue, provoking the Dutch-disease phenomenon that destroys the competitiveness of the local economy.

## Is the Sahel a cause for despair?

The list of problems facing all the nations of this region should not lead us to despair, but rather to sound the alarm not only in the countries of the Sahel and West Africa but also in France and Europe, which will be directly affected by the situation. The issue is a geopolitical one involving the shared interests among the Sahel, France, and Europe; it is not about charity. If poorly managed, these issues are likely to have a direct impact on our security by causing migration to Europe—and to France in particular—on a scale we have not yet witnessed. The situation is already serious enough in Syria, Iraq, Yemen, Somalia, Libya, Afghanistan, South Sudan, and Central Africa without adding the five or six French-speaking countries in the Sahel whose collapse would likely lead to the destabilization of the coastal nations, particularly Nigeria, Cameroon, and Cote d'Ivoire. There is a great deal that can be done over the next few years, however, to defer the reckoning and begin to address the key challenges.

Taking action on demographic trends is difficult, certainly, but it is possible. Strengthening government institutions is also difficult, but possible. So is stimulating small-scale farming so it can offer employment and reduce the destruction of soil and the process of desertification. Managing urban growth of 5 to 6 per cent a year is also difficult but possible. Promoting labour-intensive industries is complicated, but not impossible. In all of these areas, primary responsibility lies with the elites in the countries concerned. The scale of the problems is such, however, that without considerable financial, technical, political, and, in some cases, military support from the West, the chances of success are very slim.

The experience of the last 30 years has unfortunately shown that the outcomes produced by international aid in countries with limited administrative structure, or those that are emerging from conflict, leave a great deal to be desired. The case of Afghanistan, where the failure of aid has been glaring, sparks concern for the Sahel if the same old recipes and practices that have proved ineffective and even harmful in Afghanistan—as well as in DRC, Haiti, and elsewhere—are employed here.

If there is one thing that all the support, both civilian and military, provided by the West to Afghanistan since 2002 has illustrated, it is this: intervention that is badly conceived and aid that is poorly targeted and managed can easily become part of the problem rather than the solution. An analysis of the failure of Western aid and intervention in Afghanistan, symbolized by the almost complete withdrawal of international troops in 2015 without having achieved a single one of the strategic objectives intended to return peace to the country, cannot help but provide useful lessons for defining an effective strategy in the Sahel.

Building or rebuilding a fragile state is a difficult and complex thing to do; restoring security is a key element of any effective process in this area. Afghanistan, sadly, offers a dramatic counter-example, but one that is full of lessons if we analyse them seriously: negligence, business as usual, and incompetence in terms of aid—approaches that are known to be harmful, clumsy, and counterproductive in restoring security—and dogmatism in imposing a democratic model that is entirely unsuited to the country. Afghanistan clearly offers an example that merits analysis and review in the interests of the Sahel, as well as in our own interest.

# CHAPTER
# NINE

## Afghanistan—Lesson One: Security Cannot Be Entrusted for Long to Foreign Forces

### Should we view Afghanistan as a failure?

The Taliban has not yet settled in Kabul. Why should we then say that the West failed in Afghanistan? First, the recent decision of President Trump to send back US troops to Afghanistan is not a sign of success. Second, in reality, the objective of the Western intervention was threefold: liquidate Al-Qaida and remove the Taliban regime that sheltered it, install a peaceful democracy with a stable economy to prevent any return of the terrorists, and restore peace and security in this country.

### Has Al-Qaida disappeared?

The Al-Qaida, far from being liquidated, has withdrawn to the Northwest Territories in Pakistan, where jihadist groups have proliferated for 20 years. We know that it is now flourishing in Yemen and that one of its branches is very active in Syria, and another in Libya. It is certainly slowing down in global terms, but to the benefit of the ISIS, which seems even worse.[1]

This weakening of Al-Qaida should not be considered definitive. In 2015, Mullah Omar's[2] successor, Mullah Mansour, acknowledged the authority of the head of Al-Qaida, Ayman Al Zawahiri. Mullah Mansour was killed by a US drone in May 2016; his successor, Haibatullah Akhundzada, is a religious figure with limited military experience, and most of the power has apparently shifted to the son of Jalaluddin Haqqani, who was the main protector of Al-Qaida in Afghanistan from 1996 to 2001. Some observers even believe that Mullah Mansour's death has resulted in a de facto takeover of the Taliban movement by the Haqqani network, well known for its ruthlessness.[3] Several training grounds have recently been established by Al-Qaida in the south of Afghanistan, some of which were bombed by the US Air Force in October 2015. It is worth remembering that the presence of such training grounds was a key element in the US decision to intervene in Afghanistan in 2001.

### Has democracy been established?

Regarding the establishment of a peaceful democracy in Afghanistan, in the last presidential election, in 2014, massive fraud on both sides made it impossible to determine how many people had voted for each of the two candidates, and the breakdown of votes cast was not even published. Ultimately, enormous pressure imposed by the US helped achieve a negotiated solution—albeit a shaky one—after more than two months of discussions.

---

[1] Now, in 2018, it is interesting to re-read the forward-looking study produced in 2010 by the well-known British think tank, the International Institute for Strategic Studies, which concluded on a note of cautious optimism for 2015: Dodge, Toby and Nicholas Redman (eds), 'Afghanistan: To 2015 and Beyond', IISS, Routledge, 2011.

[2] Head of the Taliban, Mullah Omar died in 2013, but his death was made public only in 2015.

[3] This group was the first to launch kamikaze attacks in Afghanistan.

The new president, Ashraf Ghani, is quite a remarkable man, but the conditions under which he was elected have gravely undermined his legitimacy, and his deadlock with his main opponent, Abdullah Abdullah, appointed chief of staff with an uncertain mandate, is losing Ghani a lot of credit. Former President Karzai, who lives in a house he had built immediately adjacent to the presidential palace, is already scheming and possibly planning a return to power. He has no qualms about undermining the authority of his successor by criticizing some of his major political choices, such as the attempted rapprochement with Pakistan, despite its offering the best chance for any kind of political agreement with the Taliban.

Appointing the new government took seven months of laborious discussions and, again, strong pressure from the US. Almost ten months were lost between the second round of the presidential elections in July 2014 and the appointment of the government in the context of a dire budget situation, and a seriously worsening security context. As if Afghanistan could operate on automatic pilot like Belgium!

Finally, the government of national union which had been promised to John Kerry when he negotiated a way out of the political deadlock with Ghani and Abdullah has not been established. The constitution that should have been modified to take into account the setup of the position of chief of staff for Abdullah Abdullah has not been changed and the 'Loya Jirga', the grand assembly that was supposed to vet such change, has not met. Legislative elections that were supposed to take place in 2016 could not be organized due to insecurity. In such circumstances, opponents to the government consider that it has no legal basis.

### Has security been restored?

In terms of peacekeeping and the disappearance of the Taliban, in spite of more than USD 1 trillion in military spending solely on US troops, the Taliban's activities continue to expand. The rapid withdrawal of Western forces—which in late 2017 reached a low level of 13,000 troops (of which about 8,400 were American soldiers), compared with 132,000 in 2012—had left a hastily formed Afghan army to deal with a rebellion that shows no sign of giving up. The national army is seriously underequipped in terms of air support, artillery, tanks, and logistical resources. The White House's initial announcement of a total withdrawal by the end of 2016 can only have dashed the government's hopes and strengthened the Taliban's resolve not to enter into negotiations.

A report from the International Crisis Group on the subject,[4] published in May 2014, was already extremely disturbing. It highlighted the progress of the rebellion in most regions, including those that had previously remained calm. It also pointed to the Taliban's increased capacity for setting up operations involving large units, and an equivalent level of losses between Afghan and rebel forces, suggesting a balance between the two sides. One particularly disturbing symptom was that the Afghan army's losses in combat in 2014 alone were higher than the total losses suffered by Western troops between 2001 and 2014. Fighting over who would succeed Mullah Omar, the historic leader of the rebellion, has tended to aggravate rather than reduce the violence, and as of mid-2018, the situation has gone from bad to worse. The government has basically lost control of about one third of the rural districts and almost daily terrorist attacks in Kabul launched by both the Taliban and now ISIS take a heavy toll on both the civilian population, expatriates and the afghan security services.

In spite of the temporary occupation of the 300,000-inhabitant provincial capital Kunduz by the Taliban in October 2015 and again in October 2016,[5] the presence of about 14,000 US troops is denying the rebellion any hope of occupying Kabul. However, the Taliban strategy of territorial encroachment and controlling the roads will, if it continues, lead to some towns' being gradually cut off and able to receive supplies only by air. The governor of Kunduz has publicly acknowledged that he cannot travel out of the town. A Taliban takeover of a couple of provincial capitals and the inability of Afghan forces to take them back could have a domino effect.

In general, the military situation has been deteriorating since the withdrawal of foreign troops. The Taliban summer offensive

---

[4] 'Afghanistan's Insurgency after the Transition', ICG, 12 May 2014.
[5] US forces were needed to take back control of Kunduz.

in 2016 seriously dented the morale of the regular army, and the Taliban now seems to have full control of about 40 per cent of the countryside and about 35 per cent of the population. No road in the country is safe to travel. Even the heavily protected embassy district in Kabul was recently struck by a terrorist attack that killed 160 people and maimed about 500, triggering huge protest demonstrations in Kabul. Finally, in mid-2017 President Trump had to follow the Pentagon's advice and reluctantly send back first 3,000 troops to try and prevent several important provincial capitals from falling to the Taliban. About 6,000 thousand more are expected by mid-2018. An increasing US military presence in Afghanistan is clearly not a sign of success. And the balance of power has been made particularly precarious because funding, not only for the army but also for a sizable proportion of the state apparatus, is provided by Western countries.

## A collapsing war economy and a drip-fed budget

The regime is currently surviving on a drip-feed of external funding, and it is somewhat ironic that the man who, thirteen years ago—at the time a very lucid Minister of Finance—was the first to denounce the ineffectiveness, disorder, and abuse of aid in his country, is now so dependent on international funding. The security and economic situations are extremely concerning.

The progress achieved by Afghanistan in economic and social terms between 2002 and 2014 should not be underestimated. Economic growth was more than 9 per cent on average between 2003 and 2012, and gross domestic product (excluding the opium trade) doubled between 2007 and 2012, from USD 10 billion to USD 20 billion. Of course, the 2010 Kabul Bank scandal in which hundreds of millions of dollars disappeared after huge loans were given to the bank's main shareholders—including people with business and family links to President Karzai and vice president and strongman Fahim—demonstrated the fragility of the financial sector and the abysmal level of corruption in the upper levels of the government. Despite President Ashraf Ghani's efforts and IMF support, and in spite of the progress made in collecting taxes and managing public finances, the security efforts required against the rebellion are unsustainable in budget terms.

The country is so dependent on international aid that the very survival of the regime is in the hands of the West. Western countries are currently funding more than 50 per cent of budget spending, even though non-budget spending covered directly by donors is still considerable. It now appears that the remarkable growth in the economy depended mainly on the local effects of military spending and on civilian and military aid flows, which exceeded USD 15 billion in 2010—an amount equivalent to the Afghan GDP at the time.

Growth has collapsed with the departure of Western forces. Under these conditions, the economic forecasts produced by the World Bank in 2014 were already showing very high external funding requirements over the long term. The World Bank's assessment was that around 25 per cent of the Afghan GDP would be needed as budget support in future years—that is, around USD 7 billion to USD 8 billion, as early as 2016. As it turned out, those figures were unrealistic because they were based on highly optimistic growth assumptions, which proved wrong, and on a reduction in military personnel—in effect, implying a political agreement with the rebels that never materialized.

These funding requirements are marginal compared with past Western military spending. But aid budgets differ from military budgets, army salaries cannot be paid with promises, and history has demonstrated, in both Vietnam and Iraq, the US Senate's lack of enthusiasm once the US finds itself in a 'cut-and-run' situation.

Finally, such budget issues should not mask the huge challenge of creating jobs for the 400,000 young people arriving on the labour market each year, in a country where industry is negligible, services are collapsing, and agriculture is dependent on climatic conditions. We must, therefore, hope that Afghanistan can achieve a broad political consensus across the democratic spectrum, not only so it can move away from being ruled by warlords, factions, mafias, and corruption, but also to convince the West not to abandon the country.

## Disappointment on both sides

The great Western disappointment, a source of immense frustration and mistrust, stems from the fact that after 14 years of the

Karzai presidency, and in spite of international aid that reached colossal levels in some years, Afghanistan has not been able to build a credible administration, a reliable army, or a government capable of producing a serious development and post-conflict strategy. Hence the temptation for many Western countries to write it off as a bad deal and, now that most of the boys are back home, forget about Afghanistan and move on to something else.[6] President's Karzaï's responsibility for this state of affairs seems to be overwhelming. As mentioned by Carlotta Gall,[7] President Karzaï 'excelled at internal politicking but never had time nor interest for details on governance, rule of law, security. ... [H]e allowed some of the worst war criminals and mafia bosses access to power.... In the end he decided not to fight the strongmen and chose to tolerate the corruption that swelled to obscene proportions under his administration.'

But the disappointment is mutual, and the relationship between President Karzai and the Americans had deteriorated to such an extent by the end of his presidency that Karzaï—no doubt keen to rebuild his reputation as a nationalist patriot, and exasperated by criticism of the appalling level of corruption he was willing to tolerate—refused to sign the protocol needed to allow US troops to remain in Afghanistan.

One terrible symbol of failure was that, having emerged, for a while, from almost ten years of darkness, the lights went off again in Kabul in the winter of 2014–15. Arriving in the city at night by plane, one was struck by the fact that only the lights from traffic suggested Kabul was there. For years, the whole of Kabul had been dark because a major mafia warlord who headed the Ministry of Energy had dissuaded donors from investing seriously in this area.

---

[6] The progressive disillusionment felt by most Western ambassadors as they discover the complexity of the situation and the impasse their countries have unwisely gotten themselves into is superbly described by the former British ambassador Sherard Cowper-Coles in his book *Cables from Kabul, The Inside Story of the West's Afghanistan Campaign* (HarperCollins, 2011).

[7] Carlotta Gall, *The Wrong Enemy: America in Afghanistan, 2001–2014* (Mariner Books, 2014).

Although Kabul had finally been connected to the grid by about 2010, lack of maintenance allowed a series of pylons atop the Salang Pass to collapse under the weight of snow, cutting off the entire electricity supply to the capital. As ice and snow prevented equipment from being taken up the mountain for several months, many residents of Kabul spent the winter of 2015 using oil lamps or candles for light and warming themselves by burning old tires. The pollution caused by this and the thousands of small generators running in more affluent neighbourhoods was appalling.

Given the colossal scale of the military and financial efforts of the Western coalition, here is the billion-dollar question: why such a failure, with Western forces leaving before the enemy had been destroyed, without a stable regime able to stand on its own two feet with a healthy economy being established, and without the opium trade being eradicated?

## Afghanistan in 2001 was not Côte d'Ivoire in 2011!

First of all, it is important to draw a distinction between 'failed' states, in ruins and severely damaged, and states that have been through periods of conflict and very severe crises but have kept their state apparatus relatively intact. The latter was clearly the situation in Côte d'Ivoire, where, as noted previously, green spaces were still being maintained in Abidjan although the country had been split in two. In these cases, reconstruction is effectively a problem of political stabilization and 'good' economic policies, which help bring back private investment. I have already referred to the rapid economic growth that occurred once the conflict between the 'two presidents of Côte d'Ivoire' ended in 2011 and reasonable policies reintroduced with the arrival of the Ouattara government.

In 'failed' states, however, the situation is altogether different. The social situation is appalling, the economy is paralysed, and the public administration has practically disappeared. This was the situation in Cambodia in 1979, in the Democratic Republic of the Congo and in Afghanistan in 2001, and in South Sudan and Somalia today. We are now witnessing the collapse of Syria, Iraq, Yemen, the Central African Republic, South Sudan, north-eastern Nigeria, northern Cameroon, and Libya, among others, and may well be witnessing Mali's collapse tomorrow. The obvious concern now is that countries in the Sahel do not also tip into chaos, with the risk that they will drag with them the northern parts of countries on the Gulf of Guinea, and thus destabilize the whole of West Africa. These situations are regional, or even global, problems that present the international community with challenges it does not know how to tackle.

Over the last 15 years, having long neglected these issues, Western countries have taken steps to try to restore long-term security in countries such as these, to relaunch their economies, and to mitigate the terrible destitution faced by the people living there. The World Bank made this the theme of its World Development Report in 2011.[8] Yet, in spite of the considerable political, financial, economic, technical, and military efforts made—costing tens of billions of dollars—the results of Western interventions and the aid they have provided to severely damaged countries remain fairly distressing. Is it because their military interventions were poorly designed or their aid poorly managed or poorly targeted?

Insofar as Afghanistan is, by far, the country that has benefited most from the support of the international donor community, we should seek out and learn the lessons of our failed interventions there before we pour additional billions into the Sahel.

## Reconstructing a 'failed' state emerging from conflict requires more than promises.

It would be unreasonable to assign primary responsibility for the general deterioration of the situation in Afghanistan to international aid. Corruption under President Karzai's regime reached, as we already mentioned, levels unequalled since Mobutu's reign in the Congo. In a context where a mafia system corrupts most institutions, the ambitions of the Pakistani army and its special branch, the ISI, to control Afghanistan has certainly been a key element. This is the main message of Carlotta Gall's book, already quoted. But neither should we underestimate the responsibility of

---

[8] *World Development Report: Conflict, Security and Development,* World Bank, 2011.

the George W. Bush administration or that of the whole international donor community in the collective failure in Afghanistan.

First, let's be clear about one thing: there is no miracle solution in these circumstances. But it does now seem clear that applying the usual procedures and working methods quickly leads to an impasse. A legitimate question is whether sufficient financial efforts were made to reconstruct the country. We know that a lot of announcements of aid do not necessarily materialize in practice.

As far as Afghanistan is concerned, it is important to distinguish 2002–07 from the period that followed. During the 'relatively calm' period of 2002–06, before the security situation seriously deteriorated under the major Taliban offensives in the summer of 2006 and 2007, which threatened Kandahar in the south of the country, the role of aid in its various forms (humanitarian, economic and financial, technical, institutional, and so on) could have been crucial. During the post-2007 period, however, aid efficiency declined rapidly in response to the increase in insecurity. During the initial period of just over five years, the commitments made by donors were considerable, reaching USD 25 billion in civilian aid alone.

Although much lower than military spending—around USD 130 billion over this period for the United States alone[9]—it was still a colossal figure. When I recently cited this USD 25 billion figure to the Prime Minister of the Democratic Republic of the Congo, he was taken aback at the sheer scale of it. Indeed, at the time, it equalled some five years' worth of aid provided by the World Bank to the whole of Sub-Saharan Africa. Afghanistan, alone, was promised an amount identical to that received from the World Bank by 48 African countries!

The actual amount of civilian aid disbursed over this period was lower—slightly less than USD 15 billion. The difference between the USD 25 billion announced and the USD 15 billion disbursed caused a controversy when the figures were released, with some taking the view that the missing USD 10 billion had been 'stolen.'

[9] We should note that in 2008 alone, US military spending in Iraq was over USD 140 billion, or more than six years' worth of military spending in Afghanistan, which is a clear indication of where its priorities lay.

This was not the case. The money probably was simply caught up in the financial 'pipeline,' moving slowly through the inevitably convoluted bureaucratic machinery. It was probably spent over the next few years.

Returning to the question of the quality of aid, there are several aspects to consider.

## Timely money, correctly used ...

### Beware the vagaries of 'tied' aid.

Most aid to Afghanistan in 2002–07 was of US origin, a fair proportion from the Pentagon, and was 'tied,' meaning it could only be used to buy Afghan or American goods and services. In this case, the resources were mainly used to pay major American firms (such as Halliburton, of which Vice President Cheney had long served as president), which operated as prime contractors, and subcontracted a wide variety of tasks to other companies, either in the US or Pakistan which, in turn, subcontracted to Afghan businesses created specifically for this purpose, and so on.

The result? It is probably fair to say that around a third of this aid was likely used to pay the abnormally high margins associated with most operations with a marked lack of transparency. As a consequence, in the six years during which one might have hoped that international aid would be particularly effective, neither USD 25 billion nor USD 15 billion, but rather the equivalent of around USD 10 billion of 'real' aid was probably disbursed, or somewhat less than USD 1.7 billion a year. This proved completely inadequate for rebuilding a country that is larger than France and whose road, urban, and energy infrastructure was in ruins.

### Timing is everything when mobilizing funds.

Putting resources in place between 2002 and 2007 was therefore a very laborious process. Compared to that sum of around USD 10 billion over six years, aid in both 2010 and 2011 exceeded Afghanistan's GDP at the time—that is, around USD 15 billion.[10]

---

[10] How can aid reach the same level as GDP without increasing the latter accordingly? Quite simply because aid is calculated based on the

At that time, however, the insurgency was on such a scale that development efforts were almost paralyzed. Of course, half the aid provided was to support the Afghan army, while strictly civilian aid was 'only' USD 7 billion to USD 8 billion. But this still equalled about 50 per cent of the Afghan GDP. These excessive amounts were paid too late for the funds to be used effectively. They resulted in a significant level of waste and prompted severe distortions in the local economy.

If a fire breaks out, a single, carefully aimed hose might be able to put it out when it first starts; but once it has turned into a major blaze, even mobilizing all the firefighters in the region might not be enough to bring it under control. The problem is the same for development aid in a context of increasing insecurity. It is futile, and can even be harmful, to sprinkle aid on a region in flames, as Afghanistan was after 2008/10—in other words, once the fire had spread. It can be harmful because providing too much aid can trigger the notorious condition known as 'Dutch disease,' which strangles the economy.

The difficulty is that donors are initially not inclined to abandon old habits, which dictate that resources be allocated, as a priority, to well-managed 'good pupils' They have to wait until Western political leaders come to fear the deteriorating situation and finally exert strong political pressure, which is the only way of significantly increasing aid. But, by then, as we have seen in Afghanistan, it is too late.

### Beware poor management of technical assistance.

In addition to financial support, Afghanistan has also benefited from a significant amount of technical support for running its administration and public corporations, and preparing and supervising investment programmes. In 2007, Afghan authorities raised concerns about the abnormally high cost of the technical assistance

---

records of the expenditures borne by donors. Yet, much of this spending includes various margins and takes place in the donor's own country, so it bears little relation to the financial flows actually transferred and spent locally.

provided and its cost–effectiveness. They asked me to carry out an audit, which revealed that spending on technical assistance, which was often difficult to identify, amounted to some USD 500 million a year throughout this period, an amount equal to twice the annual budget for civil service salaries. This also meant that, of the USD 10 billion in 'actual' aid received over a six-year period, about 30 per cent was related to technical assistance.

The analysis also revealed the exorbitant margins earned by consulting firms, which billed for their 'experts' at four or five times their actual cost; the inability of authorities to control technical assistance and get it working properly; messy power struggles among firms; and, most serious of all, the systematic influx of the least-qualified experts into a country that was incapable of monitoring what they did![11]

### Target aid effectively.

We will see later on that it is essential to use these resources to finance well-defined, strategic priorities and that it cannot be left solely to donors, who are guided by their public opinion or political objectives in their own countries, to assess how resources should be allocated. For instance, in the situation Afghanistan found itself in, in 2001, was the immediate priority to build schools, as all the donors rushed to do?

## The population's main desire is for day-to-day security.

Experience gathered in 'failed' states and/or countries emerging from conflict shows that the population's main desire is for security. This is the top priority, even ahead of access to food and health care. The key error committed by the Bush administration was to ignore this point and subcontract the issue, in 2002 and 2003, to the Northern Alliance forces and to the 'commanders' who had previously supported the Taliban and then switched sides. In 2001, the CIA and the Pentagon had given them broad

[11] I do not, of course, include in this category those with an untiring affection for the country who continue, and will continue, to work there in spite of all the difficulties and risks.

responsibility for conducting the military operations that helped defeat the Taliban, and they, similarly, subcontracted to the 'commanders' most issues of security and local administration from 2002 on.

It should be noted that US leaders had their sights firmly set on Iraq. They therefore left just 8,000 men in charge of security for a country of then 30 million inhabitants. Moreover, they initially restricted the NATO security mandate represented by the International Security Assistance Force (ISAF) to the city of Kabul.[12] The ratio of international forces to population was therefore around 1 per 3,750 inhabitants. Though this in itself is deceptive, given that the forces' mandate was not to ensure the security of the population but to pursue Al-Qaida. I recall that the same ratio was indeed 1 to 40 at the end of the war in Kosovo, 1 to 112 at the end of the conflict in East Timor, and 1 to 205 at the end of the war in Bosnia.

The transfer of power to both minor and leading warlords, some of whom were notorious criminals, recreated the type of mafia system that had plunged the whole of Afghanistan into chaos in 1992 after the collapse of the Najibullah regime.[13] The resulting disorder had already made it easier for the Taliban to conquer the country. Instead of supporting the creation of a modern state, this practice helped to strengthen a Merovingian-type power system that was actually a step backwards compared to the relative 'order' brought by the Taliban in institutional terms.

*International military intervention is common and sometimes badly needed.*

It is quite astounding that no attempt was made in 2002 to establish an international peacekeeping force along with a temporary

---

[12] The book by US ambassador James F. Dobbin, who had supervised reconstruction efforts in Bosnia and Kosovo and was sent to Afghanistan to help form a government in November 2001, is damning about George W. Bush's administration, which was entirely preoccupied by its adventures in Iraq.

[13] Najibullah had been installed by the Soviets shortly before they left the country.

civilian administration and adequate financial resources, to launch an initial emergency stabilization and reconstruction programme. But what did we do in Libya after we had bombed Gaddafi's supporters to pieces? Such negligence goes against all the experience of post–conflict resolution gained during the twentieth century. We have previously noted that failed states are generally marked by a deterioration of security and the disappearance of any form of sovereign authority (justice, police, local administration, et cetera.), starting with the peripheral regions.

As we previously explained, this collapse in the state apparatus quickly leads to the emergence of militias, which raise taxes, take over the failing state apparatus, and strip it of its legitimacy. Let's not forget that, apart from the exceptional case of the Antarctic, there is no area of the world where a particular power does not exercise control. The disappearance of the state simply means that other powers have taken its place. The change in Libya over the last six years is, therefore, not surprising. In Afghanistan, the Taliban regime had at least largely broken or controlled the mafias and provided security, and a degree of (admittedly cursory) justice throughout the part of the country it controlled. Its collapse, combined with Western shortcomings in terms of security and local administration, resulted in the failure of the Afghan state.

From 2004 on, as the situation began to deteriorate—due as much to the crime, racketeering, vendettas, settling of old scores, and acts of violence committed by minor warlords, as to the return of the Taliban, who took advantage of the chaos—the Western coalition tried to implement its own military response to restore security, initially using US forces from 'Operation Enduring Freedom,' who acted along strict military lines and bore the brunt of the war effort in the first few years.

*Foreign soldiers are quickly seen as an occupation force.*

ISAF forces were mobilized as the conflict spread. Like others before them, they demonstrated a fairly significant level of ignorance of local cultural sensitivities and made extensive use of air power to save the lives of their own troops. The collateral damage obviously helped alienate Afghanistan's rural population and fed the Taliban's very skilful propaganda,[14] with the result that the foreign soldiers were soon locally regarded as an occupation force.

The military was aware of these problems and the inadequacy of a purely military approach, but also of humanitarian and development needs at the local level, prompting its leaders to examine the situation in detail. They sought support from international aid agencies, which is no easy task in an insecure environment. Aid agencies are reluctant to endanger their own staff while NGOs, which sometimes accept high levels of risk, lack the resources to have a significant impact.

Keen to 'win hearts and minds,' echoing the terminology of the Vietnam War, the various foreign contingents[15] in Afghanistan set up an ambitious civilian-military programme with a significant development component, the 'Provincial Reconstruction Teams' or PRT programme. Insofar as it is a fairly traditional approach in this context—not dissimilar to the 'Sections Administrative Spéciales' (SAS) established by the French army during the Algerian war of independence—it might be useful to analyse the performance of this type of programme.[16]

### Foreign soldiers cannot provide a long-term response to local demand for development.

The conclusions we can now draw from the action of these 'reconstruction' teams is very disappointing. The aim of these units was twofold: to provide a military presence on the ground to protect the actions of the development agencies; but also to run small development activities directly, with funding from military budgets. Contrary to the official declarations, when I interviewed officials from the major aid agencies in Kabul in private in the late 2000s and early 2010s, they felt that these programmes should

[14] Cf. the remarkable study by Gilles Dorronsoro: 'The Taliban's Winning Strategy in Afghanistan', Carnegie Endowment for International Peace, Washington, 2009.

[15] But not France, which set up a programme based on the involvement of the AFD in the zones for which it was responsible, particularly in Kapisa.

[16] A similar approach is being considered for northern Mali.

either be radically reoriented or put to bed. They continued, however, for reasons related largely to the foreign forces' communications policies. What else could be shown to visiting officials? A
school, needless to say, is more presentable than Taliban corpses.

Most notable, perhaps, was the extent of amateurism[17] on the
part of soldiers, who had plenty of goodwill but no experience
in development work. The fact that they came from 13 different
countries also meant that they took 13 different approaches. They
generally took over from each other every six months and tended
to operate in silos, with no opportunity to share their experiences.
The intervention came too late and only moved up to full gear in
2009–10—much too late, given that both the level of insecurity
and the political situation had reached dramatic proportions.[18] In
addition, serious consideration was never given to whether projects would be viable once the Western forces had left.

The initial failings were gradually corrected, particularly by
the Canadians, the British, and, above all, the Americans, once
General Petraeus took control of the US Central Command
covering Afghanistan in 2008. Structured civilian technical teams
were then recruited and provided considerable resources in 2010
and 2011. But once again, the timing was poor and the aid arrived
too late; the deteriorating security situation led many of the PRTs
into a 'bunker' mentality, limiting their willingness to venture
outside their fortified bases.

*Foreign soldiers cannot respond to administrative needs or the de-
mand for better local governance.*

It was not possible to correct the other major defects of this
approach, given the nature of the operations. The PRTs were
obviously incapable of meeting the population's demands for better governance at the local level. Constant complaints concerning

---

[17] See the very lucid analysis: Barbara J. Stapleton, 'A Means to What
Ends? Why PRTs are Peripheral to the Bigger Political Challenges in
Afghanistan', *Journal of Military and Strategic Studies*, Autumn 2007.

[18] The budget for development activities by the US PRTs was just
USD 52 million in 2004 out of a total authorised US aid budget of more
than USD 2 billion.

the lack of justice, acts of violence perpetrated by the police, and corruption among district leaders simply had to be ignored. Western soldiers, even if they were informed about life in the villages, could not get involved in resolving local problems, particularly once an embryonic local administration was in place, even one that lacked resources.

Above all, the actions of the PRTs, like the actions of a fair proportion of the main donors, were not in any way coordinated with Afghan institutions. Their activities were developed in isolation from the local budget processes being implemented and without consultation about regional priorities defined by local authorities. The PRTs' response to the systematic failings of Afghan institutions was simply to take over, which actually made Afghan institutions weaker in practice.

### Anticipation is essential.

This remark does not constitute a criticism, because there is no simple procedure for conducting development activities in an insecure environment. These areas usually fall under humanitarian aid, which is another field entirely and is extremely difficult to implement in this type of context.[19] An initial conclusion is therefore that, regarding development programmes, *anticipation is essential.* For instance, it is important to intervene as early as possible, before, or as soon as, signs of security deterioration begin to manifest, and certainly before the situation gets out of control. This is a lesson that needs to be carefully considered for the Sahel. If PRTs had been established much earlier, between 2002 and 2005, they might have constituted a provisional solution while capable Afghan institutions were built over three or four years and international aid programs were implemented. As it happened, their introduction, and efforts to move them up a gear, came too late.

The PRTs also turned into permanent mechanisms, at least until the departure of the Western forces. Given the weakness

---

[19] Readers interested in the lessons that can be learned from the Afghan conflict about managing international humanitarian aid might want to refer to Pierre Micheletti's book *Afghanistan, gagner les cœurs et les esprits* (Presses Universitaires de Grenoble/RFI, 2014).

of institutional progress in the Afghan countryside, most of the activities PRTs were supporting ended in 2013 and 2014, when the Western forces withdrew. The PRTs' mission had remained unclear, but would undoubtedly have gained from focusing on support for the Afghan institutions being created. In particular, the PRTs could have provided technical support and funding for the provincial bodies being established—not only the provincial development committees, but also the Community Development Councils established by the Ministry of Rural Reconstruction and Development. By largely ignoring these institutions, the approach taken contributed, once again, to their marginalization.

## Not in Roosevelt's league ...

President George W. Bush had clearly forgotten that in 1945, his great predecessors Presidents Roosevelt and Truman had carefully planned the re-establishment of the German and Japanese administrations, in particular the sovereign bodies, once they had been cleared of their Nazi and militarist elements. They had even planned the administration of France in 1944, to the fury of General de Gaulle.

Any serious reflection (as Secretary of State Colin Powell had engaged in, albeit to no avail) would have shown that the demand for security and local administration was clearly the first priority for a population traumatized by more than 20 years of warfare. One of the first demands was the rapid creation of a national police force, a national army, local justice, territorial administration, and—given the disastrous state of the countryside after the destruction wrought by the Soviets—a dedicated Ministry of Reconstruction and Development.

But, because it would take a minimum of three or four years to create such institutions, a temporary PRT system had to be established for the transition period as a matter of urgency, and be very well-resourced both technically and financially to address the most serious shortcomings. All of this meant mobilizing significant military and civilian resources. Conversely, the role of the temporary administrative system should be to support the national and local institutions being created and then, ultimately, it would be dissolved; under no circumstances was it intended to replace them.

In fact, it is clear that in Afghanistan—though the same was also true in Iraq[20]—the Bush administration reacted to events instead of planning its actions on the basis of serious analysis, thus gradually reinventing a counter-insurgency process more than 30 year after Vietnam. The situation is all the more shocking given that Colin Powell was acutely aware of these questions, yet—highly lucid but powerless—had to watch as the disaster unfolded. Clearly G.W. Bush was no Roosevelt.

We must accept the reluctance of the Bush administration vis-à-vis the general reconstruction of the Afghan system of government. But, considerable sums were also allocated to the reconstruction of the Afghan national army. How is it that Western forces had to support the bulk of the military effort until 2013–14?

## One, two, buckle my shoe: Who wants to fund the Afghan army?

A new Afghan army was created with considerable US support and grew after 2004 at the instigation of the Minister of Defence, Wardak. Until 2009–10, however, its size was entirely out of step with the security challenges it faced. Until 2005 and the UN-led disarmament programme, the forces of certain warlords, such as those of 'General' Fahim (who was also Minister of Defence at the time)[21] and 'General' Dostum (Ashraf Ghani's fellow candidate in the 2014 presidential elections, present Vice president... and now key opponent!), were also much larger and better equipped than the national army, even in terms of heavy weapons. At the time, militias under the main warlords comprised about 100,000 fighters. Much criticism was voiced at that time regarding the UN disarmament programme, as these 100,000 fighters lost their jobs overnight and found themselves without resources, a situation not dissimilar to the dismissal of the army and the policy of 'de-Baathification' in Iraq in 2003. A sound approach would have

[20] On the failure in Iraq, I would recommend: Thomas E. Ricks, *Fiasco, The American Military Adventure in Iraq* (Penguin, 2006).

[21] And President Karzai's fellow candidate in the 2009 presidential elections!

been to implement the disarmament programme progressively in order to integrate, over time, these 100,000 men into the new army.

The national army was arbitrarily limited to some 30,000 men because neither the United States nor any donors were willing to make a long-term commitment to funding it. Its size was, therefore, based from the outset not on security needs, which could easily be estimated based on international comparisons, but on what US analysts viewed as the future financial capacity of the Afghan budget. As it turned out, it took time to reach the objective of 30,000 men; in 2006, only 14,000 men had been trained and were very thinly stretched across the territory. In this respect, US support could hardly be viewed as serious.[22] In 2005, for example, Rumsfeld refused a request that Minister Wardak increase the size of the army to 70,000 men.[23] At one point, the United States even wanted the cost of the army to be covered out of the Afghan budget, causing panic in the Ministry of Finance, where I was working at the time—in time, the US changed its mind.

The result: operational forces barely numbered 57,000 men in 2007. It was not until the arrival of General Petraeus to head the US Central Command in 2008 that reason was restored and an urgent programme to construct a modern army of the right strength was launched in 2009–10. Between 2009 and 2014, the number of troops increased from 60,000 to around 240,000; combined with the police force, the aim was have a total of 352,000 men serving from 2014 on. We should note that in 2012, shortly after the departure of Petraeus and following the unexpected death of Richard Holbrooke,[24] who had experience of Vietnam, US authorities began to work on rapid reduction

[22] After the departure in 2003 of General Eikenberry, who was initially responsible for coordinating US support for the army, US Air Force generals took up the reins despite having no skills whatsoever in this field.

[23] At the same time, while the Taliban was starting to establish its political infrastructure in the south of the country, Rumsfeld was transferring about 1,000 US soldiers to Iraq.

[24] President Obama's special envoy for Afghanistan and Pakistan.

scenarios for the security forces for 2016–17, clearly in order to create savings.

After so much time had been lost, however, the increase in numbers was too fast for the quality of the institution. Between 2006 and 2009, morale in the Afghan military was seriously affected by the general deterioration in security. Since 2013, it has also been deeply shaken by the announcement of US disengagement, logistical failings, the lack of air support, the absence of an effective system for evacuating the wounded, and threats against troops' families by the Taliban. Given these circumstances, few Pashtuns now come forward to volunteer, and the army is losing its role as an interethnic melting pot.

The most serious issue throughout the period from 2002 to 2012 was that the ISAF's Western armies had to bear almost all the military effort as the Taliban made headway. In doing so, they gradually became an occupation force in the eyes of the population—bombing and searching houses, offending the sensibilities of a population whose culture was profoundly alien to them, and thus feeding the Taliban's skilful propaganda, but without ever reaching the critical mass needed to occupy the country. As in Vietnam, they won almost all the battles, but clearly lost the war.

## Three, four, knock at the door: Who would like to tackle the Augean stables of the Afghan police?

Although the task of reforming security-sector institutions is crucial, it does not fall within the purview of the major multilateral aid institutions, such as the World Bank. Bilateral aid is generally sought to tackle these issues.[25] Even this has proved incapable, however, of meeting the challenges in Afghanistan. The police force, which was in a catastrophic state in 2008,[26] has

[25] Multilateral aid agencies, such as the World Bank or Asian Development Bank, are subject to strict intervention rules developed a long time ago, which exclude spending on security from their field of action. Conversely, bilateral aid agencies, which depend on the political authorities in each donor country, are much more flexible in this respect.

[26] The Economist Intelligence Unit report on Afghanistan in October 2008 stated, 'The state of the police is abysmal.'

improved only marginally since then. In June 2015, for example, the International Crisis Group published a devastating article on the behaviour and lack of discipline of the Afghan police and the lack of any clear distinction between police forces, militias, and simple bandits.[27]

Germany, which had initially been tasked with restoring order in the police force but had not assessed the scale of the problem, limited its involvement to providing training and equipment to an organization that needed to be rebuilt from scratch, starting with the clearing out of almost all its senior personnel. The United States began to grow concerned about the problem in 2004 in response to increasing complaints about the police. But Rumsfeld refused to support the request from Interior Minister Jalali for a 'clean-up of the government, the Ministry of the Interior, and the administration.' It should be noted that Jalali's request was opposed by President Karzai, who was keen not to endanger his alliances with the warlords and local 'commanders'.[28]

As there is no national gendarmerie or federal police force in the United States likely to provide this type of institutional support, it subcontracted the job of supporting the police force to a private security company (DynCorp), which specialized in aircraft maintenance(!), had no experience with this type of work, and whose main concern was to fulfil its obligations under a profitable technical assistance contract. In the end, various US administrations argued over who should supervise the operation.

It was only in 2008, six years too late, and under international pressure, that the Herculean task began. But the rapid removal of Minister Hanif Atmar, who had been tasked with this extremely difficult job late in the reconstruction process, and the lack of political will at the highest level, meant that the work was not undertaken with the necessary vigour. Threatening the upper hierarchy of the ministry of interior and the police as Hanif Atmar tried indeed meant threatening powerful people close to the Presidency. Once again, precious years were lost.

[27] Graeme Smith, 'US funded Afghan police prey on those they are paid to protect', *Reuters*, 15 June 2015, ICG.

[28] This refusal led to Minister Jalali's resignation and exile to the United States in 2005.

Mafias and 'commanders' still make the law outside areas controlled by the Taliban.

For its part, the territorial administration suffered from a shortage of financial and human resources, disorganization, corruption at the Ministry of the Interior to which it was attached, and the nepotism that governed the selection of leaders. It was only partially taken back in hand in 2007, when it was removed from the Ministry of the Interior, converted into a separate organization (the Independent Directorate of Local Governance), and entrusted to a serious executive coming from the NGO sector, Jelani Popal.

Under President Karzai's regime, the selection of local leaders, governors, and district heads was rarely based on competence.[29] The human and financial resources of the Directorate of Local Governance were also limited. Consequently, now that the PRTs have withdrawn, actions by local governments are hampered by the deterioration in security, the corruption of many officials, and the harmful role played by the 'strongmen,' 'commanders,' and mafia-like gang leaders with whom Karzai's regime entered into opportunistic alliances.

International experience can help define the ratio of security personnel to population needed to improve security in a country at risk of a resurgence of civil war, as was manifestly the case in Afghanistan in the 2000s. This ratio is around one security officer (police, military, or militiaman) per 50 to 100 inhabitants—or a total of 300,000 to 600,000 for a country such as Afghanistan. This figure is in line with the target set by Petraeus in 2008 and the number of army and police officers put on duty in Algeria during the civil war that began in 1993, when the Algerian population was roughly equivalent to that of Afghanistan's. Similar numbers existed in the Iraqi security services (army and police) that collapsed under the onslaught from IS in 2014.[30]

[29] Rumours about district head positions going to the highest bidder were rife in Kabul.

[30] An interesting research paper was recently published to try to determine the optimal size of the Malian army: Stéphane Kader Bombote, 'Quel effectif pour les forces de sécurité du Mali', November 2015, which confirms these estimates.

It is clear that unless the country's mining reserves can be exploited—which is doubtful given the current security context—the Afghan budget will never be able to support these expenses at this level. The refusal by the international community to help establish an adequate security apparatus goes a long way toward explaining the current situation. The Obama administration and General Petraeus rediscovered these realities in 2008, as the Nixon administration had done 40 years earlier, following the Tet Offensive in 1968. But the US had missed the opportunity provided by four to five years of relative peace from 2002 to 2006, to establish these institutions properly. As a result, the Taliban became such a political and military force that the future is very worrying and a cause of deep anxiety for the Afghan population.

A similar situation can be found today in the Democratic Republic of the Congo. Since 2002, the international community has preferred to continue the costly funding of the 16,000 demotivated soldiers[31] deployed with the United Nations MONUSCO force in the DRC, rather than take the necessary steps to strengthen the country's state apparatus. The stability of the DRC is, therefore, still threatened by the lack of discipline and disorganization of its army, which was created by combining multiple militias and bands of looters, the aim being to bring them together to reduce their intrinsic harmfulness. MONUSCO's discipline and commitment in combat were so mediocre that until 2014,[32] it was unable to establish even a minimum level of order in Kivu. However, of course, President's Kabila's quite special governance and disregard of the DRC constitution would have made this option of international support to build the Congolese army politically unrealistic.

---

[31] It is the countries that supply the troops, rather than the unfortunate soldiers, that pocket the tidy sums paid by the United Nations.

[32] It took the mobilization of a new brigade made up partly of South African soldiers, with combat helicopters, to (partially) resolve the problem.

# CHAPTER
# TEN

# Afghanistan—Lesson Two:
# Aid Agencies Cannot Be Left
# to Do as They Like

## Did donors follow a common, carefully considered intervention strategy?

There were clearly doubts and incoherence in the West, particularly the US, concerning the best way to restore security in Afghanistan. As we have already seen, the fundamental errors were over-reliance on the Western armed forces, not having taken steps quickly enough to create a national army and police force able to deal with the security issues in question, and the failure to rebuild local sovereign institutions. The Bush administration began by sending in the US Army before it had thought through the options.

It is, in this regard, telling that the US Marines, deployed in 2009, chose their own intervention area, Southern Helmand, where the fighting was particularly violent, and built their base there without conferring with the International Security Assistance Force (ISAF) commander-in-chief, even though he was American.[1] By opting for a mainly desert area—home to less than 1 per cent of the Afghan population—where they could make the best use of their firepower, they were at odds with the new doctrine of counter-insurgency defined by General Petraeus, who demanded protection for civilians, which meant prioritizing intervention in densely populated areas. This aside, moving on...

With military coordination already lacking, consultation between civilians and armed forces was also limited. No serious concern was expressed for the necessary interlinkages among the three most urgent tasks, namely establishing security, maintaining it, and building the state apparatus. The military was involved in either 'peacekeeping' or 'warfare,' and civilians did not dare get involved with questions concerning sovereign institutions, which fell outside their usual area of competence. According to Carlotta Gall, General Richard, who took command of NATO forces in Afghanistan in 2006, considered 'the lack of coordination among the Afghan government, the foreign military and western donors as anarchy'.[2]

In fact, until General Petraeus arrived, there were no clear, common objectives in Afghanistan; some forces were busy 'killing bad boys' (to use the terminology of the time), while others were working to combat poverty. But the military was not alone in terms of shortcomings: did the major aid agencies have a common strategy? Were their activities implemented as part of a clear strategic vision, under the authority of a clearly identified leader, aimed at fulfilling relevant and carefully chosen objectives?

It is important to remember that aid is effective when its actions are concentrated, and efforts coordinated in specific areas by all sides. It is not by chance that the number of pupils enrolled in schools in Afghanistan increased from less than one million to more than nine million—including almost four million girls—between 2002 and 2014, or that significant progress was made in terms of public health. However, it is also true that much of this progress is quantitative rather than qualitative—the quality of

---

[1] Ahmed Rashid, *Pakistan on the Brink: The Future of America, Pakistan, and Afghanistan* (Viking, 2012).
[2] Carlotta Gall, *The wrong enemy: America in Afghanistan, 2001-2014* (Mariner Books, 2014).

teaching still leaves a lot to be desired, a situation not dissimilar to that found in Niger or Mali.

Although laudable efforts have led to encouraging results in the field of education, the allocation of aid has clearly not corresponded to the most obvious priorities, either by sector or by geographical area.

## Was anyone in control of international aid?

The lack of strategic management of aid was manifest first in the marked lack of coherence in allocations of aid resources at the sector level. For example, about 75 per cent of the Afghan population lived in rural areas at that time. Yet, of the USD 15 billion actually disbursed between 2002 and the end of 2007 (a third of which, remember, most likely represented costs and margins which are difficult to class as actual aid), just USD 500 million was spent in the agriculture sector. General Petraeus, with whom I discussed this matter when he gave a lecture at Sciences Po in Paris in late 2010, was very open in recognizing the problem. He assured me that spending on civilian aid in rural areas of Afghanistan, at the time, stood at more than USD 800 million a year. But once again, what a waste of time!

In a country of fairly arid lands, where rain is often unpredictable and the amount of land available for cultivation limited, water management is essential for farmers. Irrigation is as important in Afghanistan as it might be in Niger or Burkina Faso. Yet, in Afghanistan, not only has the development of traditional networks not kept pace with demographic growth, but many of them were destroyed or very severely damaged by the scorched-earth policy practiced on a large scale by the Soviets. This has been aggravated by a dramatic lack of maintenance over the last 20 years. By 2003, the World Bank considered that the irrigated area represented only a third of that available in 1993 (following the destruction caused by the Soviets) and that residual areas were functioning at only a quarter of their capacity, with the presence of Soviet mines adding to the difficulties of rehabilitation.

Except for the World Bank, which funded a remarkable rehabilitation programme that began in 2003, and subsequently attracted several tranches of additional funding, there was a general lack of enthusiasm for small-scale irrigation among donors, though this is essentially what sustains villages in the valley bottoms. The reason for this is perfectly understandable—it has to do with the technical difficulty of rehabilitating thousands of small structures dispersed throughout the mountains. Overall, donors preferred to concentrate their interventions on rehabilitating or extending large and medium-sized facilities that affected broader areas.

## The lack of donor efforts in agriculture has been a shame in Afghanistan; it is still a shame in the Sahel.

I cannot criticize my colleagues for this—if I'd been faced with the same choice, I undoubtedly would have done the same as they did. But, rather than being given the choice, they should have been pressured to try to rehabilitate as many small hydraulics schemes as possible as quickly as possible. This was feasible until 2006–07, after which the increasing level of insecurity made this type of work extremely dangerous in many regions. Even so, the World Bank, multiple NGOs, a number of donors, and the Provincial Reconstruction Teams (PRTs) have continued efforts in this area, though their plans have often been paralyzed by insecurity. Reading the World Bank's irrigation project completion report sends shivers up the spine as successive incidents are described (with the inimitable detachment characteristic of the administrative style of the institution), providing, in passing, the names of construction staff members who were kidnapped and, in most cases, killed.

In spite of these efforts—and the sometimes astounding efforts made by villagers—many Afghan valleys still face a truly Malthusian drama exacerbated by the return of a good proportion of the 5 million people who took refuge in Pakistan and Iran. This rural population now faces not only a shortage of land, but land that has very limited potential due to the lack of investment in irrigation and roads to bring inputs in and get surplus production out.

As in the Sahel, there are no local jobs for young people. Instead, they crowd into the cities and swell the ranks of the urban unemployed. Following the departure of the international forces and the jobs associated with their presence, the only options for them now are to emigrate, get involved in the opium trade, or join the Taliban, which offers attractive salaries. As an Afghan tribal chief told the *New York Times* in 2009: 'The vast majority of Taliban in my region are young men who need a job. We just need to give them work; if we can put them to work we will weaken the Taliban.'[3]

The lesson to be learned from this situation, plus the inevitable length of time it takes to implement any vast, decentralized irrigation programme[4]—and I'm thinking about the Sahel, of course— is the fundamental importance of massive investment in small irrigation schemes, by the international aid community, very early on in any stabilization process. But increasing investments of this kind assumes that there is both adequate capacity for the strategic management of aid and an ability to focus it on priority issues—an issue we will examine in more detail below. It also assumes that there is significant implementation capacity in the field.

Village demand and capacity for local initiatives for this type of programme are very high. I still remember the astonishing image of an improvised dam built by the farmers at the bottom of a steep valley. It consisted of ten or so hulls of Soviet armoured personnel carriers and tanks that had been shoved down from the road above—a sight my friend Farouk Baroukzaï took me to see, carefully following the little painted pebbles that showed where there were no land mines.

### Inadequate efforts in rural areas have driven the boom in the opium trade.

The lack of efforts in rural areas during the five or six years when it was 'relatively' easy to work there, along with a lack of interest among donors and/or their lack of resources during these early years, goes some way toward explaining the spectacular growth of

---

[3] Hajji Fazul Rahim, cited by the *New York Times*, 28 November 2009.

[4] It took more than ten years to disburse the USD 125 million of the World Bank Irrigation project in Afghanistan devoted to these rehabilitation works, which covered a very small fraction of needs. In 2013, the project benefited around 900,000 farmers, which is remarkable, but the Afghan rural population was around 24 million. A national programme of around USD 1 billion was needed.

the opium trade. In 2014, poppy fields reached a record 224,000 hectares and production was more than 6,400 tonnes.[5] As already noticed it reached an all-out record level of 9,000 tonnes in 2017 leading to a drop in farm prices. This sector now represents revenues measured at the border of USD 3 billion to USD 5 billion, depending on the year, and employs more than 400,000 farmers. Frédéric Bobin, special correspondent in Afghanistan for *Le Monde*, who knows the country well, wrote: 'The failure of efforts against the drug trade is unquestionably the most crushing defeat suffered by the international community in Afghanistan. A textbook case of political failure.' This is true but one should not either underestimate the complexity of the task.

Opium and insecurity feed off each other, according to Avetisyan, the former local United Nations Office on Drugs and Crime (UNODC) manager responsible for preventing drug trafficking. In addition to the very high level of income it generates per hectare—which is about four times higher than wheat—the immense advantage of opium is its high value-to-weight ratio. People, therefore, do not need the almost non-existent rural roads to carry it to traders and instead use donkeys or motorbikes.[6] Another advantage of opium production is the highly efficient system of contractual agriculture, based on extremely well-designed credit and marketing mechanisms implemented by the trafficking networks.

Overall, opium is a lifesaver for Afghan farmers, and any campaign to eradicate it would now lead to a dramatic increase in rural poverty, which would inevitably consign the country to yet more conflict and bloodshed.[7] Opium is highly profitable and not only allows people to buy cereals if there are food shortages,[8] but

[5] Frédéric Bobin, 'La guerre perdue contre l'opium,' *Le Monde*, 28/29 December 2014.

[6] See Christopher Ward, David Mansfield, Peter Oldham, William Byrd, 'Afghanistan: Economic Incentives and Development Initiatives to Reduce Opium Production', World Bank-DFID, February 2008.

[7] Cf. the remarkable study: Jean-Bernard Véron, 'L'économie de l'opium en Afghanistan et ses implications en termes de développement, AFD, December 2008.

[8] See the study: '*Immediate Priority Needs of Vulnerable Farmers engaged in Opium Poppy Cultivation*', Urgence Réhabilitation Développement (URD), January 2008.

also gives them access to basic consumer goods and benefits such as motorbikes, tin roofs, and better health services. However, the consequences of the sharp rise in the drug trade are now catastrophic in Afghanistan and Iran, where heroin consumption is increasing rapidly, not to mention, of course, the consumption in Russia and Northern Europe.

A programme to control and then reduce the trade would require specific efforts to increase the cultivation of alternative crops. Such programmes do exist. One example is cotton cultivation, which was successfully launched in the north of the country by the French Development Agency (AFD). With only limited resources, it helped increase production from 3,000 to 80,000 tonnes, but it has reached only a quarter of its potential—the country was producing more than 300,000 tonnes 40 years ago. Other crops with high added value, such as saffron, have also been tried, but on a small scale.

The drug economy is now deeply rooted in the Afghan countryside. It is one of the funding sources for both the rebellion and the local power base of the warlords and 'commanders.' The drug networks have also penetrated senior levels of the political hierarchy. It is hard to see how the trade can be controlled in the future, given the current insecurity and the failure of numerous eradication campaigns in the past. This is another major challenge for the president Ashraf Ghani, on whom the West is bringing pressure to act.

### Failure is predictable when aid is concentrated in combat zones.

Although there was no coherent strategy for the allocation of aid by sector, its geographical distribution was based on two clear priorities: for a long time, it remained focused on Kabul, where it is at least easier to work; and at the military's insistence, it has systematically followed the combat zones. In 2007–08, for example, when the insurgency was increasing in power, it reached USD 450 per inhabitant in the Nimroz and Helmand provinces, which were severely affected by the fighting, in an attempt to win 'hearts and minds.'

In the quieter provinces, aid was minimal—for example, around USD 50 per inhabitant for the same year in Wardak, which was (then) still peaceful. The result: resources were largely wasted in areas where insecurity prevented any serious development. Nor did the policy help rebuild the quieter regions. In 2009, the 'quiet' Wardak region tipped into insurgency; many villagers have commented that, ultimately, it was the insurgency that brought in the aid! I now notice the strong pressure the French military put on AFD to urgently launch development programmes in the north of Mali and around the lake Chad where the level of insecurity is likely to paralyze development efforts, while development aid should rather be focussed on areas still quiet...

## Coordinating donors' actions in fragile countries: Doomed to failure?

There has certainly been no lack of dedication or talent in the field of international aid. Up until 2004, when on mission to Afghanistan, ten or twelve of us from different aid institutions frequently slept on the ground, on poor mattresses in windowless dormitories, stifled by heat in summer and shivering with cold in winter. No one complained. On the contrary, there was genuine enthusiasm (even though some people missed their missions in the Seychelles...). Conditions have obviously changed, and now the Hotel Serena offers palatial luxury, though it is barricaded like a prison following several terrorist attacks in which guests and many guards lost their lives.

Nor was there any shortage of good analysis; it was not for lack of information that the right decisions were not taken.[9] On the contrary, there are countless studies of remarkably high quality. The lack of logic in the sectoral and geographical distribution of aid comes from the lack of strategic management. The problem is both institutional and political and can be found in all countries with a low level of institutional capacity. This issue merits further exploration.

Whole forests have surely been felled to print reports on aid coordination, a subject that mobilized myriad experts in major international conferences—first in Paris in 2005, then in Accra in 2008, in Busan in 2011, and so on. These events were useful

[9] William Byrd, 'Responding to Afghanistan's Development Challenges', World Bank, 2007.

insofar as they raised awareness among senior figures and defined a set of best practices.

Simply stated, there are two types of situations regarding aid coordination. Some countries, such as Vietnam or Morocco, are well organized at the administrative and political level, and local authorities take a negative view of any attempt at coordination by the donors who support them, seeing it as the donors setting up a sort of syndicate to try to dictate policies. In such countries, aid coordination is managed by local authorities, and it usually works well. When I was leading programming missions as the AFD chief operations manager in countries such as these, I sometimes had very detailed discussions with local political figures and managers, but there was no sense that I could fly in from Paris and make decisions on their behalf about what we were going to do for them.

On the other hand, in countries that are poorly organised at the administrative level—and 'failed' states are obviously the worst— coordination among donors is essential to avoid duplication, errors, or the neglect of certain areas, and, above all, to ensure that their actions fit into a sensible overall strategy. Experience shows, however, that coordination often amounts to only superficial exchanges of information. It rarely translates into real strategic management that focuses resources on the sectors and regions where they will be most useful, thus providing a temporary substitute for the lack of national budget-planning mechanisms.

## The laudable aid-coordination principles are not implemented in fragile countries.

This problem of aid coordination is very difficult to resolve. First is the fact that the decision-making centres involved in international aid in these fragmented countries are divided among 15 or so main actors, each trying to play its own part in isolation. Begin with the central actors, whose responsibilities are split among the ministries of finance, budget, planning, cooperation, and foreign affairs; just as in France (at least until President Macron took office), the number of ministerial posts has to increase to keep one's friends happy and avoid concentrations of power. Not so long ago, under President Hollande, we even had seven ministers in 'Bercy', sharing the French Ministry of Finance, Economy, and Budget, leading as expected to much confusion! Then there are, at least in most fragile states, ten or so peripheral actors—the ministries for each sector. The situation is often chaotic, with each of these actors talking to some donors and ignoring others or, in the case of the sector-specific ministries, trying to attract donors to fund 'their' initiatives.

The aforementioned conferences obviously recommended putting a senior national figure in charge of aid. But it is not as easy as that. A good option would be for the Prime Minister to take charge at the operational level but, in many countries, it is either a key post and the Prime Minister is already overloaded or the post of Prime Minister does not exist—as was the case in Afghanistan during the Karzai period[10]—or it is a purely political position that is given to a figure who has no intention of getting mixed up in logistical issues of this kind. Sometimes the post is even given to an opponent and therefore carries only symbolic power.

In such situations, which occur very frequently, finance ministers often attempt to establish a degree of order. This is exactly what happened in Afghanistan in 2002–04 with Ashraf Ghani, who had all the necessary experience thanks to his time at the World Bank. In a remarkable chapter dedicated to the role of aid in the book he published with Clare Lockhart in 2008, following his departure from the Ministry of Finance, Ashraf Ghani explained:[11]

> From the user's perspective, the fragmented system is costly. Ministers who are responsible for coordinating policy must create consensus not only with other cabinet members but also with dozens of donors and agencies and hundreds of NGOs, each with their own budgets, priorities, rules, and preferences. In Afghanistan, the Minister of Finance in the post-Taliban period spent more than 60 per cent of his time on coordination. Had the aid system united around a single flow of financing and rules, the number of reforms carried out within the government's core systems would have risen exponentially. Moreover, each donor agency tends to

[10] It now has a position of chief executive officer whose responsibilities and authority are unclear.

[11] Ghani, Ashraf and Clare Lockhart, *Fixing Failed States* (Oxford University Press, 2008).

build alliances with different ministries, further fragmenting cabinet unity. Instead of becoming catalysts for orderly policy management, donors become instruments of division and chaos.

What Ashraf Ghani did not write was that any Minister of
Finance attempting this coordination also comes under fire from
his colleagues, who find it difficult to accept that one of them
would grant himself the considerable power implied by controlling the financial flows of international aid. This is what happened
to Ashraf Ghani, who was forced to leave the government in
December 2004 after some serious clashes with his colleagues and
with the President.[12] Unless a country has a prime minister who
really feels involved in these issues and has the political authority
to impose his will in this domain—such as Kablan Duncan in
Côte d'Ivoire[13] or Matata Ponyo in DRC, whose staff tracked
these issues week after week so that they could report to them—
institutional and political problems usually prohibit aid from being
managed according to the precepts established at the international
conferences cited above.

## Is herding cats feasible?

In fragile countries today, officials are usually asked to prepare
a so-called poverty reduction strategy paper—the famous PRSP
(the acronyms vary)—to help provide a logical development

[12] As an aside, when I made a courtesy call to Ashraf Ghani in 2005,
shortly after he left the Ministry of Finance and became Chancellor
of Kabul University, he spoke in exceptionally harsh terms about the
behaviour of donors, picking up on almost all the points outlined above.
One more detail: as he left his office to accompany me back, his two
secretaries in the waiting area leapt to their feet as a mark of respect. I
had been somewhat surprised by the long coats they were wearing. In
fact, they concealed Israeli Uzi submachine guns they had on their knees,
magazines loaded, which they had to place on their desks to stand up. I
felt that to take such precautions, the political career of this man, whom
I held in the highest esteem, was probably not over.

[13] Who, in 1995–96, received monthly reports on the disbursement
rates of all the major programmes funded by donors and used to call us
directly in Washington to give us a dressing down if he was unhappy with
the results.

strategy to guide the actions of the various donors. My experience is that countries with limited capacity often see this request as an additional bureaucratic demand imposed on them by the donors, do not take it seriously, and frequently have it produced by teams of foreign consultants.

Too often, this results in formal exercises aimed at donor conferences, which have so many priorities (forty for the Afghan Development Strategy produced for the London conference in 2006) that nothing achieves priority at all. Defining priorities is a highly political exercise that cannot be delegated to foreign consultants. It was not until the donors' conference in Kabul in 2010 that a strategy document was developed reducing the scope of its ambitions to more realistic ten priorities. Still, there was no link between the multiple activities listed, the country's budget capacity, and the donors' available financial resources.

In some cases, this exercise becomes one of pure political communication, illustrated with magnificent graphs and colour photographs, as I saw in Madagascar at the end of the Ravalomanana regime. But this superb document, which the President presented to his visitors, outlined a programme costing at least four times the resources one could have hoped to attract. It was simply something to dream about.

This way of working leaves donors a lot of leeway for 'cherry-picking'—deciding which of the projects on a long list align best with the aspirations of their public opinion and political patrons and the pressure groups that try to influence them. It is, therefore, their own institutional and political constraints, rather than the country's most urgent needs, that determine their programme of action. They tend to focus on social sectors, such as education and health, which are rarely controversial. Meanwhile, they forget the urgent problems of maintaining rural roads, refurbishing irrigation networks, or providing electricity to rural communities; not to mention, the need to restructure the justice system, the police, the Ministry of the Interior, the local administration, and more.

Yes, these are all complex areas. But they are not insurmountable unless each donor tries to tackle them on its own, particularly without the political weight and courage to raise the issue of incompetence and corruption among senior officials. Ultimately, each donor does as it chooses and, to quote an ambassador I met

## The temptation to return to the colonial governor

There is thus a great temptation to identify a coordinator among the donors. The UNDP representative often assumes this role and holds coordination meetings, to which aid agency representatives send their most junior staff. The World Bank would have the capacity to act as a coordinator, but does not have a mandate to do so. And what could it have done in Afghanistan, where the two largest donors, the Pentagon and the United States Agency for International Development (USAID), were barely speaking to each other in the early 2000s?

I discussed this matter in 2010 with the president of the World Bank, Robert Zoellick, and Professor Fukuyama at a small seminar on managing aid in post-conflict situations. We talked about the role that could be played by a senior United Nations representative on the ground who would have the requisite legitimacy and who could be backed by a technical team from the World Bank. Unfortunately, there was no follow-up to the joint proposal we drew up.

This was, however, the solution that allowed the UN representative in Mozambique, Aldo Ajello,[14] to manage the post-crisis situation in this country, although it involved stepping outside the very traditional lines of his mandate. There is, therefore, some logic to this approach which, to my knowledge, has not been properly tested anywhere and which undoubtedly requires exceptional qualities in terms of personal authority and negotiating skills. Finally, if donors need to organize themselves for a limited time when a country is clearly unable to do it, I see only three solutions.

The first is for the bilateral partner with the highest level of political, and possibly military, involvement to take charge of coordination. Unfortunately, in Afghanistan, the United

[14] Aldo Ajello, *Brasiers d'Afrique: Mémoires d'un émissaire pour la paix* (L'Harmattan, 2010).

States—which could have taken on this responsibility—was unwilling to do so because of its focus on Iraq and its opposition to anything resembling 'state building.' The first US ambassador, Zalmay Khalilzad, who had grown up in Kabul, knew the country well enough to take on this kind of role. He also had very clear ideas and spoke a lot of common sense about the priorities for reconstruction; he felt that the first thing to do was to build credible national institutions and to focus on rural development.[15] The Bush administration, however, soon sent him to be ambassador in Baghdad when the security situation in Iraq collapsed in 2005.

The second option was proposed in Kabul in 2007 by the British, who were well aware of the ongoing disaster in aid management. They proposed the appointment of an aid coordinator with extensive powers, including the ability to monitor consistency between military and civilian actions. With support from the US, the British proposed Lord Ashdown for the role, a man of experience and authority, a former captain in the Royal Marines and former UN High Representative for Bosnia. But upon seeing his CV, President Karzai was up in arms, saying, 'You're trying to impose a colonial governor on me!'

The third option is to create a parallel budget that is effectively managed by the donors until capacity can be strengthened at the local level. A solution of this kind implies that donors agree to put their money into a single pot with a dedicated governance structure—or what is known in jargon as a trust fund—through which most aid is channelled. This formula, which reflects the wish expressed by Ashraf Ghani and Clare Lockhart[16] to have access to a single income stream and common rules, was used to great effect with the creation of the 'Afghanistan Reconstruction Trust Fund' managed by the World Bank. Unfortunately, it applied to only a tiny fraction of international aid.

[15] Interview with Zalmay Khalilzad cited by Seth G. Jones: Seth G. Jones, *In the Graveyard of Empires, America's war in Afghanistan* (Norton, 2010).

[16] Ashraf Ghani and Clare Lockhart, *Fixing Failed States* (Oxford University Press, 2008).

## The dilemma of balancing between urgency and long-term actions

One factor that particularly outraged successive Ministers of Finance in Afghanistan was that it was impossible for them to control anything other than a few crumbs from the billions provided in international aid. Indeed, funds from donors systematically short-circuited the Afghan authorities and their budget in a very harmful way. Behind the practice of donors implementing projects and programmes directly, using their own procedures and resources—in some cases without even informing the local authorities—lay the suspicion that their funds would otherwise disappear into insecure channels and/or get blocked in the Afghan administrative machine. Regarding the workings of the budget and the Ministry of Finance, these suspicions were largely unfounded after the tenure of Ashraf Ghani, who had rebuilt a functional ministry and secured the public-procurement process.

Such concerns were more justified when one of the local institutions was used as an executing agency. The dysfunction of local institutions, given the level of corruption that exists and the famous 'Potemkin' effect, is a source of significant ineffectiveness in most fragile countries and all 'failed' states. Nonetheless, the habit of operating outside the budget and short-circuiting local institutions is harmful once local channels have been returned to a proper footing, in that it leaves local authorities feeling dispossessed as they simply watch the bulldozers go by.

This way of working is particularly harmful because it gives donors an exorbitant amount of power to do exactly what they want, how they want, and where they want, sometimes in a rather haphazard and irresponsible way. Of course, aid that goes through official channels can get caught up in the local administrative machinery and be lost in the process, or take years to reach its intended recipients. But depriving the authorities of any control over what you are doing in their country diminishes the prospects of those activities continuing over the long term once the initial project is done and the donor has gone home. Many schools built on this basis now have no teachers.

International aid has to sometimes strike a balance between urgency, effectiveness, and respect for local procedures. The US methods referred to above—in which contracts are awarded, without solicitation of bids and proper procurement procedures, to companies equipped to implement projects as soon as possible—are understandable in emergency situations. It is very expensive, and transparency suffers, but projects such as building major roads do get completed. The Chinese do the same. Yet, there are considerable disadvantages to this approach. It can generally only be used for major infrastructure works, and we have seen the additional costs it generates. The most serious problem is that it does not foster local institutional capacities to ensure the long-term viability of the work carried out. Who, for example, will deal with maintenance, and where will the resources come from?

This somewhat crude approach is particularly inappropriate for activities that are dispersed over a wide area—for example, a decentralized irrigation programme that requires hundreds of small, detailed technical studies and thousands of hours of discussion with villagers. The problem is that, very often, the NGOs that are the only organizations equipped to carry out these projects implement them in secret, often without even informing the state about what they are doing. This creates countless frustrations and major difficulties relating to the long-term viability of the projects after they have left.

## Emergency actions that carry on result in serious impasses.

In failed states such as Afghanistan in the early 2000s, the dysfunction of local institutions became an even more fundamental problem: not only were the institutions (the ones that still existed) in a mediocre state, but their qualified staff had also disappeared. Confronted with a serious shortage of qualified staff, donors— whether they were bilateral or multilateral agencies or NGOs— proceeded in Afghanistan as they usually do in this kind of situation: they set up what are known as 'project implementation units,'[17] recruiting the few competent Afghan technical personnel available, often found in exile in Pakistan, Iran, or even Europe and the United States, for each project they were funding.

[17] The term 'Project Implementation Unit', or PIU, is found systematically in donors' technical documents.

Since aid agency managers found themselves facing a shortage of local executives, they competed to recruit the few individuals available; as a result, their salaries rose rapidly and, in the end, were based on those paid by UN agencies (which also became some of the country's largest employers). The scale of financial aid effectively resulted in the formation of a parallel administration, funded by donors, starting in 2003–04.

In early 2014, this parallel administration (known by Afghans as the 'Second Civil Service') still employed around 120,000 technicians, engineers, and executives—three or four times the number of highly qualified personnel employed by the traditional administration. That same year, this parallel administration was still managing hundreds, if not thousands, of projects, if those run by NGOs are included. The defects in this system, which can be seen in all fragile countries, were striking in Afghanistan. As Ashraf Ghani wrote in his book, *Fixing Failed States*: 'The aid complex undermines state capacity to perform essential functions. To address the most serious of the world's problems (among them poverty and global terrorism) the aid system must orient itself around the tasks of building effective, functioning states'.

The usual differences in salary between this parallel administration and the public administration trying to establish itself, are extreme. Technical-project staffers who might earn USD 200 to USD 300 per month working for the public administration are routinely paid USD 1,000 to USD 6,000 by donors. One of the obvious drawbacks to this practice is that, while public administration and state services struggle to develop, the system encourages their qualified personnel to move to the parallel administration.

## The parallel administration is strangling state institutions.

Project implementation units disappear once projects have been completed and the associated foreign funding has come to an end. This parallel administration is therefore subject to a constant process of creating and destroying capacity, at least while external funding continues. Nothing sustainable can come of it. Given the lack of alternatives, attempts to coordinate aid and define sector policies, which are the responsibility of the central administrative authorities, also have to be entrusted to project implementation units funded by donors.

As we move up the hierarchy, we see that many senior Afghan officials, including at the ministerial level, were still part of these project implementation units at the end of the Karzai regime in order to take advantage of the salaries offered. The system is unstable and used to cost almost USD 1 billion a year. It can continue only if international donors agree to fund it. Of course, Ashraf Ghani has tried to bring some order to the situation, but the corresponding collapse in income leads to an exodus and high unemployment among qualified staff. Other consequences of this salary inflation are that it prevents industrial development due to the obvious lack of competitiveness and undermines the survival of many service activities that developed in line with the international presence.

In 2013, I was chatting in Kabul with a young Afghan executive I had once known as an assistant at the World Bank—and who had just been let go by an accounting firm that was closing—about his job prospects. He shared his hope of finding a job at the same salary as the one he had just left: USD 6,000 a month. When I told him that in France, someone with five years' post-secondary education often started at less than USD 2,000, he was astounded.

The problem is now critical in Afghanistan but in no way confined to it. I worked, on several occasions, in Cambodia at the request of the World Bank, which was aware of the impasse the country found itself in after an entire generation of educated people had been slaughtered by the Khmer Rouge. Donors tried to make up for the shortage of local executives and the disorganization of the administration by increasing the number of project-implementation units employing Cambodian executives from the diaspora. The cost of the system clearly undermined its long-term viability, and the salaries paid made the administration weaker by causing an exodus of the most qualified staff, as had happened in Afghanistan.

Strong economic growth in Cambodia made it possible to plan for a rapid increase in salaries in the civil service. The negotiations I launched with both the donors present in Phnom Penh and local authorities led to a rational capping of the salaries paid by the projects. As a result, it became possible to think about integrating the project implementation units into the administration in the fairly short term and then dissolving the former.

Donors do not always have perfect discipline, however, as illustrated by a mission from The Global Fund to Fight AIDS, Tuberculosis and Malaria, that arrived during one of my stays in Cambodia. The Global Fund had no representatives there and did not meet any of the donors or administrative authorities involved in the issues I was discussing with them. Without consulting anyone, it introduced a salary structure for 'its' project that was around twice the ceiling we had agreed on. When people in the Ministry of Health found out about this unrealistic pay structure, the staff went on strike, demanding a re-alignment of their salaries with the Global Fund's proposals...

## The impasse of poorly managed technical assistance

Project implementation units cannot cover all the functions for which the central administration is responsible. There is a minimum amount of work that needs to be done by the central administration in any country. Managers cannot find the qualified staff they need unless they are able to pay attractive salaries. Ultimately, the easiest option for local managers is to ask for technical assistance, which they view as a free service.

Given the costs of providing security for these staff hires and the abnormal margins imposed by international consultancies in 'at risk' countries such as Afghanistan, donors are paying USD 30,000 to USD 40,000 a month for foreign experts to work on tasks that, admittedly, could not be done by local executives paid USD 300, but would be better done by Afghan executives paid between USD 1,000 and USD 3,000. Technical assistants are working in a country where they know neither the language nor the culture, where they do not have local contacts, where local managers can neither clearly define nor monitor their work, and where their loyalty to the Afghan government is questionable because their careers depend on the companies that employ them.

Their presence causes a threefold problem: an obvious financial problem, a political problem because perceptions of technical assistance are increasingly negative, and, finally, the problem of who takes over as aid becomes scarcer. The project implementation units have not been able to train local executives to replace them, as they all left to work on the donors' projects as soon as they were trained. The country thus finds itself at an impasse, with everyone critical of the quality of technical assistance provided, which has markedly deteriorated as security conditions have worsened. But no one knows quite how to manage without it. The government team led by Ashraf Ghani faces an extraordinary challenge in sorting out this incredible mess.

Let me be clear: in some circumstances, provided it is delivered in accordance with best practices, high-quality technical assistance can be very valuable. But it cannot be sprinkled randomly whenever there is an emergency or on the basis of uncoordinated requests from various sides or, worse, on proposals from donors looking to 'place' staff they do not know what to do with.

Technical assistance of this kind represents a significant amount of money—up to 30 per cent of the aid provided to some countries. Yet, it is really effective only if it is aligned with coherent strategies for building institutions. The most bizarre element in all of this is that we have known about these problems for a very long time. The question was already being asked in Africa in the 1970s and 1980s. Tangible solutions had then been put forward by Professor Berg in the early 1990s.[18] Although some donors have abandoned such practices, others have simply found it easier to keep on using them, and the same errors are unfortunately being repeated in the Sahel today.

[18] Elliot Berg, 'Rethinking Technical Cooperation', UNDP, 1993.

# CHAPTER
# ELEVEN

## Afghanistan—Lesson Three: In Fragile States, the Priority is to Build Modern, Efficient, Sovereign Institutions

In early 2000, the new vice-president for Africa at the World Bank, Callisto Madavo, appointed me as his senior adviser to his cabinet and, knowing of my interest in the subject, asked me to prepare a report on the most appropriate ways for the World Bank to respond to the needs of countries emerging from conflict.

As I presented my initial conclusions, which emphasized the importance of rebuilding sovereign institutions, I was astonished when he said, 'Serge, you're undoubtedly right, but I won't be able to sell your proposals in-house. State-building is too complicated for us.' Bang! This response from a man with extensive experience and for whom I had much respect—but who had just torn my arguments to shreds—perplexed me completely.

Callisto had a talent for spotting what people call the 'zeitgeist.' He had already internalized what was about to become the US administration's deep hostility towards anything that might be considered state building—that is, a rational approach aimed at rebuilding a 'failed' state.

Although nothing explicit was ever said, the attitude of the Bush administration throughout the interventions in both Iraq and Afghanistan was effectively determined by the belief that a good American-style constitution, free elections, and the destruction of the terrorists would inevitably result in a democracy—and that such measures, with the support of the US Army, of course, would help good triumph over evil and bring peace to countries steeped in conflict and bloodshed through the murderous misadventures of their leaders. Yet, this ideology was commonplace in the major aid agencies throughout the 2000s, strengthening conservative attitudes and, undoubtedly, indirectly contributing to the Western failure in Afghanistan.

## State-building? A difficult art

In a sense, Callisto was right: state-building is, indeed, a difficult art. But difficult is not the same as impossible. What I propose here is not a standard formula that will work anywhere, at any time, but an approach based on my own experience, limited as they may be.

One major problem is that the aid institutions are always reluctant to tackle the fundamental problem of (re)building sovereign institutions in these countries head-on. They are more accustomed to helping redevelop the Ministry of Finance or Ministry of Agriculture, energy companies, or development banks. But the army, police, gendarmerie, territorial administration, and even justice fall outside both their mandate and their areas of technical expertise. In this respect, aid institutions underestimate the fundamental role they could play as intermediaries between sovereign institutions in well-managed, developed countries and institutions that need to be rebuilt in fragile and poorly managed countries.

Unfortunately, the World Bank's 2011 World Development Report on the aid provided to countries in crisis (cited above), despite being a remarkable piece of work, actually helped bury the idea of the organization involving itself in this area, by taking a very pessimistic view of efforts to rebuild failing national institutions. It based its position first on the mediocre performance of most projects implemented to reform broken public institutions, without examining the often-questionable way these operations had been designed. Second, it relied on some troubling historical statistics indicating that it had generally taken at least a generation for institutions in emerging countries to reach their current levels of effectiveness. Ultimately (and paradoxically, for a piece of work of this quality), the message was basically one of 'laissez faire.'

But the analysis ignored the fact that leaving things alone is not an acceptable option in many circumstances. Indeed, where will the countries that are currently 'failing,' or even some that are simply 'fragile,' be a generation from now if their institutions do not evolve? And why would their institutions spontaneously become effective? Can these countries really wait 30 years for their institutions to get back on their feet? If it takes 30 years for the sovereign institutions of the Democratic Republic of the Congo to become effective, will the country still exist, or will there instead be five or six countries in ruins after an appalling period of crises and wars? Finally, how can it be that Rwanda, also a victim of genocide and civil war, took less than ten years to build a state apparatus of such remarkable effectiveness that this exceptionally small country was able to invade the DRC twice? Imagine Luxembourg invading Germany!

## The challenge of constructing effective 'modern' institutions

As we have already noted, the fragility of states is broadly linked to the fragility and ineffectiveness of their institutions, and the best way of strengthening them is to build or rebuild those institutions, particularly the sovereign institutions. Various examples show that doing so is perfectly possible, within reasonable time frames of three to five years, even in a country as complex and difficult as Afghanistan. One typical example was the construction of a Ministry of Reconstruction and Rural Development (MRRD) by Hanif Atmar in the early 2000s.

Atmar's approach was simple. His view was that ethnic and political networks and nepotism had utterly corrupted Afghanistan's public institutions, which had lost any hope of effectiveness as the networks simply sought to extract rents and profits. Combating such corruption, Atmar believed, meant getting back to the fundamentals that determine the effectiveness of modern institutions: recruitment based on merit; promotion based on performance; an organizational structure that allows management by objectives; defining clear procedures so sanctions are decided on an objective basis; selecting executives via an open process based on competence and integrity; job descriptions and skills-assessment to remove people who are not performing effectively; and setting salary levels on the basis of market prices. Atmar turned the entire situation around. The results were spectacular.

Comparing the MRRD, which has functioned remarkably well for more than twelve years, with almost all other Afghan institutions today—even though some have received considerable support in the form of technical assistance, training programmes, internships abroad, motivational seminars, multiple bonuses, and such—reveals that there is one good, but many bad ways to reform institutions that have gone adrift.

In fewer than four years, a ministry built and run by a leader who combined charisma and managerial capability was functioning as any modern institution elsewhere would, and its achievements could be seen across the country. The remarkable National Solidarity Program, which provided small grants to fund projects identified by villagers was, unfortunately, underfunded for a long time, but it proved essential in that it made it possible to start organizing things at the village level and established an embryonic form of grassroots democracy by creating development committees to manage the funds.

I met Hanif Atmar on several occasions when he was Minister of Reconstruction and Rural Development and again when he moved to the Ministry of Education, which was in chaos[1]. I also got to know some of his close colleagues well as I observed and tried to understand his extraordinary achievements. He is certainly one of the men from whom I have learned the most and who has impressed me most with his strategic vision, his leadership, and, not least, his courage: his efforts in 2008 to reorganize the Ministry of the Interior and fire the mafiosi running it—before he was removed for his insistent activism—was an extremely dangerous undertaking.

---

[1] And where when he took over, about one-third of teachers were illiterate.

Institutional reconstruction based on the principle of merit was
also implemented at the Ministry of Finance and the Central Bank
by Ashraf Ghani, and at the Military Intelligence Department
under the authority of another remarkable man, Amrullah Saleh.
Based on these successful experiences, we can conclude that,
technically, it was perfectly possible to build effective, modern
institutions in Afghanistan in a short time frame. On a larger
scale, it also seems clear that—again, *technically*—a well-organized
Afghan state apparatus, including at the decentralized level, could
have been in operation around 2006–07, a time when security
was becoming a serious problem and the Taliban were mounting
their first major spring offensives. It seems that a trick was missed.
Why was no attempt made to build an effective state apparatus
based on methods that have traditionally ensured effective organizations? There were clearly serious reasons for this.

## Not insignificant technical and financial obstacles

The costs involved—for audits, technical support, and bonuses
to attract qualified staff—are not insignificant. Indeed, low salary
levels in the public sector are a serious problem in many countries—the classic result of successive budget crises and/or years
of inflation. In Afghanistan, as in many fragile countries, the
low taxation capacity makes it impossible to generate the budget
margins needed for significant salary increases; the discrepancy is
particularly marked for executives and highly qualified technical
staff (IT specialists are a classic case). This leaves governments in
most fragile countries reliant on the goodwill of donors who, in
turn, are reluctant both to fund the civil service and to make a
long-term commitment, essential as these steps are.

An overly rapid rise in salaries could also prompt a significant
increase in inflation, which is already driven by injecting considerable volumes of aid, which in turn triggers the famous 'Dutch
disease.' But, even if increasing salaries is necessary, it is far from
sufficient to guarantee a qualified administration. Respecting the
principles that underpin a meritocratic system is also important—
and obviously runs counter to the pervading nepotism.

To resolve the financial problem, Hanif Atmar mobilized the
resources of a small experimental project established with the

support of the World Bank, as a first attempt to reorganize the civil service. The Priority Reform and Restructuring Program (PRR), launched in 2004, was a pilot project aimed at improving the public administration's performance by introducing professionalism and merit in the recruitment process and supporting reform through bonus payments and premiums. Because the ups and downs surrounding this operation are symptomatic of donors' mistrust in this area, it's worthwhile to reflect on a few points.

This small experimental operation had a number of flaws that could easily be corrected, and a new phase was being considered based on a fairly modest cost increase of around USD 50 million over five years; this new phase was being prepared by a joint Afghan and World Bank team, of which I was a member, in 2005–06. After a lot of hard work, we were disappointed to have our proposal rejected by the institution's hierarchy as being 'too risky.'

We were instead asked to do a detailed study. I dug my heels in and refused to participate, though the work involved some high-calibre experts who produced a beautiful report with colour graphs and photos—a truly remarkable document that I believe I am the only person to have kept a copy of outside the archives of the World Bank.[2] The report explained clearly what needed to be done as a matter of urgency in 2006—which was not very different from what we had proposed a year earlier. But, given that it was published in late 2007, when the situation was deteriorating seriously and Kandahar seemed likely to fall as the result of a Taliban offensive, it was no longer of much interest to anyone. A window of opportunity had clearly been missed.

Conversely, in 2013, I was asked to urgently examine the terms of implementation of what turned out to be practically the same project, this time already validated and approved in the panic that had gripped all the aid agencies when the departure of US troops was announced. Meanwhile, to my surprise, the project's budget had increased to USD 250 million so it could simultaneously benefit almost all of Afghanistan's ministries and administrative bodies, though there had been no opportunity to test the process on a smaller sample, as had originally been planned. This chain of mistrust, followed by panic leading to

[2] *Afghanistan: Building an Effective State, Priorities for Public Administration Reform* (World Bank, 2007).

untested proposals being implemented too late, is unfortunately a fairly common scenario.

I produced my recommendations. They were well received by the ministers concerned, who gave me an unexpectedly warm welcome. Then, at the end of 2013, it was time for elections, and I heard nothing more about the project since then.

## But the real obstacles are political

It is naive, perhaps, to think that one can form a government only of brilliant technocrats who cannot represent local political forces and equilibriums. We saw how long Mario Monti's government survived in Italy.

In Afghanistan and elsewhere, it would have been futile to seek to extend the experiment run by Hanif Atmar with the MRRD to all public institutions. It was necessary to leave room for the heavyweights of Afghan politics, some of them obviously war-lords, mafiosi, and criminals; but they were no doubt less harmful inside the government than outside it, and they were capable of commanding the votes of tens of thousands of electors. A reason-able solution would have been to target the six or seven most important institutions and build on the success of these experi-ences to gradually extend them.

This option was never considered at the time because both the CIA (an important actor during the 2002–04 period) and President Karzai had made the political choice to form an alliance with the warlords and local 'commanders.' Although perhaps necessary in the chaotic context of the time, this was also incompatible with building a modern administration based on impersonal relation-ships and rejecting nepotism. Subsequently, contrary to the hopes of the Afghan intelligentsia, President Karzai persisted in exercis-ing power while maintaining his opportunistic alliances with the power brokers, mafiosi, and 'strongmen'. How is it possible to build a modern state under these circumstances?[3]

---

[3] See the powerful argument by one of the best US experts on Afghanistan, on the need to put an end to the power and impunity of the power brokers: '*Afghanistan's Uncertain Transition from Turmoil to Normalcy,*' Barnett R. Rubin, Council on Foreign Relations, March 2006, and his major work, *The Fragmentation of Afghanistan: State Formation and Collapse in the International System* (Yale University, 2002).

Finally, the strategic choice made by President Karzai led to the formation of political and ethnic networks inside each institution; and membership to these networks, rather than merit, determined recruitment and promotions. The logic was strong but contrary to any aim of achieving effectiveness. Throughout the Afghan government, ministers with sometimes rudimentary levels of education blindly managed institutions whose missions were vague, their organization defective, internal procedures non-existent, and senior personnel selected on the basis of ethnic and political criteria, with a little mediocre technical assistance sprinkled on top. The evident defects in the system increased the level of mistrust among donors, who were already terrified of the risks of corruption and outright disappearance of their money. This context strengthened their conviction that only project units whose staffs they selected, closely monitored and paid for could execute the projects and programmes they were funding. It had come full circle.

## So, mission impossible for President Ashraf Ghani?

It is no doubt becoming clear why building a new Afghan government after the 2014 presidential elections took more than eight months. Indeed, the problem was not only about finding a balance between Ashraf Ghani's candidates and those of his opponent, Abdullah Abdullah (and not upsetting Karzai, who was still lurking in the shadows). It was also about finding the complex balance between the technocrats with whom Ashraf Ghani would have liked to surround himself and the famous heavyweights of Afghan political life. Ashraf Ghani must have had to mellow a great deal to select 'General' Dostum—a historic warlord viewed by many as a war criminal, who controlled the Uzbek vote—as a running mate for the elections. Given that all cabinet posts, following the US model—an absurdity in the Afghan context— must be approved by a parliament packed with 'strongmen,' the selection process of any government may take many months.

In spite of the handicaps associated with the complexity of Afghan society and its political game-playing, and above all the hesitancy of President Karzai, a few Afghan institutions have, as we have seen, managed to organize themselves, recruit high-quality executives, implement coherent policies, and, finally, implement

BOKO HARAM

**Legend:**
- Geographic origin and diffusion of activities of the sect since 2009
- Main area of activity of the sect 2014
- Arms trafficking
- Nigerian states with Sharia law

**Ethnolinguistic areas**
- Kanuri
- Hausa
- Yoruba
- Ibo

In just a few years, Boko Haram, initially a tiny sect, has effectively destabilized a whole region.

*Source*: OECD/SWAC (2014), *An Atlas of the Sahara-Sahel: Geography, Economics and Security*, OECD Publishing, Paris. http://dx.doi. org/10.1787/9789264222359–en

This map is without prejudice to the status of or sovereignty over any territory, to the delimitation of international frontiers and boundaries and to the name of any territory, city, or area.

## NIGER FACED WITH REGIONAL THREATS

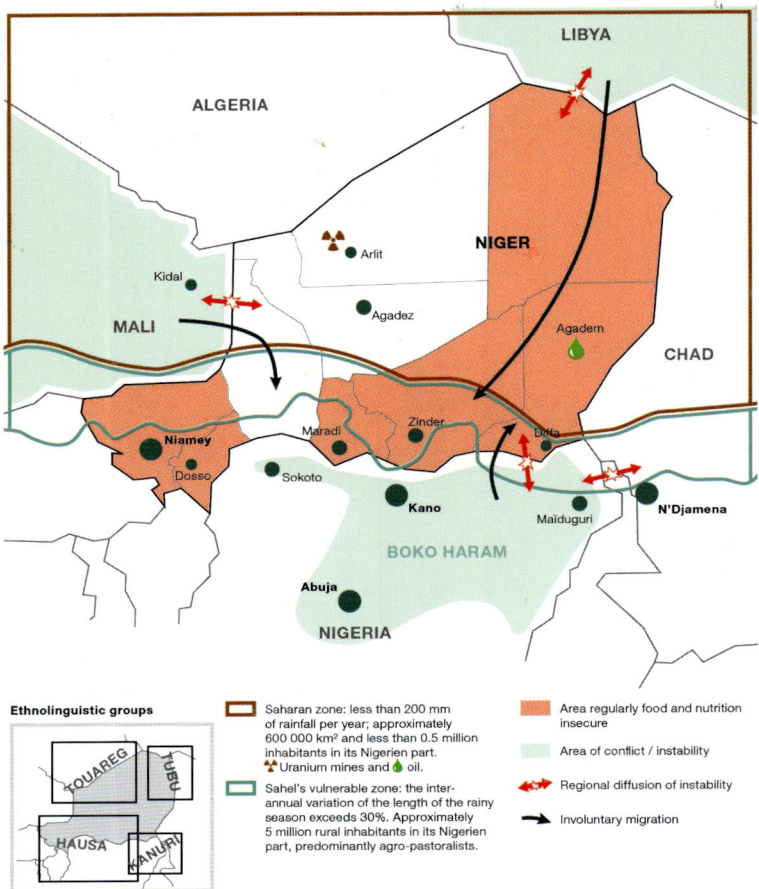

Niger faces security threats from all directions—from Mali, Nigeria, and Libya. Its tiny army is constantly on the move to address security emergencies.

*Source*: OECD/SWAC (2014), *An Atlas of the Sahara-Sahel: Geography, Economics and Security*, OECD Publishing, Paris. http://dx.doi.org/10.1787/9789264222359-en

This map is without prejudice to the status of or sovereignty over any territory, to the delimitation of international frontiers and boundaries and to the name of any territory, city, or area.

## COCAINE FLOWS

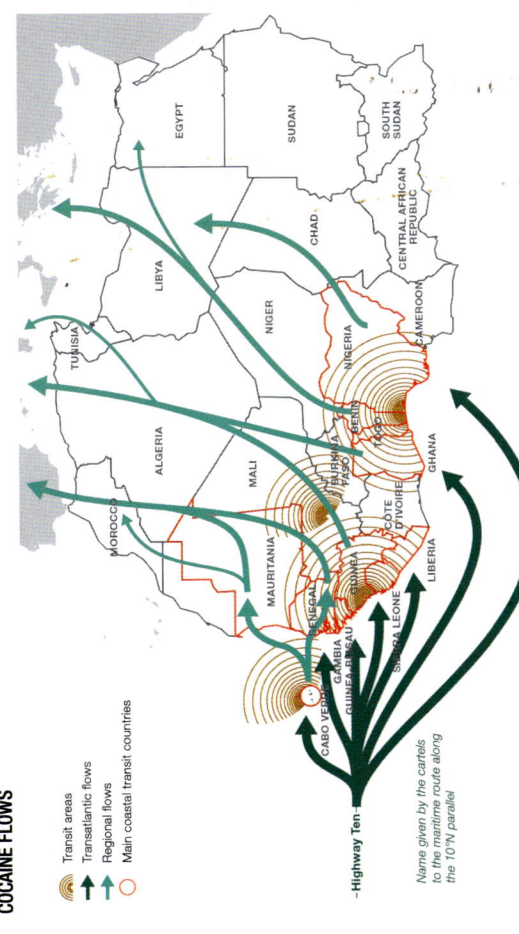

Legend:
- Transit areas
- Transatlantic flows
- Regional flows
- Main coastal transit countries

Highway Ten

*Name given by the cartels to the maritime route along the 10°N parallel*

Source: UNODC 2013

Thanks to its uncontrolled borders, West Africa—particularly the Sahel—is a key area of transit for cocaine coming by boat from Latin America for the European market.

*Source:* OECD/SWAC (2014), *An Atlas of the Sahara–Sahel: Geography, Economics and Security*, OECD Publishing, Paris. http://dx.doi.org/10.1787/9789264222359-en

This map is without prejudice to the status of or sovereignty over any territory, to the definition of international frontiers and boundaries and to the name of any territory, city, or area.

## FERTILITY TRANSITIONS (CHILDREN PER WOMAN)

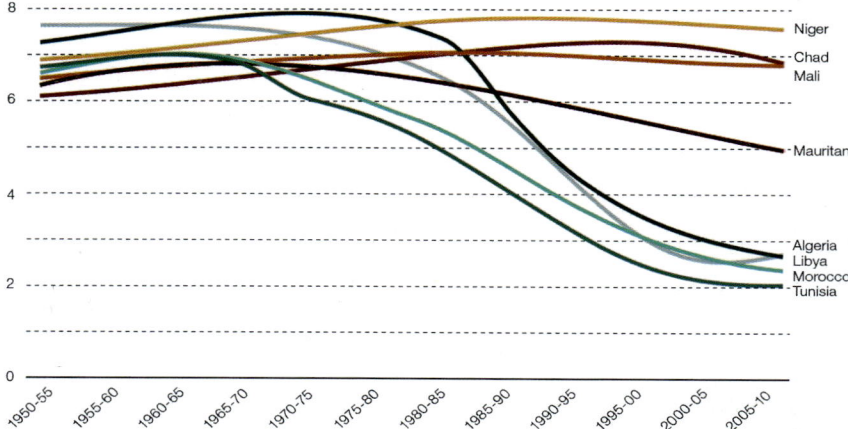

Source: DESA UN, *World Population Prospects: The 2012 Revision*

It took more than thirty years to the Maghreb countries to achieve their demographic transition. Niger, Mali, and Chad have not even begun theirs.

*Source*: OECD/SWAC (2014), *An Atlas of the Sahara-Sahel: Geography, Economics and Security*, OECD Publishing, Paris. http://dx.doi. org/10.1787/9789264222359-en

This map is without prejudice to the status of or sovereignty over any territory, to the delimitation of international frontiers and boundaries and to the name of any territory, city, or area.

## COEFFICIENT OF VARIATION FOR ANNUAL PRECIPITATION, 1901-2006

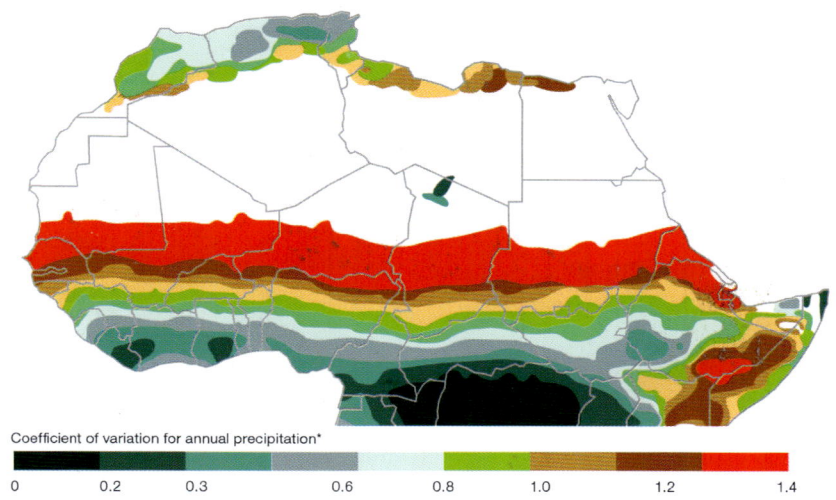

Coefficient of variation for annual precipitation*

| 0 | 0.2 | 0.3 | 0.6 | 0.8 | 1.0 | 1.2 | 1.4 |

*standard deviation normalised by the mean,
only regions with annual precipitation > 10 mm/year

Source: UK Met Office Hadley Centre; University of East Anglia Climate Research Unit (CRU)

The area in red, which includes most of the Sahel, is highly unstable in terms of annual rainfall. That instability will increase considerably over the next 30 years due to global warming. Yields for major food crops, such as sorghum and millet, are likely to drop by at least 25 per cent.

*Source*: OECD/SWAC (2014), *An Atlas of the Sahara-Sahel: Geography, Economics and Security*, OECD Publishing, Paris. http://dx.doi.org/10.1787/9789264222359-en

This map is without prejudice to the status of or sovereignty over any territory, to the delimitation of international frontiers and boundaries and to the name of any territory, city, or area.

## THE TRUNCATED PERCEPTION OF ETHNIC GROUPS IN MALI

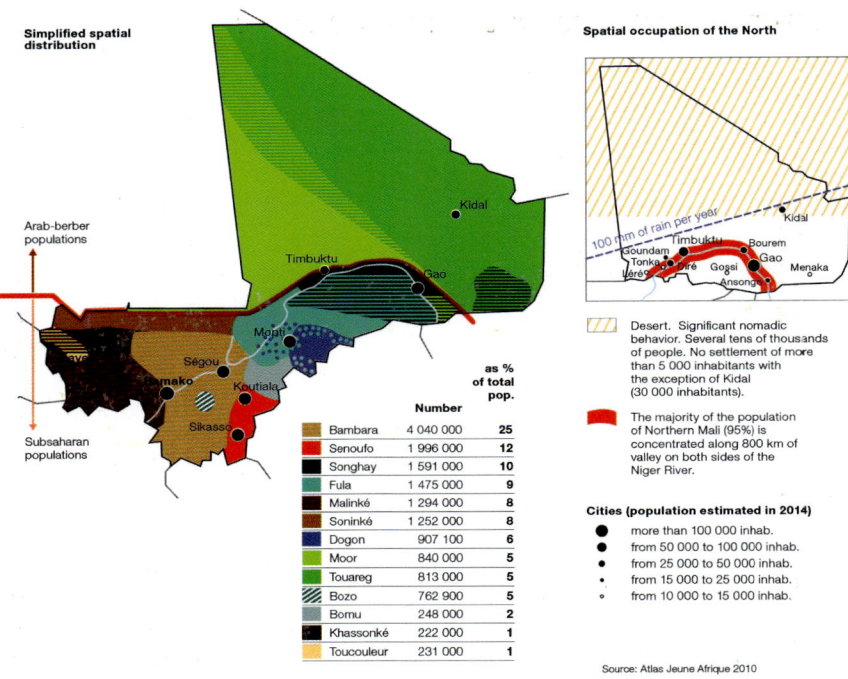

**Simplified spatial distribution**

Arab-berber populations

Subsaharan populations

Kidal

Timbuktu

Gao

Mopti

Ségou

Bamako

Keutiala

Sikasso

| | Number | as % of total pop. |
|---|---|---|
| Bambara | 4 040 000 | 25 |
| Senoufo | 1 996 000 | 12 |
| Songhay | 1 591 000 | 10 |
| Fula | 1 475 000 | 9 |
| Malinké | 1 294 000 | 8 |
| Soninké | 1 252 000 | 8 |
| Dogon | 907 100 | 6 |
| Moor | 840 000 | 5 |
| Touareg | 813 000 | 5 |
| Bozo | 762 900 | 5 |
| Bornu | 248 000 | 2 |
| Khassonké | 222 000 | 1 |
| Toucouleur | 231 000 | 1 |

**Spatial occupation of the North**

100 mm of rain per year

Kidal

Goundam  Timbuktu  Bourem  Gao

Tonka  Diré  Gossi  Menaka

Léré  Ansongo

Desert. Significant nomadic behavior. Several tens of thousands of people. No settlement of more than 5 000 inhabitants with the exception of Kidal (30 000 inhabitants).

The majority of the population of Northern Mali (95%) is concentrated along 800 km of valley on both sides of the Niger River.

**Cities (population estimated in 2014)**

- more than 100 000 inhab.
- from 50 000 to 100 000 inhab.
- from 25 000 to 50 000 inhab.
- from 15 000 to 25 000 inhab.
- from 10 000 to 15 000 inhab.

Source: Atlas Jeune Afrique 2010

Most Sahel countries are characterized by a considerable ethnic fragmentation. Mali is no exception.

*Source*: OECD/SWAC (2014), *An Atlas of the Sahara-Sahel: Geography, Economics and Security*, OECD Publishing, Paris. http://dx.doi.org/10.1787/9789264222359-en

This map is without prejudice to the status of or sovereignty over any territory, to the delimitation of international frontiers and boundaries and to the name of any territory, city, or area.

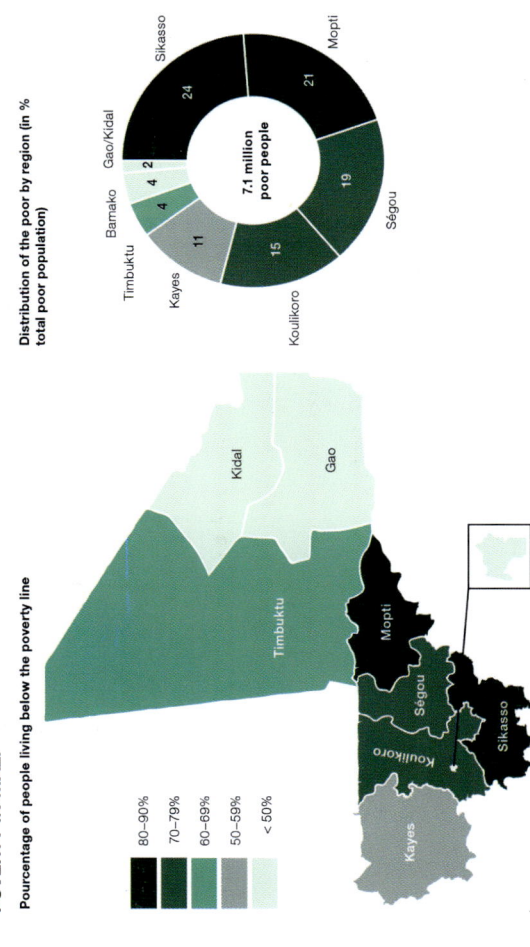

**POVERTY IN MALI**

Pourcentage of people living below the poverty line

- 80–90%
- 70–79%
- 60–69%
- 50–59%
- < 50%

Kidal

Gao

Timbuktu

Mopti

Ségou

Koulikoro

Sikasso

Kayes

Bamako

**Distribution of the poor by region (in % total poor population)**

Sikasso 24

Mopti 21

Gao/Kidal 2

Bamako 4

Timbuktu 4

Kayes 11

Koulikoro 15

Ségou 19

7.1 million poor people

Source: World Bank 2013

Puzzling as it may seem, the poorest areas in Mali—Mopti and Sikasso—are the regions with the best agricultural potential, while the most affluent regions have the lowest potential. But these more affluent regions are either the main areas of migration to France (Kayes) or are heavily involved in various traffics through the Sahara (Gao and Kidal).

*Source:* OECD/SWAC (2014), *An Atlas of the Sahara-Sahel: Geography, Economics and Security*, OECD Publishing, Paris. http://dx.doi.org/10.1787/9789264222359-en

This map is without prejudice to the status of or sovereignty over any territory, to the delimitation of international frontiers and boundaries and to the name of any territory, city, or area.

## MIGRATORY MOVEMENTS

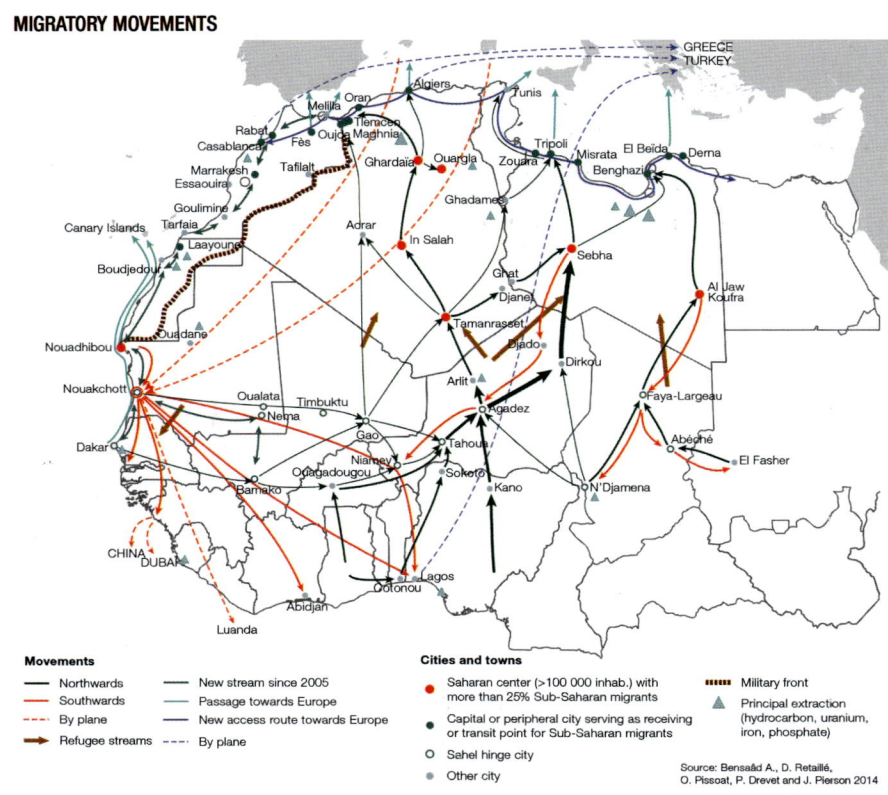

**Movements**

| | |
|---|---|
| —— Northwards | —— New stream since 2005 |
| —— Southwards | —— Passage towards Europe |
| - - - By plane | —— New access route towards Europe |
| ➤➤ Refugee streams | - - - By plane |

**Cities and towns**

● Saharan center (>100 000 inhab.) with more than 25% Sub-Saharan migrants

● Capital or peripheral city serving as receiving or transit point for Sub-Saharan migrants

○ Sahel hinge city

● Other city

▰▰▰▰ Military front

▲ Principal extraction (hydrocarbon, uranium, iron, phosphate)

Source: Bensaâd A., D. Retaillé, O. Pissoat, P. Drevet and J. Pierson 2014

Migrations through the Sahara are controlled by powerful mafias and have become a highly profitable business. Libya is a key platform for this activity. It is estimated that by the end 2017 some 350,000 migrants were waiting in private concentration camps there, and being submitted to human rights abuses and sometimes slavery.

*Source*: OECD/SWAC (2014), *An Atlas of the Sahara-Sahel: Geography, Economics and Security*, OECD Publishing, Paris. http://dx.doi.org/10.1787/9789264222359-en

This map is without prejudice to the status of or sovereignty over any territory, to the delimitation of international frontiers and boundaries and to the name of any territory, city, or area.

effective programmes of action. Let's look back and dream for a moment. If Afghanistan had been able to mobilize six or seven ministers of the calibre of Hanif Atmar, who had the support of the head of state and the trust of the international community, in order to raise the billion dollars needed over three or four years to rebuild the main sovereign and economic institutions, the state apparatus would not be in the dire situation it finds itself in today.

It would have a backbone, would be built coherently, and would not have its functions split among hundreds of project units that risk collapsing at any time if the aid stops flowing, while the administration will also be abandoned by technical-assistance personnel who have been unable to train their replacements. The state apparatus would have been able to get the country back on track. It is a tragedy that Ashraf Ghani, a leader with clear ideas and a firm commitment—who has even developed a theory for the problem he is now facing[4]—has arrived on the scene so late and is tied down by the multiple agreements and compromises that were required for him to get into power under an ill-conceived constitution. He is now even more tied down by the compromises he has to make to remain there, such as the recent official welcome, in the Presidential Palace, of Gulbudin Hekmatyar, the head of the Hezb e Islami, who made a triumphal entry in Kabul with his own personal army.[5] This Islamist warlord has, for years, been associated with the Taliban and stands accused of many atrocities.

It seems to me that part of the approach outlined in this analysis of the Afghan experience was implemented with some success by President Saakashvili in Georgia between 2008 and 2013. He was convinced, in a country worn down by mafias and deep-seated hatred, that he needed to form a government based on merit and that this, in turn, meant bringing in a new generation. I have visited Georgia only once and do not know a great deal about it. But having been invited to dinner at the President's residence

[4] Ashraf Ghani and Clare Lockhart, *Fixing Failed States* (Oxford University Press, 2008).

[5] This weird alliance being an answer to the establishment of a strong opposition coalition led by several warlords including General Dostum (the present Vice President!) and General Ata.

overlooking Tbilisi one evening in 2012, as part of a delegation, I found myself sitting between two brilliant young women who could easily have been my students at *Sciences Po*. As we chatted, I realized they were both government ministers, and when I asked the President about his miracle cure for getting his country back on its feet, he said, 'No ministers over the age of 35! After 35, they are already too influenced by what has been done in the past.' It was clear there was little chance of my becoming a minister in Tbilisi.

## Doesn't democracy have to be built from the ground up?

Finally, I must say I am perplexed that the international community is now systematically imposing a Western democratic model on these fragile countries emerging from conflict. I have already expressed my doubts about the 'calming' nature of the type of democratic process imposed by the international community on presidential and parliamentary elections in complex heterogeneous societies. We have seen how tensions in multi-ethnic countries can become more acute at election time, and I fully share Paul Collier's reservations on this subject.[6]

Although elections following a period of conflict can help get a country out of a political impasse, many newly elected heads of state find it difficult to step down after they lose out on re-election. We have seen what happened in Côte d'Ivoire in 2010. The same occurred in Gabon very recently. The international community is beginning to realize that 'democracy' does not automatically make the political game any calmer. But because the international community does not know what else to do, it persists in imposing elections in often unreasonable circumstances. The latest elections in the Central African Republic, when the country had no administration in place and was forced to adopt an unrealistic timetable, left me bewildered and was most likely intended to allow France to begin planning a discreet withdrawal.

Let's not forget that the parliaments produced by elections of this kind are not entirely made up of enlightened democrats.

---

[6] See Paul Collier, *Wars, Guns and Votes, Democracy in Dangerous Places* (HarperCollins, 2009).

Take the Afghan parliament: while it undoubtedly contains some exceptional figures, including some remarkable women, it also includes mafiosi and gang leaders who have bought their seats and, as a result, immunity, which they quickly strengthened by voting in an amnesty law. Some of the parliaments in these countries are caricatures. Obviously, there are no miracle cures in this area, but it would sometimes undoubtedly be better to accept temporary solutions under a provisional UN administration instead of rushing into national elections.

People in all 'failed' states and many fragile states sometimes suffer because of the lack of an effective state apparatus; sometimes because of acts of violence the state perpetrates, and sometimes because of the same acts committed by local 'strongmen.' Constitutional reform projects will be needed in all these countries to introduce control mechanisms and re-establish a balance of power. At the same time, it will be essential to build real grassroots democracy, probably on the basis of structures similar to Afghanistan's Community Development Councils and by giving substance to the provincial bodies created on paper but which, as can be seen today in Mali, have neither resources, capacity nor authority.

This ambitious project in Africa should, in time, allow centralized states, which sometimes exist only on paper, to become more decentralized. Many constitutions in French-speaking Africa were written in a rush by young French constitutional experts in the late 1950s, so a 'tidy up' would certainly be in order. An approach aimed at building a grassroots democracy based on a 'bottom-up' process also reflects the vision of Hanif Atmar, who quickly found himself 'opposed' by President Karzai when he attempted to push this idea, because the president feared it would be used to establish a political constituency that would benefit a potential rival. How wrong could Karzai have been!

That said, precautions do have to be taken, even at the grassroots level, for democracy to function. The time I have spent in villages and poor urban neighbourhoods has convinced me that the thirst for democracy there is immense. But I have also seen that many local actors, from traditional chiefs to local thugs, are constantly on the lookout for any new mechanism that might strengthen their own power by distorting basic democratic rules.

Although introducing real democracy at the village level reflects strong local demand, it also requires numerous precautions to prevent it from becoming a caricature.

## The collapse of Libya reminds us that military intervention in a fragile country raises obvious questions about subsequent stabilization.

The complexity and difficulty of both, building an effective state apparatus and establishing democracy in fragile or 'failed' states makes it easier to understand the risks of foreign military intervention in such situations. We clearly have not finished paying for the cowboy nonchalance of the Bush administration in Iraq, which has led to the ISIS catastrophe which will certainly not end with the recapture of Mosul. We are already paying a high price for the same nonchalance in Libya, a tribal country with no real sovereign institutions, where France and Great Britain, with US support, intervened by bombing, carefully staying above 3,000 meters to avoid air defences—all this without even securing or destroying arms depots. Saddam Hussein and Gaddafi were abominable tyrants, but before we toppled them, did we really assess the complexity, cost, or feasibility of subsequently establishing functional democracies?

It is instructive to compare this nonchalance regarding the issues around security, justice, and local administration once the regime has been toppled in a fragile or 'failed' state, with the approach taken by Vietnamese leaders in Cambodia. When the Vietnamese invaded Cambodia in 1979 to bring down Pol Pot's regime, they made short work of his army—just as the US did in Afghanistan in 2001. But, unlike the US in Afghanistan, the Vietnamese feared that a Khmer Rouge rebellion might take advantage of the ongoing chaos and strengthen its position by embedding itself in the countryside. So, the Vietnamese consistently imposed strict order in rural Cambodia by establishing a strong military presence and rapidly rebuilding local administrations.

I have discussed these issues on many occasions with Cambodian leaders, who insisted on the importance of rapidly establishing a police force and a competent local administration. They found it more difficult to acknowledge that, given the lack of educated Cambodians (the pro-Vietnamese communists and almost all educated Cambodians having been massacred by Pol Pot's regime), they had turned to members of the Khmer Rouge to build local governments.[7] Supervision by the central authority, however, was tight.

When I raise these questions with my students, or during lectures, I am routinely challenged: 'Surely you're not thinking about intervening on the ground in Libya!' No, I'm not. Such an intervention would mean sending a multinational contingent—and for how long? Given that any significant Western force on the ground would provoke an enormously hostile reaction that could quickly descend into a holy war, I would hope that any intervention in Libya would be conducted by local forces, properly strengthened, or by Arab forces. If truly essential, given the deteriorating situation in late 2017, Western powers should limit their intervention to small special-forces units supporting a rebuilt Libyan army. Between the Egyptian army, which is already bogged down in the Sinai by jihadist groups, and the Algerian army, which is reluctant to step outside its own border (unless it can do so very discreetly), it is hard to see a solution. In fact, Sarkozy, should you not have been asking yourself this question about future stabilization before you decided to send in the Rafales?

## Could the last war in Afghanistan have been avoided?

As to the reasons for the Western failure in Afghanistan we must, sadly, conclude that the ability of foreign military interventions to re-establish (and maintain) peace in a country prone to civil war is quite limited. That failure also suggests a poor understanding of the complexity of the political context in the case of Afghanistan, not to mention the very stupid decisions[8] made by Paul Bremer leading to a catastrophe in Iraq. It also seems clear that, while aid seems to be the only obvious option in the Western toolkit,

---

[7] For more on this, see: Evan Gottesman, *Cambodia after the Khmer Rouge, Inside the Politics of Nation Building* (Silkworm Books, 2004), and Henry Kamm, *Cambodia, Report from a Stricken Land* (Arcade Publishing, 1998).

[8] Such as dismantling the army and firing most civil servants.

its efficiency in fragile countries, whether they are in crisis or simply very disorganized, is also limited. Finally, aid as presently organized does not help maintain security. Restoring peace and maintaining security in such countries cannot be achieved according to some simple equation.

In retrospect, was the outcome of the war in Afghanistan (that began in 2001, following 23 years of conflict that had already cost more than 1.2 million Afghans lives) inevitable? Obviously, it is easier to rewrite history after the event, in the peace and quiet of one's office, than to experience it live in the stress and urgency associated with positions of authority, on the basis of fragmentary and contradictory information, and under pressure from opinions and emotions. But, I was so struck by the comments made to me independently by several Afghan friends that I feel obliged to repeat them here.

When the Soviets began their withdrawal from Afghanistan in 1987, they installed Mohammad Najibullah, to cover the transition, as president—he was the former head of the Afghan secret service, who was no choirboy but was at least an energetic and highly capable man. Najibullah inherited the Afghan army created by the Soviets: a solid force of some 300,000 men that routed the Mujahideen forces on several occasions following the Soviets' departure. He also inherited a country where the regime in power had little control, except in the cities and a small part of the countryside. The collapse of Najibullah's regime was followed by a civil war among Mujahideen groups and then, the deliberately opaque Taliban system which destroyed what remained of the government structures that had existed under the monarchy.

Najibullah surrounded himself with a team of high-calibre technocrats who can now be found in many important positions[9] and whose support for communism was entirely opportunistic. This team would probably have been capable of resisting the Mujahideen rebellions funded by the CIA, Pakistan, and Saudi Arabia if it had continued to receive financial support from Russia following the collapse of the USSR. But, the end of Russian

---

[9] Most of them were removed from important posts because they were viewed by the US as 'unreliable former communists.' Hanif Atmar was one of them.

funding caused the collapse of the Afghan army and of Najibullah's regime in 1992; Najibullah was later hanged by the Taliban.

In the opinion of several of my Afghan friends, Najibullah's army was a great deal more professional than the current Afghan army; its officer corps, trained by the Russians for ten years, was much more experienced than current Afghan officers, and Najibullah was a 'modernist' far removed from Islamism. In their view, if the United States—rather than seeking a complete victory over communism in 1992, had had the wisdom to take over the army and sovereign institutions' funding from the Russians, Najibullah and his team would have switched sides, and a moderate, 'modernist,' pro-Western regime would probably have been established. Afghanistan would have avoided both the Taliban regime and 15 years of war—war which is still not over. Other friends have purported that the Pakistani secret service, the famous ISI, would never have tolerated a regime of this kind. Can we ever know?

## Would a serious negotiation with Pakistan have avoided war after 9/11?

Let's continue rewriting history. On 12 September 2001, the day after the World Trade Centre attacks, Deputy Secretary of State Richard Armitage had a difficult discussion with General Mahmood, head of the Pakistani secret service (ISI), who happened to be passing through Washington. The ISI had been providing the Taliban with financial and military support for years. Armitage sent General Mahmood a stark message: 'You are either with us or with the terrorists.' On 13 September, he sent him a memo—effectively an ultimatum—saying that a cabinet meeting had concluded that if Pakistan did not help the United States, it risked coming under attack by US forces.

Difficult discussions between President Musharraf and Secretary of State, Colin Powell, continued by phone in the following weeks. In broad terms, Powell offered the leaders of Pakistan two options: 'Either you're with us and you give us your full support for the invasion of Afghanistan we are about to embark on to destroy the Taliban and Al Qaida, or you're against us and we are prepared to send you back to the Stone Age.'

We know what happened next: Pakistanis were forced to follow a policy contrary to what they believed to be in their historic interests and were accepting aid from the US while simultaneously supporting the Taliban. The evidence supporting this was clearly established following the major Taliban offensives in southern Afghanistan in 2007, when US officers found communications equipment that the US had supplied to the Pakistani army. But the Americans were in such dire need of Pakistani logistical support that they preferred to look the other way and accept the ambiguity, sparking anger from officers who found evidence of Pakistan's duplicity—the result of imposing political objectives the country did not share—on the ground.

Some of my Afghan friends are convinced that if, instead of rushing in to destroy the Taliban and Al Qaida before the snow fell in the mountains, the American government had taken the time to enter into proper negotiations with Pakistan, which would have taken several months, the latter probably would have managed to have Bin Laden executed and have Al Qaida driven out of Afghanistan by the Taliban, over which the Pakistani government could exert considerable pressure. There was indeed significant unease among the Taliban leadership regarding what they should do with Bin Laden after 9/11.

Of course, the Saudis had, a few years earlier, asked for Bin Laden's head and been rebuffed, to their great displeasure. But 9/11 vastly changed things. The council of clerics, the highest religious authority in Afghanistan, asked that Bin Laden leave the country. According to Carlotta Gall,[10] Colonel Imam, the key Pakistani interlocutor of the Taliban leadership and an influential ISI official, travelled to Kandahar in the days following 9/11 to meet with Mollah Omar and 'urged him to ignore demands to hand over Bin Laden and to resist the American attacks.'

A few days later, the head of Pakistani intelligence, Lieutenant General Mahmud Ahmed, travelled to Kandahar twice to meet Mollah Omar and conveyed a message counter to the instructions of President Musharraf, 'who wanted that they should come to some sort of compromise and allow Bin Laden to be sent away

[10] Carlotta Gall, *The Wrong Enemy: America in Afghanistan, 2001–2014* (Mariner Books, 2014).

or handed over to the Americans.' Instead, Mahmud, 'who was deeply caught up in the Taliban cause and a committed Islamist, told Omar to hold on to Bin Laden and resist the attack.' Clearly Musharraf was not in control of the ISI. If given some more time, he might have been able to establish his authority and have Bin Laden expelled from Afghanistan.

We might recall the saying attributed to Talleyrand: 'A good agreement is always an agreement between hidden motives'—that is, based on the two parties' actual, if unexpressed, reciprocal interests. By embarking on a war based on an agreement with an ally that fundamentally disapproved of the intervention, America got itself into a difficult situation. A war that has already lasted 17 years could have been avoided. More than USD 1 trillion and, more importantly, tens of thousands of lives could have been saved. Of course, we cannot rewrite history, and it is fair to say that US public opinion, which was crying out for vengeance, might not have tolerated four or five months of waiting before action was taken.

In fact, the main aim of this historical reconstruction is to remind us that rapid military action as the first option in situations of this kind, without assessing the difficulty of political stabilization and the rebuilding of complex societies that must accompany it, should be avoided as much as possible. Before embarking on any military action in these countries, we should carefully explore all the diplomatic options, particularly those involving regional actors.

## What can we learn about the Sahel from all this?

France can no longer reasonably act as a regional police force in Africa. This comment does not apply to Operation Serval in Mali, which prevented the collapse of the country and the occupation of its capital, Bamako, by jihadist forces in early 2013. The risk of 6,000 of our fellow countrymen being taken hostage in Bamako was clearly too high. But, it must prompt us to ask questions about interventions of the type that France has embarked on in the Central African Republic, a country in which a long-term stabilization is difficult to imagine.

First and foremost, I draw the same conclusion about our intervention in Libya in 2011, which resulted in chaos that was worse than the appalling dictatorship that preceded it. Finally, I even disapprove of French intervention against ISIS in Iraq and Syria. Our military action in these countries can have only a marginal impact at best; it is impossible to see how long military action might last and what the political outcome might be. It spreads thin our military forces just when we need them both in the Sahel and in France; and, most important, fighting against both Bashar al-Assad and Daesh is unreasonable because, in any conflict, as Churchill reminded us in June 1941, it is crucial to identify the main enemy. The chaotic situation in Iraq and Syria is primarily the fault of President George W. Bush; we would have been better advised to keep our limited military resources available to deal with unexpected developments in the Sahel or in Libya.

We now, more than ever, need to be wary of decisions taken in the heat of the moment for domestic political reasons or under pressure from public opinion in the traumatic wake of terrorist attacks. I fear that French and, sometimes, American laudable ambitions regarding human rights might drag us into operations as senseless as those undertaken by the Bush administration and its neo-conservatives. Armed conflicts in fragile countries are not like squabbles between tribes armed with spears that a battalion of marine infantry might have settled in the era of oil lamps and men-of-war.

The combination of demographics, Kalashnikovs, and IEDs[11] has significantly changed the situation. I remember the drawing by the French cartoonist Plantu in *Le Monde* in which Baroness Ashton, who was responsible for European foreign policy, gently admonished the Libyan combatants who were busy massacring each other: 'Now, now, children, calm down.' We can understand the aims set for Operation Barkhane by our political leaders. But, how do we get out of the mess we have gotten ourselves into?

---

[11] 'Improvised explosive devices' are improvised bombs set off remotely using a mobile phone. They were responsible for almost half of the American losses in Iraq.

# PART IV

## What Is to Be Done?

# CHAPTER
# TWELVE

## Key Security Lessons for the Sahel drawn from the West's Failure in Afghanistan

The first question to be addressed is whether the comparison between Afghanistan and the Sahel is really relevant or just an editorial 'trick.' The Sahel is not Afghanistan, but as I have already explained, there are major similarities between the two regions, particularly regarding demographic issues, a poorly performing agricultural sector, youth unemployment, the weakness of state institutions (and their absence in many dilapidated areas), illicit trafficking, spreading insecurity, and the rise in some regions of insurgencies, mafias, and parallel authorities in a context of spreading militant Islamism.

The successful outcome of the March 2015 elections in Nigeria is, perhaps, the beginning of a new era for West Africa. If political stability can be attained in Nigeria and Cote d'Ivoire for two solid decades, these countries have the potential to bring the entire sub-region along with them, putting it on the path to emergence. The significant imbalances in the Sahel and the chaos that could become widespread there, however, could derail that scenario.

Fortunately, in many ways, the Sahel is in a better position than Afghanistan.

## Afghanistan and the Sahel present major differences.

A key difference is that the French-speaking Sahel has never experienced conflicts on the scale of those that have been tearing Afghanistan apart since 1979. To use terminology adopted by the Afghans, there was the 'Russian war' from 1979 to 1989, when the Russians implemented a scorched-earth policy in rural areas controlled by the Mujahedin. Then there was the 'Mujahedin war' between 1990 and 1992, when various factions fought each other with heavy weaponry, particularly in Kabul, which was partially destroyed.[1] Next came the 'Taliban war', intended in principle to halt the chaos caused by the victors over the Russians. Between 1992 and 1995, the Taliban conquered the vast majority of the country, with the exception of the Panjshir Valley in the north, which was defended by the famous commander Masood. The 'American war' lasted just a few weeks at the end of 2001, though the aerial strikes resulted in a great deal of damage. Finally, the long war against the Taliban guerrillas remains unfinished even after 15 years. The Sahel has been spared such a series of misfortunes.

### The French-speaking nations of the Sahel are not (yet) failed states.

Unlike Afghanistan in 2002, the French-speaking nations of the Sahel all have genuine administrative structures in place. In particular, their finance ministries—which are generally good, an important starting point—have long been supported by the French financial authorities, the IMF, the World Bank, and the Central Bank of West African States. When I visited the Finance Ministry in Kabul in early 2002, on the other hand, it was an alarming sight: in the middle of winter, in the snow, the windows had shattered. The walls were full of bullet holes. The offices were deserted and emptied of their furniture. There was no electricity

[1] Here I refer readers to William Maley's book, *The Afghanistan Wars* (Palgrave Macmillan, 2002).

and no heat. The doors had been stolen—even their hinges were gone. I'd seen the same kind of devastation in Brazzaville just a few days after fighting ended in October 1997, but at least it was not so cold there, and the minister waiting for me at the top of a tower (without an elevator and with its large windows shattered) had two chairs brought into his empty office so we could sit and talk.

The situations in Mali, Burkina Faso, Chad, and Niger have little in common with this distressing picture. Back in the same Afghan ministry the following year, doors and windows had been installed, makeshift furniture had been brought in, and American consultants and Afghan professionals were busy at their computers. The only problem was that there was still no heat in the meeting room where we sat in hats and fur-lined jackets and with blankets that had been kindly loaned to us. A brazier under the meeting table brought the temperature up to a few degrees above freezing so we could have our discussion.

This is to say that, in 2005–06, the capabilities of the financial heart of the Afghan government were perhaps not so different from those in some Sahel countries today, yet there is still a huge disparity due to the extreme level of destruction (and refuelled hatred) that years of war have wrought on Afghanistan.

### Fortunately for the Sahel, Pakistan is far away.

We have observed how destabilizing Pakistan's ambitions to control Afghanistan in its global fight against India have been for the country. Time and again, Pakistan has helped equip and fund the Taliban. It has constantly meddled in Afghan affairs with the clear purpose of keeping the country weak and divided. Pakistan has hosted and offered protection to the Taliban leadership since 2001, imprisoning or killing those willing to negotiate with the Afghan government or the Americans and systematically supporting the extremists. This double game was fully exposed when Osama bin Laden was finally discovered and killed in a safe house in Abbottabad. Carlotta Gall's main message in her 2014 book was to highlight this double game and its pernicious impact.

Fortunately for the Sahel countries, Pakistan is far away and unconcerned about the region. A key source of instability is, of course, an unstable Libya, where various groups are still confronting each other. But now that ISIS's presence in Libya has been significantly weakened, no regional power has the destabilization of the Sahel as a key political objective. Regarding the future course of events, a lot will depend upon Algeria's political and security stability, which are both highly uncertain over the medium to long term. Despite its strong army, Algeria is indeed a fragile country. It strongly resents the French army's presence close to its borders, and its secret services have long been manipulating Algerian-led Malian insurgent groups.[2]

### Ethnic groups opposing established governments are very much a minority.

The Tuareg of Mali and Niger are actually very limited in number—about 1.4 million in Niger and 800,000 in Mali. These peoples of the southern Sahara pay no attention to borders and rely on support from their 'brothers' in Algeria and Libya. The Afghan Pashtuns, from whom the majority of the Taliban and similar groups were initially recruited, represent at least 40 per cent of the Afghan population, or more than 15 million people, and also enjoy support from a Pashtun population in Pakistan of double that number.

On the other hand, many groups besides the Tuareg live in the vicinity of the Sahara: the Toubou in northern Chad who, with support from their 'cousins' in Libya, have been in almost constant revolt against the central government since the end of the 1960s; Arab and Fulani communities, large numbers of whom live throughout the northern Sahel region; the Moors; and more.

---

[2] Many well-informed observers consider, for instance, that Iyad Ag Ghaly, the head of Ansar Diine, who pledged his oath of allegiance to the head of Al-Qaida, Ayman al-Zawahiri, is protected by the Algerian secret services, which allows him and some of his group to travel freely from Algeria to northern Mali. Cf., for instance Joseph Brunet Jailly: 'Aveuglement-Mali cinq ans après l'attaque fratricide où en sommes-nous?', September 2017 (not yet published). Iyad Ag Ghaly has in 2017 formed the 'Groupe de Soutien à l'Islam et aux Musulmans' (Jama'at Nusrat al-Islam wal Muslimeen), the united front of jihadists in Mali.

Chad is a different case because the Zaghawa people, an ethnic group from the northeast of the country, are largely in charge, and face hostility from groups of other ethnic and geographical backgrounds despite the central government's constant negotiations and attempts to create alliances.

Despite the differences with Afghanistan and the relatively positive elements just listed, two very troubling transnational phenomena persist.

## The Sahel and Afghanistan are subject to similar—and troubling—transnational influences.

*Under the influence of Wahhabism, conflicts are likely to move beyond ethnic boundaries.*

As the cases of Afghanistan and other troubled areas clearly show, once set in motion, crises and conflicts initially rooted in ethnic tensions and ancient prejudices cause social breakdowns that take on their own dynamics and move beyond their initial ethnic boundaries. In Afghanistan, for instance, Taliban groups now include not only Pashtuns but also Tajiks, Uzbeks, Hazaras, and others. This explains their ability to now intervene in all of the country's provinces. In this regard, the ongoing insecurity spreading in the centre of Mali between Segou and Mopti, where various militias, particularly the *'Front de libération du Macina,'* are attempting to establish themselves, is essentially based upon a sense of neglect and marginalization by Fulani groups. The Fulani are an important group spread throughout West Africa; they represent a major part of the population in Guinea and, contrary to the Tuaregs, their demographic weight is significant in West Africa. Their insurgency may become a threat to the whole region. In addition, if the insurgent Fulani groups succeed in taking root there, the religious dimension of their insurgency may well overtake the ethnic dimension.

For the last 30 years, the Sahel has indeed experienced an accelerating increase in Islamic fundamentalism, Salafism, and particularly Wahhabism, largely financed by foundations based in Saudi Arabia and the Persian Gulf. The growing influence of these groups has led, in Mali and Niger, for example, to the rejection of draft family-code bills; and demonstrations and church burnings took place in Niger, including in Niamey, in protest against the participation of the Nigerien president in the show of support held a few days after the *Charlie Hebdo* attack in Paris in 2015.

### The same tidal wave of Islamic extremism is sweeping across the Sahel region.

Among young African people from rural or poor urban backgrounds, as Philippe Hugon notes, there is a general tendency to 'discredit the political class and criticize corruption and signs of Western modernity.'[3] Jean-Pierre Olivier de Sardan, a French anthropologist who has lived for half a century in Niger, recently told me that 'radical Islam in Niger has won the ideological battle by standing in opposition to the current authorities and through support from religious and political leaders.' He sees the religious arena as increasingly favourable to fundamentalist versions of Islam. Followers of moderate versions of Islam are afraid; they are keeping quiet and not leading the ideological battle. Even more troubling are the supportive echoes of armed jihad among young people from rural areas. He added, 'These movements are the receptacles for all frustrations, as they take on not only the elites and the state, but also the West and its values.'

In tandem with the collapse of Marxist ideology, the rise of the religious dimension (Christianity as well as Islam) in politics is widespread, as demonstrated by the long-running war that led to the secession of South Sudan. Even more surprising and troubling is the borrowing, from Maoism, of propaganda and population-control techniques by a group like the Islamic State; and the use by it, as well as by the Taliban, of a very Maoist strategy of taking power in the countryside and progressively strangling towns. Islamic State propaganda, extremely well-designed and presented, is circulating throughout the Sahel as it is in Europe.

The Sahel is not Afghanistan, but certain groundswells are reminiscent of those that have swept Afghanistan since the 1980s.

---

[3] Philippe Hugon, 'Les devises de la République à l'heure des manifestations dans le monde à propos de Charlie Hebdo', unpublished working paper, 2016.

The rise of extremist Islamism has led to the radicalization of a significant proportion of a population that previously practiced a very moderate form of Islam. All things considered, given the similarities and differences, the comparison between the Sahel and Afghanistan is fully justified, at least for analytical purposes, in order to draw some key lessons from the West's failure in Afghanistan. This is already true at a tactical military level—the French army recognizes that its experience in Afghanistan is extremely useful in its fight in the Sahel. It is also useful with regard to managing aid and even to selecting an overall intervention strategy. So let's now summarize the key lessons, the '12 commandments' that should be drawn from the West's debacle in Afghanistan in order to avoid a new catastrophe in the Sahel.

## Lesson 1: Lasting security cannot be provided by foreign or United Nations troops.

As we observed at the beginning of this book, Sahel countries are confronted by huge new threats that constitute multiple flashpoints and bushfires that are ready to spread. In short, the Sahel countries have become highly flammable powder kegs. Facing up to the threats confronting the Sahel region thus entails both extinguishing the bushfires and also—above all—neutralizing the powder kegs. Is this possible? *Yes*—provided the Sahel countries, the French government, the European Union and the international donor community do not continue their 'business-as-usual' approach.

Let's begin with basic principles. Essentially, extinguishing such 'bushfires' requires military means. But, dismantling the powder kegs requires the implementation of complex strategies combining security measures, political negotiations, development programmes, humanitarian assistance, and more. First up: how to deal with flashpoints and bushfires.

*Foreign troops should be used chiefly to extinguish flashpoints as quickly as possible.*

Flashpoints and bushfires threatening to spread swiftly may require external military intervention, as when French forces conducted a high-impact operation to stop a military offensive led by jihadist groups in Mali in 2013. This case was exceptional, as the fighting took place in a semi-desert environment where air support and heavy weaponry could be used without much risk of collateral damage. The Jihadist groups were moving with columns of pick-ups and were easy targets for the French air force. The involvement of foreign military forces in densely populated areas, such as central Mali or the North West of Niamey in Niger, where Jihadists generally move with just two or three pickups and a few motorbikes, or remain hidden among the population raises more complex issues.

If Malian authorities believe, as it seems to presently be the case, that the French army will take care of its jihadists—and that there is no urgency in reconstructing its army, gendarmerie, and bureaucratic machinery because it will create too many political problems with friends and cronies—Mali will soon find itself in an Afghanistan-type crisis that no foreign army will be able to sort out. If the new French government continues with the purely military approach to Sahel problems that was its predecessor's choice, it will soon find itself as embarrassed as the present US government, confronted today with the uneasy choice of sending troops back to Afghanistan or facing humiliating defeat. Finally, if the international donor community continues with its current disorganized and unstructured approach, the billions in euros and dollars spent in the region are likely to sink into the sand.

Clearly, this type of conflict can neither be settled by foreign armies nor solved by military means alone. 'Winning the war is not enough to win the peace,' the former chief of staff of the French armed forces, General de Villiers, wrote recently in the influential *"Le Monde"* newspaper.[4] The destruction of the main rebel armed forces alone does not resolve the conflict. On the contrary, the cancer is likely to spread and expand if the underlying problems—the powder keg—are not addressed. Moreover, experience shows that these conflicts are rarely resolved in a few months but, rather, require decades. And it is folly to expect that foreign forces should remain involved in a conflict of this kind for decades.

[4] *Le Monde.fr*, 20 January 2016.

What should be feared in most Sahel countries is similar to what is taking place today in central Mali and around Lake Chad. In these regions, small armed groups take advantage of local weaknesses of the state to exploit economic, social, and political difficulties and establish footholds in densely populated areas; if foreign armies were to intervene, they would quickly be perceived as occupying forces. Clearly, action limited to extinguishing flashpoints by 'neutralizing' jihadists (to use the official wording), though necessary, is insufficient; a powder keg that is not defused will produce more jihadists than the armed forces can eliminate. This is what occurred in Afghanistan. Only local forces, and the strong presence of efficient administrative and security apparatuses, will be able to maintain basic security once jihadist forces have been degraded and dispersed by foreign forces.

## United Nations peacekeeping forces have a very limited capacity.

Assessment of the performance of UN peacekeeping forces in the face of these new threats is critical. These forces can help maintain a minimum level of security in a region if the situation has not degraded too much, but their operational capacities are very low. For example, the main concern of the MINUSMA force in Mali today is the protection of its own bases and of key roads to ensure their supply chain. One reason for the weak capabilities of these forces stems, in part, from their heterogeneity (29 countries are represented in MINUSMA in Mali in 2017, many of them with merely symbolic forces). But the main reason for their weak capability is the poor quality of troops sent by the countries providing the forces, and their lack of motivation.

In fact the inefficiency of UN Peace Keeping forces in the world in now a major source of concern. Thierry Vircoulon, a former staff of International Crisis Group and now researcher at the French IFRI think tank has recently written a devastating analysis[5] of the general causes of their inefficiencies, which according to him "get quickly bogged down, and unable to resolve conflicts just satisfy themselves with accompanying them".

[5] Thierry Vircoulon, https://theconversation.com/le-maintien-de-la-paix-version-onu-radiographie-dune-impuissance-84942?utm

According to Vircoulon these forces have only a military look but cannot be a military force due to restrictive mandates that they in addition apply restrictively. They have no coherent conflict resolution framework, and with their doctrine ill-suited to the nature of modern internal conflicts, they are condemned to be powerless.

These countries receive good income[6] from the United Nations while sending untrained and unmotivated personnel who are sometimes not fully equipped. Providing troops to the UN has become a profitable 'business' for some countries. What can the level of motivation be, for example, for Bangladeshi soldiers locked up in their bastion in Kidal in northern Mali, or traveling in the desert on impossible roads without ever coming across the enemy, but who witness the death of brothers-in-arms who step on improvised explosive devices or suffer incoming mortar shells at night? The MINUSMA force has suffered significant losses in Mali—more than 140 deaths since it was set up in 2013—revealing the inadequacy of its mandate, structure of forces relative to the enemy they are expected to fight, and its modes of action.

It is thus reasonable to question the cost-effectiveness of these forces, whose cost in Mali exceeds USD 1 billion per year, especially if their maintenance over 15 years proves necessary, as is the case, for instance, in the DRC. In addition, the mandate of the forces is often inadequate to the situation, or blurred, and may give rise to varying interpretations on the ground resulting in culpable inaction.[7] These constraints do not allow the forces to carry out pre-emptive actions or even engage in aggressive responses to attacks.

[6] A country that sends a battalion as part of a United Nations peacekeeping operation receives about USD 15 million per year. The salaries it pays its soldiers might be between USD 2 million and USD 4 million, or sometimes less, if expatriation and risk premiums are not paid, as has been known to happen. This demonstrates the profitability of what, for some countries, becomes a business. Note that the discrepancies between billed and actual costs mean that private security companies (which are interested by such 'business') could offer a much better service for less.

[7] It is for this reason that the head of UNMISS in South Sudan was recently relieved of his duties after allowing a massacre of civilians to take place before his eyes.

On the other hand, as General Lamine Cissé[8] recently pointed out to me, that if this type of force is made up of regional African contingents, they are able to equip and train themselves while incorporating rules concerning respect for fundamental rights as well as a capacity to operate with forces of diverse origins. These assets would give them greater efficiency both on the spot, where they are easier to motivate than when they return to the armies of their countries of origin, and in future African regional permanent forces.

This analysis—and the understanding that MINUSMA will never be up to the task—is clearly one of the reasons for the establishment of a regional multinational 'G5 force' of 5,000 men, which will be composed of soldiers from the armies of the G5 countries. The force, whose establishment was announced at the G5 summit in Bamako on July 2, 2017, will be trained and supported by the French Barkhane operation and may improve the military capacity in the field. However, its cost as initially assessed by member countries was on the high side, and questionable, and its funding has only been partly identified.[9] Finally, as we have noted, of course, the military dimension is just one facet of the security problem.

## Lesson 2: Sovereign government institutions need to be consolidated or rebuilt.

Clearly, these fragile nations are complex, crisscrossed by multiple ethnic, religious, social, intergenerational, and territorial divisions, where unemployed young people constitute a ticking social time bomb and where a simplistic, totalitarian ideology conceals itself beneath the veneer of Islam. Under such conditions, to believe that foreign military forces belonging to a completely different culture are, by themselves, capable of bringing peace, is unreasonable.

[8] Former chief of staff of the Senegalese army and former commander of the United Nations office in West Africa.

[9] This cost had been assessed, by the African military of the G5, to be 423 million euros, which is unrealistically high. A more accurate figure should be in the range of half this amount. The European Union has decided to provide (only) 50 million euros.

*There is no alternative.*

Despite their restrictive rules of engagement, ISAF troops in Afghanistan were unable to avoid blunders, from errors during aerial bombing raids to conducting searches in women's areas. These blunders were cleverly exploited by Taliban propaganda. From 2007 on, I saw men spit at passing patrols in Kabul. These scenes called to mind the reactions of people in France during the 1950s—manipulated, of course, by the Communist Party on orders from Moscow—when faced with the simple presence of American soldiers who had liberated the country.

In some cases, the intervention of foreign forces can prove essential, as we saw in Mali in 2013. It is unrealistic, however, to believe that eliminating 'terrorists' will lead to a restoration of peace if the political, economic, institutional, and social conditions that enabled the crisis are not also 'treated.' In a previous book, I compared these countries to kegs of gunpowder and the extremists present there in large numbers to torches suspended above the kegs. It would take just one minor incident to cause one of the torches to fall into a keg. A foreign army will never be able to extinguish all of the torches; *the real problem is the keg.*

The figures speak for themselves. At the height of the rise of US power in Afghanistan, when international forces numbered some 150,000 troops, ISAF still did not really occupy the country. Had it done so, would it have been able to administer justice? Settle land disputes? Issue identity papers? Hunt down kidnappers? Provide jobs for young people? Bring in supplies? Let's be honest. The era when marine troops and Senegalese 'tirailleurs,' the military wings of the colonial system, would assume these functions in Sahel year-in and year-out, acting under the authority of a local colonial commander, are long gone. It is precisely because justice has not been administered, government no longer exists, livestock thieves and kidnappers operate with impunity, and young people have no jobs, that these torches are able to set off explosions. Dealing with these issues is vital if the goal is to ensure stability in these countries.

If police, local governments, and legal systems in the Sahel are not restored to order, in some cases even 'reconstructed' on different basis and if genuine rule of law is not established not only in the capitals and major cities but throughout the countries concerned, there is every likelihood that the overall situation will deteriorate. Sorting out the legal system is no doubt a particularly tricky task. I do not have sufficient knowledge of the legal systems in the countries of the Sahel to make a judgment, but I have reviewed the legal systems in other African countries and know that sometimes, corruption goes all the way to the top. The most corrupt magistrates are the most vigilant with respect to the independence of the legal system and the first to claim that it is being destroyed if the executive branch attempts to clean things up.

Here too, however, experience offers options for improvement: publication of all legal decisions; random review of a percentage of all legal decisions by a college of reliable magistrates; and, most important, using the opportunity of a major scandal to appoint a trustworthy senior hierarchy. Because legal systems in cities are often ill-equipped to deal with situations in remote villages located 1,000 kilometres from the capital, the option of relying on traditional systems should not be rejected in some regions.

### Strengthening or rebuilding national armies and gendarmeries goes way beyond training programmes.

On the security front, it is important to first regain control of regions and populations that are partially or completely outside the authority of the central state. Beyond any external military intervention, this requires responding to the state's shortcomings and not only strengthening the national armed forces but also consolidating—or in some difficult cases entirely rebuilding—the other state sovereign institutions. This type of consolidation can be part of an ambitious programme of security-sector reform, the scope of which must be expanded beyond current practice.[10]

It is very often the weakness, the absence, sometimes even the decay and irresponsible behavior of these state institutions that led to insecurity in the first place and, in some cases, to the establishment of parallel authorities. The need to strengthen the state

---

[10] Often, this type of reform is limited to the army and forgets the 'gendarmerie', police, and other forces.

apparatus is easy to identify, but implementing programmes to do so poses difficult technical, political, and financial problems.

At the technical level, rehabilitating the relevant institutions generally requires much more than training and equipment programmes.[11] The process requires reintroduction of the principles on which the effectiveness of institutions has always been based: rigorous selection of management at all levels on the basis of merit and performance; and the introduction of results-oriented human-resource management requiring job definitions, skills reviews to eliminate unfit personnel, and organizational structures with clear lines of responsibility. These steps often require targeted salary increases to attract and retain specialized or managerial staff.

At the organizational level, rehabilitating these institutions also requires having a hard look at the nature of the threats confronting them. Does the Malian army really need a battalion of artillery with 16 heavy guns that will never be available on time to confront an attack led by three pickups 500 miles from Bamako? Should the command structure be organized along the heavy NATO model designed to confront the soviet tanks? My discussions with French officers in the field make me believe that highly mobile light units organized along the Chadian model, with a few powerful but mobile rocket launchers, would be much more efficient than the present organizational structure of the Malian army in brigades, battalions, etc.

Basically, because the European funded training programmes of the army and other security services in Mali already mentioned (EUTM and EUCAP) do not take into account such measures, the strongest doubts can be voiced about their efficiency. For lack of political courage, European Union officials do not dare confront the Malian President and condition their support to major reforms regarding the unwritten rules regarding selection and promotion of senior officers. Combined with the inefficiency of the Malian gendarmerie and police force the result is two costly programmes unlikely to significantly improve the security services

---

[11] The limits of such programmes have been seen in the case of the Afghan police, which after 15 years of programmes of training and provision of equipment, remains the mafia it was in early 2002.

effective capacity, thus leading the French forces, as previously mentioned, into a strategic impasse[12].

The refusal by the US to quickly establish a robust Afghan army and sort out the police force, deciding instead to restore security by relying on international forces and local thugs, only exacerbated the situation. Vigilance on this point will therefore be important in the Sahel. Operating in the sparsely populated desert region of the Ifoghas hills, the French Army can deploy its firepower without fear of collateral damage. But, in the Niger River Loop region of Mali between Segou and Mopti, once frequently visited by tourists, where a new insurgency is developing, it is difficult to imagine the French army going in and freely deploying its firepower.

Some time ago, a young lieutenant involved in Operation Barkhane explained on French television: 'It is not easy—it is impossible to know who the enemy is. The Tuareg who goes past with his goats could be the guy who has just buried his Kalashnikov after firing at my soldiers from behind'—a statement that brings back bad memories of other conflicts.

### Nepotism is a major obstacle.

The greatest obstacle to implementing such institution-building programmes is political in nature. Reform of this type requires abandoning practices that are common in multi-ethnic countries where loyalty, tribal links, and nepotism often take precedence over capability and efficiency. Real reform of the security sector, for instance, requires profound changes in human-resources management of armed forces, police forces, local government, and more. Lasting results cannot be expected where nepotism, ethnicism, and corruption reign supreme.[13] In this respect, the new and

---

[12] At the suggestion of a few French Officers who cannot express themself, I recently developed these points in a well-known French review: '*Mali, une guerre sans fin* ?' Revue de la Défense Nationale, février 2018.

[13] For example, vehicles bought at great expense are plundered (as was the case in Iraq) or their tires found for sale in the market (as is still the case in Mali), arms and ammunition are resold, and units that are ready to fight on paper are in fact ghost troops, like those that fled before the jihadists in Mosul in 2014.

very lucid Malian Minister of Defense, appointed in April 2017, explained in a recent interview on Radio France International that he could not rebuild the Malian army if he was constantly pressured to recruit friends and relatives of powerful politicians. In his own words, 'Such recruits only come for the pay and are afraid of the enemy.'[14] The quality of every institution—and the institutions responsible for security are no exception—depends above all on the quality of their personnel and especially on the quality of those who lead them.

### The poorest countries lack the resources to strengthen their state apparatuses and fund their security expenses.

A major difficulty is that Least Developed Countries (LDCs), which include the Sahel countries, cannot finance both their development[15] and state apparatuses able to meet the threats they now confront, especially since the state apparatuses must be deployed throughout their territories. In a characteristic case, Niger[16] was forced to multiply its military spending by a factor of 3.7 between 2009 and 2015. Neither Niger, nor Mali, nor the other countries of the Sahel sub-region possess economies or tax bases that enable them to meet their immense social and economic needs, as well as the security emergencies they face.

The fiscal capacities of these countries rarely exceed 17 to 18 per cent of their GDPs. Faced with threats, they are forced to reduce development spending to finance security spending, which approaches 6 to 7 per cent of GDP in many places, and as much

[14] RFI 30 May 2017, interview of Tiena Coulibaly, new Minister of Defense in Mali.

[15] Social expenditures are currently exploding because of demographics: 40 to 50 per cent of the population is under 15 years of age.

[16] Niger is one of the first countries in the world to have benefited from a detailed analysis by the World Bank, of the sustainability of its security spending based on various assumptions about its pace of growth. The analysis, carried out in 2015, based on data from 2013, showed that if security expenditures were to increase over the period 2013–16 at the same rate as 2009–12 (154 per cent), the budget deficit would become intolerable. However, the country's security spending in 2016 has already exceeded the World Bank's most pessimistic expectations.

as 9 per cent in Chad. Even this level of security expenditure is insufficient to cope with the new threats they face. These exceptional costs reduce the resources allocated to economic and social development, thus increasing future risks without guaranteeing security. These countries are therefore caught in a double impasse that is both budgetary and security-related. As a result, they risk falling into conflict traps.

Recall that the American refusal, until the arrival of General Petraeus in 2008–09, to accept serious financial responsibility for the Afghan army largely explains its poor performance. The entire state apparatuses of these Sahel countries—including army, police, local administration, justice, and customs—urgently need consolidating and funding. In the Sahel region, only countries with significant oil or mining revenues—as was the case of Chad prior to the collapse of oil prices—would be able to do so.

## What role can aid agencies play in the security sector?

Aid agencies have developed knowledge and expertise about strengthening institutions in the sectors in which they traditionally intervene. They know how to help restructure ministries of finance, planning, energy, public works, education, health, and the like, as well as public companies operating in the relevant sectors. These institutional issues are the core justification for their intervention, since any bank can finance a power station—'hard' infrastructure in development jargon. On the other hand, 'soft' infrastructure, or restoring order to institutions—which in the energy sector, for example, might involve restructuring an electricity company, reviewing its performance contract, and redefining the responsibilities of the relevant ministry—is usually the main component of a sector intervention by the World Bank or the French Development Agency (AFD).

But what should the role of these aid agencies be when it comes to reorganizing police forces, armies, local governments, and territorial administrations? Changing the mandate of the major international agencies in these areas could take decades. It is therefore important to restore the role of bilateral aid agencies, whose capacities—because they were considered relics of the colonial era—have tended to be denigrated over the last 30 years. The bilateral agencies could pool resources and work in groups of two, three, or four to remove the 'return-of-the-colonists' charge that might be attached to an intervention carried out by a single bilateral agency. They have much quicker reaction times than the big multilateral bureaucracies and could fund studies and pilot projects that could later be used by multilaterals. The skills and technical capabilities of the major European bilateral agencies— the UK's Department for International Development (DFID), Germany's KfW and GIZ, and France's AFD—are certainly equal to those of the best multilateral behemoths.

These agencies, of course, have no expertise in fields related to national sovereignty. Hence, their role should be different from the role they play in their normal sectors of expertise. First and foremost, they should act as intermediaries between the relevant sovereign institutions in their own countries and the recipient countries. This should include offering experts from their own country's army, police force, interior ministry, and so on, as well as expertise in institution-building. They can also facilitate mobilization of expertise from other developing countries. Finally, they can play a financial role: the French police, for example, cannot be expected to fund any support it might offer to Niger or Mali from its own operating budget. This implies that these agencies should have access to funding specifically for this purpose.

On this point, I admit to having been aghast at the end of 2001 by a meeting held in the high-security basement of the General Secretariat for Defence and National Security in Paris when I was the head of operations of the French Development Agency. The aim of the meeting was to identify what kind of aid France would offer Afghanistan. Sitting around the large table were some 50 representatives from the main French departments expected to offer contributions. At the end of the meeting, we had a random list of things Parisian ministries did not know what to do with: three academy inspectors, 50 tonnes of seeds, ten police instructors, three drug-sniffing dogs and their instructors, and, worst of all, a decision not to take part in the joint UN–World Bank mission that was going to make an initial assessment of the most urgent needs.

## Lesson 3: Most security expenditures will have to be supported by the international community.

In a context in which security expenditures reaching 6 to 9 per cent of GDP are now supplanting development spending, strengthening or rebuilding national armies (some of which are 'Potemkin' in nature) requires substantial financial support.

### *Political and ethical problems should be carefully considered.*

For an external player, this poses many problems. The first is a political one. What is the legitimacy of the political power that will have authority over this army? If it is a democratic power, does it provide opportunities for minorities to express their views or does it, on the contrary, seek to suppress them? Strengthening an army that seeks to oppress minorities or political opponents would be adding fuel to the fire. A political analysis should therefore be conducted.

What, also, are the risks of setting up an army composed of a single ethnic group or religion? We have witnessed the abuses of an Iraqi army that ostracized the Sunnis who constituted its backbone. Because it was established too late—after the majority of Pashtun regions had already fallen under Taliban control—the Afghan army is largely Tajik. This means it cannot be the crucible in which a new nation can develop. It also means that in Pashtun areas, where the Tajik forces do not speak the local language, the army is almost as lost as the American troops were.

Would an ethnic mix that was, in principle, capable of creating this embryonic nation be acceptable to political leaders in the Sahel? Would it be acceptable to the troops themselves at a time when refuelled hatred among ethnicities has created a climate of constant suspicion? We must not forget that the almost mono-ethnic Tuareg units formed at great expense by the Americans in Mali before the 2012 crisis wound up deserting *en masse* when they were sent in against their brothers from the National Movement for the Liberation of Azawad (MNLA). Would political leaders—who often fear their own armies and rely on presidential guards, often drawn from a single ethnic group or tribe—accept a strengthening of the army without a concomitant strengthening of their presidential guard forces?

*Costs to donors are likely to remain manageable.*

Funding of at least part of these countries' security costs by the European Union or a group of donor countries is the most urgent measure needed to prevent further deterioration of security. This support should not be limited, as it is now, to training personnel and supplying miscellaneous equipment. Instead, it should include payment of wages and fuel, reforming human-resources management, equipping units with appropriate equipment, building new barracks, and most important, reforming governance of security forces.

The problem for the international community is not financial. With sound management, equipping, training, and funding a Sahel battalion for one year costs about 20 million.[17] Instead of setting up high-cost peacekeeping forces, the United Nations would be better off funding local security forces—on the condition that it seriously oversees their complete reorganization. The rehabilitation and reconstruction of the Malian army, for example, certainly would not cost the billion dollars a year mobilized for the UN peacekeeping force. Moreover, the conditions likely to accompany funding from aid institutions would help improve the governance of those forces. The failure to properly reorganize the Afghan police should remind us that foreign support limited to provision of training courses and the donation of equipment can never hope to seriously restructure a security institution.

Such a cost-sharing approach is easy to justify. Financially, it would be far less expensive than a foreign military intervention;[18] moreover, the political cost would be much lower because the international community does not take kindly to the return of its children in coffins. Secondly, the security of these vast regions

[17] Recall that the cost of MINUSMA for Mali alone is on the order of USD 1 billion per year, the cost of the Barkhane operation is more than 650 million euros, and the budget of the 11th European Development Fund (EDF) covering the 2014–20 period is € 30 billion.

[18] A Western military intervention would, in any case, lead to an impasse in view of the available forces, the size of the territories in question, their populations, and the inevitable friction between a population and armed forces from very different cultures, sometimes representing the former colonial power. The Sahel represents about 7 million square kilometers and will have a population of 150 million in 10 years. The Barkhane force consists of 4,500 men.

constitutes a regional, even global, public good and therefore justifies a cost-sharing approach. Also, this is the only credible way to ensure the security of these areas and to avoid a process that might be called 'Afghanization.'

*However, opposition to international funding of security expenditures is considerable.*

Multilateral organizations have long funded institutional restructuring programmes in their usual areas of intervention. The irony is that these aid institutions know there can be no development without security and no security without development, yet they apply rules that clearly contradict their own observations.

Within multilateral aid organizations, legal experts rely on 70-year-old statutes that prohibit any involvement of donors in the security sector. Officials at these agencies also fear that resources devoted to security will reduce those devoted to traditional development activities, and so take a dim view of new demands on limited budget resources. Finally, many representatives of civil society argue that aid is not meant to fund security, security budgets are often opaque, and funding them under such circumstances constitutes a gift to corruption. Given these conditions, altering the practices of the principal donors will clearly take time and considerable lobbying.

Still, it is important that the governments of the countries concerned, especially the Sahel countries, exert pressure on the multilateral aid institutions to recognize the obvious contradiction between their understanding that there can be no development without security and their practice of ignoring that fact. The OECD Development Assistance Committee (DAC) is well aware of this contradiction and is working on the subject,[19] which makes it possible to anticipate some progress, even if it remains very timid for the time being.

The goal of the World Bank study of the sustainability of security spending in Niger—the first of its kind in a country facing serious threats—was to achieve agreement among the major multilateral

[19] See Annex 2 of the declaration issued by the high-level DAC meeting of 19 February 2016, entitled 'ODA boundaries in the field of peace and security.'

partners within three to five years to fund at least non-military security spending, focusing primarily on local administration and justice, followed by equipping police and similar forces in non-lethal equipment.

Among multilateral bodies, only the European Union (EU) is beginning to get involved in these issues—in particular, by funding training programmes for security forces such as the European Union Training Mission in Mali (EUTM). However, if funding is restricted to training or purchasing non-lethal equipment, as currently envisaged—without providing for proper military equipment (and civilian control over military forces)—it remains inadequate. For now, the EU is still hesitant, and its expertise in this area is very limited.

The recent EU proposal to provide about 50 million euros to help support the G5 multinational force for the Sahel is a positive first step, but it is insufficient. The force should cost about 220 million euros, but the budgets of the G5 countries will not provide funding given the fiscal crisis they currently face due to already exploding security expenditures. Comparing this offer of 50 million euros by the EU with the security costs directly supported by the G5 countries of the Sahel which must be in the range of USD 2 billions shows that the EU has not yet understood the magnitude of the problem; and relying as has now been decided upon Saudi Arabia to fund the G5 military force is basically asking a pyroman to extinguish a fire he has contributed to start...

Through the mobilization of the human resources of their own state institutions, bilateral donors (US, UK, France, and Germany) have the best expertise in this field. But the US is far less concerned than Europe with security in Africa, Great Britain has little interest in Francophone countries, and European countries have limited resources with which to finance support for capacity-building and institutional restructuring.

*International funding for local security costs requires their rationalization and transparency.*

Due to donors' reluctance to fund military expenditures, an indirect approach can be used. Military and security needs of low-income countries can be met without direct funding of military expenditures by aid partners. The solution would be to show, in the usual financial statements discussed with the IMF, the actual costs instead of the widely underestimated amounts currently presented, and to fund the increased deficits as budget support, whether unallocated (ideally) or even earmarked to social or development expenditures. This last option would create room to maneuver in the budget in that the fungibility of budgetary resources would allow for the indirect funding of security spending.[20] However, this mechanism involves finding solutions to several problems.

To reassure donors, these countries should abandon the purely reactive approach to security emergencies that currently holds sway, and introduce mechanisms for the rational programming of security expenditures based on serious threat and security analyses. The first step should be the preparation of white papers carefully analyzing current and future threats. This should lead to the preparation of multi-year military programming laws setting out requirements for the military and other state-security institutions.[21] Subsequently, it is important to move away from an accounting approach that leads most of the countries concerned— all of which are under IMF programmes and supervision—to scale down their security budgets to bring them in line with available resources, and not in accord with the nature and extent of actual threats.[22] They tend to respond to security emergencies with

[20] For example, the Algerian government met the budgetary cost of a large part of its security expenditures linked to the outbreak of the civil war in 1993–94 with indirect financing through the IMF.

[21] It is desirable that the countries concerned have this work validated by the partners who support their military efforts, in particular France, the US, Germany, and the UK, depending on the case. However, this approach requires still greater transparency in security budgets— including the military budget—which must be capable of being audited by the financial partners, as is commonly the case with the education and health budgets that receive budget support.

[22] Following this accounting reasoning, the Afghan army was sized to very insufficient levels (about 30,000, with only 14,000 trained men until 2006, and 50,000 until 2007–08), leaving foreign forces with the responsibility of fighting the rebellion. Given the extent of the rebellion in 2008, General Petraeus estimated the need to urgently build a local force of 350,000 men.

supplementary budgets that widen deficits and lower development spending. Such a highly constrained and unplanned budgetary approach does not provide an effective response to real security needs.

Implementation of these principles requires a high level of awareness among bilateral partners—in particular France, Germany, the UK, the Nordic countries, and the US—including EU bodies. They must recognize the crucial problem of security in these regions, the inevitability of increased budget deficits linked to the military and security efforts required, and the need for external funding of these deficits on a multi-annual basis in order to avoid financial gaps and security impasses each year.

Once such an agreement has been reached, in principle, in the Sahel countries' negotiations with the leading European governments, it is also desirable that these countries raise awareness among the governments with influence in both the IMF and the World Bank, in particular the US, Canadian, Japanese, and Chinese governments. It would then be easier, in negotiations with the Bretton Woods institutions, to integrate the real costs of security into budgets and anticipated financial operations with greater transparency.[23] If the resulting financial gaps can be covered by bilateral aid or by the European Union, agreement from the IMF and the World Bank should be easy to obtain.

---

[23] One my wonder whether the difference between the initial cost of the G5 force as assessed by the G5 countries (423 million euros), and a more reasonable assessment which is in the range of USD 220 million, was the 'rent' some G5 countries had expected to extract from possible donors.

# CHAPTER
# THIRTEEN

## Other Key Lessons for the Sahel and Donors drawn from the West's Failure in Afghanistan

It is clear, by now, that defusing Sahel's powder kegs requires implementing complex strategies that combine political and social actions, security measures, ambitious development programmes, and, ultimately, ideological struggles. Politically, it will be necessary, sooner or later, to reach balanced political agreements to reduce tensions that have accompanied or contributed to ongoing conflicts. These tensions are often linked to perceptions of marginalization and, in some cases, to actual discrimination. This was the case of some Tuareg revolts in both Mali and Niger, and it appears that feelings of political and economic marginalization are behind the recent formation of the Macina Liberation Front by Fulani groups in central Mali. The launch of stabilization programmes, however, should not wait until proper political agreements have been reached, since this could take years, or even decades.

## Lesson 4: Launching stabilization programmes cannot wait for full political agreements.

The sooner political agreements can be reached, of course, the easier it will be to resolve conflicts. But, if political negotiations drag on, as has been the case in Afghanistan for 40 years and is currently the case in Mali, the conflicts have every chance of becoming entrenched, especially if, as is often the case, certain actors benefit greatly from them. It is usually very difficult to reach a political consensus at the outset of or even during a conflict, as is hoped by many observers and by an impatient public. The international community often underestimates the depth of political tensions affecting these countries and pushes for unrealistic, early agreements that usually fall apart.

Unfortunately, it is often necessary to wait until a conflict unfolds like a Greek tragedy, before a political agreement can be reached. This means that political agreements cannot be a prerequisite for launching ambitious security, social, and development actions. This point is critical because, while reaching political agreement or relative consensus is always difficult, if not impossible, in acute conflicts, a stabilization strategy cannot wait.[1]

## Lesson 5: Forcefully addressing the job issue is critical to stabilizing rural areas.

Given the demographic constraints confronting these countries, along with the critical need to maintain security and govern regions where peace has been recently restored, or that are at risk of insurgency, a key priority for the international community is to help create jobs. At least in the short term, this means focusing on the rural sector, where there are considerable employment possibilities. Revitalizing the rural economy in areas severely affected

---

[1] In Côte d'Ivoire, in 2011, when the tensions and disagreements among the parties to the conflict were still extreme, priority was given to disarmament, demobilization, and reintegration programmes, as well as an ambitious reform of the security sector even as politicians were still involved in discussions. Where the external partners strive to obtain the agreement of all parties before acting (as in the case in the CAR), the situation solidifies, then degrades.

by instability and underemployment should therefore be a key priority, which has not yet been the case in the Sahel. The goal is to reduce the temptation for young men to join the ranks of traffickers, who are often linked to jihadi groups. At least six main measures are required here.

## Increase budgets for the rural sector

Changing the scale of resources allocated to the rural sector means increasing national budgets and international aid to this sector. It is essential that the share of national budgets allocated to agriculture escapes its current range of 3–8 per cent and reaches a level more consistent with the proportion of the population that makes a living from agriculture—somewhere between 55 and 80 per cent in the Sahel. Agricultural spending on the order of 20 per cent of the total budget would provide appropriate funding for national agricultural institutions, including research centres, extension programmes, and agricultural schools, and for local public goods such as all-weather rural roads and soil restoration.[2] Such budget readjustments would also enable the creation of non-agricultural jobs in rural areas, particularly in activities such as soil regeneration, opening rural roads, and the like.

It is crucial that donors, at the very minimum, double their financial contributions devoted to this sector, which currently represent, depending the countries, around 4–8 per cent of international aid, even if that means cuts in areas that can more easily be financed by banks, the private sector, and/or support granted on market terms. Of course, donors' current lack of technical teams with strong expertise in tropical agriculture remains a major obstacle.

## Clarify the agricultural development model

The priority given to modern, small-scale farming, working wherever possible under contract with private wholesalers or local

---

[2] A usual justification that I heard many times for small budget allocation to the rural sector is the lack of projects and the weak absorptive capacity of this sector. But this is sheer nonsense. Building the relevant absorptive capacity should precisely be a key priority.

processing companies, is the best option capable of responding to the relentless problem of rural unemployment. This option should not, of course, exclude some agro-industrial operations that, to secure a return on an accompanying processing plant, require that part of the area be devoted to highly mechanized agriculture—a model that has proven effective in Côte d'Ivoire. Planning to rely solely upon sophisticated and highly mechanized agriculture to solve rural problems, however, would only create additional unemployment. Distributing tractors in the hope of recreating a European or American model in which 5 per cent of the population feeds everybody else is not a serious option.

### Strengthen sector institutions

I emphasized, in the previous chapter, the need to rebuild or strengthen institutions dealing with security issues because we usually operate on the assumption—which has not always proved correct—that the other institutions in the Sahel have long been monitored and supported by donors and received technical support and funding from external actors. I also warned that disasters generally hit sectors neglected by donors. This is particularly true with agriculture and local-development public institutions. Indeed, many were literally destroyed by the structural-adjustment programmes of the 1980s and 1990s and the anti-government ideology that accompanied them. It is, in fact, unrealistic to think that the private sector can do everything alone in this area.

Agriculture in the Sahel desperately needs public institutions capable of developing coherent sector strategies and facilitating their practical implementation. It is disheartening that the countless agricultural-development strategy documents produced by both national bodies and donors—most of whom combine a lack of experience with being distant from the field—are unrealistic. Agriculture in the Sahel needs support structures capable of overcoming market failures by maintaining roads or facilitating access to inputs, areas where the private sector is often absent. At the institutional level, however, the problem is often complicated.

Should the dormant and dysfunctional agriculture ministries be painstakingly rebuilt? Should they be reduced to empty shells, making way for grand initiatives based upon regional agencies built from scratch along the model of the old development companies (the famous *'Sociétés de dévelopement'*) in Cote d'Ivoire? What is certain is that these issues cannot be resolved by uncoordinated approaches, project structures that are not set up for the long term, and simple injections of cash, as the main donors are currently attempting to do. It is imperative that the institutional issues be seriously dealt with.

## Mobilize African and international expertise

Agriculture in the Sahel region is a difficult and risky undertaking and needs highly qualified expertise. While aid at the international level has largely turned its focus away from this sector,[3] there is still considerable expertise. Seasoned experts who gained a great deal of experience in the Sahel when it was still possible to travel safely in the region can be found scattered throughout the World Bank and other institutions, such as the International Fund for Agricultural Development (IFAD) and the Food and Agriculture Organization (FAO). Finally, one should not forget that there is a great deal of African expertise that is underutilized, or not used at all. The problem is, as we already discussed, both institutional and financial.

## Launch major regional rural development programmes

Programmes focusing on agricultural and pastoral development, small-scale economic infrastructure at the local level, rural and pastoral water supply, rural electrification, decentralization, and

[3] These issues are more complex than is usually imagined, since the classic 'technical top-down' approaches consisting of proposing turnkey projects to rural populations have an unfortunate habit of failing. During a seminar held in 2003 in Rabat, the World Bank came to the conclusion that half of the rural development projects it had financed in Africa had failed (cf. Zana M. [2003]. *Préparer et financer les projets dans la coopération au développement,* ARISSALA, Rabat). The fact is that this institution, unlike the AFD and French development NGOs, had largely lost sight of the importance of participative approaches, local design, and high-level expertise in tropical agriculture.

related issues should concentrate on effectiveness rather than causing a stir in the media. It is the success of actual projects that is important in securing stability, not announcements of funding in the press. Such programmes should be part of coherent, medium-term expenditure frameworks taking into account comprehensive budget constraints and a realistic assessment of the ability to mobilize external funding.

### Strongly Support Municipal and Community Development

Since the mid-1980s, various kinds of local development programmes based on direct support by government budgets and donors to municipalities or rural communities have been initiated in the Sahel. In Mali, throughout the 1990s, for example, French aid financed so-called rural-development-fund programmes.[4] Since then, resources provided to such funds by donors have been decreasing, and donor actions have often short-circuited rather than strengthened these institutions. Most are now unfunded, and the institutional setups have remained idle. While such programmes allow direct funding of poor rural communities by donors, present transfers often amount to less than one cent of a dollar per beneficiary per year.

The Sahel countries should study the achievements in this area by the Afghans, thanks to the National Solidarity Program. I have already mentioned my admiration for the work done in Afghanistan by Minister Hanif Atmar and his team at the Ministry of Rural Reconstruction and Development (MRRD), as well as by the World Bank teams that monitored and financed the programme for more than twelve years. As I noted, this type of operation involves offering small grants to village councils so they can implement projects important to them. This sounds simple, but programmes of this type are extremely complex to manage when they cover an entire country and encompass tens of thousands of small projects—about 60,000 in Afghanistan, spread throughout 28,000 rural communities—especially if projects are

---

[4] Cf. M.J. Demante and A. Félix, '*Répondre au défi du développement local en milieu rural: l'exemple du Mali*', in Serge Michailof, '*À quoi sert d'aider le Sud*' (Economica, 2005).

to be technically sound, so that small dams are not swept away by storms and a serious, participative, democratic process is to be set up.

In Mali, the *Fonds National d'Appui aux Collectivités Territoriales* (National Support Fund for Local Authorities) is functioning, but has been completely starved of resources. A similar institution has been established in Niger and a pilot project is also implemented by the *"Haute Autorité pour la Consolidation de la Paix"* under the supervision of the Prime Minister. Why not strengthen and re-energize these institutions, check their procedures, and see if they can be made into instruments capable of channelling significant resources to municipalities and rural communities with success similar to that of the National Solidarity Program?

## Lesson 6: Acceleration of the demographic transition should be at the top of the international development agenda.

I have noted the reluctance of international aid agencies to commit to funding family-planning programmes, which are very sensitive in nature. But for Sahel countries in the grip of a demographic boom that is essentially trapping them in poverty, *there is in reality no alternative* if they hope to avoid the Malthusian collapse that awaits them. Such a collapse might take the form of a chaotic security situation, which would precede and provoke the kind of famine described by Malthus more than two centuries ago.

Today, we have enough data and experience to implement comprehensive programmes that have a good chance of accelerating the demographic transition in the Sahel. Such programmes should combine the provision of general health services at village level, information campaigns, increased education efforts for girls, legal prohibition of early marriage (as Chad has recently adopted), and access to modern contraceptive devices. High-quality family-planning services need to be made available to women in both urban and rural areas. This is a difficult issue, we know, and the first task will be to tackle societal norms in the Sahel that favour high birth rates. But it is essential that governments recognize the urgent need to take action in this area and unambiguously support programmes that offer family-planning information, advice, and services. Despite numerous publications and conferences on the subject, these goals are still a long way from being realized.

The success achieved in this area in countries such as Indonesia and Bangladesh—two Muslim countries, just like the nations of the Sahel—which have seen birth rates decline from six or seven children per woman at the end of the 1960s to about 2.2 today, provides a clear illustration of the path to take. Of course, for obvious ethical and political reasons, the programmes implemented must never be coercive and should fully respect the rights of individuals.

The patriarchal structure of families in the Sahel and the practice of early marriage for young girls pose considerable obstacles. Just remember the outcry when the contraceptive 'pill' was introduced in France! Any programme seeking to control birth rates must rely on parallel actions that use financial incentives to keep young girls in school as long as possible and help improve living conditions for women by focusing on such matters as access to drinking water, microfinance, and improvements to homes and sanitation. These activities need to be complemented by communications campaigns against early marriage and by providing improved health care, which presupposes the strengthening of primary healthcare coverage.

Over the last 15 years, donors have shown that when they mobilize in support of clear objectives, such as reducing infant mortality, results can ensue. They now urgently need to raise to the top of the international-development agenda the issues of sensible fertility control and informed access of all women to contraception. I fear that this is a long way off. The cost of family-planning programmes can be contained within very reasonable limits—the problem is essentially political. In 2012, the Gates Foundation and DFID organized a family-planning conference in London, the aim of which was to mobilize USD 8 billion and launch an extensive family-planning programme, to run until 2020. So far, donors appear to not have responded to this initiative with the necessary alacrity.

In this crucial area, Sahel governments and aid agencies alike must now show courage, launch awareness campaigns as soon as possible, and restructure existing—and ineffective—family-planning services. Initiatives such as the Oasis programme of the

University of California, Berkeley have been distributing accurate
information on these subjects for years. Such initiatives need to be
openly supported by the major international donors. The Afghan
experience teaches us, however, that to avoid 'fishing for projects'
and to focus international resources on the sectors and activities
most capable of meeting clear objectives, strategic management of
international aid resources is essential.

## Lesson 7: Establish in each country a mechanism for strategic management of international aid.

We have noted the shambles created by the international aid
agencies' desire for independence in Afghanistan—and explained
that the problem is not easy to solve. The desire for donor independence in Afghanistan was not the result of stupidity on the part
of those running the agencies; the instructions came from their
political masters in London, Berlin, Washington, and Manila—I
am not including Paris, since France had virtually no money to
spend in Afghanistan—all of whom had ideas about what would
be good for Afghanistan, but were thinking mostly about public
opinion in their own countries.

   Unfortunately, a disorganized, incoherent profusion of projects about which decisions are made by foreign partners does not
constitute a development policy, as Ashraf Ghani reminded me
curtly during one of my first meetings with him at the Finance
Ministry in Kabul in the early 2000s. At the time, he was still trying to control the 'herd of cats,' of which I was, of course, a part.
The lack of organization certainly was not unique to Afghanistan,
though it did reach particular heights due to the large amounts of
money involved.

### It is not simple, and even some intelligent attempts fail

In 2006, I was hired as a consultant by the World Bank to help
prepare its country strategy for the Democratic Republic of the
Congo. This huge country, almost as large as Western Europe,
was emerging from a long civil war, so it was a delicate exercise. In the World Bank system, the country strategy is important
because drawn up with the participation of local authorities, it

'defines, in some detail, the operations to be financed by the Bank over the next four or five years. The Bank's regional director for DRC had the excellent idea of consulting the two other major donors, the United Nations and the European Union, to prepare a joint document. This document would have the benefit of forcing the three principal donors—who would, over the next few years, give several-hundred-million dollars to the country—to work together and harmonize their approaches.

The work proved complicated, since the visions of the three external partners differed on many points, and the DRC government often did not have well-established positions on the subjects. This is a classic problem and often raises the question of coherence among the activities of the big multilaterals (World Bank, IMF, regional development banks, UN institutions), which often have the same shareholders. There are, nevertheless, significant differences in approach and perspective where, to simplify things, there are finance people on one side and diplomats on the other.

The work was further complicated when, seeing the three main donors cooperating behind their backs, all the other donors asked to participate in the work. This was an entirely sensible idea and allowed an attempt at cooperation at a very early stage. So, with a team that had become very large, and often working at cross purposes, we prepared a document reflecting the approaches that had been coordinated and discussed at length with the authorities. All this work produced a programme with financial commitments from multiple donors. A great result, right?

Five years later, I was invited to Kinshasa by a group of donors to lead a seminar aimed at reviewing the procedures for coordination among them, which they had already named the 'Kinshasa Agenda'. In my naiveté, I imagined we would be taking stock of the multi-donor programme developed in 2006. But my interlocutors had all changed, and with the exception of the local World Bank representative, who treated the document as the Bible supposed to determine his work programme, no other donor was even aware that it existed. Being a consultant is sometimes a frustrating job...

This example illustrates how the constant and much-too-rapid staff rotation within donors' technical teams is itself a problem in fragile countries. In well-structured countries, institutional memory exists within national institutions. In countries where local institutions have largely disintegrated, there is often no institutional memory. Everyone has to reinvent the wheel.

During this time, I was also making regular visits to Afghanistan to support the commission responsible for reforming the civil service. Each time, I went to see the USAID experts dealing with the issue because USAID was co-financing some of the commission's programmes. I was always impressed by the quality of my American interlocutors, all with diplomas from prestigious universities, familiar with most of the literature on Afghanistan, and full of good intentions. As a result of crazy security rules, they lived in air-conditioned barracks that looked like containers in one of the courtyards at the US Embassy. They were protected by security guards from a private US company who were equipped, to my surprise, with Chinese Kalashnikovs rather than American M16s—a clear sign of globalization. These experts were virtually prohibited from going out except in armored cars accompanied by security guards and their Kalashnikovs. They might as well have been behind their computers in Houston. Every time I went, I gave them a rundown of the commission's activities and options for reforming the Afghan civil service. They were absolutely delighted. But I gave the same rundown every time because I never spoke to the same people twice. Of course, life in those containers was not fun.

## Two ways are suggested to get out of the impasse.

These examples suggest the difficulty of coordinating aid in countries without any real technical capacity, and particularly without the institutional architecture that would allow the centre of economic and development decision-making to be clearly defined. This centre must be located as close as possible to the seat of political power—the prime minister's office, if there is one, or the presidency, or, if need be, a finance minister with extensive powers and a significant level of technical capability.

To avoid expanding the present aid 'bazaar' in Sahel countries, it is important to quickly put in place a politically powerful committee in each country, to coordinate and manage aid. Such a committee also needs to be technically capable. But this is no small undertaking. The power of such a committee will necessarily encroach on that of other ministries and risk rendering the planning ministry obsolete, which generally has neither resources nor authority. This committee must precisely define the working procedures of the various donors. Taking into account the time necessary to set up and equip such a committee, define the procedures, and ensure that budgetary mechanisms are properly established so donor funds can be handled without risk that they will 'evaporate,' several years can go by.

In the short term, if establishing such a governing body of donor resources takes time, a good option is to set up a 'common pot' to receive as much as possible of donors' resources. Pooled in a trust fund, the money is then managed according to objectives specified by a board made up of representatives from the government and the donors providing the funds. This preliminary step usually forces the establishment of a powerful governing body.[5]

By pooling resources, it is possible to avoid the temptation that each donor plant its own little flag on 'its' project—which is precisely what makes donors reluctant regarding such pooled resources; because they love these little flags. Now, this approach which I am here suggesting for Sahel countries is not really new: I saw such a mechanism work successfully in Côte d'Ivoire in 1977.

## Lesson 8: Sahel countries must also reinvest in strategic thinking.

I have previously mentioned the contradictions in some World Bank's recommendations for the development of African countries, and highlighted the somewhat contradictory recommendations in its 2008 and 2013 World Development Reports, dealing respectively with agriculture development and job creation to end poverty. I do not suggest that this is an easy subject. I remain unsure myself, as taken as I am with the recommendations in

---

[5] The Afghanistan Reconstruction Trust Fund (ARTF), primarily led by the World Bank, enabled the genuine strategic management of part of the aid given to the country. Unfortunately, it received only a small fraction of the billions of dollars spent in Afghanistan.

my bedside reading materials from my time studying at MIT and my work during the 1970s as part of McNamara's team involved in rural development. These books, now almost impossible to find,[6] focused on the driving role that a vibrant agricultural sector should play in the economic development of a poor country. Impact of these recommendations was also reinforced by my observations, during five years, as AFD's deputy director resident in Côte d'Ivoire in charge of funding this sector in the 1970s and '80s, of the progress made there thanks to agriculture.

That said, my missions and visits to Vietnam and China have strengthened my conviction that, to provide jobs in countries experiencing rapid demographic growth, integration into the value chains of industrial globalization should not be overlooked. Despite their enormous handicaps, the Franc CFA being one of them, I am convinced that the French-speaking countries of the Sahel should keep in mind the success of the Asian model, and try in the future to take advantage of the expected increased costs of production in Asia and relocations from China to low-cost countries, as Ethiopia has done. However, we know that in order to succeed in this field, the required efforts will be considerable particularly to improve the business environment and align salaries on effective productivity.

What should Sahel countries also make of the options chosen by India from the 1960s through the 1980s to combat unemployment and underemployment? I retain strong impressions from the months I spent traveling around India and talking to local experts in the 1970s, studying the astonishing experiences of small-scale Indian sugar mills with a team of French specialists from the sugar industry, on behalf of the French scientific and technical research directorate (DGRST). We learned how India, for decades, provided jobs for a large proportion of its population using inexpensive technologies with relatively low productivity: the famous 'intermediate' or 'appropriate' technologies adapted to the technological environments of rural towns and villages—provided that there was electricity, of course.

[6] Such as the previously cited work by Michael Lipton, *Why Poor People Stay Poor*, or *The Political Economy of Agrarian Change* (Macmillan, 1974).

On this point, the works of the British economist E.F. Schumacher are impressive.[7] Now quite old, but still gripping, they focus on combating mass unemployment and underemployment by developing the technological level and managerial skills of an informal or 'semi-formal' sector that is somewhere between local craft production and small-scale industry. Such a sector is able to offer products that meet the needs of a very poor population. In the context of globalization, where China has become the workshop of the world, are the recommendations of this economist who was clearly 'thinking outside the box' still relevant?

And what are the possibilities of applying to the Sahel, the recommendations of Peruvian economist Hernando de Soto,[8] about supporting the development of micro-capitalism? What prospects are offered today by the development of the popular urban economy, a place of resourcefulness but also creativity, so dear to Jacques Bugnicourt, the founder of the French and Senegalese NGO ENDA (Environmental Development Action), with whom I spent many evenings in some of the poorest districts of Dakar? These are ideas that Sahel economists should study with an open mind.

These questions warrant a great deal of reflection, with employment being the major goal. Bruno Losch[9] from the CIRAD research institute emphasizes the importance of regional development, of creating a network of large, well-equipped rural towns capable of establishing links that are currently missing between town and country. He also stresses 'decompartmentalizing' public policies and, in particular, moving away from opposition between urban and rural areas toward an integrated approach.

Also of major importance, I believe, is building the capacities of African think tanks. I have already mentioned my high regard for the African Center for Economic Transformation (ACET) in Ghana, the competence of its experts, and the high quality of its

[7] A good start is: E.F. Schumacher, *Small is Beautiful: A Study of Economics as if People Mattered* (Blond and Brigg, 1974).

[8] See his classic works, *The Other Path: The Invisible Revolution in the Third World* (Harper and Row, 1989), and *The Mystery of Capital: Why Capitalism Triumphs in the West and Fails Everywhere Else* (Basic Books, 2000).

[9] Bruno Losch, 'Urban Africa still needs agricultural Africa to meet the continent's challenges,' CIRAD, Demeter, *Économie et Stratégies Agricoles* (Economy and Agricultural Policy, 2014).

analysis. There is a genuine need for more such institutions, which
will know, better than anyone, how to advise African political
leaders in the future. This requires sizable funding to attract and
retain African experts who will otherwise be drawn to posts in
Washington, London, Beijing, Brasilia, or Ottawa. It also entails
establishing partnerships with institutions like the *Fondation pour
les Etudes et Recherches sur le Développement International* (FERDI)
in France. In this field, it is essential to aim for *excellence*, because
the cost of errors in economic policy is, as France has witnessed
for almost 40 years, utterly astronomical.

## Lesson 9: Donors' 'software' and priorities need to be revisited.

International aid agencies long ago lost interest in fragile countries,
lumping them in the same category as 'problem countries.' The
thinking being that through corrupt and inefficient institutions,
these countries made poor use of the funds provided to them,
so it was better to keep a distance. The agencies, quite logically,
preferred to fund 'good students' in order to maximize the global
impact of their support. Plus, it was easier, and the hotels were
more comfortable.

The downside, as we have seen, is that these 'good students'
were, in general, the countries that least needed international
aid and could fairly quickly gain access to international capital
markets, and derive maximum profit from private investments.
Following these precepts, aid lost interest in troubled countries—
those on which it ought, in fact, to have been most focused.

The world is beginning to understand that these 'failed' states
are veritable 'global public bads,' and that the road from fragility
to failure can be very short. Clearly, fragile and 'failed' states can
no longer be ignored because the latter cause problems we are
all too well aware of: terrorism, maritime piracy, hostage-taking,
epidemics,[10] locust swarms,[11] drug and weapons trafficking, refugees, circulation of arms, mass migrations, and more.

---

[10] These epidemics are linked to the disorganized state of medical
services and the movements of refugee populations.

[11] Instability results in an inability to gain access, within a useful time
frame, to treat the locusts in the areas where they reproduce.

The Busan International Conference in South Korea in 2011, which followed conferences in Paris in 2005 and Accra in 2008—all devoted to the issue of aid effectiveness—adopted a 'New Deal for Engagement in Fragile States.' Advocating an integrated approach covering political, security, and development aspects, the New Deal was a significant step that coincided with publication of the 2011 World Bank's World Development Report focusing on fragile states emerging from conflict.

But it was still a small step. Aid should now be *massively* refocused on the most fragile countries and 'failed' states, or those at risk of becoming failed states in the near future. Ultimately, this decision can be made in the donor countries only at the highest political levels, but we are far from seeing such a refocusing. Most of the major aid institutions, such as the World Bank, still allocate their resources to beneficiary countries in line with performance indicators (the CPIA[12] in the case of the World Bank), which allows the 'dunces,' the 'average students,' and the 'good and very good students', to be identified according to a mysterious calculation that has long remained secret.[13]

Of course, as with Afghanistan, these institutions are sometimes obliged, under political pressure from major donor countries, to 'bend' their principles and allocate sufficient resources to 'failed' states. Experience proves, however, that these 'acts of generosity' are usually approved too late to provide much hope of rectifying the situation. In fact, behind this 'charade,' political horse-trading is usually going on. This is what enabled East Timor and Afghanistan to receive colossal sums despite their highly dubious governance, while the Central African Republic was neglected. (Of course, they speak French there...) But, beyond the important issue of resource-allocation rules lies the more fundamental problem of the objectives set for international aid.

[12] Country Policy and Institutional Assessment rating.
[13] I recommend that those who might be interested in these issues, which have long fascinated economists, read a critique I published in a special edition of the journal *Revue d'Economie du Développement,* analyzing aid allocation principles, No. 2-3, September 2005.

*'Saving' fragile and 'failed' states should now become a genuine priority for the major aid agencies.*

I explained in a previous book[14] that the objectives of the major aid agencies have varied enormously over time depending on circumstances, and that their current objectives are the product of history. To summarize, aid was first of all a tool for intervention during the Cold War, ensuring that countries likely to be tempted by communism would remain in the West's camp. In this respect, it was very useful during the 1950s in Greece and Turkey and in the 1960s and 1970s in South Korea, Taiwan, and Thailand during the Vietnam War. French aid was, for a long time, guided by the desire to facilitate both decolonization and indirect 'control' of some countries in francophone Africa; its effectiveness in this regard was seen in Côte d'Ivoire. During the 1970s and 1980s, this objective faded but did not completely disappear—note the very stupid aid granted to Mobutu's regime throughout this period.

In subsequent years, aid was largely focused on the structural-adjustment programmes that became crucial as a result of the impact of the 1973 and 1978 crises on fragile and poorly managed economies in countries in the Southern Hemisphere. The aid was ultimately used to help refinance a debt that had become insupportable, but which no one wanted to cancel. Not until the previously discussed HIPC initiative was launched in the 1990s by the World Bank was a solution to this trap found. For the most part, these adjustment programmes were successful at the macro-finance level (although we saw how they failed in Côte d'Ivoire), but they had a catastrophic impact on social sectors and, paradoxically, contributed to increasing poverty in these countries. The analogy with today's Greece is, unfortunately, quite striking.

Subjected to virulent attacks from NGOs, churches, and the media, aid agencies decided in the mid-1990s to repair what they had unintentionally helped destroy, by focusing on the reconstruction of social sectors and the fight against poverty. All of this crystallized in the Millennium Development Goals (MDGs) approved during an extraordinary meeting of heads of state and

[14] Serge Michailof, *Notre maison brûle au Sud* (Fayard, 2010).

government at the United Nations in September 2000. They established clear, universal objectives for poor countries, to be met by 2015, and this became the Bible for donors, scrupulously guiding their strategies. The goals provided an opportunity to largely rehabilitate aid in the eyes of public opinion, mobilize significant resources, and obtain results in the social sector.

Two key needs were unfortunately forgotten, however: agricultural and rural development (unbelievable!), and controlling fertility rates,[15] which is essential if certain poor countries are to escape a genuine poverty trap. The MDGs also played a key role in how aid was directed, since the basic assumption that supported the approach—the addition of resources for the sectors concerned—never materialized. In reality, there was a transfer of resources to social sectors at the expense of basic urban and rural infrastructure projects (such as rural electrification) and rural development. In very poor countries such as those in the Sahel, which cannot mobilize much private financing to fund basic infrastructure, considerable funding deficits have accumulated in these areas since 2000.

The new 'Sustainable Development Goals' (SDGs) approved for the next 15 years (at the end of a participatory process led by the United Nations involving an unbelievably labyrinthine system)[16] have a different aim entirely. They are intended to be universal, and will therefore apply to the US as much as to China or Niger. They are the result of an unlikely merger of the Sustainable Development Goals Agenda (itself a product of the Rio Conference on Environment and Development in 1992) and the MDG approach. But are they really adaptable to fragile countries' priorities?

## Lesson 10: Beware of the new Sustainable Development Goals in fragile countries.

The goals, in the opinion of many observers—including some representatives of the US and British governments—are a list of

---

[15] Note that the problem of shantytowns and deprived areas was also neglected.

[16] This participatory process was expected to involve more than a million people.

pious hopes that cheerfully combine measurable microeconomic objectives, laudable ambitions concerning global public goods, and Universalist dreams. All told, there are 17 major goals, difficult to classify in a coherent manner, and 169 targets focused primarily on sustainable development, green growth, and climate change. These goals are fundamental to the survival of our planet and the wellbeing of my grandchildren, and I hope they will one day be binding on the United States and China through an agreement along the lines of the 2016 Paris climate agreement. Unfortunately, President's Trump policies do not seem favourable in this respect.

I sincerely doubt, however, that these goals can significantly aid the poorest and most fragile countries that are emerging from conflict, or those that are at risk of being plunged back into it[17]. Niger, where only 10 per cent of households have access to electricity, provides a vivid example. The country currently depends on electricity from Nigeria and from old diesel power plants that are unable to meet the demand. Obviously, solar energy has huge potential in Niger, but solar energy is not yet capable of meeting the demand of large cities at a reasonable cost. To produce energy for its main cities at an acceptable cost, Niger—which has sizable coal deposits—is urgently in need of new thermal-power stations. But will the donors Niger depends on refuse it this option? Will they force it to rely exclusively on solar or wind power, which can meet the needs of remote villages but cannot satisfy urban demand? China or India will, of course—paying no heed to the SDGs—continue to build coal-fired power stations at the rate now of maybe one per month instead of one per week, but poor Niger, reliant on the goodwill of donors, will have to forget its coal (which, indeed, it hardly dares mention in its development plan).

Ashraf Ghani and Clare Lockhart offer some stark comments on international aid in their previously mentioned book:[18]:

---

[17] Consult for a full development on this issue: "*Un défi pour la planète, Les objectifs de développement durable en débat*", Patrick Caron et Jean Marc Chataigner ed, IRD editions, 2017.

[18] Ghani, Ashraf and Clare Lockhart, *Fixing Failed States* (Oxford University Press, 2008).

This is not to argue that international institutions are not an indispensable part of any practical and sustained attempt to combat the most serious challenges in the contemporary world, ... the aid system is facing a crisis. ... Good intentions are wasted without positive effects. Even though the development system sometimes acknowledges that weak states are a central issue, it continues to fall short in efforts to strengthen fragile institutions. ... The aid complex—the series of ways in which the international aid architecture works—undermines states' capacity to perform essential functions. To address the most serious of the world's problems (among them poverty and global terrorism), the aid system must orient itself around the task of building effective, functioning states.

We know that aid objectives are the product of history, and of context. As we watch Syria, Iraq, Afghanistan, Yemen, the Central African Republic, South Sudan, Libya, north-eastern Nigeria, and now Mali collapse before our eyes—and with the other countries of the Sahel, on which I have focused, at great risk—is it not time for the major aid agencies to review their priorities? Embracing green growth and fighting poverty in emerging countries is important; but surely it is the geopolitical priorities that should be at the heart of their concerns.

Consider again the wise words of Ghani and Lockhart:

At the level of individual projects or sector and structural adjustment, the aid system has met with much success. ... We can and must learn from these successes. In more recent years ... it is those countries that followed an unconventional path driven by leadership, management, and untried and imaginative thinking that have broken out of the poverty trap. There is a great deal of tacit knowledge in the aid system that must be turned into active knowledge to provide the basis for state-building strategies.

*Charitable activities and 'green growth' cannot be the sole objectives of aid in troubled nations.*

Clearly, the most fragile countries and 'failed' states should attract much more rigorous attention from the international community; dealing with their problems should not be left to the military, as is the case with France, or treated as a secondary priority behind the new SDGs. What is the point of creating more schools for girls if the girls are going to be kidnapped on their way to school because no one has taken responsibility for restoring security by sorting out the police? And beyond that, knowing that if the kidnapper is ever caught, there will be no judge to sentence him, and not even a prison or penitentiary system to keep him removed from society!

Help for very fragile countries, or countries emerging from serious conflicts, demands that the international community change its software. Before he was elected to the Afghan presidency, Ashraf Ghani expressed his frustration with donors in a video conference (available online): 'The aid system is broken!' he exclaimed. As someone who knows the system well, he added: 'One dollar of aid could be 10 cents; it could be 25 cents; or it could be four dollars. It depends on what form it comes in, what degrees of conditionality are attached to it.'[19] Brian Atwood, the former USAID Administrator and former Chair of the Development Assistance Committee, and Emmanuel Faber, the CEO of Danone, a French multinational, say more or less the same thing.[20] I am absolutely in favour of green growth and in favour of fighting poverty. But was that the priority in Afghanistan? And is green growth really the priority in the Central African Republic or in Mali today?

The mandates of the major international agencies prevent them from participating in operations that are fundamental in these countries—reform of the security sector, restoring order to a police force that has lost its way, taking charge of local government and administration in an under-populated area, and, perhaps above all, reorganizing an army. Adding to the difficulty is the fact that intervening to strengthen an army may entail—horror of horrors—reinforcing a presidential guard force at the same time. All of this is of course difficult, highly sensitive, and requires sound political judgment.

## Lesson 11: Address nepotism head-on.

Institutional weaknesses most often result when leaders are selected on the basis of criteria that have nothing to do with expertise

[19] Ashraf Ghani, 'How to Rebuild a Broken State', TED Global, 2005.

[20] Quoted in O. Lafourcade, *L'aide au développement, un état des lieux, des interrogations* in *Techniques financières de développement*, December 2014.

or managerial talent. Very often, nothing serious can be done without changing the officials at the top levels of institutions. This, of course, gets into the realm of interference, a particularly thorny matter when it comes to sovereignty issues. The situation can be complicated and delicate—in some cases, impossible to resolve. Naturally, hasty decisions and superficial judgments must be avoided, and it is essential to remember that the competence and managerial abilities of leaders have nothing to do with their mastery of French or English.

None of this is easy, but neither is it, in principle, impossible, because the availability of substantial financial resources gives the external actor the ability to discuss options. Over the course of my career, I have always tried to avoid interfering in this area. But to achieve results, it is necessary to be frank in some cases. I recall one episode that was particularly delicate due to the personality of the main interlocutor, who was a head of state.

President Biya of Cameroon—not an easy man to talk to, despite his politeness—once sent me a message that he was counting heavily on the World Bank to help cancel Cameroon's foreign debt via the HIPC mechanism.[21] The financial stakes were as high as the Cameroonian debt, but using the HIPC mechanism required that Cameroon make significant progress in social sectors, particularly basic education and health. Unfortunately, the group of ambassadors posted to Yaoundé, who had invited me to a working lunch, believed any progress to be impossible in these sectors, given the mismanagement, corruption, and laxity in the relevant ministries.

Taking note of their opinion, which seemed difficult to argue with, I went to see the President. I told him that he certainly had the support of my institution but, from the perspective of the best international observers present in the country, it was impossible for Cameroon to join this mechanism and see its debt reduced significantly—at least as long as the ministers responsible for the health and education sectors remained in place. I could see on the President's face his intense displeasure at my remark.

He did not reply, but two months later, two excellent technocrats were appointed to those posts, and a few years after that,

---

[21] Heavily Indebted Poor Countries initiative.

Cameroon was admitted to the HIPC initiative, enabling a large part of its debt to be cancelled. There is no doubt that social sectors are less 'sensitive' than sovereign sectors. But, this example serves as a reminder that it is important to talk frankly with our interlocutors, and also useless to spend billions if certain preconditions are not met.

## Lesson 12: Ad hoc mechanisms established to launch development programmes in insecure areas should remain temporary solutions.

Insecurity is, of course, a major obstacle to the proper management of development programmes. In many areas, the lives of expatriates and local officials are put at risk, as was the case with a World Bank-funded small irrigation project in Afghanistan, where many local engineers and technicians were kidnapped and sometimes killed. One option in such situations is to entrust projects to specialized military or mixed civilian and military teams, as was done in Afghanistan with the ISAF military and the Provincial Reconstruction Teams (PRT). This type of action, however, should be carried out only on a temporary basis until normal development programmes can be implemented.

Two main lessons can be drawn from this experience. First, such civilian–military programmes must not only fund and sometimes execute physical projects (small bridges, small dams, and the like); they should also work to strengthen local governments and not bypass or replace them. This might lead to delays and less efficiency, but is important for building local capacity and ensuring maintenance and long-term viability of the investments. The other lesson is that financial resources made available to such programmes should be significant, but not excessive.[22] The objective must always be to hand over social and development programmes to development agencies and local civilian authorities as soon as possible.

---

[22] The resources were insufficient in the early years in Afghanistan, and subsequently excessive, resulting in a great deal of waste and in marginalization of local authorities. Today they are ridiculously low for the Barkhane operation, at €300,000 for 2016.

Finally, because insecurity constitutes a major obstacle to development agencies in the field, development efforts should be conducted in safe regions as close as possible to the areas of greatest insecurity to stem the spread of conflagration.

## Is it still possible to stabilize the Sahel?

The cases of Boko Haram and Mali show that security cannot be ensured solely by strengthening security measures—it is essential to address the full range of social and development challenges. Even a superficial examination of the social and economic situations in most of the rural areas of the Sahel reveals the magnitude of the challenges confronting the region.

*Addressing such huge challenges will require a kind of 'Marshall Plan'.*

The social and economic upgrading of these countries, and especially of their deprived rural areas, presents such a challenge that a kind of 'Marshall Plan' will be required. Such an effort implies the simultaneous launching of vigorous programmes for rural and municipal development, education and basic technical training, infrastructure development, and access to drinking water and electricity. Most of these initiatives, at least in the poorest countries, will have to be financed by international aid. Yet, their implementation will require that local politicians pay them much greater attention than in the past and focus on effectiveness and results on the ground rather than on the fanfare associated with project launches.

Donors are beginning to respond to this need: development aid to the Sahel is now about USD 4 billion per year. The World Bank has earmarked USD 3 billion on its IDA 18 envelope for the next three years until 2020. Does this increased development aid represent a magic weapon for lowering insecurity? There is a tendency to mock aid and minimize its importance, and most African leaders would be glad to do without it. At the global level—about USD 140 billion a year—we already noticed that development aid has become almost marginal compared to private-investment flows to developing countries or remittances from migrants. Yet, these figures mask the important role it still plays in LDCs and all very poor countries, including the Sahel where, apart from the mining and oil sectors, private investment has been notably absent.

In the very poor countries of the Sahel, international aid easily represents 8 to 10 per cent of GDP, about 60 to 90 per cent of their investment budgets, 60 to 70 per cent of their net foreign inflows, and 40 to 50 per cent of their tax revenues. If well-targeted and well-managed, these transfers should contribute significantly to the economic development of beneficiary countries, where it is important that young people find proper jobs in order to reduce the temptation to join the ranks of traffickers or of jihadist groups.

*Remember, however, that aid in Afghanistan quickly became part of the problem.*

We have noted that the total volume of aid to Afghanistan has been colossal, in some years exceeding the country's GDP; aid reserved strictly for development between 2009 and 2012 exceeded 50 per cent of GDP. But, after almost 15 years of sometimes-massive aid efforts, Afghanistan still ranks 171st out of 190 on the Human Development Index. Insecurity reigns even in the embassy district at the heart of Kabul, where a truck full of explosives recently killed more than 150 people. No road can now be traveled in safety, and the government truly controls little more than the key cities.

## The agenda for dealing with the new threats confronting the Sahel is ambitious and hard to implement.

*African governments will have to consolidate or rebuild their state apparatuses.*

To ensure the security of their territories, they will have to extinguish the flashpoints and bushfires to the extent possible, using their own strengthened militaries, without expecting to rely on foreign or United Nations forces. And they will have to complement this military approach by reinforcing their entire state apparatuses. They must overcome the dual fiscal and security impasse that forces them to choose between security and development spending. They must not only rebuild their failing sovereign institutions, they must also strengthen major economic and social institutions that are revealed to be largely failing. Absent the reorganization of key administrations, countries may find themselves unable to launch necessary investment programmes and implement necessary reforms.

*They will have to negotiate exceptional financial, technical, and political support from the international community.*

Given that the vast majority of people with the lowest incomes live in rural areas and make a living from agriculture or raising livestock, any effort to generate massive employment and reduce poverty will require the stimulation and modernization of agropastoral systems and the rural world. This goal must be both long-term and ambitious, as these countries also suffer the effects of global warming. They urgently need to revitalize and intensify their traditional, rain-dependent cereal crops. This requires significant public investment in soil defense, protection, and restoration, rural roads, market organization, agronomic research, adapted farming practices, more widespread use of animal-drawn cultivation, and more ecological agricultural practices. They will also need to pursue and accelerate investments in irrigation, especially small-scale systems, and restructure their transhumant and sedentary livestock systems. Finally, CFA Franc Zone countries should consider adopting a flexible system to adjust the parity of the CFA according to their own economic objectives.

The overall aim should be twofold: to ensure food security in the medium term and to increase the number of jobs in more intensive agriculture and livestock farming and associated support functions both upstream and down. Achieving these goals will require enormous efforts in many areas, including literacy, targeted training, legal and regulatory measures, and investment in rural areas, along with sustained efforts to expand drinking-water infrastructures and rural electrification. These actions will require innovative, decentralized approaches that have been successfully implemented in other countries. However, to achieve the goals, governments will have to regain control of international-aid spending and reorient it, to the extent possible, toward the factors that fuel insecurity, particularly rural poverty.

*These countries will have to undertake wide-ranging reforms of their education systems and vocational and technical training programmes.*

The aim must be to facilitate the creation of jobs for young people in their own countries, in the sub-region, and, where appropriate, via migration outside the continent. It is also to provide these countries with the human capital necessary to secure an economic upswing. They will most likely need to focus on primary education, reorient secondary and tertiary education toward vocational, technical, and scientific subjects, launch ambitious adult-literacy programmes associated with basic-skills-training programmes for artisans in the informal sector, and revitalize post-primary education. Such programmes constitute huge challenges for the countries concerned; they will not be able to fund them alone. It will therefore be necessary to mobilize development partners in this area.

*The massive creation of jobs demanded by the region's exceptional demographic dynamism also means facilitating the development of a dynamic private sector.*

This objective will require a radical rethinking of the generally restrictive business environments and rapidly enhancing the availability, quality, and costs of using basic infrastructure. These cross-cutting measures will have to be supplemented by programmes that could give rise to ripple effects such as the implementation of support projects for training and equipment in the informal-services sector and urban and rural handicrafts.

*These multiple efforts will remain insufficient if the rate of population growth is not brought down to a level compatible with countries' economic capacities.*

Population growth is so high, and natural resources so limited, that these countries cannot expect economic growth, urbanization, income growth, and girls' education to progressively and spontaneously reduce the birth rate. They have no choice but to implement population-control policies.

Doing so will require major changes in current norms and values in the sub-region, which in turn will require exceptional communication and pedagogical efforts. Programmes aimed at controlling demography in the Sahel have been prepared and adopted in the past, but have never really been implemented. Yet, other poor countries with rural majorities and of Muslim faith, such as Bangladesh, have found ways to do so. The countries of the Maghreb, Saudi Arabia, and Iran, have all succeeded. As in these countries, several levers that are immediate determinants of fertility are available to authorities. These principally include access to modern contraceptive techniques, dissuading the practice of early marriage, lengthening the period of breastfeeding, providing proper education to girls, launching information and communication programmes on family planning, etc. They should be used simultaneously.

*Governments will have to engage in a courageous struggle against Islamic fundamentalism and jihadist ideology.*

The restoration of security throughout the region implies an ideological dimension that cannot be underestimated. For more than 40 years, Salafist preachers returning from the Haj have traveled across the rural Sahel. Throughout that period, funding from Saudi Arabia and other Gulf countries has enabled the proliferation of mosques and Koranic schools which, along with the building of major works and prestige investments, has bought the support—or at least the neutrality—of the political elites for the expansion of a conception of Islam that does not reflect the tolerant tradition of local Sufism.[23] As early as 1985, Moriba Magassouba was challenging the lack of adequate response of the Senegalese authorities to imported Wahhabism, denouncing the 'integrist virus.'[24]

African leaders must absolutely regain control and halt the process of radicalization and resulting intolerance that prepares

[23] Classic reference works such as *L'Islam Noir* by Vincent Monteil (Seuil, 1964), are no longer representative of the reality of today's Islam in the Sahel.

[24] Moriba Magassouba, *L'Islam au Sénégal, demain les mollahs?* (Karthala, 1985).

young people for jihadism. This may well be the most difficult task of all because political leaders with the courage to engage in the ideological battle will have to confront the hatred of the preachers of intolerance in the mosques, the markets, and the poll booths. They may even have to fear for their lives. However, this struggle, which must necessarily accompany any demographic reduction-and-control programme, cannot be avoided.

*The success of such a comprehensive response to the security challenge presupposes that these programmes constitute an interdependent and indivisible whole.*

These ambitious programmes cannot be approached in a selective manner, *but must be implemented almost simultaneously*. In fact, the interconnections among them constitute the key to initiating a chain of virtuous circles. This type of comprehensive response to the security challenge is inevitably a lengthy undertaking that will require significant additional resources from financial partners over the long term. But, the overall cost of such a mobilization does not require excessive amounts and is perfectly possible and realistic.

Yet, government officials must demonstrate the political will to act in tandem on these various axes by building political coalitions based on the scale of the challenges they face. They will need to build political consensus way beyond their own majorities in order to protect such programmes against future political changes. The challenges confronting the Sahel are indeed so huge, and the agenda for their implementation so extraordinarily difficult, that the related action programmes will need to become what may be called 'state programmes',[25] able to be implemented over very long periods despite successive political changes. This will certainly be difficult, but such key "state programs" will be critical for the future stability of this region.

[25] An example of such 'State programmes' developed over long periods independently of successive political majorities is for instance a fifty years' reliance on a defence policy based on dissuasion and the development of an independent nuclear force in France.

# Conclusion

It is now time to ring the alarm—and also to respond to eventual accusations of Afro-pessimism that will surely be directed at this analysis.

To the reader who finds this book exaggeratingly dark, I recommend the remarkable 20-year vision report prepared by Nicole Gnesotto and Giovanni Grevi in 2006 for the European Union.[1] This report is fascinating on two counts. First, it is not an autonomous work but rather the synthesis of dozens of vision documents drawn up by the most renowned research institutes, universities, think tanks such as the RAND Corporation, and even confidential reports of intelligence agencies such as the CIA, MI6, and France's secret services. Second, it was written more than ten years ago, which lets us compare its predictions with actual events at the halfway point, brushing aside the usual objection to vision documents that, because they are focused on the future, no one can trust or deny their accuracy.

This remarkable work dwells on the possible development of the major regions of the world, identifying, in particular, the growing gap between population and employment as being the most worrisome issue for both the Middle East and Africa. The

---

[1] This report has also been published as a book: Gnesotto, Nicole and Giovani Grevi, *The New Global Puzzle: What World for the EU in 2025?* (Institute for Security Studies, European Union, 2006).

upheavals that are now unfolding in Iraq, Syria, and Yemen. The
chapter on Sub-Saharan Africa is deeply disquieting.

The general conclusion of the study is that the world in 2025
will be 'more populated, more exploited, more arid, and more
polluted than it is today. In other words, it will become a far
less hospitable place. The wellbeing of billions of people will be
put under more severe strain. ... [T]he outlook for some critical regions, such as Middle East and North Africa and parts of
Sub-Saharan Africa, is negative and seems to be getting worse.
The envisioned deterioration of other structural factors, such as
demography and the environment, could endanger the stability
of those countries which are failing to adjust to globalisation and
losing ground compared to emerging economies. Moreover, the
perception of disparities, and the awareness of the challenges and
threats looming ahead, will be magnified by the globalisation of
information and perceptions.'[2]

I looked for recent texts by Nicole Gnesotto to see if her vision
for the future had altered. In a special issue of the French review
*Esprit*[3] about the 'new global disorder,' she lists what she calls
strategic paradoxes: 'A more violent world, but a more impotent
international community. A more unstable context, but less regu-
lated international security. More active extremism, and more
uncertain democracies.' She adds: 'It is before these challenges
that the collective impotence of Europe appears to be the greatest
political waste of the early 21st century.' In another article in the
review, co-authored with Marc-Olivier Padis, she observes: 'No
process of history is leading the world towards greater democracy and international law, nor towards hope for the pacification of rivalries, and for a reduction in identity-based hatred and
warmongering.'

You may consider me a pessimist, but I regard myself as a real-
ist along the lines of Nicole Gnessoto's thinking.

---

[2] Gnesotto, Nicole and Giovani Grevi, *The New Global Puzzle: What
World for the EU in 2025?* (Institute for Security Studies, European
Union, 2006), pp. 192-193.

[3] Special issue of the review *Esprit* on the new global disorder, Nicole
Gnessoto, 'Political globalisation does not exist', August-September 2014.

### Europe and the whole western world face a major geopolitical risk in the Sahel.

Any analysis focusing on the medium and long terms faces the difficult task of identifying and interpreting multiple signs and indicators. Media and political leaders, being focused on the short term, rarely apprehend these signs, or if they do, they usually have neither the time nor the inclination to decrypt them. Apart from General De Gaulle, no one thought in 1960 that the Muslim population in French Algeria would exceed 40 million people half a century later—obvious as it should have been—and thus pose a major integration problem to French society.

In fact, many intelligent men and women, including leading politicians and high-ranking military officers, believed that France should remain forever in Algeria and Algeria be a French province; they fought to impose this mad idea on the French government and even organized a coup against President De Gaulle in 1961. As Jean-Claude Mallet comments in the same *Esprit* review, 'A government is, perforce, short-sighted. It is obsessed by the short term. ... The real difficulty lies in distinguishing and correctly interpreting the signs. The facts are there, they must just be translated.'

In 2010, almost three years before the upheavals in Mali, having analyzed these myriad signs, I predicted in a previous book (unfortunately not available in English), borrowing a sentence from former President Jacques Chirac:[4] 'Our common house in the South is on fire.' Now that the flames are clearly visible, should we continue ignoring it?

For reasons of history, language, and geographic proximity, France and Belgium are on the front line in the event of a major tragedy in the Sahel. Our European neighbours—apart from Germany and Great Britain, which are beginning to worry and begin sending some men and a few equipment[5] to the Sahel—have little interest in these matters apart from the markets they can win in 'emerging Africa.' In short, the other Africa does

[4] Who had clearly recognised the problem but had, frankly, done nothing about it.

[5] The United Kingdom recently sent 3 helicopters to the Sahel....

not concern them. They forget that our European frontiers are
porous and there is little chance that a massive wave of migration
to France would stop in Strasbourg. The recent terrorist attacks
in the Sahel—as in France, Belgium, Germany, and the United
Kingdom—are but a preview of the threats to come, which are
largely determined by demography. The most urgent and problematic situation is, of course, the case of Mali, where both the
political and security situation are quickly deteriorating.

I sincerely hope the Malian authorities soon realize that the
situation cannot be stabilized unless the economy, particularly the
rural economy, is thriving and the state machinery is properly
consolidated (meaning in some cases, such as the army and police,
being rebuilt from scratch). A key issue is to free Malian public
institutions from the tentacles of clientelism.

Important foreign financing is now being mobilized to facilitate the stabilization process, and Mali is expecting at least about
USD 2 billion dollars a year in foreign aid. About USD 4 billion
dollars a year are now earmarked for aid to the Sahel. But these
resources are not directed—or are only marginally so—towards
the previously mentioned critical issues. If there is one lesson
to be learned from the disastrous management of foreign aid in
Afghanistan, it is that disordered and ill-managed aid quickly
becomes part of the problem instead of the solution. The big,
white land cruisers with long radio antennas that usually carry
donors in crisis countries are now clogging the streets of Bamako.
Unfortunately, from my visits to Mali, meetings with Malian
friends and former colleagues, and reading of many reports, it
seems to me that it is precisely the disordered way aid is managed
in Mali that dims hope for satisfactory results.

## The war in Mali is not over, and both Sahel countries and West Africa are at great risk.

Jihadists in Mali lost a battle and many fighters in 2013, but they
have not lost the war and remain a serious threat. The Mujao
is developing roots in the highly populated region of the Niger
River crescent around Gao and Mopti, which has good farming
potential and considerable irrigated land. It is no longer possible
to visit the once-popular tourist spots of Mopti, Djenne, and

Timbuktu. Like the Taliban in Afghanistan in 2003–06, jihadists in this region are not necessarily fomenting highly visible trouble, though they did blow up a car laden with explosives in Gao in January 2017, killing 80 people on a military base close to the airport. They mainly resort to laying mines in the roads and would of course kidnap any imprudent foreigner or official. As a result, state authorities, particularly the "gendarmerie" have left and these regions have become lawless areas. The Jihadists are marrying local women, distributing money to the needy, controlling the main roads, levying taxes and engaging in trafficking. They also threaten, and systematically kill, local elites who are hostile to them.

Other armed groups in the centre and south of the country, such as the 'Front de Liberation du Macina', are mobilizing Fulani people who feel marginalized. The root of this new conflict is land disputes based on ethnic and economic differences—Fulani stockbreeders can no longer travel freely with their livestock in an increasingly populous and cultivated region. With the administration's abandonment of the region and the army's heavy-handed repression, armed groups have sprung up. A source of concern for neighbouring countries is that the Fulani people are widely distributed throughout West Africa and represent a large minority (if not a majority) in nearby Guinea. Once again, the failure of civil authorities and excesses of uncontrolled police and armed forces spurred the rebellion, adding to old grievances among ethnic groups, as is clearly explained in an International Crisis Group (ICG) report.[6]

In this insecure environment where local police forces have withdrawn to the main cities, villages are organizing militias to protect themselves, adding to the mess. The next risk is that AQMI-related[7] armed groups establish kernels of parallel administration for ensuring local security and meting out justice. This may already be happening under cover. Well aware of the futility of direct combat with international forces, armed groups are using guerrilla tactics against the Malian army, as well as UN and

[6] 'Central Mali: An Uprising in the Making?', ICG, July 6, 2016.
[7] AQMI is the French acronym for Al-Qaida in the Islamic Maghreb.

French forces, planting improvised explosive devices IEDs and launching mortar attacks on camps at night.

These activities are exhausting a dispirited Malian army and discouraging the UN force. Unlike 2013—when the French air force destroyed jihadist pickups by the dozens—a French pilot recently told me that there are no longer any valuable targets for fast-flying aircraft, and he felt idle. This does not mean security is improving—just that the enemy has become invisible. If France, the former colonial power, were to try to substitute for a vitiated Malian state apparatus in these highly populated regions, it would only lose a guerrilla war conducted under the constant surveillance of social networks.

In a situation where a new type of war is developing—a low-intensity insurgency trying to control a rural population and harassing government forces—it is of the utmost urgency to help Mali rebuild its state apparatus. Only with a revamped military, a solid police force and gendarmerie, a reliable local administration, a judiciary with integrity—and a flourishing rural economy—can Mali meet these challenges. Yet, these issues were completely absent from the aid agenda presented in October 2015 at the Paris donor conference. Instead, the agenda was still the standard 'fight against poverty'—basic donor business as usual.

As already noted, the risks are equally high in Niger. The nation's small army is fighting on four fronts—way too much for its capacity. Security is seriously deteriorating on its border with Mali, where military and police posts are under regular attack. In Nigeria's northeast region, close to Niger's southeast border—where Boko Haram is still present—by mid-2017 more than 2 million people were suffering from a critical lack of food, in part because of scanty rainfall, but mostly because the lack of safety had paralyzed local trade.

Each Sahel country is, of course, a specific case. But all of them face major risks. Sooner or later Chad, which is in a critical fiscal situation due to its military expenditures, the drop in oil prices and the way it has mortgaged its oil revenues, will have to face the succession of President Deby, who rules his country with an iron hand. And Burkina Faso, surely initially the best-structured and organized country, is grappling with a complex political situation since President Compaoré's ouster, and is now threatened by jihadist groups and home-grown rebel militias even way beyond its border with Mali. Local religious and political leaders fear—and sometimes genuinely support—this radical Islam in its ideological war, even if it puts them in opposition to the government. These radical movements, a combination of frustrations, attack the elites and the states, as well as the West and its values.

Another unwelcome piece of news—courtesy of a video released through the Mauritania press agency—was the official announcement on 1 March 2017, of the union of four major jihadist groups in the Sahel under the name *'Groupe de Soutien à l'Islam et aux Musulmans.'*[8] In the video, one could see the leaders of the four jihadist groups[9] pledging allegiance to Al-Qaida together and appointing Iyad Al Ghali, founder of the Ansar Dine jihadist group and a well-known warlord long involved in trafficking and kidnappings, as the overall leader of the union.

Only the experienced and dangerous Algerian leader Mokhtar Ben Mokhtar—who fought in Afghanistan and with the GIA and GSPC rebel groups during the Algerian civil war in the 1990s, and who orchestrated the January 2013 assault on the In Amenas Algerian gas complex—was missing from the family photo. Such a union formalizes the close collaboration among these groups that had been going on since 2011.[10] Behind the union may also be a decision to compete for regional influence with ISIS, which has made some rapprochement with Boko Haram. Yet, beyond a desire to coordinate their actions and clarify their respective trafficking zones, the announcement also indicated a determination to expand their influence regionally, particularly in Libya and Burkina.

Therefore, beware: the war in Mali is not over, as both President Hollande and the French public thought in February 2013, and the war in the Sahel has only just begun. The increase in suicide attacks since the one in June 2015 in Ndjamena, in which 24 persons were killed, heralds a new phase in the deteriorating situation.

---

[8] Group in support of Islam and Moslem people.

[9] Ansar Dine, the Macina katiba, the Al Mourabitoun group, and AQMI.

[10] And attests to the freedom these jihadist leaders enjoy to travel and meet.

This kind of attack, which first occurred in Kabul about fifteen years ago, is but a warning of graver dangers to come, which now threaten the entire Sahel region—a vast, landlocked zone with scant natural resources, agriculture threatened by droughts that will be aggravated by global warming, and unchecked population growth.

## In the face of these problems, it is urgent that france get organized.

Given the disinterest of most European countries and the insufficiency of current international aid, France and Europe must get organized. In France, apart from the Ministry of Defence, which is preoccupied with the quagmire in which its troops have landed, most administrations have, until recently, conducted business as usual. Until President Macron assumed power and immediately flew to Gao, there was little sense of urgency vis-à-vis the Mali crisis, and the Sahel in general, among the ministries concerned, which used to function without much coordination among them.

Symptomatic of the business-as-usual attitude was the omission of Mali and the Sahel from the ODA annex to the 2014 French finance bill. Some French parliamentarians had sent me the first draft of the annex for comment in mid-2013—about six months after Operation Serval was launched in Mali. During those six months, newspapers had run daily front-page accounts of the French military action in Mali. Then, two remarkable parliamentary reports on the crises in the Sahel and in Mali, signed by the President of the Senate and a former Defence minister, were published. Yet there was no mention of Mali and Sahel in the finance bill on aid for 2014! But even more puzzling, by end 2017, the new ODA annex to the 2018 French finance bill still makes no mention of the Sahel and the word Mali does not even appear in the 98 pages of this document. In what kind of bubble are our Treasury bureaucrats living?[11]

---

[11] Since parliamentarians reacted quite strongly to this omission, in the final version of the annex the words 'Sahel' and 'Mali' were sprinkled almost at random—but the resource allocation had not been modified!

Apart from functioning in silos and being ignorant about the real world, the French institutional mechanism on aid, with the exception of AFD, is so complex that it is unintelligible to the nation's partners and leaves even specialists flummoxed. There is little consistency among military, political, and development actions, which are conducted in a disorderly fashion by multilateral institutions. Given how firmly President Macron and the new French government have taken the Malian problem in hand, much better coordination in this area is now ongoing. But in the meantime, precious years have been needlessly lost.

### It is also crucial that Europe not leave France to face the Sahel crisis alone.

A crisis-ridden Africa will not be limited to northern Nigeria or the French-speaking Sahel. The United Kingdom, as an article in *The Economist* entitled 'Jihafrica'[12] pointed out, has openly expressed concern about the creation of a 'Shabab-land' in Kenya, where Somali al-Shabab militants, who are recruiting followers from the Somali Kenyan ethnic group, have transformed a coast that was once a popular tourist destination into an area where no Westerner dare set foot anymore. In the eastern region of the country bordering Somalia and Ethiopia and right up to the border with Tanzania in the south (which has not been spared, either), jihadi militias are a threat, murdering local elites and supporting imams who preach hate.

Links have been established among jihadi outfits in Libya, Mali, Nigeria, Sudan, Somalia, and Kenya, and their tentacles have wound their way into Tanzania, Ethiopia, and Uganda. Their interactions range from exchanging propaganda techniques to circulating military know-how about producing improvised explosive devices (IEDs) and promoting highly mobile combat modes using Toyota pickups in accordance with the modus operandi perfected long ago by Chadian rebels.

These movements feed off poverty, the unemployment of local youth, and the abandonment of regions lacking any economic growth. They also feed off the brutality and excesses of

[12] 'Jihafrica,', *The Economist*, 18 July 2015.

the army and local police forces, which blindly repress them, as in Nigeria and Mali. Al-Shabab also recruits youths from refugee camps, regardless of ethnic origin, and nurtures the ambition of establishing a caliphate on a religious and not a tribal basis. Amidst such rural distress, the ideological and religious dimension of these movements poses a singular challenge. Europe can no longer afford to ignore crisis-ridden Africa and assume—as Angela Merkel once hinted to François Hollande—that these issues are France's responsibility.

## The Sahel's problems are way beyond France's capabilities.

The Sahel's problems can no longer be France's sole responsibility for two main reasons: first, its troubles will soon affect all of Europe, and second, the problem has moved far beyond France's capabilities. Thirty or forty years ago, France might still have hoped to influence the political, economic, and social developments of some African countries. A marine infantry battalion was then capable of restoring order in a country and even replacing a head of state, as happened when President Giscard D'Estaing had 'Emperor' Bokassa replaced in September 1979. But that is a bygone era. The French armed forces, which had thought themselves capable of restoring order after civil war broke out in the Central African Republic in November 2013, wound up having to limit their ambitions to restoring precarious order only in the capital city of Bangui and some key arteries.

In the Sahel, political problems have become too deep-rooted, the economic and social situation too grave, and the circulation of modern weapons too widespread for such interventions to be able to stabilize a crisis-ridden country with deteriorating security. Today, we see the limits of this kind of action in Mali which, despite the French and UN military presence, continues to tip gradually into insecurity because none of the foundations of stability has been restored, despite the formal legitimacy of the regime.

The Tuareg problem in the north is yet to be resolved, and a new Fulani problem has appeared in the centre and south of the country; the Algiers agreement has not been implemented; the rural economy is as badly managed as ever; and the state apparatus, including the military, is prey to a clientelism that dooms it to inefficiency. The former colonizer can neither bear the expenses of restoring order nor raise its voice to impose rigor. Because France will soon be out of breath, the European Union will have to take the lead.

In the coming years, Europe, and particularly the European Union, must be prepared for interventions in the Sahel that will include military action as and when required, extensive police and gendarmerie work, and a long-term effort to reform the security sectors of Sahel countries. In most cases, it will be necessary to rebuild the core ministries and institutions of sovereignty in these countries. This work should go hand-in-hand with major development aid for the aid-orphan sectors, particularly the rural economy, local and municipal development and family planning. The trouble is that Europe does not possess armed forces, and its main instrument for economic action, the European Development Fund (EDF), is so cumbersome that it has great difficulty adapting to emergencies.[13]

Europe will therefore have to improvise as and when urgent situations arise. On the military front, it can rely on the French armed forces, but cannot leave them to deal with such troubles alone; now that the United Kingdom has opted for Brexit, other European militaries must intervene, especially the German armed forces. A German contingent is already helping train the Malian military. Aware of the mind-boggling complexity of EDF procedures, the European Union also instituted the EU Emergency Trust Fund for Africa in 2015 for migration prevention, stability, and security in the Sahel, the Horn of Africa, and North Africa.

This trust fund does not collect funds from other external sources and does not really aim at rationalizing and coordinating their distribution, which is usually the role of such funds in principle[14] (and was the kind I recommended in vain that the French government establish for Mali in 2013). Its aim is merely to create

---

[13] The actions are programmed under the NIP, or 'National Indicative Programs,' which are five-year action plans that are set one year in advance.

[14] This was, in fact, the very aim of the multi-donor Afghanistan Reconstruction Trust Fund overseen by the World Bank in the country.

a procedural window in the internal regulations of EU instruments, which helps simplify procedures and accelerate action on exceptional grounds. It is certainly better than nothing, and attests to the fact that European bodies have taken note that 'Europe's neighbouring houses,' particularly in North Africa and the Sahel region, are burning.

But, it is critical that European Union procedures become faster and that new instruments be developed dedicated specifically to the Sahel in order to facilitate collaboration with bilateral aid agencies by pooling analyses, expertise, and resources. An independent audit of the EDF's procedures and modes of intervention should probably be undertaken so that this instrument, which frankly does not know how to spend its funds, is capable of addressing new challenges. All this may appear complicated, but small steps are already showing the way forward. Fortunately, Europe and the Sahel can count on a new generation of responsible Sahel executives and leaders who must show that they can rise to the occasion during this critical period.

### The chief hope: Competence among the new generation of African decision-makers.

Ultimately, we know that the aid mechanism I am trying to dust clean and reorient is important, but it is secondary to the competence of the men and women, officials and political leaders, who will carry out the required reforms in the Sahel and all over Africa. I am always filled with wonder when in every country, including the most fragile and sometimes the 'worst,' I come across decision-makers perfectly aware of the problems facing them and determined to remedy them. I have expressed my admiration of Hanif Atmar, whom I barely know but whose extraordinary work in Afghanistan[15] I have seen. There are numerous leaders of such calibre in Africa, too.

When I was at the World Bank, the Central African Republic (CAR) fell in the zone under my charge in the late 1990s. There was an acute shortage of experienced managers in this country,

[15] Hanif Atmar is now in charge of supervising security in Afghanistan in the President's office, a hopeless task...

and I had thus greatly appreciated working with the then-Prime Minister, Dologuélé, a man of quality and good will (who, by the way, was defeated in the last presidential election). Ousted by President Patassé, an unreliable and unstable head of state, Dologuélé wrote me a thoughtful letter upon leaving office, thanking me for my efforts and commenting without rancor that my efforts, like his, had had little effect on his unfortunate country.

It is sometimes in the worst of situations that we find men and women of quality holding high posts, but who come a cropper against the real seats of power. Dologuele is not an exception. His predecessor, Jean-Paul Ngoupandé, was also a remarkable man who, having had to face the stark realities of power in his difficult country, later gave a brilliant account of the crisis that rippled through the CAR in 1996–97[16] and his own powerlessness in controlling it.

It is such a pity to see outstanding leaders paralyzed by parallel networks or heads of state who have completely different agendas. Hanif Atmar was blocked many times by Hamid Karzai—as when he wished, for instance, to extend the democratic process to the grassroots level in the Afghan countryside—and was unceremoniously sacked when he tried to clean up the Ministry of the Interior, which was in the grip of criminal networks.

Many African ministers and prime ministers became friends of mine. I saw some of them take courageous, farsighted, and resolute actions. I sometimes clashed with them when the interests or vision of the institution I represented did not match theirs. But I have always had deep respect for them. I once was even played by a particularly wily and accomplished minister of finance, which got me in trouble with my Paris headquarters. At the time I felt resentful towards him, but I later understood his reasons and he, too, became a good friend.

Most often, I tried to support them to the best of my ability, which enabled me to gauge the obstacles they encountered. Time and again, I have seen them sinking in impossible quagmires, falling into traps deliberately set by their enemies acting from the shadows. I remember a weekend in Washington spent

---

[16] Jean-Paul Ngoupandé, *Chronique de la crise centrafricaine (A Chronicle of the Central African Crisis) 1996–1997* (L'Harmattan, 1997).

on the telephone with a Cameroonian minister in charge of the reform programme who had firmly decided to restore order in his country, which was then almost in ruins. He was dictating to me the conditions of the World Bank's support programme to his country, and every three hours we had to readjust them as he discovered devious last-minute stratagems designed to torpedo the reforms. We were not in the kind of unhealthy relationship that existed between Greek authorities and the famous European 'troika,' but rather in a situation in which the minister used my institution as an instrument to strengthen his action.

How many of these exceptional men and women have been 'broken' by their presidents? Some, whose success put their 'boss' in the shade, were even thrown in jail and are still imprisoned on highly dubious grounds.

So many African institutions are true Potemkin buildings, infested with hidden networks that often hold the real power behind the officials' backs. Hence, even determined leaders require enormous courage to overturn such mechanisms and dare to embark on what often resembles open warfare. Some run considerable personal risks. Ngozi Okonjo Iweala had to increase her bodyguards fourfold when she started seriously attacking high-level corruption in Nigeria. Her grandmother was even kidnapped to exert pressure on her. Thanks to the degree of trust she had been able to build with the finance ministers of major OECD countries, she was able to negotiate an important debt-rescheduling programme, with what is referred to as the 'Paris Club,' without having to jump through the usual IMF hoops. It was quite an achievement. But did Ms. Okonjo Iweala have any authority over the oil sector, the protected preserve of the president and shadowy men?

## Even at the highest echelons of responsibility, the most qualified persons are rarely in the drivers' seats.

In 2009, I was called to audit the operations of the Prime Minister's Office of the Democratic Republic of Congo at the joint request of the then-Prime minister and the World Bank. Donors had been driven to despair by the fact that this key office at the heart of the state's machinery functioned like a black hole into which files systematically disappeared. The very old politician who preceded this Prime Minister had made the institution an asylum for the needy cadres of his party. I don't think I'd ever seen such a mess in my life.

Offices for six people with only four chairs, teetering towers of unprocessed files randomly stacked on the floor, antediluvian computers—not that it mattered, as there was no electricity in most offices—a thick layer of dust, and—well, I'd really rather not remember the worst. The new prime minister perused my analysis and suggestions, and we discussed the matter for hours. So interested was he that I almost missed my plane one evening— and experienced the worst fear of my life when his escort car drove me to the airport at full speed, using the wrong lane on the newly built highway in order to avoid traffic! At my suggestion, he tasked two experienced non-Congolese African experts (both are now ministers in their own countries) to help him develop a programme for restoring order. Ultimately, no doubt having weighed the risks he would have to take, he postponed a decision, realizing that he would have to fire the bulk of his party cadres, which had colonized the 'Primature.'

It took mere months for his successor, Matata Mapon Ponyo— who assumed the position in 2012 and had already straightened ill-managed public finances—to change the dysfunctional institution into one that very ably steered and coordinated the government's action during his four-year mandate. To do so, he followed the age-old principles for restoring order in a crisis-ridden institution: after carefully defining the institution's mission, a new organizational structure, and the associated job descriptions, he carefully selected his managers on the basis of merit and experience, recruiting them, when he saw fit, from the diaspora and the youngest on their graduation from university. What about the incompetent staff? They were shown the door. Of course, by doing so in an African society crisscrossed with influential family and ethnic networks, he did not make many friends.

Some years ago, he received me very early in the morning, as was his habit, along with my friend Tertius Zongo, another former African prime minister of great experience who was working with me as a consultant. It must have been around 7 o'clock in the morning when he proudly took us on a tour of the impeccably ordered new offices. His staff, busy working on their computers since dawn, were discussing the agenda of the daily cabinet meeting held at 7:30 a.m. At 9:30, I went to the World Bank office located nearby. The staff had just begun filing in, coffee mugs in hand. Of course, we all knew that the real power resided in none of these offices—not the Prime Minister's or the World Bank's, but in the 'palace' a little farther on, near the banks of the river...

Because a major disaster in DRC is now brewing, allow me to provide a few comments. Matata Mapon Mpoyo as a Prime Minister never had any control on the mining sector and its huge contracts with foreign firms where the big corruption takes place. He never had any control over security issues, be it the police force or the army. At the end of his mandate, poverty in his country misgoverned since its independence, was still abysmal; but at least he controlled public finances with a firm grip, had reduced inflation to a minimum, had stabilized the exchange rate, initiated a few key reforms and launched the country on a growth path. But then the "palace", probably in need of additional resources, imposed upon him one of its cronies as minister of finance... before firing him.

Now, god knows where DRC is going! As I write these line by end March 2018, the President has lost all legitimacy since the constitution is barring him from running for a new term, and he has again and again postponed presidential elections that were supposed to take place in 2016. In rural areas security is fast disintegrating as 70 or so rebel groups have taken up arms. 10 out of 26 provinces are in the grip of armed conflict. The country is on the verge of sliding into a new war which may equal or be worse than the 'Great Congo War' of 1998-2003, considered to be the 'bloodiest conflict since the second world war'.[17]

While Mali and the Sahel may well have the potential to destabilize most of West Africa in about a decade, a misgoverned DRC as big as Western Europe, with a population of about 80 million, and may be 150 million in 20 years, can destabilize *all* Central Africa. Unless a satisfactory political solution is soon negotiated and a capable government team urgently put in place, a new

[17] Gerard Prunier, *Africa's World War, Congo, the Rwandan Genocide and the Making of a Continental Catastrophe* (Oxford University Press, 2009).

tragedy is on its way in the heart of Africa, mostly due to appalling mis governance.

## The key to success is the political will of the Sahel elites.

We should not forget the lessons learned from the blunders and missteps in Afghanistan. We know that, in the long term, only private investments will enable the countries of the Sahel to emerge from extreme poverty. But for the time being, beyond sometimes unavoidable military interventions such as the one in Mali in 2013, an upgraded version of development aid, with new allocation rules and management methods, is likely to be the chief instrument for helping stabilize the Sahel region.

We must not labour under illusions, however. Aid, regardless of the amounts distributed, is no substitute for political will and for courage on the parts of the local elite and political leaders. Unlike ex-President Karzai, the latter must accept the indispensable modernization of their political and institutional systems, which are too often in the grip of nepotism. Unlike ex-President Karzai, they must lead a strenuous fight against the festering corruption that, in many states, arouses distrust of the leaders. Again, unlike ex-President Karzai, they should agree to combat drugs and other illegal trafficking activities, which will otherwise swiftly pervade and corrupt state apparatuses.

Even more important, an ideological battle against radical Islam is inevitable. African leaders in the Sahel must have the courage to oppose Salafist ideology, which is incompatible with the universal values of progress, democracy, and human rights. Only the local elite can lead this fight, but it demands committed mobilization, which many are reluctant to engage in. Opposing demagogy is never easy, and taking Islamic extremism head-on is a risky proposition, both politically as well as for one's personal safety.

The looming apprehension is that, faced with too many obstacles and difficulties, the local elites and state authorities will lower their guard and end up, like ex-President Toumani Touré, entering into a pact with jihadists with the hope of 'buying' peace. President Touré's failure, his hesitation in modernizing and reforming Malian institutions, his refusal to combat corruption and drug-trafficking, his refusal to engage in an ideological fight—just like President Karzai's failure in the very same areas—clearly show the path that Sahel countries must *not* follow.

If the leaders of these countries are not firmly and intelligently supported politically, financially, technically, and sometimes militarily, the obstacles they will soon face could be impossible to overcome. Let us therefore rise above our natural selfishness. The problem is not a question of charity. *As Europeans, this is in our direct interest* if we wish to avert the malignant influence that the chaos in Sahel will spread to our suburbs and lay at our very doors.

The Syrian and Libyan tragedies already show us what a narrow barrier the Mediterranean is. This is why I today strongly believe—to borrow a sentence from René Billaz's book—that *'making the Sahel a prosperous area is a major geopolitical urgency.'*

# Epilogue

### *How the World has Changed a Lot in Some*
### *Ways and Hardly At All in Others*

## From the remote arctic that was once inaccessible ...

A little over fifty years ago, fuelled by my passion for anthropology, traveling alone on foot, I reached the remote Eskimo
encampment of Kriketardiuk on the east coast of Igloolik Island,
located in the Foxe Basin in the far north of the Canadian Arctic.
Tracked for 36 hours while crossing the island by hungry stray
dogs that were more frightening than wolves, I could neither
sleep nor even lie down to rest. Finally, exhausted, I was warmly
received by an extended Inuit family that was quite startled to see
me. I was taken into the family and given a caribou-skin parka,
sealskin pants and boots. Communicating via sign language and a
little Inuit-English vocabulary, I spent the summer with the family, most of the time on an old sailing whaleboat open to rain and
snow, hunting seals and walruses to stock up for winter, sleeping
at night on ice floes, eating raw fish and boiled seal.

One day—some two months into this life—I started feeling
acute pain in my left flank. Seeing that I was in distress, my new-
found friends harnessed some fifteen dogs to a sled and drove me
across forty kilometres of successive snow, marshland, rocky bars,
and grassland to the main village of Igloolik. The 'village' was

merely a cluster of tents and stone foundations awaiting the construction of igloos for winter. Dozens of leashed, howling dogs greeted our arrival. Father Fournier, the French oblate missionary who had been living there almost twenty years, treated me as best as he could. I owe my life to him, the sole non-Inuit within a hundred kilometres. Seeing little hope of curing in Igloolik what turned out to be case of acute renal colic—and with no radio, telephone connection, or any other means of communication—Father Fournier dispatched me with an Inuit family on a sailing whaleboat headed south. I spent three days and three short nights in a semi-comatose state, writhing in agony on the floor of the boat, showered by sea spray and apprehensive about being lost due to thick fog; compasses are useless so close to the magnetic pole. At first dawn—around two o'clock—on the third night, I spotted on the horizon, beautiful in the rising sun, the radar dome of the US DEW line[1] of Foxe Main that my companions were seeking for me, and I knew I was out of the woods.

A few months ago, I happened upon a Canadian television report on the Arctic set on Igloolik Island. Obviously, I was keenly interested. The report started with a shot of the film crew's luggage and equipment arriving on a conveyor belt, as at any modern airport. The next shot showed half a dozen airplanes parked at the airport, then a view of the town of Igloolik with streets laid out in perfectly straight lines, pretty modern houses of wood painted in all hues, and a Ski-Doo parked behind each house. The TV crew loaded into a gleaming SUV and set off to visit several Eskimo families. The camera followed the crew into a spick-and-span interior where a bunch of kids lay sprawled on couches watching television and eating chocolate bars. Their fathers were off playing pool and drinking beer in the local pub.

All this clearly stressed the scale of the Canadian government's efforts to bring material progress to these areas, and its largesse in granting them allocations and subsidies which enabled them all to shop at the little local supermarket, a scene on which the camera dwelt for a while. Next, the crew accompanied a few

---

[1] 'Distant Early Warning line': line of radars installed in the late 1950s by the US Air Force to the northern extreme of Canada for detecting Soviet bombers. These radars were dismantled in the 1980s.

Inuit hunters on a high-speed boat. The latest sniper rifles and up-to-date binoculars had replaced the nineteenth-century spyglasses and Lee-Enfield guns dating back to World War I that I had used fifty years earlier. The hunters chatted constantly with their families and the other boats via VHF radios. But we didn't see a single seal. No ice, either. Probably the result of climate change.

For a long time I had been toying with the idea of returning to Igloolik, which I knew was now easily accessible. But this TV report cured me of the desire. The once-isolated society, then surviving in conditions unimaginable today, now lives indolently off the fortnightly state dole that Canada sends like a good mother. The Arctic has clearly changed.

## ... To the north of the Sahel, so near and now inaccessible!

Niamey, 11 November 2015. I emerge after a four-hour audience with President Issoufou, whom I first met more than thirty years ago when he was a mining engineer running the Somaïr uranium-mine operation. He was still the perceptive, frank, resolute, and direct man I had known. I am still impressed by his lucid vision of the vast problems and threats that face his country, and his determination to address them. But I also see his worry over the huge political constraints that brake his desire to act and his concern about an administration atrophied for decades by the constant interference of political networks. He was also deeply concerned by the fiscal crisis linked to the security threat. Niger is not Singapore!

As I board my flight a few days later, I compare my latest impressions with recollections of my first encounter with the country in 1970. Niamey was then a big village; it is now a metropolis with more than 1.5 million inhabitants. Women who used to roam around with their heads bared now resolutely cover them. On the other hand, bikers, who used to wear helmets—the poor sometimes using a simple calabash secured with a string for fear of the police—now ride without any head protection all, wantonly flouting the rules. Asking my driver about this, I'm told: 'This is democracy.'

Drivers, too, have clearly forgotten traffic rules, and within a few hours my chauffeur narrowly escapes two serious collisions (reminding me of Cairo in more glorious times). The traffic jams at the city's centre during peak office hours are a real problem, exacerbated in no small measure by the hulking SUVs of embassies and UN agencies. In the evening, the light mist hovering over the river greets me as it did in bygone times, but there are no caravans of camels loaded with wood on Kennedy Bridge at nightfall as there were in the Eighties.

I lose my bearings as I move through the city because high walls topped with rolls of barbed wire cut off my view of the houses and low-rise buildings that used to guide my way. I cannot even find the AFD office building unaided, though I worked there for five years. The house I used to live in near the banks of the river is now hidden from view by these walls. An urban highway is under construction close by. But the oldest district in the city's centre has barely changed, though a few buildings have shot up amidst the network of congested alleys and small shacks made of mud-brick and metal sheets. Even in the dry season, the gutters are overflowing. My car soon gives up any ambition of moving between trucks being unloaded and children kicking a ball around.

I take advantage of the opportunity to chat and visit a concession. The courtyard has practically disappeared, swallowed up by new structures stuffed into the space to accommodate the latest arrivals. Everyone lives in the alley. Construction is so dense that there are no toilets, no place for personal sanitation; as for collective sanitation, there's been talk about it for the past forty years. I'm told there are public toilets nearby. There is no running water in the concession, but water sellers are still there, pushing their carts loaded with yellow jerry cans.

The outskirts of the city are, on the other hand, completely unrecognizable. The former ribbon of a road going to Tillabery, which used to run northwest along the river, has become a four-lane highway. The city has expanded enormously. But I see the same mud-brick and breeze-block hovels, the same basic furniture, often broken, in front of small houses, the same lack of waste-treatment and drinking-water facilities as soon as one leaves the main road. The poverty I saw here during my first visit forty-eight years ago still lingers. Since then, the national per capita income has plummeted by a third.

Sometimes alternating with these poverty-stricken zones are small, private, picturesque pieces of land, some under construction, others just marked off by simple boundary stones, with no connection to public utilities, except sometimes a tangle of wires drooping to the ground for tapping electricity. In these cases, the classic TV parabolas reveal the television present inside.

There are many more children than before, running in the innumerable landfills—strewn with plastic bags—that take up all the space not claimed by dwellings. The experienced Director for Urban Planning accompanying me explains his setbacks, from the difficulty of enforcing compliance with a coherent urban plan without resources at his disposal, to the illegal constructions on the concrete platform that was to have housed a waste disposal container. There are mobile phones in everyone's hands and throngs of young people loitering in the streets in these immense, poverty-stricken districts where in the past, we used to go to see giraffes in the bush.

I do not even bother to request that the Niger government, for whom I am working, arrange for me a visit to the North, which I frequented in the 1980s with my friend Mano Dayak, who later became spokesperson for the Tuareg rebels, before dying tragically. I used to crisscross the magnificent northern desert with my family. We did so with complete peace of mind, sleeping under the stars around a campfire, sometimes hailed by enigmatic men in blue who called out greetings as they passed through the darkness with takoubas[2] slung at their sides. Venturing into the North today—even just getting out to Tillabery—is impossible for a European without military escort.

To see the North again, I have to content myself with the reports that TV5 *Monde Afrique* sometimes telecasts. Depending on the regions covered, I see the same old tents or mud-brick or straw shacks that I saw forty-five years ago, the same little gardens, the same rudimentary watering systems, with perhaps some diesel pumps, but not many. I see the same herds and the same kind of healthcare centres as the one that treated me through a bout of malaria. They now perhaps exist in greater numbers—but are

---

[2] A takouba is a long Tuareg sword.

medicines available? Mostly, what I see are lots of half-clad children running in the dust.

I feel happy to be reunited with my Nigerien friends in Niamey. Many grey-haired officials I do not recognize at first come to shake my hand warmly and fondly reminisce about the hours we spent together so long ago. I still dream of returning to the regions of the desert and north of the Sahel that I so loved, to see again the farmers and stockbreeders, the men and women who were so engaging, to whom the aid I was able to deliver thirty five years ago was but a drop in an ocean of sand. But this is no longer possible. Northern Sahel has become inaccessible.

What widely differing itineraries for these two nomadic peoples, the Arctic one (excessively) dependent on the state, the African one forgotten.

But let us not despair. Let us meditate instead on this quote from Scott Fitzgerald:

'*One should ... be able to see that things are hopeless and yet be determined to make them otherwise.*'[3]

---

[3] Excerpt from *The Crack-Up.*

# Afterword

Fifteen years of interventions, some US-led, some UN-led, some EU-supported, have left a bitter taste amongst policy-makers and in the general public. After billions spent in the Democratic Republic of Congo, trillions in Afghanistan and Iraq, the question is often asked: was it worth it? Is it an illusion to try to change countries we don't really understand? Do we know what we are doing? And such questions are asked at the very moment when development aid itself is also questioned.

At a time of fiscal constraint, domestic priorities are asserting themselves, and the temptation to hunker down behind national borders is great. For affluent countries in Europe or North America, the outside world looks both dangerous and intractable. That sentiment is particularly strong when it comes to the Middle East and Africa. The discourse of fear-mongers who brandish the threat of chaos and terrorism, and of humanitarians describing enormous tragedies to appeal to our sense of humanity, has backfired: the perception of expanding, ungoverned spaces with more human misery now risks paralysing rather than moving us into action. In Africa, the contrast between an optimistic discourse presenting Africa as the next Asia and the reality of persistent conflicts has generated much skepticism on the benefits of engagement.

This book has the great merit of charting a middle and realistic course that will help recalibrate international engagement. It is a call to action based not on fearmongering and panic, but on the decades of work of a practitioner, who has learned through experience that helping a country build a state, especially when it has been devastated, morally and physically by conflict, is an incredibly difficult task that requires humility, far from the hubris that characterized many of the interventions of the first decade of this century. But it is not an impossible task, provided the community of donors and interventionist countries redefine their ambitions and learn the right lessons from past experience; it is also a necessary task: in a connected world, we cannot afford to ignore our surroundings.

The Sahel is a case in point. Serge Michailof states some inconvenient truths about the region: while it is fashionable to present the rapid growth of population in Sub-Saharan Africa as an asset for the continent, he explains that the delayed demographic transition in countries like Niger is a time-bomb that needs to be defused now. He also goes beyond the sterile opposition that pitches those who want to address the root causes of conflict, and those who focus on the more immediate security issues. The reality that I observed as the UN head of peacekeeping is that without security nothing is possible, and the first public good that people demand in any country is to be able to sleep at night without fear. But without education and jobs, the provision of security is unsustainable, as new generations of unemployed youth turn into combatants.

There are practical answers to those challenges: I am convinced by my own experience that the primacy of politics must be restored. Technocratic approaches that ignore political dynamics have had a devastating impact in Afghanistan and other countries trying to emerge from conflict. Strengthening national institutions is the greatest contribution that foreigners can make to the stabilization of a country, but that strengthening is not a technical exercise. It is a highly political one; one that requires a good understanding of the political implications of one's efforts. Institutions will strengthen some actors and weaken others. They are a battlefield, and the naive vision of the promoters of the ' rule of law' as the answer to all the tensions of conflict does not work, all the more so as many conflict actors have no interest in the consolidation of a state: they actually benefit from its weakness.

Understanding politics does not mean that technical aid does not matter, and certainly does not justify the view that development aid can be drastically cut, as some would have it. But, it is a reminder that throwing money at the challenge is only part of the answer. As Serge Michailof puts it, a 'kind of Marshall Plan' for the Sahel is needed, and international aid is vital for extremely poor countries, where it can represent up to 10% of GDP and 90% of the investment budget. But much attention must be given to the political context in which that aid is disbursed. In the end, it is an empowered society, at the local and national levels, that can make a decisive difference. But, it desperately needs outside help, and this book is an indispensable primer on what to do and what not to do.

Jean Marie Guéhenno
Former United Nations under-secretary-general for
Peacekeeping Operations AND President and
CEO of International Crisis Group

# Acknowledgments

The French version of this book was the culmination of half a century of professional experience devoted to the economic development of poor countries spread over all the continents. It is mostly based, however, on the diagnostics, analyses, and negotiations I have conducted or supervised during the past twelve years as a consultant seeking to help countries facing crises or serious difficulties. Thus, this work is, foremost, the product of innumerable discussions with high-level government officials, experts, representatives of civil society, and ordinary citizens in countries currently facing problems of extreme poverty, economic and social disorganization, security issues, and even terrorism.

This book is also the result of reflections accumulated over a decade of teaching at the Sorbonne, and then at the Paris School of International Affairs (Sciences Po), and exchanges with my research colleagues and other experts from the Foundation for Study and Research in International Development (FERDI) and the French Institute for International and Strategic Affairs (IRIS), whom I both wish to thank especially here.

It took shape gradually from a series of conferences that obliged me to develop an analysis and argumentation that served as the framework for the book. I want to mention, particularly, the conference organized for me by the African Development Bank at its May 2013 Annual General Meeting in Marrakesh; the 2013 Crans Montana Forum in Brussels; the conference organized for me by the Gulbenkian Foundation in Lisbon the same year; my June 2014 presentation at the French Ministry of Defence to the defence attachés in Africa and the Middle East; and my presentation to the Standing Committee on Foreign Affairs of the French Parliament, in January 2015.

This book is also the product of a long conversation—begun when my previous book, *Notre Maison Brûle au Sud (Our House in the South is Burning)*, was published in 2010 in France—with friends and colleagues who share my love for Africa, my interest in development issues, and my deep concern about the Sahel's future. Although the analyses, judgments, proposals, and events reported in this book—and particularly any errors and omissions—are my sole responsibility, and all the persons cited below do not necessarily share my views and suggestions, I am extremely thankful to them for the time they devoted to reading the various drafts of my manuscript and for their suggestions, criticisms, and comments, which greatly helped me in finalizing the book.

I would like to thank, especially, Olivier Lafourcade, chairman of the Investors and Partners Board of IPDEV,(Investisseurs et Partenaires pour le Développement), member of the Board of Research for Development and the Aspen Network for Development Entrepreneurs, and former director at the World Bank, for the continuing dialogue we shared over so many years and his careful reading of my successive manuscripts, as well as Tertius Zongo, former Prime Minister of Burkina Faso, former minister of Finance, and former ambassador to the United States, for our long-term dialogue of trust and for the help he extended to me over the years in decrypting the realities of Africa. Without the encouragement of these two close friends, I probably would not have dared write this book.

I would also like to thank Harinder Kohli, founding director and chief executive of Emerging Markets Forum, founding director, president, and CEO of Centennial Group International, and former director at the World Bank, for the confidence he showed in me from the inception of this project. Without his constant support, the English version of this book would not have seen the light of day.

I am also particularly grateful to Patrick Guillaumont, founder and president of the Foundation for International Development

Study and Research (FERDI) and professor emeritus of the University of Clermont Auvergne, and Sylviane Guillaumont Jeanneney, also professor emerita of the University of Clermont Auvergne, for their remarks and comments, particularly on the concepts of fragility and vulnerability, their constant support for more than thirty years, for taking up the initiative of preparing a strong advocacy for involving donors in the Sahel even in an insecure environment,[1] and for having the FERDI foundation fund the English translation of this work. I would also like to thank Christophe Angely, former managing director with Barclays Corporate and Investment Banking Europe and currently head of strategy and finance at FERDI, for the steady support he extended to me over the past years.

My warm thanks also go to Paul Collier and Jean Marie Guéhenno, for having accepted to write the foreword and afterword of this English Version; Paul Collier is the well-known author of 'The Bottom Billion' and many other fascinating books, the former director of the World Bank's Development Research Group, a professor of Economics at Oxford University, and director of the Centre for the Study of African Economies. I also want to thank him for our regular discussions on fragile and conflict-ridden countries, on migrations, and for his perceptive analysis of my first manuscript in French. Jean Marie Guéhenno, whom I first met 25 years ago when he was leading the 'Centre d'Analyse et de Prévision' (i.e. the think tank) of the French Ministry of Foreign affairs, has been the United Nations under-secretary-general for Peacekeeping Operations, is now the president and CEO of International Crisis Group, and, as such, one of the world experts on conflicts and crisis. Comments and encouragement from these two friends were key in making me decide to have the French version of this book translated and published for an English-speaking audience.

My thanks also go out to Théodore Ahlers, international consultant and former director at the World Bank, for his very fine identification of points in my manuscript that needed clarity and his support in finalizing this work; Antoine Anfré, former

---

[1] Cf. '*Linking security and Development, a plea for the Sahel,*' FERDI Foundation, November 2016.

ambassador of France to Niger, for his comments on aspects of that country; Pierre Arnaud, former vice-president of *Compagnie Fruitière,* for his careful analysis of my first draft; Farouk Baroukzaï, former adviser to the minister of Agriculture in Afghanistan, for carefully reviewing the chapters on this country; Antoine Baux, former technical adviser and director of AFD for Côte d'Ivoire, for his invaluable comments on the chapter concerning that country; Philippe Benoit, former head of the Energy Efficiency and Environment Division at the OECD's International Energy Agency, who was my deputy at the World Bank and helped me reconstruct the history of the famous 'Chad Cameroon' project; René Billaz, former scientific director of CIRAD and former president of the NGO *Agronomes et vétérinaires sans frontières*, for his advice on the chapter on rural development; Pascal Boniface, the founder and head of IRIS, for his constant support and our regular exchanges on Geopolitics; Fréderic Bontems, director of Development and Global Public Goods at the Ministry of External Affairs in Paris, for reading and commenting on my first manuscript; Mahktar Diop, vice president for the Africa Region at the World Bank, for our many discussions on Africa, the Sahel, and fragile countries for more than 30 years, and for his constant encouragements; François Gaulme, research officer at AFD's Economic and Social Research Unit and fragility and conflict expert, for his careful review of my manuscript on those aspects; Étienne Giros, former Africa director of the Bolloré Group and deputy chairman of CIAN, who gave me his insights as an entrepreneur in Africa, and his advice; Stephen Decam, former chief operating officer of CFAO and secretary general of CIAN, and Alix Camus, deputy general secretary of CIAN, both extremely knowledgeable about African issues and the role French companies play in Africa, who compared my analyses with their own perceptions; Xavier Devictor, advisor to the Fragility, Conflict, and Violence Group at the World Bank, for his careful perusal of all the points on conflicts and the actions of donors in these contexts; Antoine Glaser, journalist, former editor-in-chief of *'Lettre du Continent'*, and a great authority on Africa and France-Africa relations, who reviewed and pointed out the weak points of my initial manuscript; Étienne de Gonneville, deputy director for strategic affairs at the Ministry of Foreign Affairs, who was so kind as to comment, in detail, on the first version of my manuscript; Alisha Grave, president of Venture Strategies for Health and Development and co-founder of *the OASIS Initiative* at the School of Public Health, University of California, Berkeley, for her comments on the French version of the book and our regular exchange of views on the Sahel; Jean-Marc Gravellini, presently coordinator of the "Alliance for the Sahel", former operations director of the French Development Agency and former vice president of *Compagnie Fruitière,* particularly for his analysis and advice on the chapter focusing on agricultural development; Jean-Pierre Guengant, emeritus director of research at the Institute for Development Research (IRD), and John May, former lead demographer at the World Bank, who both very kindly checked, and often corrected, the key section on the analysis of the demographic situation in Africa and the Sahel region and whose general comments on my manuscripts were invaluable; Philippe Hugon, senior research fellow at IRIS, professor emeritus, and renowned Africa expert, for his advice and comments on my final manuscript; Pierre Jacquemot, former ambassador to Kenya, Ghana, and DRC, chairman of GRET—professionals for fair development (France), and lecturer in Development Economics at Sciences Po, for his close reading of my manuscript and his detailed comments and advice; Dominique Kerouedan, international consultant on public health, professor of Public Health at the Paris School of International Affairs (Sciences Po), and former medical doctor in refugee camps, for our constant dialogue; Patrick Labaste, international consultant, and former practice leader for Agriculture Development at the World Bank, for his analyses and invaluable comments on the chapter dealing with rural development; Lamine Loum, former prime minister of Senegal and former minister of finance, for our numerous conversations and discussions on the questions of corruption, fragility, and conflict in the Sahel region; Jean-François Lamoureux, administrator of the NGO *Action contre la faim* (committed to ending world hunger), for his comments and encouragement; Matata Ponyo Mapon, former prime minister of the Democratic Republic of the Congo and former minister of finance, for the innumerable hours we have spent together discussing issues of fragility, conflict, and reconstruction of a failing state apparatus; Samuel

Nguembock, associate research fellow at IRIS, for his review of the manuscript and encouragement; Anne Paugam, former CEO of AFD ( French Development Agency), Jacques Moineville, former deputy CEO of AFD, and Jean-Pierre Marcelli—director of the Sub-Saharan Africa Department of AFD—for their painstaking perusal of my manuscript and our animated discussions of my often heterodox operational proposals; Erik Orsenna, former adviser to President Mitterrand, writer, member of the 'Académie Française', 'Conseiller d'Etat', and great Africa expert, for his comments, suggestions, and unflagging encouragement; Karim Pakzad, former professor of political Science at the Kabul University, presently associate researcher at IRIS, for his very careful review of my chapters dealing with Afghanistan; Philippe Perdrix, former deputy editor-in-chief of the *Jeune Afrique* magazine and CEO of the communications firm 35°Nord, for his critical but very pertinent analysis of my first manuscript; Malcolm Potts, MD, professor of public health at the School of Public Health at the University of California, Berkeley, for our many discussions on the Sahel region, its demography, and the risks there; Olivier Ray, former head of AFD's crisis-prevention and post-conflict-recovery unit, AFD director for Lebanon and Syria, for our constant dialogue on fragile states and post-conflict recovery; Rémy Rioux, CEO of AFD for his support and our regular exchanges on Sahel issues, Stéphanie Rivoal, CEO of the NGO *Action contre la faim,* for her encouragement and advice, particularly on what NGOs can and cannot do; Claude Roger, president of the NGO *Agronomes et vétérinaires sans frontières,* for his encouragement; Jean-Louis Sarbib, former senior vice president at the World Bank and present CEO of Development Gateway, for his painstaking reading, his comments, and support; Georges Serre, former ambassador of France to Côte d'Ivoire, DRC, and Cameroun, former advisor to the French minister of foreign affairs, for his very careful study and remarks on the chapter relating to Cote d'Ivoire; Michèle Tribalat, research fellow at INED (National Institute for Demographic Studies), for her comments formalizing my views on the sensitive questions of migration; Hasan Tuluy, international consultant and adviser on economic and social-development matters and former World Bank regional vice president, who took the time to make a very detailed critical analysis of my first manuscript in French; Jean-Bernard Veron, senior adviser for the *Fondation de France's* French Committee for International Solidarity and former head of the French Development Agency's Crisis Prevention and Conflict Resolution Unit, for his painstaking, critical reading of my manuscript and his remarks on my analysis of the behaviour of donors in conflict or post-conflict situations; Jean Pierre Vettovaglia, former ambassador of Switzerland and author of an anthology on the determinants of conflicts who willingly spent hours with me to share his experience; Kerfalla Yansane, former governor of the Central Bank of Guinea, former minister of Finance, former senior minister in the Guinean president's cabinet and presently ambassador to the USA, for our endless discussions on African crises and how to address them and conduct reform programmes. I would like to thank, especially, Alexandre Vilgrain, CEO of SOMDIAA and chair of the French Council for Investors in Africa (CIAN) who, without necessarily sharing my views, both encouraged and pushed me to reconsider or confirm my positions on all the disputed points. My gratitude also goes out to all the officers across ranks, serving in Africa or posted in Paris, who did not wish to be quoted but were kind enough to exchange views with me, some of whom read and annotated my successive manuscripts and shared their comments on all aspects of the military issues I dared raise.

The English version of this book gained greatly from the discussions and debates I had after the publication of the French version during a series of conferences held and presentations made between 2015 and 2017. These discussions and debates helped me focus and deepen my analyses and submit them to the successive criticisms of audiences as varied as the Institute of Advanced Studies in National Defence (IHEDN), *Institut de France,* the French Development Agency (AFD), Sciences Po Executive Master, Investors' Council in Africa (CIAN), Club Jean Jaurès, Group for Research and Technology Exchanges (GRET), the NGO *Agronomes et Vétérinaires sans Frontières* (AVSF), *Maison de l'Afrique,* Club Demeter, *Institut Open Diplomacy*, Expertise France, Proparco, French National Research Institute for Sustainable Development (IRD), Res-Publica Foundation, Embassy of the United Kingdom in Paris, and in Washington, the staffs of the US

State Department, the Woodrow Wilson International Center for Scholars, and the National Defence University.

I am thankful, of course, to both my French and Indian editors: Sophie Kucoyannis, for the quality of her work and the relevance of her comments on the French version of this book, which helped me transform what was initially a quite dry text into a book that I hope readers will find accessible and easy to read; and the team at Oxford University Press for their constant support from New Delhi and our almost daily email exchanges as the manuscript of this English version was taking shape. My thanks also go of course to Sharmila Sarkar, who undertook the English translation with great rigour; Kenneth DeCell for his remarkable editing of the English version; Alicia Saona and Mireille Olavarietta, my outstanding assistants at the World Bank and the French Development Agency, respectively, who helped me immensely in formatting the French version of the book; and, finally, Nadine Poupart, programme manager in the Division of Health and Social Protection at AFD, and one of my former staff member at the World Bank in Washington where for 20 years, she focused on human development issues, for her very attentive perusal of the final version of my English manuscript, judicious comments, and final corrections.

Last, but not least, I cannot thank my spouse, Catherine, enough for her steadfast encouragement despite all the weekends and evenings she sacrificed to leave me to my laptop, and above all, for the weeks of anxiety I caused her when I was unable to communicate from deepest Afghanistan, the east of the Democratic Republic of the Congo, or other places the Internet had yet to reach.

# Index

# About the Author

Serge Michailof had an exceptional career as a development practitioner, successively preparing development projects in Latin America, South Asia, and North Africa in an engineering firm, managing technical teams in Africa and Asia for the French Development Agency (AFD) as country director and later as the head of Operations, and negotiating development programmes and policy reforms at the World Bank as a senior advisor and country director. For ten years, he was an associate professor at the Paris School of International Affairs (Sciences Po) in Paris, and the Sorbonne. He is currently an associate researcher at IRIS (Institut de Relations Internationales et Stratégiques), the leading think tank on geopolitics, in Paris, and a Senior Fellow at the FERDI foundation (Fondation pour les Etudes et la Recherche en Développement International). He is a board member of the CIAN (Conseil des Investisseurs Français en Afrique) and the GRET (Groupe de Recherche et d'Echanges Technologiques), one of the leading French NGOs. He is also a regular consultant on fragile states and post-conflict reconstruction, working for governments and international agencies, with a specific focus on institution- and state-building. During his fifty years' career, he worked in 65 different countries on all continents.

Serge Michailof studied in France (MBA at HEC, PhD in Economics, MA in Anthropology) and in the US (MIT). The French edition of *Africanistan* (Fayard, 2015) has become a reference work in France and in French-speaking Africa.

## A FOUNDATION FOR IDEAS

## ON DEVELOPMENT

**www.ferdi.fr**

The FERDI (Fondation pour les études et recherches sur le développement international) was created in 2003 to promote a fuller understanding of economic development and the factors that influence it.

It supports research activities to study development issues, and seeks to strengthen the potential of the French-speaking world in this area.

FERDI endeavours to promote the contribution of French and European work to the international debate on major development issues, in particular on which Southern and Northern economic policies are best able to assist development by broadening capacity for individual choice and developing equality of opportunity among nations. It thus wishes to contribute to improving these policies and providing information for companies whose business depends on world markets and their outlooks.

Accordingly, FERDI's activities are driven and guided by three principles: Incisive research, outreach and capacity building.

**FERDI**
**IN CLERMONT-FERRAND**

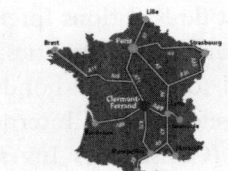

FONDATION POUR LES ÉTUDES
ET RECHERCHES
SUR LE DÉVELOPPEMENT
INTERNATIONAL

The FERDI is a foundation recognised as being in the public interest.
Together with Iddri, it implements the Initiative for Development
and Global Governance (IDGM).
It coordinates the IDGM+ Labex in conjunction
with Cerdi and Iddri.